'This book presents a trans-diagnostic view of th[e role of] compassion in treating mental disorders and the [integration of] insights from ancient Buddhist psychology as wel[l as psychol]ogy, psychedelic research and neuro-scientific find[ings. Both] personal and transpersonal approaches can comp[lement each] other. An interesting, clinically, and theoretically rich, worthwhile read for practitioners of all persuasions and for people interested in self development.'

     Leslie S. Greenberg, *Ph.D., distinguished research professor,*
          Department of Psychology, York University,
                 Toronto, Canada

'This book is an invitation to a very modern conversation about psychotherapy. Jan Benda offers a model of therapy that integrates attachment theory, schema therapy, neuroscience, and Buddhist psychology with self-transcendent states of awareness more often found on meditation retreats and in psychedelic-assisted psychotherapy. A unifying theme is helping clients to hold their emotional wounds, and themselves, in mindful and compassionate awareness. This well-documented book will inspire as well as inform clinicians from diverse theoretical orientations.'

        Christopher Germer, *Ph.D., lecturer (part-time),*
          Harvard Medical School, author of The
             Mindful Path to Self-Compassion

'*Mindfulness and the Self* is a unique and generous compendium of psychological practice and theory—prodigiously researched—clinical experience illustrated by case histories, and deep personal and transpersonal spiritual exploration, all enriched by practical exercises for both professionals and clients.'

     Gabor Maté, *M.D., author of* The Myth of Normal: Trauma,
           Illness and Healing in a Toxic Culture

'Jan Benda offers a unique perspective on integrative psychotherapy, characterized by a mindful attitude that permeates various theoretical articulations. The book draws on diverse therapeutic and healing approaches and outlines their distinct combination. It presents many lively examples and exercises that can directly speak to the reader. Congratulations on this achievement, which provides ample food for thought and personal reflection for psychotherapists and beyond!'

     Ladislav Timuľák, *Ph.D., Professor in Counselling Psychology,*
       School of Psychology, Trinity College Dublin, Ireland

'Jan Benda's latest work is a profound and insightful synthesis of Eastern and Western wisdom, skillfully integrating a modern neuroscientific understanding of memory reconsolidation with mindfulness-informed therapeutic practices. The result is a transformative, transdiagnostic framework for healing deep-seated trauma. Rich with clinical examples, experiential practices and a clear process for uncovering and resolving core schemas, *Mindfulness and the Self* is an essential guide for clinicians, meditators and psychonauts seeking an approach that integrates insights and self-compassion for personal growth and living an authentic life.'

Andrea Grabovac, *M.D., Clinical Professor of Psychiatry, University of British Columbia, author of* The Mindfulness and Meditation Workbook for Anxiety and Depression: Balance Emotions, Overcome Intrusive Thoughts, and Find Peace Using Mindfulness-integrated CBT

'*Mindfulness and the Self* is a profound book for psychotherapy professionals interested in integrating mindfulness and self-compassion into individual therapy. Beyond group programs like MBSR and MBCT, Jan Benda's *Mindfulness-Informed Integrative Psychotherapy* offers a more specific use of mindfulness and self-compassion in psychotherapy, offering a depth of healing often impossible in group settings. This book holds truly inspiring and integrative potential for clinicians from various orientations and spiritual seekers aiming to live a fulfilling, authentic life.'

Petra Meibert, *Diplom-psychologist, psychotherapist, MBSR, and MBCT teacher, trainer, supervisor, and author; Head of the Mindfulness Institute Ruhr and the Oberberg Day Clinic for Psychiatry and Psychotherapy, Essen, Germany*

'This book addresses relevant contemplative practice, psychopathological and psychotherapeutic issues based on insights from time-honored Buddhist psychology and mindfulness meditation practice and their convergence and integration with contemporary psychological, clinical, and neuroscientific developments, such as about the self. The author shows an outstanding depth of understanding of such issues and insights, as well as their integration. The book has important and timely theoretical as well as practical implications linked to psychological well-being, psychotherapy, and mental health, as well as contemplative practices and science.'

Antonino Raffone, *Ph.D., Full Professor, Department of Psychology, Sapienza University of Rome, Italy*

'This new volume by psychotherapist Jan Benda is an excellent integrative work in the broadest sense. It integrates various forms of psychotherapy into a transdiagnostic approach based on mindfulness and self-compassion while also incorporating insights from transpersonal and Buddhist psychology and the use of psychedelics. Enriched with valuable practical exercises, it is a helpful resource for psychotherapists and an informative self-help guide for those with a wounded Self.'

Ivan Nyklíček, *Ph.D., Associate Professor, Department of Medical and Clinical Psychology, Tilburg University, Netherlands*

Mindfulness and the Self

The image we have of ourselves is shaped during our childhood and is often influenced by various emotional wounds. *Mindfulness and the Self* describes four types of these wounds and shows how they can be healed and transformed through developing mindfulness and self-compassion.

Grounded in the innovative Mindfulness-Informed Integrative Psychotherapy framework, this book presents a revolutionary phenomenological model of maladaptive schemas and redefines our understanding of mental disorders. It offers practical procedures to uncover hidden core beliefs and treat our most painful inner feelings—existential fear, shame, and loneliness. Beyond healing, this text will guide you in developing an Authentic and Transcendent Self while alerting you to common pitfalls on your spiritual journey. Drawing on contemporary therapeutic approaches and integrating insights from neuroscience, psychedelic research, and Buddhist psychology, the book includes 20 practical exercises and presents practices and techniques that may be used in psychotherapy and personal development.

This book is an inspiring read for therapists, mindfulness practitioners, and anyone eager to integrate therapeutic insights into their journey toward a fulfilling life. It is indispensable for all seeking to overcome emotional barriers and enhance personal and transpersonal growth.

Jan Benda, Ph.D., is a private psychologist and psychotherapist with over 20 years of experience. He draws from intensive meditation experience and integrates the wisdom of Buddhist psychology with modern psychotherapy methods.

Advancing Theory in Therapy
Series Editors

Keith Tudor, Gregor Žvelc, Maša Žvelc
About the Series
Most books covering individual therapeutic approaches are aimed at the trainee/student market.

This series, however, is concerned with advanced and advancing theory, offering the reader comparative and comparable coverage of a number of therapeutic approaches.

Aimed at professionals and postgraduates, *Advancing Theory in Therapy* will cover an impressive range of theories.

With full reference to case studies throughout, each book in the series will

- present cutting edge research findings;
- locate each theory and its application within its cultural context;
- develop a critical view of theory and practice.

Books in this series:

Constructivist Psychotherapy
A Narrative Hermeneutic Approach
Gabriele Chiari, Maria Laura Nuzzo

Lacanian Psychoanalysis
Revolutions in Subjectivity
Ian Parker

Gestalt Therapy
Advances in Theory and Practice
Edited by Talia Bar-Yoseph Levine

Existential Therapy
Legacy, Vibrancy and Dialogue
Laura Barnett, Greg Madison

Integrative Psychotherapy
A Mindfulness- and Compassion-Oriented Approach
Gregor Žvelc, Maša Žvelc

Mindfulness and the Self
Mindfulness-Informed Integrative Psychotherapy
Jan Benda

Mindfulness and the Self
Mindfulness-Informed Integrative Psychotherapy

Jan Benda

Routledge
Taylor & Francis Group
LONDON AND NEW YORK

Designed cover image: Shutterstock.com

First published in English 2025
by Routledge
4 Park Square, Milton Park, Abingdon, Oxon OX14 4RN

and by Routledge
605 Third Avenue, New York, NY 10158

Routledge is an imprint of the Taylor & Francis Group, an informa business

© 2025 Jan Benda

The right of Jan Benda to be identified as author of this work has been asserted in accordance with sections 77 and 78 of the Copyright, Designs and Patents Act 1988.

All rights reserved. No part of this book may be reprinted or reproduced or utilised in any form or by any electronic, mechanical, or other means, now known or hereafter invented, including photocopying and recording, or in any information storage or retrieval system, without permission in writing from the publishers.

Trademark notice: Product or corporate names may be trademarks or registered trademarks, and are used only for identification and explanation without intent to infringe.

Published in Czech by Portál in 2024

British Library Cataloguing-in-Publication Data
A catalogue record for this book is available from the British Library

Library of Congress Cataloging-in-Publication Data
Names: Benda, Jan, author.
Title: Mindfulness and the self : mindfulness-informed integrative psychotherapy / Jan Benda.
Description: Abingdon, Oxon ; New York, NY : Routledge, 2025. | Series: Advancing theory in therapy |
Identifiers: LCCN 2024032604 (print) | LCCN 2024032605 (ebook) | ISBN 9781032823331 (hbk) | ISBN 9781032823324 (pbk) | ISBN 9781003504061 (ebk)
Subjects: LCSH: Mindfulness (Psychology) | Psychotherapy.
Classification: LCC BF637.M56 B459 2025 (print) |
LCC BF637.M56 (ebook) |
DDC 158.1/3--dc23/eng/20240916
LC record available at https://lccn.loc.gov/2024032604
LC ebook record available at https://lccn.loc.gov/2024032605

ISBN: 978-1-032-82333-1 (hbk)
ISBN: 978-1-032-82332-4 (pbk)
ISBN: 978-1-003-50406-1 (ebk)

DOI: 10.4324/9781003504061

Typeset in Sabon and Optima
by KnowledgeWorks Global Ltd.

To Manuela and Sára Antonie

Contents

Figures, Tables, and Exercises   xi
Acknowledgments   xiii
Series Preface   xiv
Preface   xvi

Introduction   1

Part I. Mindfulness-Informed Integrative Psychotherapy   5

   1. Mindful Diagnosis of Mental Disorders   9

   2. Early Childhood Experiences and Development of Psychopathology   18

   3. Maladaptive Schemas   24

   4. Narrative Self and Mental Disorders   30

   5. Universal Solvents for Mental Difficulties   47

Part II. The Wounded Self   51

   6. The Lost Self   56

   7. The Abandoned Self   64

   8. The Inferior Self   71

   9. The Inflated Self   79

   10. Healing the Wounded Self   88

Part III.	**The Authentic Self**	**97**
11.	The Mindful Adult	101
12.	The Drama Triangle and How to Get Out of It?	107
13.	Adult Responsibility and Its Limits	115
14.	Self-Compassion and Protective Anger	124
15.	Courage to Separate and Courage to Be Close	130
16.	Meditation, Psychedelics, and Their Pitfalls	139
Part IV.	**The Transcendent Self**	**149**
17.	Non-Dual Awareness	153
18.	Integration of Transpersonal Experiences	161
19.	Mindful Zombie, Spiritual Narcissist, and Enlightened Nerd	171
20.	Master of the Two Worlds	178
	Conclusion	183
	Recommended Reading	186
	References	187
	Index	236

Figures, Tables, and Exercises

Figures

1	Phenomenological model of maladaptive schema	25
2	Daniel's maladaptive schema	34
3	Amy's maladaptive schema	36
4	Zoe's maladaptive schema	37
5	Eve's maladaptive schema	39
6	Simon's maladaptive schema	41
7	Veronica's maladaptive schema	43
8	Ryan's maladaptive schema	44
9	The Wounded Self and unfulfilled needs	54
10	Personal and transpersonal development	140
11	Selfhood triumvirate	150

Tables

1	Defense mechanisms and ego states	52
2	The Lost Self	62
3	The Abandoned Self	68
4	The Inferior Self	76
5	The Inflated Self	85

Exercises

1	Identifying the feeling preceding anger	15
2	Emotional bridge to the past	21
3	Abstractions and generalizations	28

4	A loving letter to your Authentic Self	45
5	Re-experiencing loving attention and care	49
6	Shedding omnipotent guilt	62
7	Saying yes to your grief	69
8	From inferiority to humility	76
9	Descending from the pedestal of superiority	85
10	Your core belief on a billboard	93
11	Who am I?	105
12	Transcending the drama triangle	113
13	Learning to understand your warning lights	121
14	Anger as a guardian animal	127
15	Open your heart in relation to others	137
16	Do I Have a Healthy Functioning Authentic Self?	145
17	Transpersonal disidentification	158
18	Saving a feeling of wonder and gratitude in your inner database	168
19	What does life want from me?	176
20	Integrity of values	181

Acknowledgments

I want to express my heartfelt gratitude to all my clients, first and foremost, for their trust and courage. Through this trust, we have been able to explore together, throughout the years of therapeutic encounters, how to heal our deepest wounds. The healing has always been mutual, and this book would never have come into existence without my clients' profound openness and willingness to share their struggles within the therapeutic relationship. My thanks go to my partner Manuela for showing me what genuine closeness in a relationship looks like and for her patience throughout the writing process of this book. I am grateful to all the members of the Kayumari community and the Stargate School for allowing me to experience the power of mutual human support and the healing effects of a well-functioning and learning community. Special thanks to Henk Barendregt for assisting me in creating a *phenomenological model of maladaptive schemas* inspired by Buddha's "Discourse on Dependent Origination" in the garden of the Amsterdam café Dignità in July 2018. Further gratitude goes to Maša and Gregor Žvelc for their friendship and inspiring discussions on integrative psychotherapy that we had in August 2023 on the island of Krk. I thank Miroslav Světlák for providing an official expert review for this book. Many thanks to my colleagues Kristýna Drozdová, Veronika Nevolová, and Michaela Cmíralová for taking the time to read the manuscript of this book, for their kind feedback and many recommendations, thanks to which I was able to edit and add to the text of the book and make it more understandable and readable. I also thank Luke W. Dale and Sarah Good for their help with the translation into English and Grace McDonnell from Routledge for her meticulous editorial work—my heartfelt thanks to all of you.

Series Preface

We are thrilled to announce the 15th volume in the *Advancing Theory in Therapy* series, and the first under the expanded team of editors. For me (Keith), it is my great pleasure to welcome Gregor Žvelc and Maša Žvelc, colleagues and friends from Slovenia to the co-editorship of the series, who, four years ago, contributed an excellent volume on *Integrative Psychotherapy* to the series. As a team, we are committed to rejuvenating and expanding the series, already have another book in production, and several proposals under review, so watch this space!

This series is dedicated to the evolution of psychotherapy theories, and to promoting the integration of established theories with groundbreaking research and innovative thinking. Jan Benda's *Mindfulness and the Self* is such a book and meets our high standard of advancing theory by challenging contemporary authors and ideas. Jan builds on modern mindfulness-informed psychotherapies, enriching them with his *phenomenological model of maladaptive schemas* and his theory of the self. He also brings the phenomena of transpersonal experiences into the core of psychotherapy theory and practice.

We (Gregor and Maša) have known Jan for many years and share his passion for using mindfulness and self-compassion in psychotherapy. We all deeply value the concept of schemas, its significance in shaping our worlds, and the search for a self that transcends the personal. We admire his sharp theoretical insights, his development of new theories, and his profound and engaging approach to working with clients. And we are all delighted to include his work in this series.

Mindfulness and the Self offers an original and detailed categorization of the self, including the Transcendent Self, and provides advanced guidance on working with different types of wounded selves. The book explores innovative ways to integrate transpersonal experiences into psychotherapeutic work, addressing how these experiences can heal wounds and transform the self. Jan skillfully integrates psychotherapy and spiritual traditions going beyond the simplistic understanding of mindfulness as a cure for stress and enhancement of personal self. In this way, the book expands the existing theories of self and touches on the subjects that are in psychotherapy not yet sufficiently explored, such as non-dual awareness. I (Keith) may say that this volume beautifully complements the previous one in this series, *Integrative Psychotherapy: A Mindfulness- and Compassion-Oriented Approach*—written by Gregor and Maša.

What further enriches this book is Jan Benda's personal experience as a Buddhist monk, meditator, connoisseur of Buddhist psychology, and expert in psychedelic therapy. His unique perspective brings depth and authenticity to his work.

Besides advancing the theory of self in psychotherapy, this book is a valuable resource for skilled therapists, featuring numerous case illustrations and exercises that also make it accessible to beginning as well as experienced therapists and anyone interested in personal growth and self-discovery as well as in advancing theory.

Maša Žvelc, Gregor Žvelc, and Keith Tudor

Preface

In June 2018, on the feast day of St. John the Baptist, inside a caravan in the Berounka River valley, I inhaled the vapors of 100 mg of dried secretions from the Colorado River toad with a single deep breath. In the following seconds, something unimaginable occurred. It was as if the entire universe transformed into an infinite embrace of emptiness. And I died. Or rather, my conception of who I am disintegrated. It was a staggering shock! A genuine upheaval. However, the impacts of this upheaval on my life turned out to be beneficial. So much tension dissipated. So much joy, trust, and love emerged. What happened? Was it some instant enlightenment? Does such a thing exist? I genuinely do not think so. I believe I simply experientially touched the reality that Buddha referred to as Not-Self (*anattā* in Pali). Before that, in meditation, I had observed and became aware of the impermanence and unsatisfactoriness of all phenomena. The psychedelic mebufotenin (5-MeO-DMT) vividly revealed to me the third characteristic of existence—the absence of any fixed, unchanging Self.[1] That's all. All notions of myself began to seem amusing to me from that moment on. Childish. Moreover, I lost interest in contemplating myself. Feelings of inadequacy or shame practically vanished from my experience. They ceased to arise when I stopped believing in the existence of a permanent Self. The experience that the Narrative Self is a mere concept has positively influenced my experience in the long term.

However, the experience of non-dual consciousness has subsequently influenced me as a psychotherapist as well. I realized, more clearly than before, that self-conscious feelings of *core pain*, which I have been focusing on in individual psychotherapy with clients in recent years (see Benda, 2019), arise based on the ideas we have about ourselves (see the mentioned *Narrative Self*). So, I became (paradoxically) more interested in the Self. Furthermore, I was surprised to find that the Self is a much-discussed topic in psychology, cognitive science, and neuroscience (see, e.g., Brown & Leary, 2017b; Frewen et al., 2020; Gallagher et al., 2024; Giommi et al., 2023; Herma & Greve, 2024; Kyrios et al., 2016b). In my practice with clients over the following years, I paid more attention to so-called negative *core beliefs* and their relationship to feelings of shame, abandonment, and existential dread (see Timuľák & Keogh, 2021). However, I also observed *ego states* and began to clearly distinguish these mental states from bodily feelings (see Lama & Ekman, 2008). I contrasted my findings with psychotherapeutic theories, current scientific knowledge, and insights about Not-Self transmitted within the Buddhist psychology of Abhidhamma (see, e.g., Armstrong, 2017; Burbea, 2014; Goodman, 2020). From these observations and contemplations, a *phenomenological model of maladaptive schemas* emerged (see Chapters 3 and 4 further). It became the fundamental inspiration for this book.

The *phenomenological model of maladaptive schemas* reveals that in the bodies and minds of clients with various clinical diagnoses, very similar *processes* are taking place. This model can assist mindful therapists in better understanding the mechanisms underlying individual symptoms of mental disorders, as well as to tailor better and target specific psychotherapeutic interventions. However, the *Transdiagnostic Theory of the Wounded Self*, introduced in this book, could also inspire contemporary psychedelic-assisted psychotherapy, which seeks to explain the mechanisms of psychedelic effects (cf., e.g., Amada et al., 2020; Cherniak et al., 2022; Gattuso et al., 2023). Psychedelic experiences and intensive mindfulness and insight meditation share many similarities (see Part IV). Among other things, they develop the so-called Transcendent Self, and in this book, we will also explore whether and under what conditions the Transcendent Self can help heal the Wounded Self and cultivate the Authentic Self. In any case, I hope that this book will help you understand yourself and all your Selves and foster a compassionate attitude toward yourself and others. Motivating readers to develop mindfulness and compassion was indeed the main intention with which I wrote *Mindfulness and the Self*.

Jan Benda
Velké Březno
January 7, 2024

NOTE

1 Observing the so-called three universal characteristics of all phenomena (*ti-lakkhana* in Pali) is a part of intensive mindfulness and insight meditation (see, e.g., Grabovac et al., 2011).

Introduction

In the world of psychotherapy, there is a notable discrepancy between the formal diagnosing of mental disorders and the way most psychotherapists approach mental disorders in practice. While, for instance, in research or communication with health insurers, therapists routinely employ diagnostic manuals *DSM-5* and *ICD-11* (see Chapter 1), in therapeutic *practice*, they often approach clients' issues differently (see the so-called case formulation or conceptualization, e.g., Goldman & Greenberg, 2015; Timuľák & Pascual-Leone, 2015). Current diagnoses do not provide much assistance in appropriately targeting psychotherapeutic interventions. Therefore, most colleagues do not only focus on the external symptoms of mental disorders but also strive to uncover and influence the *hidden mechanisms* that underlie individual symptoms. However, diagnostic manuals usually remain silent about these hidden mechanisms because it is often challenging to capture them through objective scientific methods. Nevertheless, there is a very popular tool that is most suitable for detecting these so-called *maladaptive schemas*. That tool is mindfulness, the ability to notice the processes in our body and mind in the present moment.

    In the Buddha's teachings, *mindfulness* has been employed for two and a half millennia as a means of self-discovery, self-healing, and self-transcendence. We use *mindfulness* in this book to examine maladaptive schemas in depth. We will elucidate how maladaptive schemas influence our perception, thinking, experience, and behavior, thereby causing the emergence of overt symptoms of mental disorders. Furthermore, we will demonstrate how we can "disarm" and transform individual elements of maladaptive schemas through mindfulness and self-compassion. However, special attention will be given to our conceptual Narrative Self. The *Transdiagnostic Theory of the*

Wounded Self, introduced in this book, integrates attachment theory (e.g., Cassidy & Shaver, 2016; cf. Kyrios et al., 2016b), pattern theory of self (e.g., Gallagher et al., 2024), and ontological addiction theory (Shonin et al., 2016; van Gordon et al., 2018). It offers a transtheoretical *phenomenological model of maladaptive schemas* and elucidates the role of (lack of) mindfulness and self-compassion in the etiology of mental disorders and psychotherapeutic change. It reveals the influence of our self-concept (*Narrative Self*) on the emergence of psychopathological symptoms and suggests how developing a flexible, Authentic Self and Transcendent Self can enhance resilience, emotion regulation, and the ability to form and maintain close relationships.

The book draws from the insights of ancient Buddhist psychology, Western psychotherapy, psychedelic research, and the latest findings in neuroscience. It describes how developing mindfulness and self-compassion can be used in *individual* psychotherapy. However, it is intended not only for psychotherapists but also for those interested in personal development and sincere spiritual seekers. For one of the central themes of the book is whether transpersonal experiences (whether gained through meditation or psychedelics) can contribute to the healing of our early developmental traumas. Can personal and transpersonal development complement each other? Can transpersonal experiences heal mental disorders? Can they heal our maladaptive schemas? Our "Wounded Self"? And if so, under what conditions? These are questions that the book gradually addresses. Before delving into them, however, we will clarify the crucial role of a flexible, Authentic Narrative Self in our everyday functioning. We will also emphasize the importance of *relational* experiences in cultivating self-compassion. So, what is the structure of the entire book?

In Part I, we will first acquaint ourselves with the mindful diagnosis of maladaptive schemas (Chapter 1). We will briefly discuss developmental trauma and how maladaptive schemas emerge (Chapter 2). Distinguishing the four characteristic components of maladaptive schemas—core beliefs, feelings of core pain, defense mechanisms, and archaic ego states—will follow (Chapter 3). Subsequently, with the help of seven case vignettes, we will illustrate how maladaptive schemas influence the development of psychopathological symptoms in seven selected mental disorders (Chapter 4). We will outline how maladaptive schemas can be treated through mindfulness and self-compassion (Chapter 5).

In Part II, we will delve deeper into the four types of maladaptive schemas (the four "Wounded Selves") and explain that the "Lost Self" arises when we do not feel protected and safe frequently enough in early childhood (Chapter 6). The "Abandoned Self" develops when we lack sufficient warmth and closeness or do not perceive the world as a safe place to live in early childhood (Chapter 7). The "Inferior" and "Inflated Self" emerge when, as children, we lack parental support and recognition or miss firm guidance and loving limits (Chapters 8 and 9). We will then emphasize the significance of *corrective relational experiences* and *memory reconsolidation* in psychotherapeutic change. Additionally, we will mention cognitive reappraisal of core beliefs as a suitable complementary strategy when working with maladaptive schemas (Chapter 10).

In Part III, we will focus on cultivating a flexible, Authentic Narrative Self in relationships with close ones. First, we will recall that "right mindfulness" in our daily lives should be linked to recognizing the ethical-psychological connections of our experiences and engaging in "wise consideration" of our actions (Chapter 11). Subsequently, we will explore how maladaptive schemas compel us to stage and reenact the same scripts in relationships and how to break free from these patterns (Chapter 12). We will discuss "healthy selfishness" and healthy personal boundaries (Chapter 13). Distinguishing between reactive and compassionate (protective) anger will be discussed (Chapter 14). We will hint at how our relationship with ourselves can help us find a balance between dependence and independence in relationships (Chapter 15). We will then think critically about whether corrective relational experiences can be substituted for meditation or psychedelics in healing the Wounded Self (Chapter 16).

In Part IV, we will explore the intersection of psychology and spirituality, delving into transpersonal development. We will elucidate how both meditation and psychedelics foster selflessness and gradually reshape our understanding of ourselves (Chapter 17). We will introduce a new model for integrating transpersonal experiences (Chapter 18). We will draw attention to the syndromes of Mindful Zombie, Spiritual Narcissist, and Enlightened Nerd (Chapter 19). Moreover, we will emphasize that to cope skillfully with everyday life, we need both the passive mode of mindful observation and being and the active mode of thinking and doing (Chapter 20).

Let us add that the topics discussed in individual chapters will be continuously illustrated throughout the entire book with case fragments[1] from my therapeutic practice and examples of dialogues between the therapist and the client. Experts will find valuable references in the book, totaling 278 books, 360 psychological articles, and 71 neuroscientific articles.[2] However, since understanding mindfulness and self-compassion is not easily achieved through theoretical study alone, the book includes 20 practical exercises that allow us to acquaint ourselves with mindfulness and self-compassion experientially. Dear readers, please take a moment to breathe and practice while reading, stepping away briefly from scientific concepts. You will find that your own lived experience will help you better comprehend the various aspects and connections of mindfulness and self-compassion discussed in the book than mere theoretical study.

Now that we have a broad idea of what awaits us in the book, we can move on to Part I, which introduces the foundational principles of Mindfulness-Informed Integrative Psychotherapy.[3]

NOTES

1 To preserve anonymity, the names of clients and other details that could identify them have been altered in the book.
2 Of these, 51% of the cited articles are from the last five years (2019–2023).
3 I have previously described the same "mindfulness-informed" integrative psychotherapeutic approach in the book *Mindfulness and self-compassion* (Benda, 2019). However, it is only in this book that, for practical reasons, I began to refer to it with the established and distinct term "Mindfulness-Informed Integrative Psychotherapy." Nevertheless, I want to emphasize that I am not advocating for a new therapeutic brand. I believe that the effectiveness of psychotherapy is more determined by the personality of the specific therapist than the psychotherapeutic approach itself (see, e.g., Castonguay & Hill, 2017; Wampold & Imel, 2015). Through this book, I aim to illustrate one of the possible ways in which a *mindful therapist* can uncover specific maladaptive processes in the client's mind and body while flexibly utilizing and integrating various approaches in their work with the client. If therapists understand the benefits of developing mindfulness in psychotherapy, perhaps in the future, we may see more diverse "mindfulness-informed integrative psychotherapies." And that is perfectly fine.

PART I

Mindfulness-Informed Integrative Psychotherapy

Have you ever tried entering the word *mindfulness* into an internet search engine? The results were probably overwhelming, weren't they? There are so many books, articles, podcasts, apps, courses, and workshops on mindfulness! Unbelievable! But why? Why is there such a buzz around mindfulness? What makes this topic so intriguing? Why does mindfulness capture the interest of phenomenologists, cognitive scientists, neuroscientists, psychologists, psychiatrists, psychotherapists, and enthusiastic laypeople? I believe the main reason is that mindfulness offers us an entirely new perspective on ourselves and the world around us (Benda, 2019). It allows us to understand better who we are. It enables us to overcome feelings of isolation and self-alienation, fostering instead deep connections with others, a sense of belonging, and closeness. It serves as a tool for self-discovery, self-healing, and self-transcendence. Yes, through mindfulness, we can alleviate mental difficulties. However, we can also touch upon something that transcends us, and all of this is without religious dogma, practically and experientially. That is why I think mindfulness is such a hit. That is why it captivates psychologists.

Over the past 30 years, dozens of approaches and programs utilizing mindfulness have emerged in the world of psychotherapy. These primarily include third-wave cognitive-behavioral therapy approaches, such as Mindfulness-Based Cognitive Therapy (Segal et al., 2013), Mindfulness-Based Stress Reduction (Lehrhaupt & Meibert, 2010), Acceptance and Commitment Therapy (Harris, 2019b), and Dialectical Behavior Therapy (Linehan, 1993). However, there are also existential-humanistic (Gold & Zahm, 2018; Wegela, 2014), psychodynamic (Price & Hooven, 2018; Shepherd, 2020), and integrative approaches (Alper, 2016; Benda, 2019; Žvelc & Žvelc, 2021) that incorporate mindfulness. In his book *Mindfulness and Psychotherapy*, Chris Germer describes three typical ways of integrating mindfulness in psychotherapy that we currently encounter (Germer, 2013).

1. According to him, a practicing therapist can implicitly bring mindfulness into therapy by simply being more aware of the processes occurring within themselves and on the client's side during therapy, thanks to their meditation-enhanced mindfulness.
2. If the therapist additionally utilizes traditional Buddhist concepts for their understanding, acquired through their meditation practice, Germer refers to it as "mindfulness-informed" therapy.
3. He then speaks of "mindfulness-based" therapy if the therapist explicitly teaches the client to meditate or employs various exercises to develop the client's mindfulness.

Over the past 20 years in my practice, I have developed a "mindfulness-informed" individual integrative psychotherapeutic approach (see Benda, 2019). This is because, on the one hand, I am convinced, for a couple of reasons, that the effectiveness of the most widespread "mindfulness-based" programs is somewhat limited by the fact that they take place in a group setting and typically last only eight weeks. More importantly, I do not consider meditation alone as a sufficient tool for treating mental disorders. While I do not doubt that mindfulness-based programs help participants reduce stress or alleviate depression, the question remains whether participants in such programs can use mindfulness even when they experience maladaptive schema activation,[1] i.e., precisely when they need it the most.

In my experience, a mindful and compassionate therapist can provide clients with a corrective emotional (relational) experience in individual therapy. When a therapist, at a critical moment, conveys a *compassionate attitude* toward what the client is experiencing, it leads to *memory reconsolidation* and the transformation of maladaptive schemas (Benda, 2019). However, the key to change lies in the client's new experience *in* the therapeutic *relationship* (cf. Flückiger et al., 2018; Norcross & Lambert, 2018). Therefore, I believe that no exercise performed individually by the client can replace this experience. Hence, in psychotherapy, meditation should always be complemented with other therapeutic means, methods, and techniques.

After all, the aim of mindfulness and insight meditation, in its original context, was never to address our personal or relational issues (Engler, 1984, 2003). Its purpose has always been to achieve awakening (*bodhi* in Pali), meaning the realization of absolute, unconditional reality and liberation from the cycle of rebirth (*saṃsāra* in Pali). However, this does not mean achieving mental health in our Western understanding (see World Health Organization

[WHO], 2018). In everyday life, even an awakened meditator may continue to face all sorts of difficulties (see Chapter 19). Meditation does not automatically lead to acquiring all the competencies necessary for skillful life management. Yet, that is precisely what we aim for in psychotherapy. It is a significant distinction.[2] So, let me emphasize it once again. In meditation, the goal is to break free from *samsara*. In psychotherapy, the goal is to learn to live more contentedly within *samsara*.[3]

We will delve into transpersonal experiences, meditative insights, and their integration in the final Part IV of this book. There, we will discuss experiences of non-dual awareness and ego-dissolution and how such experiences influence our experiences and daily functioning. However, most of the book will first be dedicated to self-discovery, self-healing, and cultivating self-compassion. For as Jack Engler (1984, 2003) aptly stated, we must first be somebody before we can be nobody (i.e., achieve self-transcendence). So here, too, we will follow this wise recommendation. It is worth mentioning that the transdiagnostic approach of *Mindfulness-Informed Integrative Psychotherapy*, described in this book, builds upon ideas previously introduced to readers in the book *Mindfulness and Self-Compassion* (Benda, 2019). It draws from Mirko Frýba's work (e.g., 2008) but is also significantly influenced by Emotion-Focused Therapy (Greenberg, 2021; Timuľák & Keogh, 2021) and Pesso Boyden System Psychomotor Therapy (Baylin & Winnette, 2016). It guides clients (and readers) to utilize mindfulness and self-compassion, especially during the activation of maladaptive schemas (cf. van Vreeswijk et al., 2014). Thus, it also complements Mindfulness and Compassion-Oriented Integrative Psychotherapy (Žvelc & Žvelc, 2021).

NOTES

1 A more detailed explanation of maladaptive schemas will be addressed in the subsequent chapters of this book (cf. also Benda, 2019). For now, we can mention that these are figuratively speaking the "core pathologies" underlying the majority of mental disorders. Schemas, generally speaking, are deeply ingrained emotional and relational patterns or programs that automatically and unconsciously govern our experiences. They correspond to what psychodynamic approaches traditionally referred to as so-called complexes (see, e.g., Adler, 1964) or later within the attachment theory as so-called internal working models (see, e.g., Bretherton & Munholland, 2016; Zimmermann, 1999), or mental scripts (see, e.g., Ein-Dor et al., 2011; Mikulincer et al., 2021).

2 Concerning the importance of distinguishing between absolute reality (which can be apprehended in advanced meditation) and the conventional, conditioned reality of our everyday life, the Buddhist scholar Nagarjuna wrote in the *Mūlamadhyamakakārikā* (*Fundamental Verses on the Middle Way*) at the turn of the second and third centuries (see Siderits & Katsura, 2013).

3 Freud (1952) admitted that when clients in psychoanalysis rid themselves of their pathologies, they then experience only "ordinary human unhappiness" (*gemeines Unglück* in German), which is inevitably linked to everyday life. However, Buddha sought and found a way out of this unavoidable daily suffering. In this book, we will further explore that where psychotherapy ends, meditation begins. Yet, we will also clarify that meditation cannot replace psychotherapy.

CHAPTER ONE

Mindful Diagnosis of Mental Disorders

It has been mentioned that mindfulness has offered psychologists and psychotherapists a rather specific perspective on human beings and their experiences. In this chapter, we will demonstrate that this perspective significantly alters the traditional understanding of mental disorders. Mindfulness reveals, indeed, the same transdiagnostic factors and *processes* in many mental disorders. These factors are often concealed behind external symptoms presented by the client. When a mindful therapist listens to the client, they are not solely concerned with the content of what the client is narrating. The mindful therapist continuously monitors their own feelings and states of mind evoked by the client's storytelling, as well as all external manifestations of emotions in the client (facial expressions, tone of voice, involuntary movements, gestures, body posture, etc.). In this way, the therapist discovers many essential details about the client's experience that the client is often unaware of. In crucial moments, the therapist prompts the client also to notice how they are feeling right now, what is on their mind, etc. Using this approach, the mindful therapist, *within the dialogue with a client*, gradually uncovers the client's feelings of core pain, automatic defense mechanisms, and hidden *core beliefs*. These elements of the client's experience form the basis for mindful diagnosis. Before delving deeper into it, let us say a few words about the official classification of mental disorders used in healthcare.

Currently, psychologists and psychiatrists rely on two fundamentally similar diagnostic manuals when diagnosing mental disorders, commonly referred to by the acronyms DSM-5 and ICD-11. The *Diagnostic and Statistical Manual of Mental Disorders* (DSM-5) is published by the American Psychiatric Association and is used in the United States and Canada. The *International Classification of Diseases* (ICD-11) is issued by the World Health Organization and is used internationally/worldwide. Both manuals provide detailed descriptions of conditions such as schizophrenia and other psychotic disorders. They also cover mood disorders, anxiety disorders, disorders specifically associated with stress or trauma, eating disorders, substance use disorders, personality disorders, and many other conditions. However, one rather crucial aspect is not addressed by either of the manuals—the *causes* of mental disorders. It sounds almost unbelievable. Nevertheless, it is a fact that we do not know the causes of mental disorders. Despite countless theories attempting to explain the origins of various mental disorders, there is no unified theory that all mental health professionals agree upon. It is generally assumed that multiple biological, psychological, and social factors contribute to the development of mental disorders (Borsboom et al., 2019; Dalgleish et al., 2020; Kendler, 2014; cf. Engel, 1977). However, without clarity on the causes of mental disorders, the entire diagnostic process seems somewhat precarious.

Mental disorders are diagnosed based on a person exhibiting typical symptoms or, more precisely, a distinctive constellation of specific symptoms. However, it is pretty common for the same person dealing with the same psychological issue to receive a different diagnosis from various professionals during repeated assessments. One expert may conclude that you suffer from obsessive-compulsive disorder, while another may observe manifestations of a personality disorder. Yet another professional might inform you that you have several different psychiatric diagnoses simultaneously, a phenomenon known as comorbidity. Statistics have repeatedly shown that approximately 50% of psychiatric clients show symptoms of two or more diagnoses simultaneously (Caspi et al., 2014; cf. McGrath et al., 2020). But that is far from the whole picture.

Modern neuroimaging methods have revealed changes in the same brain areas across various psychiatric diagnoses (Gong et al., 2019; Goodkind et al., 2015; McTeague et al., 2020; Parkes et al., 2021).[1] Genome-wide association studies have also shown identical genetic predispositions for different diagnoses (Brainstorm Consortium, 2018; Grotzinger, 2021; Lee et al., 2019; Selzam et al., 2018; Smoller et al., 2019). Additionally, psychiatric medications commonly assist clients with various diagnoses (Minami et al., 2019; Waszczuk et al., 2017; cf. Kelly et al., 2021). How is this possible? Many indications suggest that behind the apparent symptoms of a range of mental disorders, there are likely *common factors* not yet fully understood (Carragher et al., 2015; Caspi et al., 2014; Dalgleish et al., 2020; Krueger & Eaton, 2015; Michelini et al., 2021). Could uncovering these factors help us understand the *causes* of mental disorders? Perhaps. In any case, the current classification of mental disorders is ripe for a fundamental revision (Brunoni, 2017; Nasrallah, 2021; Newson et al., 2021). It should not surprise us that individual mental disorders have much in common. The boundaries between them are not nearly as sharp as the diagnostic categories used so far might suggest.

As experts are well aware of the fundamental shortcomings of the current classification of mental disorders, two significant scientific initiatives have emerged in the United States in recent years, aiming to unveil the hidden common factors of mental disorders.[2] These initiatives are known by the acronyms RDoC (*Research Domain Criteria*; see Insel et al., 2010) and HiTOP (*Hierarchical Taxonomy of Psychopathology*; see Kotov et al., 2017). Both initiatives deviate from the existing categorization of mental disorders and assess all mental disorders solely in terms of the degree of specific dysfunctions in a few dimensions (cf. Michelini et al., 2021). RDoC primarily focuses on the shared genetic, physiological, and neurobiological foundations of mental disorders. On the other hand, the HiTOP initiative is more oriented toward these disorders' psychological, behavioral, and social manifestations. The innovative hierarchical model of psychopathological symptoms developed within the HiTOP initiative is currently closer to practical application in clinical practice. Interestingly, at the top of the pyramid of psychopathological symptoms, HiTOP postulates a single overarching transdiagnostic factor, the so-called p-factor.[3] However, we will demonstrate here that mindful diagnosis allows capturing and describing (operationalizing) specific maladaptive cognitive and affective *processes*, based on which symptoms of individual mental disorders arise and are maintained in clients, far more precisely than both of the mentioned initiatives.

The classification of mental disorders used so far has been influenced by the post-war development of scientific psychology, which, for several decades, emphasized objective methods of investigation while completely discarding introspection (see Watson, 1913; cf. Kraepelin, 1920). Consequently, it often relies on objective, measurable, or observable criteria, such as sleep disorders, muscle tension, motor restlessness, excessive alcohol consumption, deliberate vomiting, overeating, inability to form and maintain close relationships, and so forth. However, diagnostic manuals often describe the individual's *experience* quite vaguely. They commonly use terms like worsened mood, anxiety, and stress and only exceptionally mention feelings of worthlessness, inadequate guilt, or despair. In this regard, mindful diagnosis diverges from the officially endorsed methodology.[4]

The mindful therapist, *collectively with the client*, thoroughly examines the *processes* occurring in the client's body and mind at moments that are problematic for the client and in which the client usually loses control over their experience and/or behavior. These moments often involve the activation of maladaptive schemas, either hindering the client from pursuing their desires or compelling them to do something they do not honestly want (Benda, 2019). Gradually, the therapist and client collaboratively uncover the individual elements of the maladaptive *process* (schema), including primary and secondary emotions, thoughts, states of mind, compulsive tendencies, defense mechanisms,[5] and hidden core beliefs. The consciously identified specific psychopathological mechanism becomes the subject of diagnosis and treatment. It is essential to note that the diagnosis and treatment focus on the *process*, not the client (cf. Goldman & Greenberg, 2015; Greenberg & Paivio, 2003). Let us consider a brief example.

> *Peter sought therapy due to issues in his relationship with his wife, Cristina. He worked as a crisis manager in a large company and was highly successful at work. He could make difficult decisions with a cool head and earned a decent income. He loved his wife and cared deeply for their five-year-old son. However, he frequently experienced uncontrollable fits of anger at home. He would typically explode over trivial matters and behave aggressively. He couldn't understand it himself. It was no help that, outside of the moments when Peter was seething with anger, Peter was aware that his behavior was inappropriate and that the intensity of his reactive anger was not commensurate with the relatively minor importance of the day-to-day issues he and his wife were dealing with. His wife, naturally, was troubled by this behavior. He sought therapy because he was afraid he might lose her due to his actions. Despite countless resolutions to stay calm and approach situations with perspective during the moments when anger gripped him, emotional eruptions usually overpowered him. In those moments, he felt he was losing control over himself.*

For Peter to learn to better regulate his emotions, especially in moments when he typically lost control, it was necessary for him first to become aware of the fleeting primary emotion that had escaped his mindfulness until now (reactive anger is never a primary emotion!). In therapy, the focusing technique (Gendlin, 2003; Weiser Cornell, 1996) can be employed during conversation to achieve this. Therefore, our conversation looked like this:

THERAPIST: Try to recall a specific situation when anger overwhelmed you and you couldn't control yourself. Do you remember such a moment?

CLIENT: Well ... like always when I find an unclean, wet sponge in the dish sink. I can't stand that. It breeds bacteria. I've told my wife so many times! It drives me crazy!

THERAPIST: I see. When did it happen last?

CLIENT: Last Tuesday.

THERAPIST: So, last Tuesday evening after work, you came to the kitchen, and there was a sponge in the sink.

CLIENT:	Yeah. I started swearing terribly. I wanted to throw something.
THERAPIST:	Okay. Let's try to capture that very first feeling, maybe very fleeting, that a person usually doesn't even realize. The feeling that rushed through you in the first millisecond when you saw that sponge. Can you recall that moment?
CLIENT:	It was a shock! Such helplessness! Such despair! It can't be true, I thought.
THERAPIST:	Try to recall that moment.
CLIENT:	(Tries. Takes a deep breath and exhales for a long time, unconsciously placing his right hand on his chest. Shows visible signs of emotionally reliving the imagined moment here and now as he recalls it mentally.)
THERAPIST:	What's happening in your body now? Do you feel any bodily feeling that draws attention?
CLIENT:	I don't know. Such pain. (Looks sad.)
THERAPIST:	What kind of feeling is that?
CLIENT:	I don't know, maybe helplessness ... That my wife didn't clean when I asked her to. She doesn't care.
THERAPIST:	Feeling of injustice? (Pause.) Or humiliation?
CLIENT:	(After a moment.) The feeling that I'm entirely alone in everything. I have to do everything. No one will help me.
THERAPIST:	I see. The feeling of loneliness and isolation.
CLIENT:	Yes. Sometimes I feel so alone. (His eyes light up.) Even in the middle of the family. Why? (Asks softly, but not expecting an answer. Looks surprised for a while and then contemplatively stares ahead.)
THERAPIST:	(After a while.) How is it in your body now? Has anything changed?
CLIENT:	I've calmed down. I don't feel anger at all now. Moreover, the pain in my body is gone. I guess I feel a bit relieved. How is that possible?

During our conversation, Peter mindfully noticed, for the first time, a fleeting but excruciating feeling of loneliness, to which he had always automatically responded with anger and aggression in similar situations. He thus captured the most crucial element of the maladaptive schema that governed his perception, thinking, experience, and behavior in those moments. Interestingly, the mere mindful awareness itself caused a change. The anger, as a defense mechanism, wholly disappeared. A similar shift in Peter's experience can occur in future similar situations, provided that Peter can *mindfully notice* his feeling of childhood loneliness. However, Peter's understanding of what he *needs* in those moments will also play a crucial role. When we feel lonely, we need to feel closeness and compassionate understanding. This is what Peter was able to experience in therapy *in* his *relationship* with me, the therapist. Yet, to prevent Peter from getting stuck (or giving up) in a state of desperate childhood abandonment when he mindfully notices his loneliness in the future, he will need to learn to *be compassionate with himself*. This may take some time. Still, mindful awareness of the feeling of loneliness is an inevitable first step. The fact that Peter shared this feeling with me and could *in relationship* with me experience that I stayed with him, did not abandon him, and understood what he was going through can be an essential corrective experience for him. An experience that will gradually help him break the learned childhood helplessness and develop *self-compassion* as well.

However, with mindful diagnosis, it will be possible to uncover another crucial and deeply hidden element of Peter's maladaptive schema: A core belief that chronologically precedes the emergence of the painful feeling of childhood loneliness. The genesis of feelings of core pain[6] is always conditioned by some idea (belief) usually fixed in childhood, and it is also possible to work with it in therapy using mindfulness.[7] For Peter, it might be a belief like "I am unlovable, no one cares about me, I don't belong anywhere." When Peter mindfully notices that the feeling of loneliness actually arises from such an internalized assumption, he will have the opportunity to challenge the absolute validity of this belief through adult reasoning. Moreover, he will be able to realize that, unlike in childhood, he is no longer dependent on whether he is loved by someone externally. As an adult, he can be kind and caring to himself. He doesn't have to abandon himself, even if the whole world were to leave him. Such awareness can be liberating for him.

Using Peter as an example, we have briefly illustrated the mindful, phenomenological approach to a mental disorder.[8] It should be apparent that our focus is not on whether, according to ICD-11 or DSM-5, Peter meets the criteria for "intermittent explosive disorder" or "emotionally unstable personality disorder." From a mindfulness perspective, such diagnoses merely capture an external phenotype of the disorder. They tell us nothing about how Peter's aggression originates or how he can transform his reactive anger without merely suppressing it. On the other hand, mindful diagnosis focuses on the details of what happens inside Peter at the typical moments that trouble him and what brought him into therapy. It systematically identifies crucial emotional and cognitive elements of the client's maladaptive schema, their interactions, and potential looping (cf. Borsboom & Cramer, 2013; Hájek & Benda, 2008). In addition to core beliefs and feelings of core pain, it typically uncovers long-established defense mechanisms and their impact on maintaining enduring states of mind typical of certain disorders. This approach lays the groundwork for therapeutic interventions precisely aimed at influencing specific maladaptive *processes* that covertly sustain individual symptoms of the disorder.

Years of therapeutic practice covering a broad spectrum of diagnoses have revealed to me that, from a mindfulness perspective, there are remarkably similar maladaptive mechanisms underlying the majority of mental disorders. These mechanisms govern clients' perception, thinking, experience, and behavior when they encounter a trigger specific to them. In my experience, the lack of mindfulness and self-compassion causes these maladaptive processes to typically "defy" clients' conscious efforts to regulate their experience and behavior (see common factors). Mindful awareness of feelings of core pain (1), understanding the unmet *needs* these feelings signal (2), and "seeing through" the limited truth of fixed and often unconscious core beliefs (3) are, in my view, critical drivers of therapeutic change. Generally, it is about becoming aware of certain experienced phenomena and changing one's *attitude* toward them. Now, let us delve into how maladaptive emotional (relational) schemas occur during our development and where our core beliefs and heightened emotional vulnerability come from. This will help us at least partially understand the causes of mental disorders.

EXERCISE 1
Identifying the feeling preceding anger

When we experience anger, it's a clear signal that a *secondary* emotion has surfaced in response to a *primary* one. As mindful therapists, our task is to skillfully identify these *primary* emotions. Let's try this recognition exercise together.

Start by recalling a situation when you felt angry. Dive into the details, pinpointing the *triggers* of your anger. If it involved an interaction with another person, was it their words or how they expressed them that angered you? Did their actions or inactions provoke your anger? Recall the initial thought that crossed your mind in the heat of the moment.

Now, take a moment to pause your thoughts and look at what you feel in your body right now when you are reminded of the situation. Bring your attention to your body. At what place in the body does the bodily feeling occur? What is that feeling? Acknowledge that the situation has stirred anger within you, and that's okay. Allow yourself to feel the anger. However, can you identify the *primary* emotion that precedes the anger? Try to capture the feeling that arises in your body before anger flares up.

If you've identified a physical feeling drawing your attention, attempt to find a word that best encapsulates that feeling. Ask yourself: Is it fear, shock, dismay, or a feeling of injustice? Do you feel abandoned, betrayed, diminished, or humiliated? Is there a feeling of failure or inadequacy? Inquire within: What feeling precedes my anger? What is my "inner Child" experiencing? Mentally go through each of the words above, pausing after each, and observe any shifts in your bodily feeling. Has anything changed in your body? If not, slowly move on to the next word. What word best describes the feeling you're experiencing right now? What do you *need* to feel better? Take a moment to observe your bodily feelings with kindness and compassion.

By entertaining the possibility that beneath anger lies another poignant *primary* feeling, you open yourself to recognizing your vulnerability and nurturing a compassionate attitude toward yourself. You might find a word that resonates with your feelings during this exercise, bringing relief. Alternatively, you might acknowledge an unpleasant bodily feeling without fully understanding it. If, after ten minutes, the feeling persists, gently place your open palm on the area where you feel it, and three times in succession, say in your mind the wish: "May all my painful feelings pass! May I be well!" How do you feel now?

NOTES

1 Creating our concept of Self, which we will delve into in this book, appears to be primarily associated with the activity of the ventromedial prefrontal cortex and other parts of the so-called default mode network. Numerous studies confirm changes in these brain areas in mental disorders (cf. Koban et al., 2021).
2 In the United Kingdom, existing classifications of mental disorders also face significant criticism. The British Psychological Society has offered an alternative perspective on functional psychiatric diagnoses in the document *Power Threat Meaning Framework* (PTMF; see Johnstone et al., 2018).
3 The HiTOP model further categorizes symptoms of mental disorders into three (or six) general categories, describing (1) psychosis (further divided into thought disorder and detachment), (2) so-called externalizing disorders (subdivided into disinhibited and antagonistic), and finally, emotional (internalizing and somatoform) disorders (Kotov et al., 2017; Watson et al., 2022). The focus of this model on specific maladaptive processes is much closer to mindful diagnosis than the nosology of DSM-5 or ICD-11.
4 Carl Rogers (2021) wrote about the still-used method of diagnosing mental disorders, stating that it "is unnecessary for psychotherapy, and may actually be a detriment to the therapeutic process."
5 In Mindfulness-Informed Integrative Psychotherapy, for distinguishing defense mechanisms, we utilize the Abhidhammic phenomenological matrix of "mental defilements" (*kilesa* in Pali; see Benda, 2019; Benda & Horák, 2008).

6 In alignment with Emotion-Focused Therapy, this book delineates three variations of core pain: (1) existential fear, (2) loneliness, abandonment, and (3) inferiority, shame. We will get acquainted with them in more detail in the book's second part (see also Timuľák & Keogh, 2021).
7 Heinz-Peter Röhr, a famous German psychotherapist and author of many books, refers to core beliefs as "secret programs." He refers to maladaptive coping strategies as "antiprograms" (see Röhr, 2022a, 2022c).
8 It appears that the mindful, phenomenological perspective on mental disorders allows for a better understanding of psychopathological processes occurring in our brains, also at the biological level (see, e.g., Guendelman et al., 2017; Vago & Silbersweig, 2012; Wielgosz et al., 2019; cf. Zarate-Guerrero et al., 2022).

CHAPTER TWO

Early Childhood Experiences and Development of Psychopathology

Psychotherapy has always been interested in the *development* of our personality and specific early *relational* experiences from our childhood since its inception. Sigmund Freud (e.g., 1942) and later Erik Erikson (1998) described critical developmental stages[1] through which children pass, associating the emergence of pathological *complexes* with "fixation" or "stagnation" at certain lower levels of our development. However, contemporary psychotherapeutic approaches most often draw from the theories of John Bowlby (1976, 1982, 1983) and Donald Winnicott (2017, 2018b, 2018c). These theories emphasize the significance of our early experiences *in relationships* with primary caregivers. In brief, it is primarily about the fact that, as small children, when we *need* something, we are entirely *dependent* on whether our caregivers recognize and fulfill that need. We cannot do it ourselves (see the concept of learned helplessness—Seligman, 2005). So, if attentive and caring parents adequately attend to fulfilling our needs in childhood, a feeling of basic security and trust gradually shapes and strengthens within us. We also internalize the impression that we are worthy of love and that the "world" accepts us. However, suppose our needs are chronically not met. In that case, we experience "annihilation anxiety," "unspeakable terror," or "primitive agony" (i.e., core pain—cf., e.g., Hurvich, 2018). In contemporary terminology, we form very negative and general core beliefs about ourselves, others, and the world around us (see, e.g., Beck, 2021).

Leading world experts in attachment theory, Mario Mikulincer and Phillip Shaver, posit that positive early childhood *relational* experiences form the foundation for the gradual development of mindfulness and compassion toward others and ourselves (see Shaver et al., 2017). Conversely, adverse childhood experiences frequently lead to the formation of maladaptive emotional (relational) schemas and the fixation of defense mechanisms that merely *divert attention* from core pain without addressing our actual needs. The association between adverse childhood experiences and the occurrence of maladaptive schemas in adulthood has recently been confirmed by several meta-analyzes (May et al., 2022; Pilkington et al., 2021; see also, e.g., Hughes et al., 2017). Dozens of studies have also affirmed the impact of adverse childhood experiences on the development of negative core beliefs (see Aafjes-van Doorn et al., 2020; cf. Aafjes-van Doorn et al., 2021).[2] The formation of maladaptive schemas, however, is not solely conditioned by experiences such as domestic violence, psychological or physical abuse, abandonment, sexual abuse, substance abuse, etc. *Trauma* leading to the creation of maladaptive schemas is often much more subtle (cf., e.g., Teicher et al., 2006).

INVISIBLE TRAUMA

When Zoe reminisced about her childhood, she most often recalled being alone in her little room and feeling bored. From the age of two, she lived with her mother, who usually watched TV upon returning from work and was "glad to have some peace." Nothing dramatic happened in their home. Zoe had enough food and clean clothes. However, virtually nothing was happening at all. They never had any visitors. They never went anywhere. They didn't talk much. Zoe knew that her mom "had a lot on her plate," was tired, and she didn't want to "add more work" for her. She felt that she was bothering her mom with her chatter. "I'm terrible," she thought sometimes when she saw her mom's expression in response to her childish questions. To make her mom happy, she gradually learned to be a "good girl," which meant not talking much and not asking for anything. Then her mom was content, and sometimes she even stroked her hair. At school, Zoe tried hard. However, how she and her mom lived together seemed natural and normal. Nevertheless, she often felt somewhat strange. "I must be somehow odd," she thought.

The example of Zoe is typical in that, at first glance, it doesn't seem like she experienced any *trauma* in childhood. No one physically tortured her, nor did anyone sexually abuse her. She had a childhood similar to many other children of her generation. Nevertheless, it is indeed a trauma. It is called complex[3] (or cumulative) interpersonal, *developmental trauma* (Spinazzola et al., 2018), and sometimes also betrayal trauma (Freyd & Birrell, 2013). In this case, we can say that Zoe was, among other things, a victim of chronic emotional abuse. By learning to be a "good girl," she satisfied her mother's need ("to have peace") instead of the other way around, where the mother would meet Zoe's needs. Zoe's needs were neglected, even entirely ignored, and little Zoe experienced chronic *deprivation* and traumatization (cf. McLaughlin & Sheridan, 2016; Sheridan & McLaughlin, 2014). Zoe was emotionally rejected by her mother a million times (and, in this sense, abandoned). She didn't experience closeness, empathic connection, understanding, acknowledgment, or appreciation in her relationship with her mother (see a child's basic needs, Benda, 2019). But because she didn't know anything different, she didn't know what was missing (not until adulthood). As every small child is dependent on their mother, she couldn't leave or get angry with her mother (that could worsen their relationship). Instead, she learned to ignore her feelings, dissociate,[4] and try to meet the needs of others (originally her mother).

From the attachment theory perspective, we would speak of developing a so-called fearful-avoidant attachment in Zoe. However, from the viewpoint of the phenomenology of the maladaptive schema, it is more crucial for us to state that, due to chronic traumatization in the relationship with a passive and emotionally indifferent mother, three significant aspects have emerged in Zoe: (1) the formation of negative core beliefs about herself, others, and the world ("I am weird, awful, invisible, unacceptable, I can't rely on anyone"), (2) the development of a disposition, resulting from the potential (re)activation of core beliefs hidden in the soul, to (re)experience painful feelings of emptiness and childhood (cosmic) loneliness, and (3) the formation of tendencies to dissociate and/or compulsively focus on the needs of others. These elements still govern her experiences and behaviors whenever the maladaptive schema is activated.

Countless studies in the field of interpersonal neurobiology and cognitive, affective, and social neuroscience over the past two decades have demonstrated and extensively documented the impact of early childhood experiences on the development of the human brain (see, e.g., Cozolino, 2014; Siegel, 2020; cf. Long et al., 2020; Nemeroff, 2016; Teicher et al., 2022). Research has shown that early childhood experiences *fundamentally* influence the development of our brains' neural infrastructure and biochemistry. It turns out that typical consequences of adverse childhood experiences include elevated emotional reactivity to certain stimuli (triggers), low emotional awareness, and difficulties in emotion regulation (McLaughlin et al., 2020; Weissman et al., 2019). Studies on children and adolescents experiencing adverse experiences or deprivation have demonstrated functional and structural differences not only in areas related to experiencing and regulating emotions (e.g., the amygdala, anterior insula) but also in areas related to experiencing one's own identity or Narrative Self (including the medial prefrontal cortex, posterior cingulate cortex, orbitofrontal cortex; see McLaughlin et al., 2019; Price et al., 2021; cf. Gilboa & Marlatte, 2017). This is indeed intriguing from the perspective of the functioning of maladaptive schemas (see further, cf. also Chapter 15).

In my experience,[5] maladaptive emotional (relational) schemas typically develop during the period up to the age of seven in a child. This occurs either as a result of a single traumatizing experience or, more commonly, due to the chronic unfulfillment of some of the child's basic developmental needs (developmental trauma; see Benda, 2019). However, some theories attribute the origin of maladaptive schemas, for example, to traumatic experiences during childbirth (Grof, 1988, 2021). Memories of such experiences are not typically accessible to our consciousness under ordinary conditions. Nevertheless, they regularly surface in altered states of consciousness induced by the use of psychedelic substances (LSD, DMT, psilocybin) or during Holotropic or Maitri Breathwork. Moreover, numerous studies provide evidence for the transmission of maladaptive schemas from one generation to another, both through upbringing (see Sundag et al., 2018; Zeynel & Uzer, 2020) and through epigenetic mechanisms (e.g., Craig et al., 2021; Yehuda & Lehrner, 2018).

From the perspective of psychotherapy of particular mental disorders, it is crucial to understand that they share a very similar *etiology*, in which *traumatic* experiences of *early* childhood or the chronic unfulfillment of specific developmental needs of a child play a significant role (see Part II). These *early traumatic experiences* visibly manifest in the structure and neurophysiological functioning of our brain (cf. also Spalletta et al., 2020) and are closely related to what psychologists refer to as maladaptive schemas. Now, let us take a closer look at the phenomenology of maladaptive schemas.

EXERCISE 2
Emotional bridge to the past

Have you ever experienced emotions getting a bit out of hand and the intensity of your feelings being exaggerated and not matching your trivial situation? In such moments, our heightened emotional reactivity allows us to *understand* which developmental *need* was not fulfilled in our childhood. Thus, we can develop *self-compassion*. It's enough to ask ourselves a few right questions. Would you like to give it a try?

For this exercise, sitting upright, having both feet on the ground and hands in your lap, is suitable. So, sit in this way. And recall a specific situation when you felt emotionally overwhelmed as vividly as possible. What exactly triggered your emotional reaction at that time? What thought crossed your mind in that most intense moment? Replay that emotionally charged moment several times in your mind.

Now, having remembered that particular situation, what do you feel in your body? Where in your body does any physical feeling appear? What kind of feeling is it? Can you name it? Where from your past do you recognize this physical feeling? What childhood memories come to mind as you ask yourself these questions? (Close your eyes for a moment while recalling.)

If memories from your childhood come to mind, try stepping back from them a bit and looking at them for a moment as if you were a viewer in a cinema or perhaps from a bird's eye perspective. Remind yourself that, at this moment, you are safe and just recalling past events. You are an adult now. You are no longer a child. These are just memories. Now, as an adult, you have many options in your life that you didn't have in childhood. You are freer and more independent. However, when you, as an adult, look at these old memories, do ultimately realize what you *needed* so much back in childhood and did not have. Loving care? Understanding? Acceptance? Protection and safety? Support, recognition, appreciation? Firm boundaries? Or personal space? What did you *need* the most?

Now, realize that you can approach your wounded "inner child" with a *compassionate attitude* as an adult. Imagine, for instance, that if, as an adult, you could visit yourself when you felt a given way in childhood, you could physically touch your "inner child." You could put your hand on its shoulder, hold its hand, or hug it. You could tell your "inner child": "I love you. I care about you. I am with you, and I always will be. I will never leave you. I understand how you feel. I will care for you, support you, and protect you." Then, notice how you feel when you imagine approaching your "inner child" with compassion. Remember that feeling well. And bring your attention back to the present.

Realize that you are still sitting upright. Your feet are touching the ground. You are back here and now. Do you better understand why your feelings were so intense in that situation now? Think about how much your emotions reacted to the present situation and how much they corresponded to the childhood situation. It's great that you are not as dependent on others' help in adulthood. You can take care of your needs yourself. Realize that. Do you remember how you felt when you approached your "inner child" with a *compassionate attitude*? Could you try adopting such an attitude toward yourself the next time you encounter a similar situation?

NOTES

1 The existence of so-called critical periods in the development of the human brain is now confirmed by contemporary neuroscience (see, e.g., Lepow et al., 2021; Nelson & Gabard-Durnam, 2020).
2 The prevalence of adverse childhood experiences in Western countries is, incidentally, relatively high (up to 61%; see Merrick et al., 2018; cf. Crouch et al., 2019; Giano et al., 2020; Hughes et al., 2021; Sacks & Murphey, 2018).
3 For interest's sake, it is worth mentioning that the ICD-11, for cases of repeated or prolonged traumatizing experiences, introduced a new diagnosis called "complex post-traumatic stress disorder." The diagnostic criteria for this disorder include, among other things, the presence of negative beliefs about oneself and feelings of shame, guilt, or failure (see World Health Organization, 2018).

4 *Dissociation* is a specialized term referring to the internal detachment from one's own emotions, typically in an attempt to avoid experiencing painful feelings. As a defense mechanism, dissociation often manifests, e.g., during the experience of a traumatic event (cf. Chefetz, 2015).
5 Since I work exclusively with adult clients, I do not have the opportunity to examine maladaptive schemas in children directly. The presumed development of maladaptive schemas is primarily inferred from the recollections of adult clients who retrospectively recall when they experienced feelings of core pain in the past. In the case of experiences from the first 2–3 years of age, I estimate the impact of early experiences based on the client's heightened emotional response to their assumptions and imaginings about what happened in the first years of their life (see details further below). If there is no heightened emotional arousal in the conversation with the client about their childhood, the event we are discussing cannot be therapeutically utilized at that moment.

CHAPTER THREE

Maladaptive Schemas

Psychodynamic approaches traditionally refer to clusters of interconnected images, sensations, feelings, memories, and thoughts associated with traumatic experiences that unconsciously (autonomously) influence our perception, experience, and behavior—with the word *complex* (Shalit, 2002). The names of individual complexes often derive from mythological stories or fairy tales, such as the Oedipus complex (Freud, 1945), Icarus complex (Lear, 2019), Lucifer complex (Moore, 2003), Savior complex (von Franz, 2000), or the Medusa complex (Woodman, 1988). In psychology, however, there are many other similar concepts. For example, Stanislav Grof (1988, 2021) uses the term "systems of condensed experience," Roberto Assagioli (1993) spoke of "subpersonalities," Eric Berne (2021) of "ego states," and John Bowlby (1976, 1982, 1983) described the influence of "internal working models" on how we perceive and experience ourselves and our relationships. However, these concepts represent the same thing in different words—*programs* that control us without our awareness and often against our will. In contemporary terminology in psychotherapy, these programs are most commonly referred to as "early maladaptive schemas" (Young et al., 2003), "emotional schemas" (Leahy, 2015, 2022), "maladaptive emotion schemes" (Greenberg, 2017), or "relational schemas" (Žvelc & Žvelc, 2021). However, psychologists and psychotherapists were not the first to discover these schemas.

Long before the advent of scientific psychology, historical Buddha (*Siddhattha Gotama*) described the influence of maladaptive cognitive-affective patterns on the emergence of human suffering. He referred to these patterns as so-called *mental formations* (*saṅkhāra* in Pali; see, e.g., Bodhi, 2005). In the famous "Discourse on Dependent Origination," which serves as a foundational cornerstone for the psychology of all Buddhist traditions, Buddha explained how these formations, as latent and compelling *tendencies*, negatively impact (obscure, distort) our perception and experience (see Burbea, 2014; Hájek & Benda, 2008; Kurak, 2003; cf. Watson, 2018). Recognizing their obscuring influence mindfully, he considered a path to liberation from the endless cycle of the constant arising of all our troubles (cf. Bodhi, 2005). In this chapter, we are, in a sense, going back two and a half millennia to harness Buddha's wisdom for understanding maladaptive schemas.

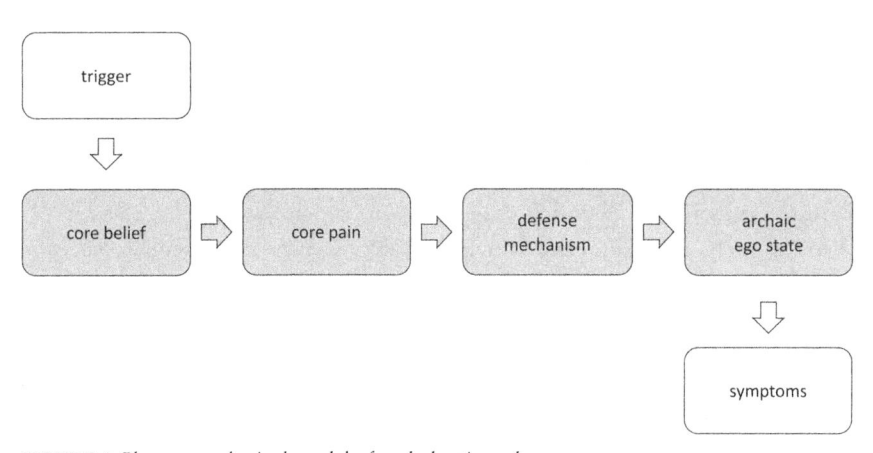

The original *phenomenological model of maladaptive schemas*, which we will introduce in this chapter, is rooted in my over two decades of therapeutic experience and inspired by the Buddha's matrix of "dependent origination" (see Hájek & Benda, 2008). It combines and integrates (1) insights from cognitive-behavioral therapy, which emphasizes, among other things, "core beliefs" (see Beck, 2021), (2) insights from Emotion-Focused Therapy, which primarily deals with the feelings of "core pain" (Greenberg, 2021; Timuľák & Keogh, 2021), (3) insights from psychodynamic approaches, which have thoroughly mapped the functioning of various "ego-defense mechanisms" (Freud, 2019), and (4) insights from schema therapy, which describes, among other things, maladaptive states of mind (so-called ego states or modes; see Arntz et al., 2021; Jacobs et al., 2020). Our model incorporates all four mentioned elements into a single procedural matrix (see Figure 1).

According to this framework, the fundamental element of every maladaptive schema is some negative, overly generalized, usually unconscious, yet profoundly ingrained core belief.[1] The model illustrates that when a trigger activates a negative core belief within us, it automatically generates a *self-conscious feeling* of core pain. Because this traumatic feeling was not adequately addressed in childhood, it subsequently triggers some "established" defense mechanism within us. Suppose we fail to mindfully notice these first three elements of the maladaptive schema, and they repeatedly emerge. In that

FIGURE 1 Phenomenological model of maladaptive schema

case, we gradually find ourselves in a state (or mode) of *narrowed consciousness*, which we can understand as an "ego state" (cf., e.g., Abramowitz & Torem, 2018). Chapter 4 will introduce us to numerous specific examples of maladaptive schemas. Let us delve deeper into core beliefs here.

According to neuroscience, our brain operates quite egocentrically. When processing information and deciding which information is of higher priority and "deserves" our attention, it automatically and rapidly prioritizes stimuli it believes are somehow related *to us* (the so-called self-prioritization effect; see Sui & Rotshtein, 2019; Yankouskaya & Sui, 2022; cf. Hohwy, 2016; Nairn et al., 2019). The brain also better remembers information somehow *related to our person* (the self-reference effect; see Cunningham et al., 2014; Sui & Humphreys, 2015). Interestingly, during the so-called self-referential processing, the brain relies on both bodily interoceptive sensations (the so-called core, Minimal Self) and our conceptual *idea* of our *Self* (the autobiographical or Narrative Self; see Frewen et al., 2020; Gallagher, 2000). But how does our notion of who or what *we* are, our so-called *conceptual, Narrative Self*, come into being?

Developmental psychology associates the formation of our *narrative identity* with the experiences we undergo *in relationships* with our primary caregivers during childhood (Marraffa et al., 2016; Siegel, 2020). According to cognitive-behavioral therapy, early traumatic experiences lead to the creation of negative (also irrational, dysfunctional, pathogenic) core beliefs to which, as children, we attribute *absolute* and total/complete validity. For instance, if one of our parents frequently criticizes or belittles us, we may easily believe that we are "*objectively*" incapable, unacceptable, and deplorable (shame). If our parents pay too little attention to us, we may easily form the idea that we are "*objectively*" uninteresting, insignificant, or weird (loneliness). Moreover, suppose our parents fail to protect us when we feel threatened or, worse, emotionally or physically abuse us. In that case, we may easily conclude that we are "*objectively*" weak, vulnerable, and powerless (existential dread). These core beliefs are, in any case, stored in our implicit semantic memory (see, e.g., Mancini & Mancini, 2018). Regardless of what we consciously *think* about ourselves in adulthood, if a maladaptive schema is activated, these beliefs re-emerge within us and influence our perception, experience, and behavior. In general, if we want to reappraise these beliefs in adulthood, we must first become *mindful* of them. Only then can we realize (gain *insight*) that these beliefs do not represent an objective and unchangeable "truth." Our adult perspective then works to "disarm" and neutralize the effects of these childhood core beliefs.

> *One of the issues that somewhat complicated Ryan's life was that he would consume five or six beers almost every day. This bothered his wife primarily, but it also unsettled Ryan that he usually couldn't*

resist the urge to have a beer, even though he sometimes wanted to. Therefore, we discussed his experiences in a specific instance just before the urge arose.

THERAPIST: What exactly was happening yesterday before you opened the first beer?

CLIENT: I was in a good mood when I came home from work. I was looking forward to my wife and little daughter. My wife, I think, was also glad that I was home. I was fine until I suggested cooking something.

THERAPIST: What happened next?

CLIENT: My wife turned pale (the trigger for Ryan's maladaptive schema). It was clear she wasn't enthusiastic about the idea. She said something about me cooking spicy food...

THERAPIST: And what was happening inside you at that moment?

CLIENT: My heart starts pounding again when I think about it now. It feels like I'm falling into some dark abyss. Everything suddenly seems distant, like behind thick glass (state of mind).

THERAPIST: What's the feeling in your heart?

CLIENT: I feel rejected and afraid that I'm doing something wrong.

THERAPIST: Ah, the feeling of rejection or abandonment, maybe even worthlessness (core pain).

CLIENT: Yes. (Nods and smiles a little. We both know we've talked about these feelings several times before.)

THERAPIST: (After a moment.) Could some hidden self-image of yours trigger these feelings? What goes through your mind when you feel that fear and worthlessness?

CLIENT: I'm afraid that I don't deserve love. That I'll never please anyone because I'm totally out of place. I'm worried that I'm messed up and different. That I'm some monster, like really "weird" (core belief). (Once Ryan says this, he feels relieved. He shakes his head. Then he looks at me with a slightly sad smile.) That can't be true!

THERAPIST: (After a moment.) A weird monster. It's a fantasy, isn't it? (We both smile at each other. Ryan reappraises his childhood perception.)

In Mindfulness-Informed Integrative Psychotherapy, working with core beliefs (cognitive interventions) typically only complements therapeutic procedures aimed at inducing *corrective emotional (relational) experiences* and transforming feelings of core pain (see Benda, 2019). If the client is already capable of consciously and compassionately addressing feelings of shame, abandonment, and existential dread, reappraising their childhood core beliefs usually poses no significant challenge for them. This was the case with Ryan. It is worth noting that, according to cognitive-behavioral therapy, besides core beliefs about ourselves, general core beliefs about other people (e.g., "Everyone just wants to take advantage of me") and the world as such (e.g., "The world is dangerous, unjust") are also shaped in childhood. However, these beliefs also have a self-referential nature as they evaluate others and the world *in relation to us*. They essentially complement our beliefs about ourselves. Within maladaptive schemas, they also lead to the emergence of similar self-conscious *feelings*. Therefore, I do not assign such importance to this distinction. So, let us instead take a closer look at our Narrative Self and its role in various mental disorders.

EXERCISE 3

Abstractions and generalizations

Have you ever experienced unpleasant thoughts or images lingering in your mind for a long time, and you kept returning to them mentally? This typically happens when we are unaware of the specific feeling we are experiencing at a given moment and/or when our thoughts become too abstract and generalizing. In the following exercise, let's see what happens when we become more aware of a particular feeling and mindfully notice our thoughts' abstract and overly general nature.

Think of a topic on which your mind easily fixates, tending to cycle into endless contemplation. It could be a personal relationship matter or, similarly, a topic that seemingly doesn't concern you much, such as politics, the environmental situation, celebrity scandals, etc. Allow your thoughts about the chosen topic to flow for a moment (2–3 minutes). Then, try to stop thinking and observe what you feel in your body when you recall that topic. Shift your attention to your body. Where in your body is there some physical feeling? What kind of feeling is it? What color could it have? What musical genre could capture it? Decide to explore this feeling more closely.

You can ask yourself the following questions: Is the feeling I am currently experiencing a form of fear? Is it a form of anger? Could it be a form of excitement? Could it be a form of resistance? Is it a form of shock, amazement, or surprise? Or is it a sad feeling? Does this feeling relate to powerlessness, humiliation, or guilt? Repeat the question of what kind of feeling it is until you truly understand your feeling or can at least categorize it into one of the mentioned categories. Then, move on to the next step.

Now, decide to explore the nature of your thoughts on the given topic. Look at your thoughts through the eyes of an external observer. And realize whether your thoughts on the subject are more optimistic and constructive or pessimistic and destructive. Are your thoughts evaluative? Do they concern the past, present, or future? Please be especially mindful of whether they are specific and concrete or have a generalizing nature. Are your thoughts sticking to particular facts, or do you derive more general conclusions from the facts? If you catch your mind tending to generalize, abstract, or derive additional assumptions and conjectures from the facts, become aware of the general conclusions or assumptions your mind is drawing about the topic. Try to formulate them as particular sentences and consider writing these sentences down if needed.

Now, distinguish which thoughts on the given topic only state facts and which thoughts further interpret the facts. What part of your thoughts is verifiable truth? If you find it challenging to admit that some of your thoughts are mere assumptions and generalizations unsupported by objective facts, why is that so? Does the possibility that reality might differ from your assumptions threaten you? Can you think of alternative ways to interpret the given facts? Try to look at the matter from a different perspective. How would your opponent interpret the issue? Finally, realize whether your attitude toward the subject has changed. What feeling do you have now?

NOTE

1 Cognitive neuroscience refers to core beliefs as so-called high-level priors (see Clark, 2015; Schoeller, 2023).

CHAPTER FOUR

Narrative Self and Mental Disorders

As hinted in Chapter 3, psychologists traditionally distinguish between two fundamental aspects of the Self: the Self as subject (*I*) and the Self as object (*Me*; for further details, see the introduction to Part IV and Figure 11 on page 150). The Self as an object, also referred to as the Narrative Self (Gallagher, 2000), conceptual Self (Rogers, 2021), or autobiographical Self (Damasio, 2000, 2010), emerges through our thinking and imagination.[1] It is our conception of ourselves as individuals with a unique past, present, and future. It is a *story about us* that we tell ourselves and others internally or aloud. A narrative that allows us to make sense and meaning of our own lives and understand the continuity of our development over time. This narrative can be concise or filled with many details and plot twists. It can be an optimistic, meaningful story full of hope or a pessimistic, meaningless tale full of despair. If the narrator of this story believes that the hero, our Narrative Self, possesses some *permanent* and *unchanging* traits, which the narrator judges, evaluates, and compares, this story can become a source of feelings of shame or inferiority and, subsequently a variety of psychopathological symptoms (cf. Benda, 2019; Brown & Leary, 2017b; van Gordon et al., 2018). However, if the storyteller believes that the story's hero can *change*, learn from mistakes, and evolve, such a story can be a source of support and hope. In any case, we need some idea of ourselves (narrative identity) for everyday life. The fact that intensive meditation can reveal the non-existence of any enduring and unchanging Self does not mean we can do without a Narrative Self (see further in Parts III and IV of this book). Meditative experiences of Not-Self only shift our perspective and understanding of who we indeed are (see, e.g., Giles, 2019).

Before we describe the Transcendent Self or Not-Self, there is still a long journey ahead. First, we should understand the role of the Narrative Self in everyday life and in the development of various mental disorders. Let us, therefore, follow in the hot footsteps of contemporary personality psychology, which, until recently, focused primarily on the role of personality traits in the etiopathogenesis of mental disorders but is now discovering the importance of the Narrative Self in mental health and illness (Adler & Clark, 2019; McAdams et al., 2021).

Psychologist Kate McLean from Western Washington University and her team recently distinguished three fundamental dimensions that capture our Narrative Self. The first dimension captures the *structure* of our life story, influenced by our ability to recall specific memories, their context, and chronological sequence. The second dimension captures the *motivational* and *affective themes* of our self-concept. This dimension is influenced by our overall sense of whether we can actively influence events in our lives and manage our emotions and behavior, our generally optimistic or pessimistic outlook on our lives, and finally, our overall positive or negative experience of closeness and understanding with others (cf. attachment style). The last, third dimension captures the storyteller's effort to give *meaning* or *sense* to their life experiences and connect them with the present moment they are in now. It relates to who we once were according to our understanding, who we are today, and the direction we want to continue developing (McLean et al., 2020).

However, let us pose the question: Why is our Narrative Self, with all the above-mentioned dimensions, so crucial in our everyday lives? Moreover, let us clarify what can happen when our ability to create a Narrative Self temporarily collapses. This occurs, for example, in the psychosis of the schizophrenic spectrum (see, e.g., Laing, 2010; Sass et al., 2018). During a psychotic episode, a person loses the sense of being the actor and creator of their actions. He alienates himself from his thoughts, feelings, and body; sometimes even feeling they belong to someone else. They lose the ability to orient themselves in time and imagine a possible future. Consequently, their life story becomes utterly incoherent and fragmented. It lacks specific details, structure, and context. The individual experiences intense and painful emotions but simultaneously loses confidence that they could influence their experiences or life in any way. They undergo chaos. They struggle to interpret life events meaningfully and relate them to the present. Understanding others and connecting with them is naturally disrupted. A person in a psychotic episode thus finds themselves in deep internal isolation (see Cowan et al., 2021; cf. Laing, 2010). It is worth noting that we can rightfully assume that so-called positive symptoms of psychosis, such as hallucinations and delusions, are likely related to the disruption or breakdown of narrative identity. However, they might also be an attempt by the psyche to give meaning, sense, or order to the chaotic experiences (cf. Evans & Read, 2020; Hasson-Ohayon & Lysaker, 2021; Perry, 2020).

In any case, the breakdown of the Narrative Self signifies, at the very least, a profound crisis or even a catastrophe in everyday life with possible long-term consequences. However, psychoses are not the only group of disorders in which the Narrative Self is involved in the onset. Numerous global experts today emphasize that *self-referential processes* are crucial in most mental disorders (see, e.g., Kyrios et al., 2016a; Shonin et al., 2016; cf. Moore et al., 2017). In this chapter, we will demonstrate how our view of ourselves (see core beliefs) influences the development of psychopathological symptoms in seven different mental disorders. This will prepare us for the healing of our "Wounded Self" (see Part II of this book).

SOCIAL ANXIETY DISORDER

Clients whom, according to the current diagnostic system (ICD-11), we would diagnose with social anxiety disorder (SAD) experience excessive anxiety in various social situations and interactions with others. They fear any public speaking or meeting new, unfamiliar people. They are afraid to initiate a conversation but also, for instance, to eat or have a drink in the presence of others. They fear humiliation or embarrassment. In social situations, their minds are filled with persistent automatic thoughts that anticipate potential threats to their narrative identity. They attentively and meticulously monitor their behavior and experiences (e.g., signs of nervousness). However, they are hypercritical of themselves and expect to be judged just as critically by others. In fact, they desire to make the best possible impression on others. Nevertheless, they expect rejection, dismissal, or ridicule (Gilboa-Schechtman et al., 2020). Deep down, their catastrophic thoughts activate negative core beliefs, such as "I am weird, uninteresting, just a nuisance" (cf. Gregory et al., 2016). This, in turn, triggers and intensifies their experience of anxiety and often leads to avoiding certain feared situations. Their tendency to experience shame in relationships makes them very vulnerable (see Riskind & Calvete, 2020).

To gain a precise understanding of all the essential components of the maladaptive schema, we may encounter in cases of SADs, let us illustrate them with the example of the client, Daniel.

> *Daniel worked as an IT specialist (developer) in a large multinational corporation. He enjoyed programming; besides cycling, it was his main hobby. He spent much time at the computer, often working into the night. However, things were going well with his wife and two children. Even though Daniel was not fond of socializing, they*

got along fine, and everything worked out. His wife had become accustomed to Daniel not liking company. She loved Daniel and appreciated that he provided well financially. Consequently, she learned to visit her parents on her own with the children. She also met friends outside of home. So, in essence, Daniel should not have any problems, except for the fact that from time to time, he had to undergo a "motivational interview" with his supervisor, participate in mandatory team building with his colleagues, or even present his results to the company's Product Manager (boss). In those moments, Daniel panicked. Suddenly, he felt like he "could not do anything." He was embarrassed about his apparent nervousness and was sure he would make a fool of himself. The idea of embarrassment terrified him so much that he even contemplated resigning. There was no communication with Daniel several days before an interview or presentation. The only thing that helped him was playing World of Tanks for hours. During the game, he could at least momentarily forget the fear of failure.

What were the components of Daniel's maladaptive schema? Furthermore, what role did Daniel's childhood-fixed self-image (see core belief about the Self) play in this schema? The prolonged state of Daniel's mind, which appeared a few days before an interview or presentation, could be, in line with schema therapy terminology, identified as the "punitive Parent" mode (see Arntz et al., 2021; Jacobs et al., 2020; cf. Calvete et al., 2013; Norton et al., 2022; Pinto-Gouveia et al., 2006). However, for psychotherapy, it is crucial to help the client also become aware of the hidden core belief that influences their experience and the feeling of core pain, which is the metaphorical emotional core of the maladaptive schema. With Daniel, we had to thoroughly examine what feeling the idea of a planned presentation to the boss evoked in him. In the interview, it first became apparent that Daniel feared embarrassment in front of his boss. When I asked him to imagine how he would feel afterward if the embarrassment occurred, Daniel named his feeling a failure, of inferiority. The core belief that this feeling triggered, Daniel expressed as "I am incapable, I am incompetent." The entire schema looked as follows: The idea of presenting to the boss initially activated the core belief "I am incompetent" in Daniel (see conceptual, Narrative Self). This belief evoked a feeling of *inferiority* and reactive self-hatred. Furthermore, that initiated the ego state of the "punitive Parent," Daniel internalized in childhood. All the essential components of Daniel's maladaptive schema are illustrated in Figure 2.

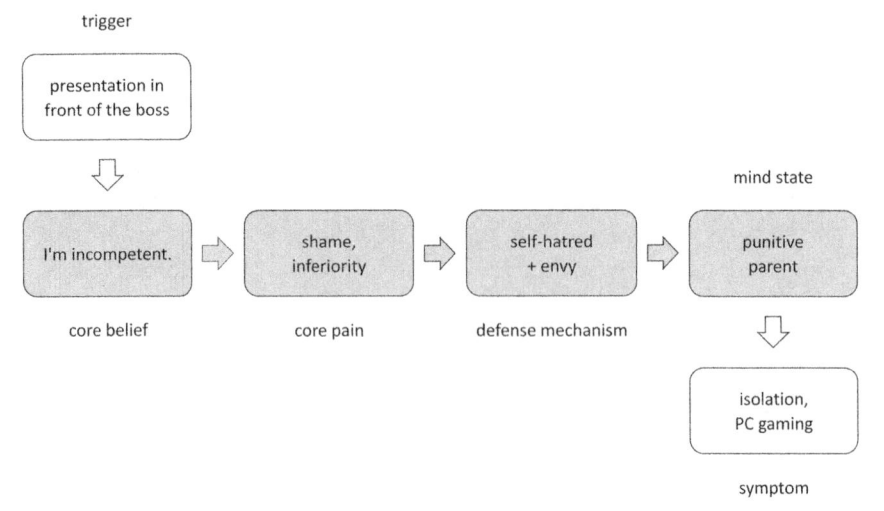

```
              trigger

    ┌─────────────────┐
    │ presentation in │
    │ front of the boss│
    └─────────────────┘
            ⇩
                                                        mind state

 ┌──────────────┐   ┌──────────────┐   ┌──────────────┐   ┌──────────────┐
 │I'm incompetent.│ ⇨ │   shame,     │ ⇨ │ self-hatred  │ ⇨ │   punitive   │
 │              │   │  inferiority │   │   + envy     │   │    parent    │
 └──────────────┘   └──────────────┘   └──────────────┘   └──────────────┘

   core belief         core pain       defense mechanism        ⇩

                                                        ┌──────────────┐
                                                        │  isolation,  │
                                                        │  PC gaming   │
                                                        └──────────────┘

                                                           symptom
```

FIGURE 2 Daniel's maladaptive schema

OBSESSIVE-COMPULSIVE DISORDER

Clients diagnosed with obsessive-compulsive disorder (OCD), according to the current diagnostic system, also experience anxiety. However, this anxiety remains in the background for them because their attention is primarily occupied by unpleasant, intrusive, persistent, and repetitive thoughts or images (obsessions) and their futile attempts to banish these thoughts or images. Typically, these thoughts or images threaten their Narrative Self (Ahern & Kyrios, 2016, Olatunji et al., 2019). They are morally unacceptable to clients because they involve issues such as dirtiness, depravity, contamination, disorder, chaos, "blasphemy," sexuality, aggression, violence, harm to someone, etc. (cf. Aardema et al., 2021). At the same time, clients often have compelling urges (compulsions) to perform certain activities, quite meaningless or at least exaggerated personal rituals, associated with adhering to very rigid and stereotypical rules. These compulsive activities bring them at least partial relief from anxiety. However, they consume an unreasonable amount of time in their lives (often many hours a day) and prevent them from engaging in more important and meaningful activities. People with OCD essentially become slaves to their rituals. Among the most common rituals are compulsive hand washing, perfectionistic cleaning, hoarding, repeated checking of everyday tasks (Did I lock the door? Did I turn off the iron?), pointless counting of things, or repeating certain words or phrases in their minds. From the perspective of mindful diagnosis, it is primarily about understanding the processes that occur in the minds and bodies of clients when the maladaptive schema is activated. This can be illustrated using the example of the client, Amy.

Amy reached out to me because of persistent and frightening thoughts that she might accidentally harm or even kill someone. The very fact that such thoughts appeared in her mind terrified her. "Am I crazy?" she asked me. "Is it possible that I am some aggressive psychopath? It feels horrible that these things come to my mind." Amy's greatest fear was related to driving. While driving, she often had the thought that she might not have noticed and accidentally run over someone. Frequently, during her journeys, she would go back and repeatedly pass through certain places to make sure there was no dead body lying somewhere. Sometimes, she even got out of the car to check if an injured person had not crawled into the bushes. Such repetitive checking understandably delayed her, and she often arrived at meetings late. However, the irrational fear that she had killed someone was too intense.

The constricted state of consciousness (ego state) in which Amy found herself during the activation of the maladaptive schema could be, in line with schema therapy terminology, labeled the "perfectionistic overcontroller" mode (cf. Tenore et al., 2018). However, a more detailed conversation with Amy was needed to determine the primary feeling of core pain accurately. It first emerged that Amy feared the (omnipotent) guilt she would experience if she ran someone over. When I then prompted her to mindfully observe this feeling of (omnipotent) guilt, she experienced whenever she imagined running someone over, she was able to recognize the feeling of *existential dread* that had previously escaped her mindful attention. The core belief that triggered the feeling of existential dread revolved around her impression that she could not trust her senses and could not control her thoughts. She expressed this belief: "I do not have myself under control, I am unreliable, I am crazy" (Narrative Self). This presumed "truth" terrified her and secondarily prompted a desperate attempt to ensure she had not run over anyone. She became very attached to the idea of the person she might have run over. Moreover, because she could not see that this idea contradicted what she perceived through her senses during the drive (a calm ride with no pedestrians on the road), she was compelled to repeatedly reassure herself and return to the "scene of the crime." All the crucial, mindfully distinguishable components of Amy's maladaptive schema are illustrated in Figure 3.

DEPRESSIVE DISORDER

Clients diagnosed with depressive disorder, according to the current diagnostic system, experience oppressive and crushing states of sadness, emptiness, and despair without apparent cause, typically lasting for several weeks. During depressive episodes, these clients practically lose interest in all usual activities. They become passive, fatigued, and exhausted. If possible, they withdraw

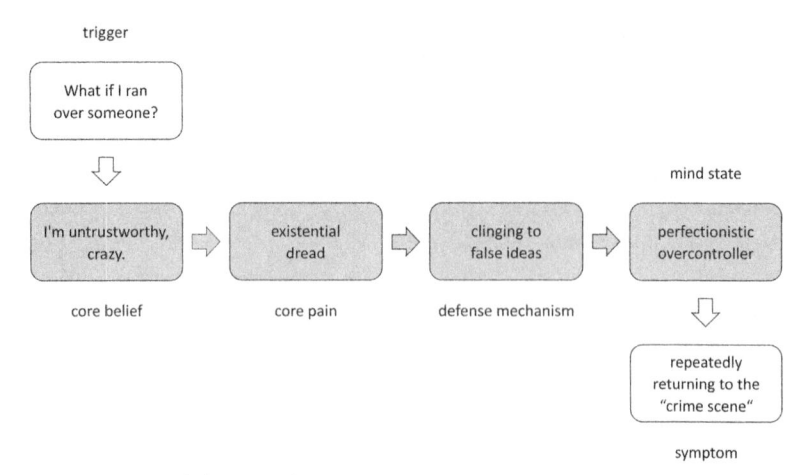

```
                    trigger
              ┌──────────────────┐
              │   What if I ran  │
              │   over someone?  │
              └──────────────────┘
                       ⇩
                                                                        mind state
┌──────────────────┐   ┌──────────────┐   ┌──────────────┐   ┌──────────────────┐
│ I'm untrustworthy,│ ⇨ │  existential │ ⇨ │  clinging to │ ⇨ │  perfectionistic │
│      crazy.      │   │     dread    │   │  false ideas │   │  overcontroller  │
└──────────────────┘   └──────────────┘   └──────────────┘   └──────────────────┘
   core belief            core pain       defense mechanism           ⇩
                                                              ┌──────────────────┐
                                                              │    repeatedly    │
                                                              │  returning to the│
                                                              │   "crime scene"  │
                                                              └──────────────────┘
                                                                       symptom
```

FIGURE 3 Amy's maladaptive schema

into solitude, struggling to concentrate on anything. They suffer from loss of appetite, sleep disturbances, and loss of libido. In terms of observable mental processes, however, depression is characterized primarily by cognitive rumination—cyclical, compulsive, pessimistic, and unproductive thinking about the same topics (Nolen-Hoeksema et al., 2008). Dozens of studies have demonstrated that the thinking of depressive clients is subject to cognitive biases, selectively focusing on negative information and memories from the past, making disproportionate generalizations, and automatically assuming the worst-case scenario for the future, among other tendencies (Everaert et al., 2017; Nieto et al., 2020). However, thinking in depressed clients is also typically very self-referential and hyper-self-critical (Bulteau et al., 2023; Cowden Hindash & Rottenberg, 2017; Davey & Harrison, 2022; Tackman et al., 2019). Clients constantly engage in negative self-evaluation and condemnation, being highly demanding and holding perfectionistic expectations. They do not forgive themselves and assess their worth solely based on achieved results or failures (Kopala-Sibley & Zuroff, 2020; Luyten & Fonagy, 2016).[2] Ruminations thus go hand in hand with the activation of negative core beliefs, such as "I am worthless" or "I do not belong anywhere" (cf. Otani et al., 2018).

For a concrete understanding of individual mindfully recognizable components of the maladaptive schema encountered in the case of depressive disorder, let us consider the example of the client, Zoe (see also Chapter 2).

Zoe worked as a teacher at an elementary school. She lived alone. She had experienced one longer relationship with a man who treated her rudely. He exploited her, insulted her, and humiliated her. There was even physical violence. Then he left her, and she struggled to cope with it for a long time. However, when Zoe came to me, she was not seeking anyone anymore. She got used to it. And, in a way, she was "glad to have peace." She did not believe that any decent guy would be interested in her. She had no close friends. Just work. She often napped in the afternoon. Everything tired her – shopping, cleaning, visiting her parents. Perhaps psychiatric pills were putting her to sleep as well. However, from time to time, she fell into states of complete despair and resignation. All it took was, for example, a colleague at work not responding to a work email. That is where it started. She felt that he had somehow realized that she was "weird." She was almost sure he did not reply because she was not worth the response. It was horrible for her. She felt deeply hurt. She blamed herself for not being able to appear more confident, not being able to make friends with colleagues, not being able to rise above such a thing, and not being indifferent to it. Moreover, the thought of what awaited her in life terrified her. She expected they would want to get rid of her at work sooner or later that they would fire her. "What kind of life is this?" she asked. However, she had no strength for anything more than her thoughts. She shut herself in at home. She crawled into bed. She just wished to sleep, to forget.

The ego state in which Zoe found herself during the depressive episode could be, following schema therapy terminology, labeled the "lonely Child" mode (cf. Stavropoulos et al., 2020). However, what primary feeling of core pain did Zoe experience? She was not too aware of her feelings. Her mind was occupied only with endless remorse and worries. It took some time before she could pause her thoughts for a moment and become aware of how she felt. Eventually, she called her feeling sadness, *loneliness*. Zoe subsequently expressed the core belief that elicited this feeling: "I do not deserve love; nobody can love me" (Narrative Self). The entire schema is illustrated in Figure 4.

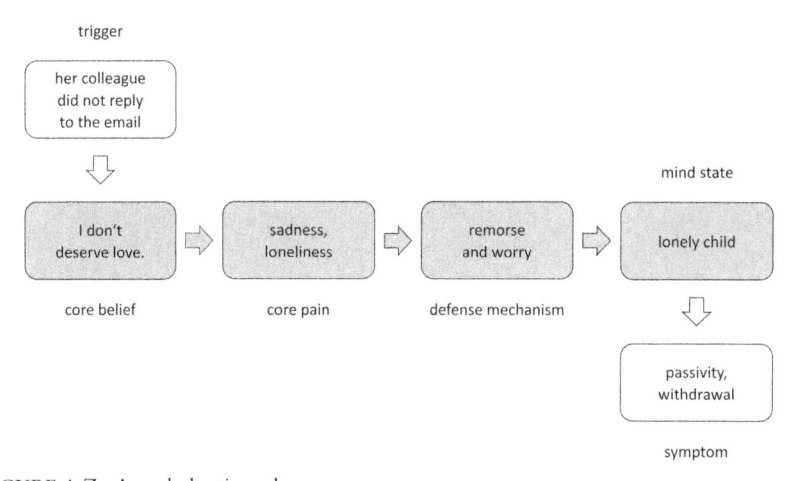

FIGURE 4 Zoe's maladaptive schema

POST-TRAUMATIC STRESS DISORDER

The development of post-traumatic stress disorder (PTSD) occurs in some clients who have experienced a shocking, terrifying, or life-threatening event. This could be, for example, a tragic traffic accident, the sudden death of a loved one (especially a child), severe physical injury, a fire, flood, destructive tornado, assault, sexual abuse, domestic violence, and so on. Typically, these are situations where the option to fight or flee is not readily available, and a person experiences paralyzing terror and helplessness (cf. Levine, 2015; Levine & Frederick, 1997). Clients with PTSD continue to re-experience these traumatic, overwhelming emotional events for months after the incident in the form of persistent intrusive memories (flashbacks) and nightmares. In their everyday lives, they often remain in a state of heightened alertness and arousal, as if constantly anticipating a threat. People with PTSD tend to display emotional numbness outwardly and may not experience common social emotions. As a result, they struggle with forming or maintaining close relationships. They also typically avoid people, situations, activities, and places that might remind them of the traumatic event.

According to statistics, approximately 70% of people will encounter a potentially traumatizing event during their lifetime (Benjet et al., 2016; Dückers et al., 2016). However, not everyone who experiences such an event will develop PTSD. Nevertheless, it appears that the presence of maladaptive schemas and negative core beliefs is among the predictors that significantly increase the likelihood of developing PTSD (see, e.g., Agorastos et al., 2019; Cockram et al., 2010; Hobfoll et al., 2020; Karatzias et al., 2016; Vasilopoulou et al., 2020; cf. Horowitz & Sicilia, 2016; LoSavio et al., 2017). Professor Golan Shahar from Ben Gurion University and his team describe the relationship between negative beliefs about the Self and the world and PTSD symptoms as a vicious circle. According to them, negative core beliefs contribute to the development of specific PTSD symptoms. However, these symptoms, in turn, reinforce these core beliefs. This vicious circle significantly complicates the recovery from the consequences of trauma (Shahar et al., 2013). Let us illustrate specific components of the maladaptive schema using the example of the client, Eve.

Eve's house burned down. Shortly after she and her husband, after years of hard work and effort, finally managed to complete the long-awaited reconstruction of their home, they were celebrating Christmas together with their children. Eve touched the tree with a lit sparkler. It caught fire, and then the curtains ignited. Before they could grab a bucket of water, the living room was already in flames, filled with choking smoke. To avoid suffocation, they were forced to run out onto the street, helplessly watching the burning house and

NARRATIVE SELF AND MENTAL DISORDERS

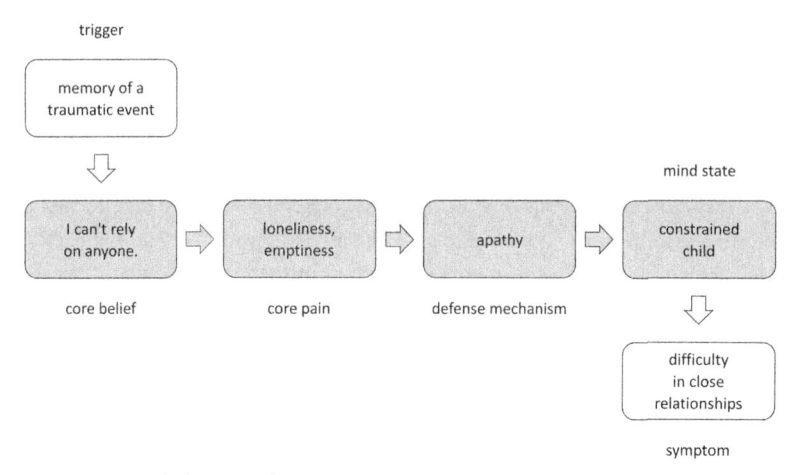

FIGURE 5 Eve's maladaptive schema

the subsequent intervention of the firefighters. Nothing was left of their personal belongings. For several months, they lived in a rented apartment. Eve gradually arranged repairs with the help of insurance money. However, she and her husband were utterly alienated. They did not speak to each other. He was angry and blamed her. Eve functioned like a robot. She felt nothing.

By schema therapy terminology, the state of mind in which Eve found herself could be characterized as the "constrained Child" mode (cf. Zaman et al., 2021). Eve's indifference, apathy, and resignation functioned as a defense mechanism. In therapy, it took several sessions before Eve could recognize the primary feelings of emptiness, loneliness, and sadness. Consequently, she expressed her core belief, which triggered these feelings: "I cannot rely on anyone." Eve had carried this belief since childhood. The fire only reaffirmed to her that it was a "reality." However, at the same time, this belief evoked deep within Eve a feeling of infinite *loneliness* and sadness, followed by apathy, which had been "protecting" her from this painful feeling. All components of Eve's maladaptive schema are depicted in Figure 5.

PERSONALITY DISORDER

Regarding personality disorders, ICD-11 describes five key personality traits typical for this disorder, namely negative affectivity, detachment, dissociality, disinhibition, and anankastia (World Health Organization, 2018; cf. also Riegel et al., 2020).[3] When we elaborate on these characteristics a bit, we can state the following: (1) Clients diagnosed with a personality disorder according to ICD-11 are

39

emotionally labile, impulsive, and struggle with regulating their own emotions. The intensity of negative emotions these clients experience (anxiety, hatred, guilt, shame) often does not correspond to the relatively minor importance of the given situation, and their reactions appear highly exaggerated. (2) In relationships with others, clients with a personality disorder typically maintain a significant distance. They avoid closeness, being reserved and measured. They stay on the surface in communication, usually not revealing their true feelings to others. Consequently, they lack genuine friends and have more acquaintances. (3) They are also highly self-centered and inconsiderate. They cannot empathize with others, showing no interest in the feelings and needs of other people. They often draw attention to themselves, expecting automatic interest and admiration from others. They consciously and shamelessly exploit, hurt, humiliate, bully, or manipulate others. When pursuing their own goals, they "walk over dead bodies." They have no moral inhibitions, lying, slandering, being rude, aggressive, and cruel. They ignore the rights of others, thinking only of themselves. (4) In decision-making, some people with a personality disorder are irresponsible and impulsive, acting based on immediate external or internal stimuli. They take risks without considering the consequences, being impatient, absent-minded, and unreliable. They do not plan much and quickly lose interest in things. They act spontaneously, focusing only on immediate gains. (5) On the other hand, other clients with a personality disorder may exhibit high rigidity and perfectionism. These clients strongly adhere to their standards, norms, habits, and rules, maintaining a consistent daily routine, emphasizing organization and order, planning carefully, and avoiding risk. They have very defined views on what is right and what is unacceptable.

However, what does the Narrative Self of individuals with a personality disorder look like? Experts exploring narrative identity in people with personality disorders describe it as painfully inconsistent, fragmented, and lacking continuity (e.g., Lind et al., 2020; Liotti & Farina, 2016). According to them, individuals with a personality disorder feel alienated from their own lives. They struggle with feelings of emptiness and unreality. Their sense of free will, or the sense that they can control their actions (sense of agency), is disturbed. They typically evaluate life as a whole negatively. Nevertheless, their life story often involves complex trauma and painful experiences of neglect, abandonment, and isolation (Luyten et al., 2020). They tend to have negative core beliefs, such as "I am terrible," "I am not normal," "I cannot change," but also, for example, "I am better than others" or "I deserve more" (cf. Akyunus & Gençöz, 2020; Beck, 2015). Let us take a closer look at the complete maladaptive schema in the case of the client, Simon.

Simon was gay. He had a boyfriend. However, he still lived with his mother. His childhood was associated with playing the piano. He practiced for many hours every day and participated in competitions. After

NARRATIVE SELF AND MENTAL DISORDERS

successfully completing the conservatory, he gave up playing. It did not bring him joy. He increasingly realized that playing had been his mother's "project." When he came to me, he seemed to be "searching for himself." It was as if he was beginning to understand who he was not. However, he did not know who he was. Nevertheless, he suffered from significant mood swings. He found it challenging to be separated from his boyfriend. He feared that his boyfriend would leave him if they did not see each other for a few days. He constantly had to reassure himself that his boyfriend cared about him and was thinking about him. When in doubt, he experienced fits of intense anger. It was enough, for example, for the boyfriend to arrive late for a meeting, and Simon would be consumed by hatred. He raged. He verbally attacked and accused his boyfriend in a very unfiltered manner. The boyfriend had to assure him of his affection. It usually took Simon many hours to calm down.

The ego state in which Simon found himself in such moments could be labeled, in line with schema therapy terminology, as the "enraged Child" mode (cf. Bach & Farrell, 2018). However, what triggered Simon's hatred? When I prompted Simon to recall what he felt while waiting for his delayed boyfriend, a fraction of a second before he began to rage, Simon discovered an excruciating feeling in his heart. It surprised him; initially, he did not know what kind of feeling it was. "It is like someone stabbed me in the heart," Simon described his feeling. With the help of focusing (Gendlin, 2003; Weiser Cornell, 1996), he gradually realized it was *abandonment*. The desperate abandonment of a small child. He expressed the core belief that triggered this feeling in the words, "Nobody can be trusted." Simon's entire maladaptive schema is illustrated in Figure 6.

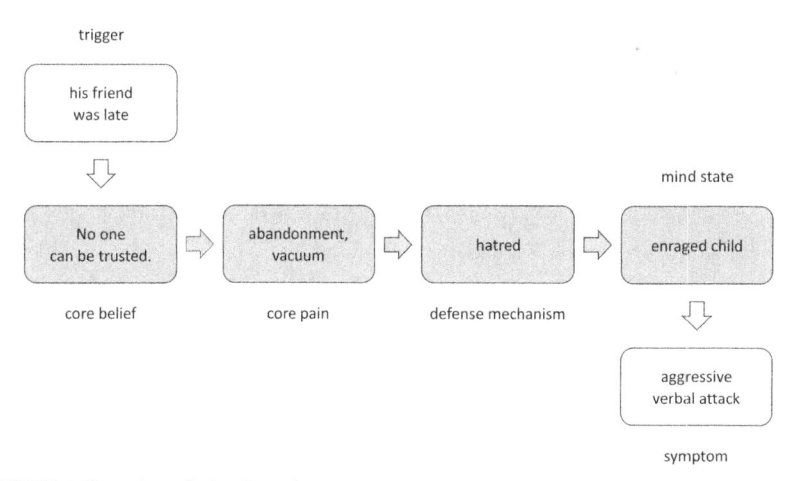

FIGURE 6 Simon's maladaptive schema

ANOREXIA NERVOSA

Clients who, according to the current diagnostic system, would be diagnosed with anorexia nervosa tend to practically identify their Narrative Self with their body, a phenomenon known as self-objectification. Since their fragile sense of self-worth is almost exclusively dependent on their body weight and proportions, they deliberately engage in extreme weight loss, starvation, vomiting, or excessively intense physical exercise. Anorexic clients consistently preoccupy their thoughts with their appearance, aspiring to achieve a perfect figure while fearing being overweight (cf. Smith et al., 2018). Simultaneously, they are excessively perfectionistic and self-critical (Bardone-Cone et al., 2020; Basten & Touyz, 2016). They are not easily satisfied, and their compulsive effort to meet high physical standards is, deep within their psyche, confronted with negative core beliefs such as "I am defective, repulsive, unacceptable" (cf. Hatoum et al., 2022). Achieving bodily perfection, however, does not free them from these beliefs. Let us illustrate this again with the example of the client, Veronica:

> *When Veronica came to me, she was studying at university and was troubled by the fact that she did not have a boyfriend or any close female friends. She envied her classmates for receiving more attention from male peers and explained it to herself by thinking she was not physically attractive enough. Consequently, she dedicated much time to physical exercise, going for a run every day. She also anxiously monitored her diet, frequently switching between various diets and fasting. However, this did not seem to help in her relationships. As Veronica went to school, she was already afraid of how her classmates would look at her. She imagined that they would find her repulsive. When she saw an interesting male classmate talking to another girl, she completely lost control over her feelings and behavior. At that moment, she hated herself intensely. In her mind, she would endlessly berate herself, and the only thing that made her feel better was to "torment" her body—perhaps by starving it thoroughly or exercising until she would faint. Nevertheless, she sensed that there must be some other way. She just did not know what it was.*

The constricted state of consciousness that Veronica experienced when trying to change her body according to her perfectionist ideas could, in line with schema therapy terminology, be labeled the "demanding" or "punitive Parent" mode (cf. Talbot et al., 2015). The core belief consciously identified by Veronica was expressed in words such as "I am unacceptable," "repulsive," or "fat." The difficulty, however, was that Veronica (1) considered her belief as

NARRATIVE SELF AND MENTAL DISORDERS

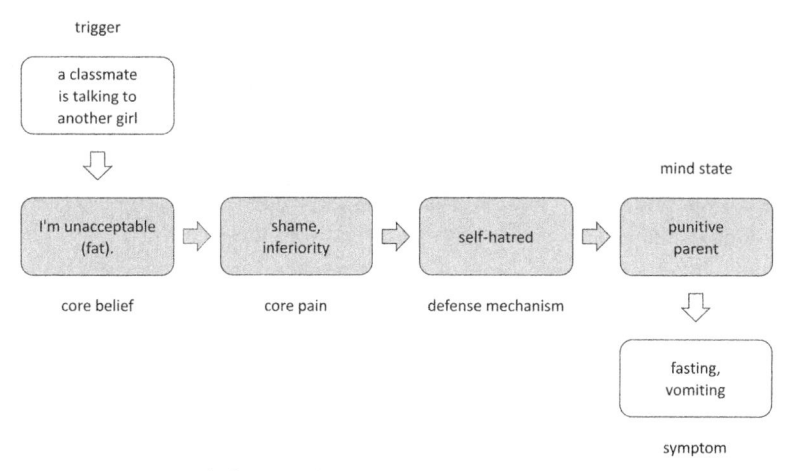

```
trigger
┌─────────────┐
│ a classmate │
│ is talking to│
│ another girl│
└─────────────┘
      ⇓
┌──────────────┐    ┌──────────┐    ┌──────────┐    ┌──────────┐
│I'm unacceptable│ ⇒ │ shame,   │ ⇒ │self-hatred│ ⇒ │ punitive │
│   (fat).     │    │inferiority│    │          │    │  parent  │
└──────────────┘    └──────────┘    └──────────┘    └──────────┘
                                                         ⇓
 core belief        core pain       defense mechanism
                                                    ┌──────────┐
                                                    │ fasting, │
                                                    │ vomiting │
                                                    └──────────┘
                                                      symptom
```

FIGURE 7 Veronica's maladaptive schema

an objective reality and (2) was not aware that she was experiencing *shame*, thus *needing* to experience unconditional compassionate self-acceptance. In therapeutic work, it was crucial to help Veronica first become aware of what she truly felt and then connect the painful feeling of inferiority with memories from her early childhood. Only then could Veronica see through the subjective and cruel nature of her childhood belief. How Veronica's entire maladaptive schema looked before we processed its individual components in therapy is illustrated in Figure 7.

ALCOHOL DEPENDENCE

The final example of a traditional diagnosis that we will discuss in this chapter is alcohol dependence. According to the current diagnostic system, we can speak of alcohol dependence in clients who struggle to regulate alcohol consumption (frequency, quantity) and excessively and repeatedly use alcohol at the expense of other personal interests even though this use damages their health, relationships, and/or functioning at work. The urge to drink (also referred to as craving) is so strong in dependent individuals that they have difficulty resisting it. However, from the perspective of mindful diagnosis, it is crucial to note that alcohol intoxication simultaneously allows the dependent individuals to avoid unpleasant self-conscious emotions (see core pain) they would otherwise experience (Luoma et al., 2019; Witkiewitz & Villarroel, 2009; cf. Brewer, 2017). Similar to all the disorders mentioned above, maladaptive schemas also come into play here (see, e.g., Chodkiewicz & Gruszczyńska, 2018; Knapík & Slancová, 2020; Straver, 2017). Dependent clients also have core beliefs deep down, such as "I am incapable, weak, faulty, inadequate, undesirable" (cf. Beck et al., 2001; Liese & Beck, 2022). The external symptoms (excessive drinking) here also arise as a result of the operation of defense mechanisms that "protect" clients from experiencing core pain.

Let us illustrate the specific processes occurring in the body and mind of a client with emerging alcohol dependence using the example of Ryan, whom we previously discussed in Chapter 3. What components comprised Ryan's maladaptive schema? The ego state that Ryan experienced while consuming his daily five to six beers could, following schema therapy terminology, be labeled the "detached self-soother" mode (cf. Kersten, 2012; Straver, 2017). The primary feeling of core pain could be described as a feeling of *inferiority* (shame). The core belief evoked by this feeling, expressed by Ryan, was "I am really weird" (Narrative Self). And the urge (desire) to have a beer served as a defense mechanism for Ryan, diverting attention from the feeling of inferiority. Figure 8 illustrates all these components of Ryan's maladaptive schema.

When we now review Figures 2–8, it will be apparent from a phenomenological perspective that clients with externally different diagnoses often undergo very similar self-referential processes. From this viewpoint, the visible external symptoms by which we establish traditional diagnoses are only the metaphorical tip of the iceberg. If we do not see "beneath the surface" (into the body and mind of clients), it is difficult to influence them. In the seven examples provided in this chapter, we could see how maladaptive schemas functioned. We could also understand the role that our irrationally held core beliefs about ourselves, others, and the world (Narrative Self) stored in childhood play in the functioning of these schemas. However, before delving into how mindfulness and self-compassion can transform maladaptive schemas in Chapter 5, let us note that many experts are currently exploring the role

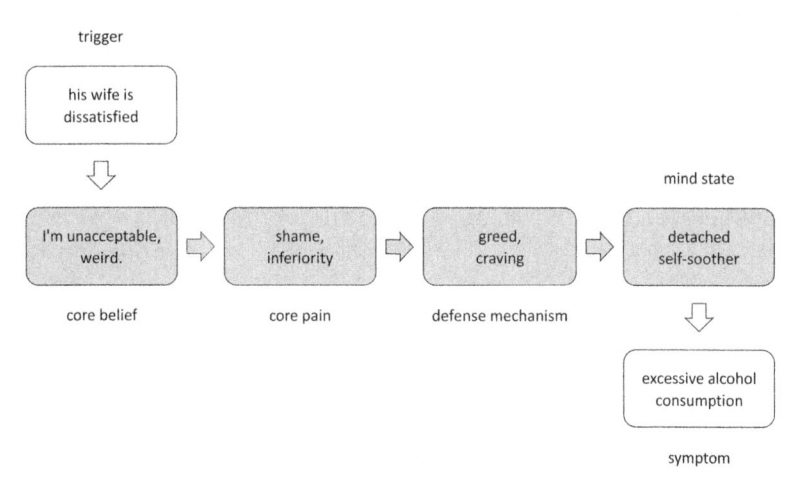

FIGURE 8 Ryan's maladaptive schema

of self-referential processes in the etiopathogenesis of mental disorders (see, e.g., Brown & Leary, 2017b; Kyrios et al., 2016b). Moreover, for example, Edo Shonin and William van Gordon, within the framework of the so-called ontological addiction theory, similarly to us, connect the emergence of various psychopathological symptoms with our mistaken belief in the existence of an inherently existing Self (Shonin et al., 2016; van Gordon et al., 2018). However, in Chapter 5, we will demonstrate that merely understanding that our Narrative Self is a mere construct may not be sufficient for transforming maladaptive schemas. There are, in fact, more essential agents of psychotherapeutic change (cf. Harrer & Weiss, 2016).

EXERCISE 4

A loving letter to your Authentic Self

Negative core beliefs about ourselves are closely linked to a lack of kindness and compassion toward ourselves. The defense mechanisms that automatically activate in our minds in response to core pain do not contain warmth or understanding. However, cultivating a kind and compassionate *attitude* toward our feelings, moods, and thoughts is necessary for transforming maladaptive schemas. A compassionate, accepting *attitude* toward core pain is actually the only healthy alternative to defense mechanisms. So, let us focus on cultivating self-compassion in the following exercise.

Find a quiet place where you can dedicate at least half an hour just to yourself. Prepare paper and a pen. Then try to look at yourself as if you were a loving person, a partner, a close friend, or a loving parent. If you were writing a loving letter to someone you really care about, and you know that they're currently going through a challenging time, how would you start the letter? Write this loving address on paper and use your name.

Start by writing a letter expressing your interest in the person you're writing to (your Authentic Self). Tell them how you feel about them. Express your love and support for them. Let them know that you're thinking of them and that they are important to you. Thank them for all the good things they do (be specific). Share with them what you appreciate about them and what you admire. Forgive them for all their mistakes and shortcomings, and instead, ask them what they need the most right now and offer your help. However, avoid giving them any advice! Trust that they can handle things on their own. Don't make any demands on them! Your task is to show them that you stand by them and will always be there for them, even if things don't go well. Write it to them. Try to encourage them. While writing, try not to be rational but express your warm feelings and loving attitude. Imagine you're writing to someone you've fallen in love with or to your child who is far away right now. What would you write in such a letter?

Once you have written the letter, take a moment to rest in the present and let your thoughts settle a bit. Notice how you felt while writing the letter. What were you experiencing? Then, read the letter aloud. Read it slowly and be aware of the reactions each sentence evokes in you as you hear them. Notice all the feelings that arise in your body and try not to suppress them in any way. Accept them. All your feelings are okay. Once you finish reading the letter, mindfully observe what you feel in your body.

NOTES

1 Contemporary neuroscience is also attempting to identify which brain regions are associated with our narrative Self (see, e.g., Tacikowski et al., 2017; cf. Araujo et al., 2015; Davey et al., 2016; Fingelkurts et al., 2020, 2022; Frewen et al., 2020; Gattuso et al., 2023; Menon, 2023).
2 Functional neuroimaging studies of the brain have revealed increased activity in specific areas of the default mode network during depressive rumination. This includes activity in the anterior medial prefrontal cortex (amPFC), dorsomedial prefrontal cortex (dmPFC), and posterior cingulate cortex (PCC). Conversely, reduced activity during rumination was observed in the medial temporal lobe (MTL; see Zhou et al., 2020).
3 The *DSM-5* distinguishes ten specific personality disorders (see American Psychiatric Association, 2013). However, the more recent *ICD-11* has abandoned this differentiation and incorporated all previously distinguished types into a single general diagnostic category called "personality disorder."

CHAPTER FIVE

Universal Solvents for Mental Difficulties

In the preceding chapters, we gradually uncovered that most symptoms clients bring to therapy result from the activation of maladaptive emotional (relational) schemas. Transforming these schemas using *memory reconsolidation* (see Ecker, 2018; Lane et al., 2015) is typically the most crucial aim in Mindfulness-Informed Integrative Psychotherapy (see Benda, 2019). All therapeutic procedures and techniques intentionally guide the client, above all, to become more and more *mindful* of all the physical and mental *processes* that are taking place in him when a particular maladaptive pattern is activated. However, transformation also requires the development of a *compassionate attitude* toward these processes (cf. Simione et al., 2021).

Mindfulness and self-compassion, in my view, are, incidentally, common effective factors in therapeutic change and play a role in virtually every psychotherapy, whether explicitly discussed or not (see Dunn et al., 2013; Goldberg, 2022; Greeson et al., 2014; Harrer & Weiss, 2016). However, understanding how mindfulness and compassion impact specific maladaptive processes can significantly enhance our therapeutic effectiveness. Let us delve into the mechanisms of the effects of mindfulness and compassion. To begin with, let us first recall that processes of thinking and mindful noticing exclude each other (see Benda, 2019). In moments of thinking or imagining, we are not mindful. However, when cultivating mindfulness, we learn to observe the *structure* of our experience and reflect on the *processes* happening right now in our body and mind without being concerned about their *content*.[1] We might mindfully notice, for instance, that a thinking *process* is occurring in our mind. From a mindfulness perspective, however, *what* we think about is not essential. A mindful therapist, nonetheless, can discern when a client thinks during a session and when they are mindful (cf., e.g., Geller & Greenberg, 2012; Pollak et al., 2014; Siegel, 2010b). Systematically guiding the client to think less and be more mindful (specific techniques outlined in Benda, 2019), the therapist enables the client to mindfully notice, for example, what they are actually *feeling* when they stop *thinking* (a necessary condition!). The client's bodily feelings, which the client often initially struggles to understand and regulate, are typically the first focus in therapy.

In general, it can be stated that *mindful awareness* and *acceptance* of any experienced feeling always interrupt the chain of *automatic* habitual reactions that would otherwise occur within us, allowing us to respond consciously and freely in a given situation (cf. Hájek & Benda, 2008; Lindsay & Creswell, 2017, 2019). However, it is precisely with *acceptance* that clients often encounter the most significant challenge, and it is precisely here that they need our assistance the most. Why? Because this is where developmental trauma comes into play (see Chapter 2).

The point is that every feeling signals a *need* that is currently unfulfilled. However, if no one repeatedly responded to this need in childhood, we have neither learned to recognize nor fulfill it consciously. The only thing left for us back then was to employ some defense mechanism (*kilesa* in Pali). This defense mechanism still automatically activates whenever we experience that particular feeling. With great urgency, it "clouds" our mindfulness and *prevents* us from being able to experience the feeling fully consciously, express it, and then *accept* it with understanding and compassion. If we are to learn this, we first need to undergo what is known as a *corrective emotional experience*.

Maladaptive schemas arise *in relationships*, manifest *in relationships* (including our relationship with ourselves), and are also healed *in relationships*. Therefore, to change the rejecting *attitude* we automatically adopt toward some of our particularly painful feelings, we must undergo a new positive experience in interpersonal *relationships*.[2] We need to experience that, at the moment we are *re-experiencing* traumatic feelings of desperate childhood abandonment, toxic shame, or existential dread, someone understands what we need and is compassionate. Only then can we internalize this new *relational* experience and gain the ability to have compassion for ourselves. This is supported by contemporary neuroscience, which describes the *reconsolidation* of specific brain circuits causing pathology in this context (maladaptive schemas stored in the so-called implicit semantic memory; see Ecker, 2018; Lane et al., 2015; Stevens, 2021). Developing a *compassionate attitude* toward the feeling of core pain represents the most crucial moment in psychotherapeutic change.

Mindfulness and compassion transform all four elements of maladaptive schemas (see Figure 1 on page 25). How does this happen? When clients come to therapy, they are usually not aware of the feelings of core pain. In some vague way, they typically describe unpleasant states that bother them (cf. so-called global distress, Timuľák, 2015). They are often aware of some defense mechanisms and repetitive, automatic thoughts that swirl in their heads (though not core beliefs). However, they either identify with these thoughts or try to suppress them, and similarly, they usually consciously "fight" with defense mechanisms (a rejecting attitude).

In Mindfulness-Informed Integrative Psychotherapy, we guide clients to become truly *mindful* of all four elements of their maladaptive schemas. This involves helping them learn to *recognize* and aptly *name* specific ego states, specific defense mechanisms (see the "Taming the Demons Within" technique—Benda, 2019), specific feelings of core pain, and specific core beliefs. Alongside clients, we uncover the original childhood traumatic experiences that once led to the formation of each element of their maladaptive schemas. We assist them in *understanding* what they *needed* and lacked in childhood (see, e.g., "Ideal Parents Technique"—Benda, 2019).[3] Connecting individual components of maladaptive schemas with early childhood experiences significantly contributes to self-compassion development. Often, only when clients *comprehend* the circumstances that once led to the formation of core beliefs and the fixation of defense mechanisms can they change their *attitude* toward these phenomena. In the case of core beliefs, they can also reappraise their absolute validity and understand (insight) that they are mere childhood assumptions, not "objective truths" (metacognitive reappraisal, cf. Dahl et al., 2015; Vago & Silbersweig, 2012).

Clear, *mindful awareness* coupled with an accepting, *compassionate attitude* toward all elements of maladaptive schemas gradually "dissolves" and transforms them, enabling clients to act as they wish without being dominated by their "wounded" child Self. However, in the subsequent part of this book, let us delve even deeper into the four most common types of the "Wounded Self" and their treatment.

EXERCISE 5

Re-experiencing loving attention and care

The following meditation exercise consists of two steps and begins with recalling a pleasant moment when someone was with you and treated you kindly or perhaps genuinely listened to you. It could be a moment when you felt understood, a moment of shared joy, play, or a moment of receiving recognition. It should be a memory of someone with whom you were genuinely happy, comfortable, and safe at that moment. A moment that you will remember fondly. If, initially, you cannot recall such a moment with a close person, you can start by recalling a similarly pleasant moment with your pet (dog, cat, etc.). Do you have such a memory?

Sit down as comfortably as possible and try to imagine what it would be like if such a pleasant moment were happening again right now. (If you repeat this exercise and no longer need to read this instruction, close your eyes). Imagine that the person is with you right now, smiling at you, listening to you, and communicating with you. Imagine that the person likes being with you, is interested in you, and wishes you the best. If you want to, you can also imagine that they are holding your hand, touching your shoulder, or giving you a friendly hug. Try to internally open yourself to enjoying the loving attention the person gives you. Notice how you feel when that person unconditionally accepts you. Is it a pleasant feeling?

After a few minutes, let your imagination slowly fade, but keep the feeling of deep acceptance. Allow your heart and mind to relax and open completely. Allow yourself a moment not to think. Let everything be and rest in an atmosphere of gentle warmth and acceptance. Then, silently express the wish three times: "May I be well! May I be well! May I be well!" How do you feel now?

NOTES

1 In this sense, mindfulness resembles Husserl's method of "bracketing," or the so-called phenomenological reduction (see, e.g., Husserl, 2012).
2 I want to emphasize here that based on my extensive experience with cultivating mindfulness and compassion in psychotherapy as well as in meditation, I find it highly unlikely that one could learn to have compassion for their core pain on their own without *sharing* this pain with someone. To all readers attempting to address their personal or relational issues independently, I recommend *sharing* your difficulties with an experienced and compassionate meditation teacher or, preferably, an experienced psychotherapist. If you muster the courage to *share* with the right person who understands you, you will save yourself a lot of unnecessary suffering.
3 The Ideal Parents Technique resembles what is known as attachment security priming (see Gillath & Karantzas, 2019) or the so-called Imagery Rescripting (see Mancini & Mancini, 2018; van der Wijngaart, 2021). However, it is much more sophisticated (cf. also "changing emotions with emotions," Greenberg, 2021).

PART II

The Wounded Self

In psychotherapy, there are various ways of dividing maladaptive schemas into distinctive types. The most detailed classification, distinguishing 21 different maladaptive schemas and 40 related ego states (known as modes), was developed by Jeffrey Young within the framework of schema therapy (see Arntz et al., 2021; Bach et al., 2018; cf. Jacobs et al., 2020).[1] However, I consider such a detailed categorization, as employed by schema therapy, unnecessary for therapeutic practice. Equally impractical, in my view, are efforts to differentiate between individual mental disorders based on purportedly typical core beliefs (cf., e.g., Beck & Haigh, 2014). In my opinion, what distinguishes various mental disorders in terms of current diagnosis (*ICD-11*, DSM-5) is neither different core belief contents nor distinct ego states but primarily diverse *defense* and *coping mechanisms* (see further) and certain individual specifics of *core pain*.

In this chapter, we will, therefore, now introduce a typology of maladaptive schemas based on distinguishing *three* typical variants of the self-conscious feeling of core pain: *existential dread, desperate childhood loneliness*, and *shame* (see Timuľák & Keogh, 2021). We will discuss the "Lost Self," "Abandoned Self," and "Inferior Self." However, since the feeling of shame can be very effectively "masked" in some cases (see the so-called hypercompensation), we will add to these three basic types the "Inflated Self." This will give us a simple typology that will allow us in practice to (1) quickly understand which basic developmental need was not fulfilled in the client's childhood (cf. Williams, 2022a, 2022b) and (2) create a specific, pragmatic case formulation and corresponding therapeutic strategy (cf. Goldman & Greenberg, 2015; Timuľák & Pascual-Leone, 2015).

Generally, from the perspective of mindful diagnosis, maladaptive ego states can be seen as a kind of "surface" of maladaptive schemas.[2] The emotional core of these schemas consists of feelings of core pain, and what determines the specific symptoms and the external clinical picture are primarily maladaptive defense mechanisms. In *Mindfulness-Informed Integrative Psychotherapy*, we use the traditional Abhidhammic phenomenological matrix of so-called *mental defilements* to distinguish individual defense mechanisms (see Benda, 2019; Benda & Horák, 2008). This matrix allows clients to gradually become mindful of their defense mechanisms without needing the therapist's feedback and interpretation (see classical ego-defense mechanisms, Freud, 2019). "Mental defilements" (*kilesa* in Pali) are specific processes occurring in the client's mind, and developed mindfulness enables recognizing them clearly. However, to gain an idea of how closely defense mechanisms within a maladaptive schema are related to the resulting ego states, for interest, let us associate them with individual modes distinguished by schema therapy (see Table 1, cf. Arntz et al., 2021; Jacobs et al., 2020).

TABLE 1 Defense mechanisms and ego states.

Defense mechanism	*Ego state (mode)*
Greed	• Reassurance seeker • Detached self-soother • Attention and approval seeker
Hate	• Angry Child • Enraged Child • Angry protector • Punitive Parent
Delusion	• Over-diligent Child • Detached protector • Funny protector
Mental torpor	• Subordinate Child • Constrained Child
Conceit	• Grandiose Child • Spoiled Child • Sulking Child • Demanding Parent • Avoidant protector • Hyper-autonomous mode • Self-aggrandizer • Bully and attack • The merciful
Clinging to delusional notions	• Compliant surrender • Perfectionistic overcontroller • Idealizer • Pollyanna/over-optimist • Pretender

(Continued)

TABLE 1 (Continued)

Defense mechanism	Ego state (mode)
Endless doubt	• Suspicious overcontroller
Restlessness	• Undisciplined Child • Impulsive Child
Remorse and worries	• Lonely Child • Dependent Child • Victimized/abused Child • Confused Child • The over-humble
Shamelessness	• Rebellious Child • Clown • Slacker
Lack of moral dread or unconscientiousness	• Dare devil • Conning and manipulation • Predator

For a mindful therapist with meditation experience (see Benda, 2011), it is not at all challenging to identify which defense mechanism contributes to forming the resulting ego state within a given client's maladaptive schema (see Table 1). However, an experienced mindful therapist also knows that a defense mechanism is an automated response to the feeling of core pain (see Figure 1 on page 25). For the maladaptive schema to be transformed (reconsolidated) in therapy, it is necessary to uncover this feeling and allow the client to experience and express it consciously. It is also necessary to provide the client with a *corrective emotional (relational) experience* that fulfils a need unfulfilled in childhood. Emotion-Focused Therapy, concerning the feeling of existential dread, addresses the unmet need for *safety and security*. In the case of the feeling of desperate childhood loneliness, it speaks to the unmet need *to be loved, understood, and connected*. Regarding shame, it addresses the unmet need for *recognition and approval* (see, e.g., Greenberg, 2021; Timuľák & Keogh, 2021). However, in Mindfulness-Informed Integrative Psychotherapy, we use a slightly more detailed distinction of five basic developmental needs, as defined by Albert Pesso and Diane Boyden-Pesso (see Figure 9 on page 54, cf. Baylin & Winnette, 2016; Benda, 2019). This distinction complements and describes the need for *place* and, above all, the need for loving *limits*, which I consider highly significant in therapeutic work (see Chapter 9; cf. also basic emotional needs, Young et al., 2003).

Because understanding unmet developmental needs is crucial for therapeutic work, we will further discuss them in the following four chapters concerning all four types of the "Wounded Self." However, we will also delve deeper into the profoundly ingrained core beliefs associated with childhood

MINDFULNESS AND THE SELF

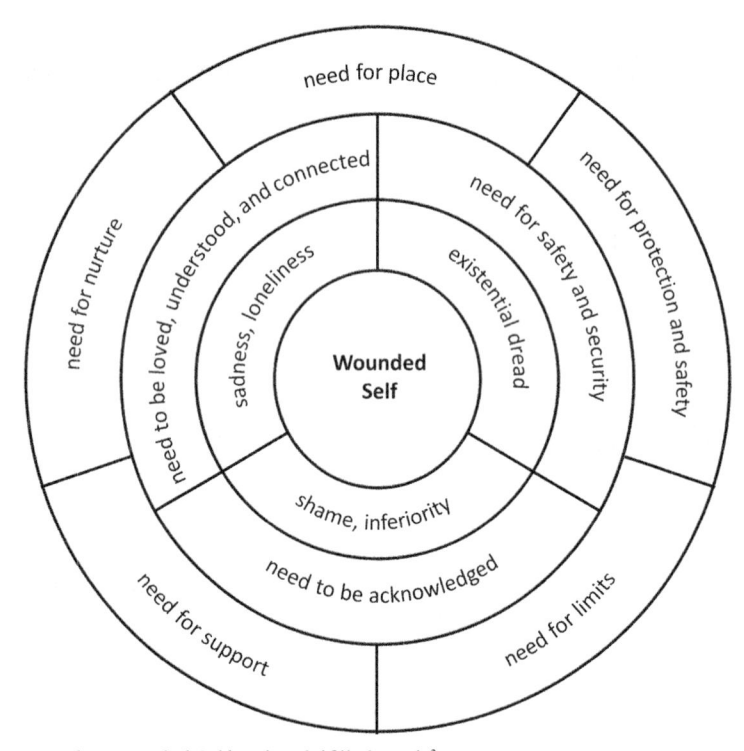

FIGURE 9 The Wounded Self and unfulfilled needs[3]

traumatic experiences and suggest how these initially often very hidden elements of maladaptive schemas can be therapeutically addressed. At the end of each chapter, professionals will find a table presenting, for each type of the "Wounded Self," its typical attachment style (cf. Bartholomew & Horowitz, 1991; Lukáč & Popelková, 2020), the typical schemas described by Young (cf. Bach et al., 2018), and typical so-called life positions (see transactional analysis, Harris, 2012). Connecting the presented typology of maladaptive schemas with these related psychological constructs can help professionals understand the typology. Now, let us introduce the "Lost Self."

NOTES

1 For comparison, Abhidhamma psychology distinguishes 50 mental formations (*saṅkhāra* in Pali) and 89 or 121 states or types of consciousness (*citta* in Pali; see, e.g., Bodhi, 2007, 2021; Narada, 1987).

2 In my practice, I do not use the terminology of schema therapy to label ego states. Instead, I always seek with each client an original and as accurate as possible naming of specific narrowed states of consciousness they are experiencing. Together, we often come up with very expressive names like "rag doll," "exhausted clown,"

"rotten apple," "decaying corpse," "king of macrobes," "Rockefeller," "savior," "avenger," "poisonous jerk," "schizoid," "demented," "totally corrupted," "broken," the state "in a bubble," "under the blanket," and so on.

3 The outer circle in Figure 9 illustrates the five basic developmental needs according to Pesso Boyden System Psychomotor Therapy. It is evident from the diagram that these five needs do not precisely correspond to the three needs distinguished by Emotion-Focused Therapy, as shown in the middle circle. However, in therapeutic practice, the general conceptualization of needs is not as crucial. What matters is whether the therapist can *empathize* with the client's situation. If so, it means the therapist can *very specifically* and vividly imagine what the client needed and lacked in childhood. This understanding enables the therapist to help the client adequately. The therapist's understanding and compassion assist the client in cultivating self-compassion. Both theoretical frameworks provide therapists only with a general guiding framework.

CHAPTER SIX

The Lost Self

In the 1980s, Edward Tronick, a psychologist from the University of Massachusetts Boston, investigated interactions between mothers and their one-year-old children, conducting experiments that became known as "still-face experiments" (see, e.g., Tronick, 2007). In these experiments, mothers initially played and lively interacted with their children. However, they intentionally stopped reacting and adopted a neutral facial expression devoid of any emotion. Initially, the children were confused and attempted to encourage their mothers to respond again. After a few minutes, though, they started crying, experiencing extreme stress, feelings of *threat*, and helplessness. Try finding these experiments on YouTube. If your impression is similar to mine, you will quickly realize that for small children, who are entirely dependent on their caregivers in every way, it takes relatively little to make them feel *threatened*. Somehow, they seem to instinctively sense that if their mother were to stop responding permanently, it would be a matter of life and death.

Children, of course, need to experience frustration as well. A certain (optimal) level of frustration helps them build resilience (Tronick & Gold, 2020). However, maladaptive schemas, centered around a *feeling of existential threat*, develop when we do not feel *protected* and *safe often enough* in early childhood. The feeling of existential vulnerability (also fear of not existing at all) in children typically arises either in situations involving violence or abuse or in scenarios where parents fail to fulfill their own needs, lacking the capacity to perceive and meet the child's needs empathetically. This occurs in situations where the child's birth was unwanted by the parents, when one of the parents lacks an adult partner, and so forth.[1] The child often feels uncared-for, left to fend for itself. They perceive that their parents are sacrificing too much for them. They become fearful and feel like a burden. Moreover, they very sensitively pick up on the parents' negative emotions, often becoming a significant stumbling block.

As children, we need parents who *shield* us from everything threatening us. Parents who show us that when faced with danger, one can actively defend oneself and then feel *safe*. Parents who visibly know how to handle all life's challenges so they are not helpless or excessively anxious themselves. And, of course, parents who do not overload us with excessive demands or expectations but can realistically assess what we can handle on our own and where we still need help. So, if a little girl starts to cry when a stranger visits, providing *protection* means that a parent might say, for example: "You don't like uncle, do you? You don't know him yet, right? Let's go to Grandma's kitchen for a while (see safety) and let Dad and Uncle talk. You don't have to talk to Uncle if you don't trust him (yet)." When a little boy is afraid of a monster under the bed, a parent might say, for instance: "Are you scared of the monster? I see. Wait, I'll check under the bed, and if there's a monster, I'll chase it away. No monster should scare you! I'll show him who's boss! Hmm, I don't see any monster... Should I stay with you for a while until you stop being afraid? Do you want to snuggle with me for a bit?"[2]

Contemporary parents sometimes try to *explain* to their children that they have no reason to be afraid. However, by doing so, they force the children to suppress their fear and only pretend not to be scared. In reality, it is only when the feeling of fear is *accepted* that it can transform. A parent should understand that protection is needed when a child is worried. And it doesn't matter why or what they are afraid of. It is straightforward—when a child is scared, the parent should provide protection, not force the child not to be frightened. The child is entitled to expect the parent to take care of protection. If a parent refuses this, perhaps because they perceive the child's fear as unjustified, it won't disappear. The child will just stop showing it outwardly. However, the fear will still be felt and perceived as something that "shouldn't be." To meet the parent's expectations, the child creates a protective "mask" (a "false self," see Winnicott, 2018a). We can say that it essentially takes on the responsibility to make the *parent* feel good. Such a mask, concealing the feeling of existential fear, is a typical accompanying phenomenon of the "Lost Self."

In therapeutic practice, we easily recognize the influence of the "Lost Self" due to clients' persistent tendency to automatically assume responsibility for others and feel complete responsibility for how others feel. These clients struggle to perceive their personal boundaries, to refuse, and to say no. If they do not meet the expectations of others, they experience irrational but intense feelings of inadequate, so-called *omnipotent guilt* (see Gazzillo et al., 2017,

2020; O'Connor et al., 1999). The compelling urge to take on responsibility in these clients originated in childhood when, as children, they felt *threatened*. They tried to "comply" (or "help") one of their parents in the vague hope that once the parent's needs were fulfilled, the roles would reverse, and the parent would start fulfilling the child's needs. However, this *survival* mechanism is ingrained in them so deeply that even in adulthood, they repeatedly feel responsible for the needs of others, resisting this tendency with incredible difficulty. The possibility of caring for themselves before others *terrifies* them at the core of their souls.

In professional or popular psychology literature, the "Lost Self" is sometimes also referred to as the "savior complex" (von Franz, 2000), "helper syndrome" (Schmidbauer, 2007), "nice guy syndrome" (see Glover, 2004), "people-pleaser" (Lue, 2023), "pathological altruism" (Oakley, 2013), or "codependency" (Lancer, 2015).[3] However, all these terms describe individuals who, long ago (in childhood), forgot about themselves. They learned not to perceive what they feel and need[4] but are very sensitive to the needs of others. In the process, they developed core beliefs such as:

- I am weak, vulnerable, defenseless.
- Nobody cares about me, I don't matter.
- I have no right to have any feelings, my feelings and needs bother others.
- I shouldn't exist at all.
- I must not disappoint (abandon) anyone, that would hurt them.
- I must be perfect/successful to deserve love.
- I must not assert myself, it's selfish.
- I can't have/do what I want. Others' needs are more important than mine.
- I can't rejoice or be happy when others suffer.
- I must listen.
- I must take care of others.
- I have no right to criticize anyone.
- Loving someone means submitting to them.

Let us illustrate the concept of the "Lost Self" with the example of the client, Kate.

> *Kate worked as the head of a large team in a bank. She was highly efficient and ambitious at work, boasting an impressive career. She earned the respect and trust of Senior management. She was a genuine hard worker. Naturally, she stayed at work every day until late in the evening, and of course, she also worked from home. However, she knew nothing but work. Hobbies were a luxury she could not afford. At home, everyone relied on her. Her husband and children*

were accustomed to Kate overseeing everything, managing everything, and making decisions about everything. Kate felt useful, but she also felt the pressure. She often stressed about work deadlines, and somehow, she was running out of breath. She was on her own in everything. She did not feel supported even by her husband. She had been contemplating the need to slow down for a long time. However, she thought it was impossible. What would her boss say? What about her family? She could not imagine how she could change her situation.

In the conversation with Kate, we focused on the feeling of urgency that accompanied her almost constantly. She felt like she "had to" do something from morning to evening. She couldn't fathom being unable to handle something or, even worse, refusing. Our conversation went as follows:

THERAPIST: How did you feel when your boss announced all those changes and new tasks?

CLIENT: It was terrible. Everything went dark before my eyes. I was afraid I couldn't handle it.

THERAPIST: Sure. And what would happen if you couldn't handle it all? What's the absolute worst that could happen?

CLIENT: I don't know. Rationally, I tell myself that it would somehow be resolved, but deep down, I fear they might fire me.

THERAPIST: Okay. That fear might be irrational or exaggerated. But for this very reason, let's explore it further. Adult reasoning may see it differently. We won't examine reality now; we'll focus on your fear. Fear has a way of magnifying things. It's like whispering to you, "What if they fire you?" What's the absolute worst that could happen if they let you go? Let's go to the extreme of your imagination. Let's say you end up under a bridge. When you imagine that, what's the worst part for you?

CLIENT: (Goggle-eyed.) I'm scared for the kids. What would happen to them?

THERAPIST: I see. What's the absolute worst that could happen to them?

CLIENT: Maybe they wouldn't handle it. They could end up in a mental institution. Or turn to drugs. They would be complete wrecks. (She looks horrified.)

THERAPIST:	What do you feel when you imagine the children turning into wrecks?
CLIENT:	That it's my fault, that I'm to blame. (She breathes heavily.)
THERAPIST:	The feeling of guilt or responsibility. Now that we've brought it into the present, do you feel that feeling in your body?
CLIENT:	Yes, it's like a tightening feeling.
THERAPIST:	From where in your past do you know this constricting bodily feeling?
CLIENT:	(Still breathing heavily.) Well… When Mom died, I was 13. Dad was often away for work, sometimes for several days. I had to take care of two younger brothers. I managed it. I had to. But once, my brother fell down the stairs. He couldn't breathe. I had no idea what to do…
THERAPIST:	What feeling did you have at that moment?
CLIENT:	I was terrified to death. I was utterly paralyzed with horror. But I had to pull myself together and take care of him.
THERAPIST:	(Nodding.) It's a terrible memory. You must have been really scared back then. (Exhales deeply.) Truly terrifying. (After a while.) Can you imagine letting your thirteen-year-old daughter care for younger brothers for several days?
CLIENT:	(Looks at me.) No way! I could never do that to her!
THERAPIST:	It wasn't fair that you had to bear such responsibility back then. Even though your dad had a hard time, unlike you, he was an adult.
CLIENT:	(Looks surprised.) I've never thought about it that way.
THERAPIST:	It was his responsibility to take care of your brothers. But he delegated that responsibility to you. What could you have done?
CLIENT:	(Tears in her eyes.) Oh my God! What could I have done? (Looks a bit angry, then sadly smiles. She realizes that her dad has shifted adult responsibility onto her. Relief slowly sets in.)
THERAPIST:	You needed someone to care for your brothers and you back then. Your safety was at stake. It wasn't a safe situation, and you were still a child.
CLIENT:	(Takes a tissue.)

THERAPIST: Your daily feeling of urgency, the "must," and the "fear of not handling it" may be connected to these old experiences from when you were 13.

CLIENT: (Nods.)

In the conversation with Kate, we transitioned from vague "global distress" to an urgent secondary feeling of *omnipotent responsibility*. However, through the recollection of her childhood, in the subsequent steps, we gradually uncovered the primary feeling of *existential fear* she experienced at the age of 13. Only this feeling is the key to initiating psychotherapeutic change. The ego state, previously referred to as the "Motor Mouse," won't cease to emerge until Kate can acknowledge, deep within her soul, that she is still re-experiencing her "childhood terror" and the associated automatic imperative "I mustn't think of myself, and I must handle it." Mindful awareness of this internal traumatic feeling is, therefore, a prerequisite for Kate to comprehend what she truly needed (and lacked) back then, enabling her to "find herself" anew.

Yes, at that time, she had no choice but to suppress her fear and *strive to meet* her father's expectation that she could essentially replace her deceased mother. She couldn't defy her father because she still needed him too much. However, today, she can learn to have compassion for herself, guard her boundaries, and, for instance, decline some tasks at work (see protective anger, Chapter 14). Her boss is not her father, and she is no longer 13. She isn't as dependent on her boss as she was on her father back then. She will survive even if her boss fires her. Kate, however, must realize that the feeling of *existential dread* she is experiencing does not correspond to the current situation but is connected to her traumatic past. Another step toward the *reconsolidation* of the entire maladaptive schema can be the experience of a corrective emotional experience (see Chapters 7, 8, and 13).

Let us add that the "Lost Self" syndrome can externally manifest itself in various ways, such as obsessive-compulsive disorder, as seen in the case of the client Amy (Chapter 4), or as "workaholism" and generalized anxiety disorder, as observed in the case of Kate, among many other forms. However, the diverse external symptoms of specific disorders in these cases always arise due to the activation of some traumatic childhood narrative (core belief) and the traumatic feeling of *existential dread*. Before the client becomes fully aware of the core pain (mere awareness of feelings of inadequate guilt usually doesn't suffice), it is challenging to influence reactive defensive and coping mechanisms. These mechanisms stem from the erroneous traumatic impression that "it is a matter of survival." Mindful awareness of feelings of *existential dread* should, therefore, always be an initial partial goal of psychotherapy. Chapters 7 and 8 will hint at how to help the client develop self-compassion and protective anger afterward.

TABLE 2 The Lost Self

Attachment style:	• anxious-preoccupied, ambivalent
Life position:	• I'm Not OK, You're OK.
Young's schemas:	• dependence/incompetence
	• vulnerability to harm
	• abandonment/instability
	• enmeshment/undeveloped self
	• subjugation
	• self-sacrifice/overresponsibility
	• approval seeking

EXERCISE 6

Shedding omnipotent guilt

Do you feel guilty simply because you haven't fulfilled someone else's unspoken expectations? Do you think you're responsible for making others (especially those close to you) happy? Do you generally find it challenging to reject or disappoint someone? Is it difficult for you to say no? If so, it's likely that you automatically take on inadequate responsibility and suffer from the syndrome of omnipotent guilt. In such a case, the following exercise might be helpful.

Much like anger, omnipotent guilt is always a secondary emotion (cf. Exercise 1 on pages 15–16). It is typically associated with an indefinite and unconscious irrational fear that not meeting others' expectations could lead to "something unimaginably terrible." The intention to become aware of this existential fear is the first step toward shedding omnipotent responsibility. So, recall a specific situation where you were convinced that you "must not disappoint someone at any cost" or that you "must not fail." How did you feel at that time? Can you recognize that the tension you felt in your body is an irrational fear? Your body was experiencing a strong feeling of threat, as if your life depended on it, right? Try to acknowledge that feeling and consciously experience it.

Ask yourself the question: Where do you recognize this feeling in your past? Perhaps this feeling has accompanied you for almost your entire life. However, when did you first experience it? In elementary school? Or even earlier? Once you recall a childhood memory associated with this feeling of threat or urgency, remember the circumstances and context of that particular memory. What were your parents doing back then? What did you (need) from them and didn't have? How could they have helped you at that time?

Ideal parents, of course, don't condition their love on their child meeting certain expectations. They are content with their lives, handling all the challenges life brings. Their fundamental life contentment is in no way dependent on what their child does or doesn't do. So, take a moment to imagine what it could have been like if, back when you were little, you had completely different "ideal parents." Envision that they would sit close to you and say something like: "We love you, even if things aren't going well for you.

We are happy and grateful to have you. And you don't have to earn our love at all. You don't have to be perfect. You know, we can handle all our problems. Therefore, you don't have to worry about our adult concerns. Leave adult worries to us, and don't stick your nose into them! Look, life is amazing! We want to share the joy of life with you. You are safe with us. You can enjoy a carefree childhood and rely on us."

How do you feel when imagining such "ideal parents" in your childhood? Try fully immersing yourself in this imagination and feeling the relief it would bring. If, through this imagination, you manage to experience a feeling of relief, you can permanently shed the feeling of omnipotent responsibility. Feel free to repeatedly return to this exercise, creating more specific, vivid, and credible visions of mature and self-realized "ideal parents." It's worth it.

NOTES

1 In this context, Albert Pesso discussed that when there are what he called "holes in roles" within the family system, children tend to "fill" them, taking on a task that is too big too soon (see Pesso, 2013).
2 When reading examples of parent-child conversations in this book, try to momentarily step out of the perspective of an adult parent and imagine yourself in the role of a one to a five-year-old child. As parents, you might think, "This is not how it works; there's no time for this in real life." However, the question is, how would you have liked such an approach from your parents when you were a child? How would you have felt as a child? Moreover, do not forget that a parent does not have to be perfect. For the healthy development of a child, it suffices when positive experiences with parents outweigh the negative ones (see, e.g., Tronick & Gold, 2020).
3 The mechanism of the Lost Self incidentally describes the so-called Stockholm syndrome, within which kidnap victims identify with their captors and their needs (see, e.g., Strentz, 1980; cf. also Fairbairn, 2013).
4 Extreme cases of the Lost Self can manifest as the so-called depersonalization-derealization disorder (see ICD-11, DSM-5; cf. Simeon & Abugel, 2023).

CHAPTER SEVEN

The Abandoned Self

Maladaptive schemas, which have at their core *feelings of sad childhood (cosmic) loneliness* and *emptiness*, emerge when we do not experience enough parental warmth and love (the need for *nurture*) in early childhood and/or when we do not frequently experience feelings of closeness, belonging, and the feeling that the world is a good place to live (the need for *place*). However, how are these needs fulfilled in childhood? As children, we primarily need to experience physical closeness. This means warm physical contact with parents—cuddling, snuggling, caressing, and pampering. Sometimes, even in this, we experience a deficit. If a small child is placed in an incubator after birth or repeatedly spends time alone in hospitals or clinics, it feels abandoned. Similarly, if parents are emotionally distant or aloof. Physical contact cannot be replaced by anything else. Let us remember the classic Harlow experiments with rhesus monkeys. Already in the 1950s and 1960s, Harry F. Harlow (1958) at the University of Wisconsin in Madison demonstrated that when he separated baby monkeys from their mothers and gave them two "surrogate mothers"—one a "wire mother" with a bottle of milk and the other a "cloth mother" without milk, the baby monkeys spent almost all their time cuddling with the "cloth mother." Monkeys that spent more time in isolation from their mothers also had later problems in relationships with other monkeys (e.g., Harlow & Suomi, 1971). For humans, it is, of course, not only about emotional but also cognitive understanding between parents and the child.

As children, we need mindful and *empathetic* parents who can empathize with us and understand what we need, even when we cannot express it yet. We need parents interested in our inner world, our thoughts, our childhood ideas, and fantasies. Also, parents who like to experience many *joint* age-appropriate activities and activities *together with us*. When parents play, go on trips, engage in sports, and create *together with us*, they provide essential "nourishment" to our children's souls. We then feel fulfilled, not empty. We feel understood, not alienated. However, it is not about parents being 100% perfect (see optimal frustration, Tronick & Gold, 2020). It suffices when our positive experiences outweigh the negative ones.

When it comes to the feeling of belonging, as children, we also need to feel that we belong somewhere (the need for a *place*). That with mom, dad, and siblings, we are one family—a team. Mutual consideration contributes to this. The fact that our parents think about us when we are not at home and inquire about our experiences at school or in extracurricular activities. Various everyday family rituals, shared rules, communal meals, holiday celebrations, and gatherings with extended family and friends play a part. When we have a genuine "feeling of home" and mutual closeness, we feel okay, worthy of love and respect, and we perceive the whole world as friendly and full of possibilities. We develop positive core beliefs. However, when our fundamental developmental needs for *place* and *nurture* are not met, when we do not experience often enough being "seen" by our parents and emotionally mirrored (see Fonagy et al., 2018; cf. Kohut, 2009, 2014), we acquire negative core beliefs, such as:

- I am unwelcome and unloved. I do not belong anywhere.
- No one can love me.
- No one can understand me.
- No one can take me seriously.
- I cannot rely on anyone.
- Opening up to others or feeling and expressing love is dangerous.
- Everyone wants to take advantage of me.
- I must be grateful if someone tolerates me.
- I must have a beautiful body/money/power to interest anyone.
- No relationship lasts long; eventually, I will end up alone.
- Accepting help would be a weakness.

Such negative core beliefs form the basis of maladaptive schemas that we can categorize under the label of the Abandoned Self. We already know that when these core beliefs are activated, we will *perceive* ourselves, others, and the world again as we did during moments of childhood trauma, even though we are now adults. In the case of the Abandoned Self, we once again feel like helpless *abandoned children*. Because such a feeling is difficult to tolerate without appropriate understanding, some defense mechanism usually automatically kicks in. It could be, for example, hatred as seen in the case of clients Peter (Chapter 1) and Simon (Chapter 4), remorse and worries as observed in the case of client Zoe (Chapters 2 and 4), or apathy as in the case of client Eve (Chapter 4). From the perspective of mindfulness-informed therapy, the key is not whether external symptoms manifest as intermittent explosive disorder (Peter), personality disorder (Simon), depressive disorder (Zoe), or post-traumatic stress disorder (Eve). The crucial aspect is to enable the client to become aware of the core pain and subsequently explore where they recognize it from their past.

Once a client in therapy begins to connect the feeling of core pain with their past and recalls relevant (traumatic) memories, it is possible to employ techniques that induce the *memory reconsolidation* process (Ecker, 2018; Lane et al., 2015). Examples include the Ideal Parents Technique (see Benda, 2019; cf. Brown & Elliott, 2016; Jencius & Duba, 2003) or the empty chair dialogue (Timuľák, 2015; Timuľák & Keogh, 2021). This can be illustrated using the example of client Peter (see Chapter 1). When I asked Peter where he recognized the feeling of abandonment, his eyes lit up. He knew that we were going to talk about his childhood and he was ready for it. He recounted how his mother left him when he was five. That memory was vivid in his mind. He saw himself, a five-year-old, standing in front of the house between both parents. His parents were arguing vehemently, shouting at each other. He was scared, yet he did not understand what his parents argued about. The scene culminated with Peter's mother angrily opening the car door parked in front of the house. She took Peter's child's backpack and threw it over the fence onto the property. She slammed the car door and drove away. His dad sat on the steps, crying. Peter never saw his mother again during his childhood.

During his childhood, Peter experienced numerous situations where he felt *alone*, lacking parental (especially maternal) *warmth* and *care*. The Ideal Parents Technique aimed to convey to him, through imagination, a *feeling of closeness and belonging* practically unknown to him—the kind he would have felt as a child if he had been born to entirely different, "ideal parents." If Peter genuinely *empathizes* with this notion under the therapist's guidance, he may *undergo* a completely new, *corrective experience*. This will then lead to the so-called *reconsolidation* of the maladaptive schema and the creation of a new, adaptive schema, which includes a *compassionate attitude* toward the feeling of loneliness (see also Chapter 10). The adaptive schema will begin to function as automatically as the maladaptive schema. This means that in situations that previously triggered core pain and reactive anger in Peter, there will be self-compassion instead of anger. Moreover, Peter will not have to strive for it consciously. Self-compassion will then calm the feeling of loneliness, allowing Peter to respond entirely differently than before (cf. Ecker, 2018; Lane et al., 2015).

In Peter's case, it was, of course, crucial to first create an image of the "ideal mommy" and subsequently envision a close, loving relationship between the two "ideal parents" (see Benda, 2019). However, this is a complex task. Therefore, in several sessions, we initially worked on the concept of a mentally mature, self-realized, and happy "ideal mommy." For the technique to work, it is fundamental for Peter to imagine that there could be a woman who understands her emotions and needs, can take care of herself, communicates as an adult, sets boundaries, and loves and expresses love to her partner and children. A woman who lives such a fulfilled life that she "has so much to give." Equally important is for Peter to imagine an honest, open, warm, and authentic relationship between the two "ideal parents." A relationship based on mutual trust, respect, admiration, and love. A relationship where both parents show affection but can also constructively address disagreements or misunderstandings. Only when Peter could imagine such "ideal parents" could we metaphorically "insert" these imaginary figures into specific childhood moments. One of several visualizations looked like this:

THERAPIST: If you had ideal parents when you were five, you would spend much time together. Ideal parents would be very interested in your child's world, all your feelings, desires, interests… Now, try to imagine yourself at that age. What interested you back then?

CLIENT: I liked nature. I admired various animals, birds, insects…

THERAPIST: I see. So, ideal parents would enjoy going with you, maybe to the zoo or outdoors, into the woods…

CLIENT: I used to enjoy being outside.

THERAPIST: Ideal parents would love going outdoors with you. They would play with you and appreciate nature together with you. If you were fascinated by a squirrel in the park, they would observe it with you. They could tell you something about the squirrel and be curious about what fascinated you. Imagine you're five, admiring a lively squirrel. Ideal parents would stop with you. Mom could sit down to be physically closer to you. Or she might pick you up so you could see better.

CLIENT: (Breathing heavily.)

THERAPIST: An ideal mom would like to touch you. She would caress you. You could cuddle with her. While observing the squirrel, an ideal mom might say, "I really enjoy watching animals with you. I'm so glad to be with you."

CLIENT: (Eyes moisten.)

THERAPIST: At this age, ideal parents, or at least one of them, would be with you almost all the time. They would sensitively perceive everything happening within you. And if you were ever sad, you could snuggle up to them anytime.

CLIENT: (Seems to be struggling with his sadness.)

THERAPIST: An ideal mom would always know when you were sad. She would gently embrace you. You could even cry on her shoulder.

CLIENT: (Puts his head in his hands and starts to sob.) (A)[1]

THERAPIST: If you cried as a five-year-old, an ideal mom would comfort you in her arms. She would caress you and might say something like, "I know how you feel right now. I'm here with you. I'll always be here." And she would hug you as long as you needed. (After a moment, I hand Peter a tissue.)

CLIENT: (After a while, he begins to calm down.)

THERAPIST: Keep imagining for a moment that you're five, and the ideal mom still holds you. The ideal dad is also with you. No one is in a hurry. You can snuggle up to her. Feel the warmth of her body, the heartbeat, and how she breathes. She gently whispers something to you. Something like, "I'm here for you."

CLIENT: (Starts to smile a little.)

THERAPIST: Can you feel that warm feeling now?

CLIENT: (Nods and smiles.) (B)

THERAPIST: Try to enjoy that feeling and keep it within you. We'll talk more in a moment. That's what you needed so much back then. The feeling of closeness, belonging, understanding...

TABLE 3 The Abandoned Self

Attachment style:	• fearful-avoidant, disorganized
Life position:	• I'm not OK, you're not OK.
Young's schemas:	• abuse/mistrust
	• emotional deprivation
	• social isolation/alienation
	• overcontrol/emotional inhibition
	• pessimism/negativity

EXERCISE 7

Saying yes to your grief

Learning to *accept* feelings of core pain with compassion is the key to transforming (and reconsolidating) maladaptive schemas. This involves voluntarily letting go of defense mechanisms that automatically divert our attention from core pain and consciously confronting this pain. Only when we acknowledge and consciously experience this pain can it dissolve. However, handling it very sensitively and with great patience is necessary. Do you want to attempt to create conditions for healing feelings of childhood abandonment within yourself? If yes, try the following exercise.

First, in your thoughts, find a personality that, in your opinion, embodies kindness and compassion in their life. It could be a living person or even a historical or movie character. Can you think of someone you are sure would understand your distress under any circumstances and would respond with kindness and compassion? Look for such a person in your thoughts until you find someone whose image makes you smile. Keep searching, even if it takes, for example, 20 minutes. Once you find such a person, imagine that they are sitting about half a meter behind you, and if it feels comfortable, further imagine that this person is gently touching your back with their palms between your shoulder blades. Only then proceed to the next step.

Recall a moment from your childhood when you felt particularly sad and lonely. Bring back that memory with all the details. What evokes the strongest emotions in you about this situation? Perhaps you envision a specific scene, hear certain words in your imagination, or become aware of your inner beliefs about the future impact of this situation on you. Observe the feelings you are currently experiencing in your heart, around your stomach, throat, mouth, abdomen, and back. Allow your body to re-experience that distant sadness and loneliness fully.

To understand firsthand what happens when you internally reject your feelings, try shaking your head from left to right for a while and silently say, "No, no, no, no, no, no, no." Say "no" to your painful feelings for a moment and notice how this mental resistance manifests in your body. What happens to your feelings of core pain when you say "no"? What happens to your heart?

Now, take a deep breath and let your feelings flow freely again. Replay the memory once more, but choose to accept your feelings this time. Allow your body to feel them again. Nod your head as a sign of agreement. Then, silently say, "Yes..., yes..., yes...." You can imagine a kind and compassionate person gently placing their hand on your back. Let your feelings take their course. Notice what happens in your body when you say "yes" to all your feelings. Do your unpleasant feelings intensify, or do they dissolve? What happens to your heart when you say "yes"? Is there anything you'd like to say? Something you couldn't say in childhood but can say now? If so, say it out loud. If tears come to your eyes, imagine that the kind and compassionate person is still with you. Then, remain seated quietly for a while and gradually let go of all thoughts, memories, and images. Rest in the present moment and maintain an accepting attitude toward your feelings. How do you feel now?

NOTE

1 Letters (A) and (B) designate moments when the client began to re-experience the feeling of core pain (A) or was undergoing a corrective emotional experience (B). Further elaboration on this will be provided in Chapter 10.

CHAPTER EIGHT

The Inferior Self

At the core of the Inferior Self syndrome lies feelings of *inadequacy* and *worthlessness*, often referred to as toxic *shame* (see Benda, 2019). These feelings emerge when, as children, we do not experience sufficient parental *support*, recognition, and appreciation. Our initial experiences of *relying* on someone are gained at the physical level. When parents carry us, lift us, hold our hands, let us sit on their laps, or pick us up, we physically *feel* that we can *count* on them and have *support* in them. Have you ever tried the exercise called the "trust fall"? In this exercise, you stand straight and fall backward, trusting someone to catch and support you. For some, this exercise is effortless, but some individuals genuinely fear trusting another person. This fear clearly indicates that these people lacked support in the past. They could not rely on others; they could not trust. However, parental support fosters healthy self-confidence in a child. The ability to trust and self-confidence develop hand in hand. When a child lacks support, he or she concludes that he or she is not entitled to it and should handle tasks independently. If, however, they cannot manage on their own, they experience *shame*.

As children, we need parents who help us discover and develop our natural potential, supporting us in *our initiatives*. So, when a little girl insists on tying her shoelaces by herself, providing *support* means a parent saying, for instance, "All right. Do you know how to do it? Want to show me? Oh, you can already make a bow. Excellent. Look, when you thread the lace here and pull it tight… Do you want to give it a try? Great. You can tie your shoelaces now." Similarly, when a young boy wants to climb a tree, a parent could say, "Wait, this tree is quite tall" (addressing the need for safety). However, proper support involves saying something like, "What if you tried that tree over there first? That seems doable, right? Once you master that, we can try the tall one.

DOI: 10.4324/9781003504061-11

Show me; I will give you a little boost. You can grab onto that branch over there. Put your foot here... See, you are already up! You have mastered climbing a tree!" The child can then feel pride (not superiority), and parents can acknowledge, "You did it!" (appreciation). It is important to note that support does not mean forcing children to do something.

Contemporary parents often strive to lead their children toward independence and autonomy prematurely. However, providing support for preschool children means doing things *together with them*. It doesn't mean saying, "Why don't you go play with those kids? Are you scared? Don't be." Support involves noticing the child curiously eyeing the other kids on the playground and offering help: "Do you like that slide over there? I see. Let's go check it out *together*. I'll say hi to the other kids and let them know we want to slide, too. We can slide together. Sit on my lap. It's a lot of fun. You'll see." The key here is proper timing. Children are initially fearful (the need for safety). It is only when their curiosity begins to outweigh the fear that it is the right time to support them. If we push them toward independence prematurely, they might later feel *ashamed* of their natural dependence, to which they are entitled (see Epstein, 2022). Additionally, parents should serve as an example and a role model. It is challenging to expect children to engage in sports when we are sitting in front of the TV. However, when children see that Dad goes running every morning and returns enthusiastic and full of endorphins, they might become interested in running. Then comes the time to run *together* with a realistic consideration of the child's performance.

Today's children often have numerous after-school clubs and extracurricular activities. However, do these activities match their genuine interests? When I see busy parents chauffeuring their children to various activities, it reminds me of the movie *Billy Elliot* (2000). In this film, a strict "macho" father enrolls his 11-year-old son Billy in boxing classes. Yet, Billy is captivated by ballet and has a natural talent for it. It is a poignant story, and there's a lesson to be learned from it. Support means allowing a child to study ballet if that interests them. Attending practices and performances with them and sharing their successes and failures. Sending them to boxing, even with the best intentions, is the opposite of support. Support and appreciation shouldn't only be linked to achievements. We need the most support when things aren't going well. Sometimes, parents try to encourage a child by saying, "You'll handle it! You're a clever girl!" However, try a little thought. Would such "encouragement" help you? When we're afraid we won't manage something, and someone tells us, "You'll handle it," we might feel even lonelier and under pressure. What if we really can't handle it? We genuinely need reassurance: "I will love you even if it doesn't work out. My love for you doesn't depend on this outcome. Go ahead, try it, and if it doesn't work out, we'll figure it out together. I'll help you." That is when we feel genuine support that "gives us wings."

Roughly until the age of 12, until we reach the formal operations stage in our cognitive development (Piaget, 2015), we are more or less dependent on others in our self-reflection. We see ourselves as if through their eyes. Our consciousness is in a stage of so-called pre-reflective identification (Welwood, 1996). This means that we essentially uncritically identify with any evaluations of ourselves that adults provide. Moreover, in this respect, we are very vulnerable. A young child does not have enough experience to assess itself in any way independently. So, when a parent tells a child, "You are clumsy," the child automatically believes it and thinks the parent is right. Sufficient parental *support* leads to adopting positive core beliefs about ourselves and the world. We gain adequate self-confidence and the ability to trust others. However, when we do not experience enough support, or when parents even dismiss, humiliate, or devalue us, we develop negative core beliefs such as:

- I am shameful, stupid, weird, incapable, uninteresting, boring, insignificant, worthless, defective, rotten, ugly.
- Nothing ever works out for me, I cannot do anything, and I will always fail in everything.
- I cannot measure up to others.
- I am unacceptable, despicable.
- I do not deserve love, recognition, or respect; I do not deserve happiness.
- I deserve to suffer, I deserve punishment.

Such negative core beliefs form the foundation of maladaptive schemas, which we can categorize under the umbrella of the Inferior Self. When activated, they place us, even as adults, in what meditation teacher Tara Brach (2004) aptly calls the "trance of unworthiness." When this happens, we feel like little children again and experience shame. Secondarily, we may react with self-hatred, as seen in the case of client Daniel (social anxiety disorder; see Chapter 4) or client Veronica (mental anorexia; see Chapter 4). Alternatively, a craving for a more pleasant experience may emerge, as seen in the case of client Ryan (developing alcohol dependence; see Chapters 3 and 4) or any other defense mechanism. However, suppose we genuinely want to break free from the influence of this maladaptive schema or permanently transform the schema. In that case, we must first become aware of (mindfully notice) the *feelings of core pain*, understand them, and subsequently learn to respond to them with compassion (toward ourselves).

In Mindfulness-Informed Integrative Psychotherapy, alongside the Ideal Parents Technique (see Benda, 2019), we occasionally employ an imaginary dialogue with a parent, metaphorically "placing" them on an empty chair to induce a corrective experience and initiate what is termed *memory reconsolidation* (see Timuľák, 2015; Timuľák & Keogh, 2021). I do this, for example, in cases where it is necessary to awaken in the client, in addition to self-compassion, the ability to actively defend oneself or assert oneself (see protective anger, Chapter 14). This was the case with client Daniel, with whom we had been exploring connections between his feelings of inferiority and the emotions he experienced in his childhood relationship with his father. His father used to mock him frequently, embarrassing him in front of others and excessively criticizing and rejecting him. In therapy, we (metaphorically) placed the father in an empty chair. The dialogue with the "father" then proceeded as follows:[1]

THERAPIST: Now, Daniel, imagine your father sitting across from you in that empty chair, okay? When you visualize him there, what do you feel inside?

CLIENT: (Looks very uncertain, squirms.) I'm scared. It's like being on pins and needles.

THERAPIST: Tell that to your father, then. (Nods toward the empty chair.) "Dad, I'm scared just picturing you."

CLIENT: (Slowly, not very willingly.) I'm scared of you, Dad. (Alternates between looking at the chair and the floor.) I've always been scared of you... You yelled at me. I don't know why you hate me so much.

THERAPIST: It hurts to realize how you've always treated me.

CLIENT: Yeah, it hurts. You've caused me so much pain. Why, for heaven's sake?

THERAPIST: Can you now switch to that empty chair? Try to react like your father, who used to yell at you so often.

CLIENT: (Moves to the chair and slowly changes expression, speaking mockingly from the father's position.) All you do is whine. Poor thing! You can't stand anything. (After a moment, with resentment.) You make me sick!

THERAPIST: (Speaking for the father.) Poor thing! I despise you. You're such a weakling!

CLIENT: (With a look of contempt and anger.) You're an utterly pathetic piece of crap!

THERAPIST: (Nods toward Daniel's original chair.) Let's go back to your chair now.

THE INFERIOR SELF

CLIENT: (Moves back.)

THERAPIST: Your father just said to you, "You're a piece of crap! You're crap!" How do you feel now? What do you feel inside?

CLIENT: I feel like a little boy. Weak..., powerless..., dirty..., humiliated. I'll never be good enough for him. He never treated me like a real dad. (Looks sad.) (A)

THERAPIST: (With a sensitive tone.) Hmm. That hurts. Ouch! Humiliation... Feelings of inadequacy... Shame... (After a while.) He never really acted like a dad... What would you have needed from him?

CLIENT: (Shakes head.) Well, what? Love... Recognition... Forgiveness for my mistakes. Sometimes, just to put his arm around me. Just like that. To be proud of me. Like I am of my kids. To support me. Have patience with me.

THERAPIST: Tell that to your father. "I needed recognition. I still need a little recognition and understanding." (Nods toward the empty chair.)

CLIENT: (Looks sad.) I never felt your love. You never stood by me. (Looks at the empty chair.) I needed a dad! Recognition. So I could lean on you!

THERAPIST: Come and sit back again. And imagine that your father is sitting there.

CLIENT: (Sits back down.)

THERAPIST: What do you feel when your son tells you he missed your love and support right now? What's happening inside you? And what will you say to him?

CLIENT: (Takes a deep breath, looks at the floor, shakes head, then stays silent for a while. Then bursts out.) I do love you! (Looks moved.) I wonder why it never worked with you. (His voice lowers.) I'm sorry about that. I wanted to raise you to be a decent man. One who's not afraid! Life was never easy for me either. I just got fed up with how your mother kept nagging.

THERAPIST: "I'm sorry I couldn't show you love. I don't know why. But I love you. Damn it!" Can you say it to your son again?

CLIENT: I love you. (Smiles shyly.)

THERAPIST:	Do you feel it?
CLIENT:	Yeah. (Looks surprised.) I do.
THERAPIST:	Go back to your chair now.
CLIENT:	(Moves back.)
THERAPIST:	What do you feel when your father said, "I love you"?
CLIENT:	Yeah. (Smiles a bit sadly.) It's good. Relief. (B) (After a while.) But he still made a negative comment about Mom. (Shakes head.)
THERAPIST:	Try to first hold on to that relieving feeling in yourself. It warms you a bit, doesn't it? When someone shows you affection and compassion... (After a while.) Well, and the sting? What would you say to him now?
CLIENT:	Dad, cut it out! You're exaggerating! Go fuck yourself! I won't listen to this, I'm not a little kid anymore.
THERAPIST:	Yeah!
CLIENT:	(Smiles.)

TABLE 4 The Inferior Self

Attachment style:	• fearful-avoidant, disorganized
Life position:	• I'm not OK, you're OK.
Young's schemas:	• defectiveness/shame
	• failure
	• perfectionism/unrelenting standards
	• punitiveness

EXERCISE 8

From inferiority to humility

The experience of shame, or the feeling of inferiority, is so uncomfortable that some defensive mechanism almost always masks it. While this defense mechanism is readily accessible to our consciousness, the feeling of shame often eludes our attention. Many people, for example, acknowledge tendencies toward perfectionism or workaholism. However, they generally don't fully realize that their craving (*lobha* in Pali) and addiction to perfection or performance stem from a feeling of inadequacy. Becoming aware of and recognizing the feeling of shame is crucial in treating the Inferior Self. If, while reading Chapter 8, you got the impression that you might be suffering from the "Inferior Self" syndrome and you're ready to confront shame consciously, then confidently engage in the following exercise. Shame (but not feelings of embarrassment and guilt) can be eliminated.[2]

Recall a situation when you felt like you were failing or had failed. Remind yourself of the cause or reason for feeling that way. Recall who was present then, precisely what happened, and all the details. Can you now bring back the entire narrowed state of your mind and the bodily feelings and urges you experienced back then (such as a rush of heat, a stabbing feeling in your face or around your heart, the desire to disappear)? Observe alternately the state of your mind and these bodily feelings like an enthusiastic scientist. It's remarkable what unfolds in your body and mind under the influence of that memory, isn't it?

Be aware, however, that the most painful feelings of inferiority will always strike at the precise moment when a hyper-self-critical thought crosses your mind. Take a moment to observe these thoughts and how they evoke a feeling of shame in your body. Can you trace how behind every self-condemning thought, there follows a physical twinge? It's interesting to mindfully observe that this feeling doesn't arise as an inevitable consequence of a given situation or the memory of it. It appears based on our subsequent (mostly hyper-self-critical) thinking.

The feeling of shame originates from a childishly naive belief that we possess an unchangeable essence that permanently determines our worth or lack thereof. It is connected to the notion of an objective hierarchy of universal human value, on which we can somehow position ourselves, and to the idea that our presumed inadequate personal value can never be altered. No matter what we do, it will never be enough. But where do these notions come from within us? When you catch a self-defeating or overgeneralizing (and black-and-white) idea in your mind related to shame, ask yourself: Where in my childhood could this idea (core belief) have originated? What person and circumstances then contributed to my feeling inadequate?

If relevant memories come to mind, continue asking yourself: What did I need back then? Imagine how you would have felt if someone who loves you had been with you then. What would it be like if this loving person embraced you or put their arm around you and said, "I love you"? Stay in that imagination for a moment, even if it might make you a little sad. You can also imagine that if you were sad back then, the loving person would gently wipe away your tears with a tissue and smile at you. How would you feel? Make sure to store that pleasant feeling within yourself.

And finally, return once more to the situation when things didn't go well for you. Can you now look at it and at yourself with a more forgiving and compassionate perspective? What lessons can you take from that situation for the future? Recognize that no one has the right to think they are more valuable than someone else. Therefore, there is no reason for anyone to feel inferior. It's possible that something is not going well for you, but that is in no way connected to your overall human worth. Genuine wisdom is always associated with humility. And humility means knowing that we don't have the right to belittle anyone, not even ourselves. And if you're tempted to criticize yourself for criticizing yourself, look in the mirror and say to yourself: "I want to love you." Nothing more. How do you feel now?

NOTES

1 This excerpt from the empty chair dialogue has been condensed yet in a manner that retains all the essential elements in the conversation.
2 The exploration of differentiating between feelings of shame, embarrassment, and guilt is addressed, for example, by Benda (2019) or Tangney & Dearing (2002).

CHAPTER NINE

The Inflated Self

The last type of maladaptive schema is, in fact, a subtype of the previous type. The core feeling of inadequacy in an Inflated, grandiose, Self is nevertheless masked by a feeling precisely opposite—namely a *feeling of godlike superiority* and *omnipotence*. When experiencing this feeling, we look at others and the world with disdain (conceit). We perceive ourselves as fundamentally more valuable than others, and sometimes, we camouflage it with an air of condescension. However, this feeling oscillates and alternates with a feeling of *worthlessness* and *shame* (Edershile & Wright, 2021, 2022; Pincus et al., 2014; Wright & Edershile, 2018). However, how does the megalomaniac, narcissistic feeling of superiority arise?

To understand the etiology of the *omnipotence* feeling, let us delve into the parenting styles distinguished by clinical and developmental psychologist Diana Baumrind in the 1960s.[1] Baumrind (1971) described three parenting styles: (1) authoritative, (2) authoritarian, and (3) permissive (liberal). In brief, according to the author, *authoritative* parents are demanding and consistent but also very loving and warm. They are interested in children's inner world, experiences, and needs. However, they also provide children with firm guidance and are unafraid to redirect their inappropriate or dangerous behavior. They lead children to a deeper understanding of significant life values, responsibility, and mutual respect. They give children a certain amount of freedom, support, and clear and safe boundaries. *Authoritarian* parents, on the other hand, place high demands on children but provide little warmth and trust. They constantly control and critically evaluate children but show little interest in the feelings or inner world of children. They do not engage in dialogue with them, insist on adherence to rules and standards, use rewards and punishments, and demand obedience without questioning. *Permissive* (liberal) parents, conversely, do not place many demands on children and are not consistent in enforcing rules. They adapt to children, always get along with them, and accommodate them. They aim for a more equal, friendly relationship with children, allowing them significant freedom. They care about making children feel "happy." Which parenting style, in your opinion, contributes to the development of feelings of omnipotence?

Research on narcissism[2] has pretty clearly demonstrated a connection between feelings of *superiority* and a permissive parenting style, and to a lesser extent, a connection with an authoritarian parenting style (see Kılıçkaya et al., 2021). This aligns more or less with classical theories of narcissism, which explained the development of narcissism either as a result of neglectful and boundary-less upbringing, lacking parental mirroring and realistic feedback, among other factors (Kohut, 2009, 2014) or as a consequence of a highly harsh and emotionally cold upbringing (Kernberg, 2000; see also McWilliams, 2020). From the perspective of meeting a child's basic developmental needs, this involves a lack of *limits* and, potentially, parental *care* or *support*. Based on my experiences, however, the fundamental antidote that prevents the emergence of grandiosity is primarily loving parental *limits*.

However, no need triggers as much controversy among contemporary Czech parents. Limits? Restrictions? Authority? Lack of freedom? We have had enough of that![3] Therefore, it is necessary to clarify what *limits* mean precisely. It is about the fact that a young child naturally experiences a range of intense emotions, whether positive, such as joy and excitement, or negative, such as fear and anger. These emotions bring with them powerful, vital impulses that can be aggressive, destructive, sexual, and so on. The child may then act hatefully, conceitedly, greedily, and recklessly. However, the child needs to feel that parents can handle these intense energies – meaning they can accept them with understanding and channel and limit them. When adequate boundaries are lacking in childhood, we internally experience ourselves as more powerful than we are (omnipotence; see Perquin, 2004). Our ordinary everyday Self is lost in such a state.[4] It becomes impotent (shame). Only when parents can provide loving *limits* can we feel that our strengths are not limitless, uncontrollable, and dangerous. We can then safely acquaint ourselves with our feelings and learn to express and utilize them. We gain a realistic self-image and self-confidence. We learn self-control. We learn to accept that there are things we cannot change. Tangibly, we also experience that we are not alone in the world, that everything does not revolve only around us, and that things have their measure and order. We learn what it is like to live in relationships and respect others.

So, when a little girl desperately insists at 7 PM that she wants to play with her neighbor Anna, setting *limits* means that a parent might say, for example, "No, unfortunately, it is not possible right now. It is time to go to bed. I am sorry. I understand you want to play with Anna (understanding), but you must wait until tomorrow. Now, it is necessary to rest first (everything has its measure)." When a young boy starts hitting neighbor Tony with a little shovel in the sandbox, setting *limits* means that a parent will physically intervene and then say, "I understand that you are angry with Tony because he took the bucket without permission. It is okay to defend yourself (understanding). However, the way you are doing it (behavior) is excessive. Tony is hurting. Try to do it differently. Ask Tony to give you back the bucket that it is yours. Alternatively, turn to me, and I will help you with it. However, do not hit Tony with the shovel." It is perfectly fine for the parent to act as a wise authority. It is acceptable for the relationship between the parent and the young child to be hierarchical, not democratic. A parent is supposed to be a mentor and role model. He is to be alpha (see Shapiro & White, 2014).[5] However, I am not talking about any abuse of power, dominance, or demeaning and belittling of the child. The parent should *limit* the child's *behavior* to protect the child from consequences it cannot foresee. The parent should not assume the child can bear the same *responsibility* in decision-making as an adult. Moreover, the parent should certainly not let the child make decisions for them in matters where the child lacks experience. That would be an educational disaster.

Contemporary parents often strive to build healthy self-esteem and the ability for their children to assert themselves in society. They try to encourage children and shower them with praise. However, in some cases, this may foster naive (illusory) childhood grandiosity. Brummelman and Sedikides (2020) warn that children need realistic feedback from us. When a parent says, "I like your drawing," they give the child appropriate appreciation. However, if they say, "That is an amazing drawing! You are an unbelievable, fantastic painter," they may unintentionally cultivate an unrealistic, grandiose self-image in the child. At the same time, it instills uncertainty in the child. What if I am not always extraordinary? Do I have to be better than others for my parents to accept me? When parents elevate a child to the skies with exaggerated praise, they do not give them a reason to continue learning and developing new skills and competencies. The child gets the impression that "I am just perfect, and I do not have to do anything for it." An overly pampered, protected, and spoiled child then expects others to always worship them without having to earn their admiration. However, love and admiration are not the same. The child undoubtedly needs to experience unconditional acceptance, even when things do not go well and they are not the best. (A parent can say, for instance, "I love you very much, even though this did not work out. I know you tried hard.") However, they also need guidance on how to learn from their mistakes and what they can do to improve next time. They learn not to perceive mistakes as failures but as opportunities for growth. They also learn that competing and comparing themselves with others is not essential, but they must evolve and grow gradually.

As mentioned earlier, it is not only indulgent, glorifying, and limitless parenting (where we perceive parents as weak) that leads to developing an Inflated Self. The shaming, devaluing, humiliating, and belittling of a child (see Inferior Self; cf. Huxley & Bizumic, 2017; Kernberg, 2000) can also lead to the formation of grandiose maladaptive core beliefs. When a child is repeatedly humiliated by a parent, they may compensate for their wounded self-esteem by developing fantasies of their power and uniqueness. In both children raised too benevolently and in those raised too authoritarian, core beliefs emerge, such as:

- I am entirely exceptional, outstanding, remarkable, and admirable.
- I am a hidden genius with unique abilities and skills.
- I am irresistible, perfect, and amazing.
- I am better, internally stronger, and more valuable than others.
- Other people do not even come close to me, they are inferior to me.
- I do not have to consider others. Ethical standards that govern other people do not apply to me.
- The most important thing is to excel. Only one can win.

In a state of an Inflated Self, adults become highly focused on their idealized self-image and show little genuine interest in others. They crave admiration from others (not love, as they disdain it), yet at the same time, they harbor deep mistrust. They fear others might expose their concealed imperfections, vulnerability, and feelings of *inferiority*. Consequently, they struggle to establish close, intimate relationships and prefer to maintain a (sometimes concealed) distance.[6] Paradoxically, they are somewhat afraid of "dependence" on others, even though they cannot distinguish boundaries between themselves and others. Psychologists describe two outwardly distinct types of narcissism, namely grandiose (overt) narcissism, and vulnerable (covert) narcissism. Both types share a sense of entitlement (in Abhidhamma, we speak of conceit; *māna* in Pali)[7] and are highly sensitive to criticism (cf. Jauk & Kanske, 2021), as it threatens their grandiose self-image and leads to a sharp shift in ego state (see Inferior Self). Grandiose narcissists, however, preempt criticism through constant self-aggrandizement, while vulnerable narcissists anxiously avoid any situations that could reveal their imperfections and/or bring humiliation or shame (Edershile & Wright, 2022; Krizan & Herlache, 2018).[8] It is also assumed that grandiose narcissism likely arises from indulgent, permissive parenting (lack of *limits*), whereas vulnerable narcissism is influenced by emotionally cold, authoritarian parenting (lack of *care* and *support*; see McWilliams, 2020; Miller et al., 2017; Nguyen & Shaw, 2020).

In my private therapeutic practice, I rarely encounter clients who precisely fit the description of narcissistic personality disorder according to DSM-5 (American Psychiatric Association, 2013). However, I do come across clients who, based on current diagnosis, would be labeled comorbid.[9] This typically occurs when something happens in their lives that "breaks through" their narcissistic defenses. This was the case with George.

> I met George about a month after his girlfriend left him. He reached out to me because, since then, he had been either raging or sinking into profound darkness and despair. He was unable to function at work or in social situations. He drowned his sorrows under the influence of alcohol but to no avail. He could not just "move on." He could not stop thinking about "it." She left him! How could she do that? He was in utter shock. "Do you think I depend on her?" he asked me horrifiedly. When she left, he packed all her belongings into boxes and threw everything onto the sidewalk in front of the house where she moved. He thought it was a way to "get back" at her and forget about her. However, it was not working. He could not understand how she could leave someone as amazing as him. After all, he has so much potential! Such brilliant ideas! Almost everyone looks up to him! She must have seen that! She knew him, didn't she? And that he used drugs? Or that he was unfaithful all the time? That is obvious! He has a perfect body. He is a fantastic lover. She could not expect to have him all to herself. He (thinks he) belongs to everyone. He is kind-hearted and selfless. Meeting him was a once-in-a-lifetime experience for all those girls. Rarely would they ever experience something more captivating. However, George felt pain. It surprised him that he felt anything. He was not accustomed to "messing around with emotions." He was genuinely confused and derailed. He did not recognize himself. He wanted to understand what was happening to him.

Inflated Self alternates with the Inferior Self. However, clients with the Inflated Self exert tremendous effort to maintain their false, idealized self-image. They, therefore, externalize their problems (see the drama triangle, Chapter 12). They perceive issues outside themselves, often blaming, attacking, competing, and envying. They are full of disdain and reactive anger (secondary maladaptive emotions). They are not in touch with their natural, primary feelings. Essentially, they are alienated from themselves (see Asper, 2018; Röhr, 2022b). Thus, in therapy, bringing awareness to primary feelings of *shame* becomes a crucial step (see Kramer et al., 2018). Our conversation with George unfolded as follows:

THERAPIST: You would like to move on from the breakup, but it seems challenging for you so far. It is still on your mind.

CLIENT: Yes.

THERAPIST:	I have found that in such cases, it is usually necessary to become aware of and process some feeling that you may not even be fully conscious of. Moreover, I do not mean anger; we know that. Would you be willing to explore your experience with me to see if such an important feeling is hidden there?
CLIENT:	Anything. If it helps...
THERAPIST:	Let us start by identifying what "bothers" you most about the whole situation, the trigger.
CLIENT:	Just that she left! That she did it!
THERAPIST:	I see. You keep coming back to that in your thoughts.
CLIENT:	Yeah. I cannot shake off that image. How she takes her bag and just calmly walks away.
THERAPIST:	Hmm. Let us pause at this image and take a very close look at what this image triggers within you. Go ahead and replay that image in your mind. You can even close your eyes. What happens within you when you evoke that image?
CLIENT:	(After a moment.) Total shock. (Shakes head in disbelief.)
THERAPIST:	Hmm. So, something like horror, terror.
CLIENT:	Well... maybe! (Looks surprised, clearly intrigued.)
THERAPIST:	You have already shared how you think about the situation. So, I can probably imagine it. However, what exactly goes through your mind right in that shock? Can you capture that?
CLIENT:	I do not know. I think: "Wasn't I good enough? Didn't she see that I am?"
THERAPIST:	I see. That sounds like a hint of self-doubt. You say, "I am great," but something seems to gnaw at your certainty.
CLIENT:	She must think something else. Something awful. I am just not OK for her!
THERAPIST:	"I am not OK." That sounds tough! Let us try to take it just as a thought, an idea. Maybe your ex-girlfriend implanted this question in your head. "What if I am not OK?" Sometimes, we may have a silent voice inside (see core belief) saying, "You are not OK." Anyway, when you replay this thought, "I am not OK," in your mind, what do you feel? Try to notice the feeling in your body right now.

CLIENT:	(Looks very serious now.) I feel like complete crap, worthless (feeling of inferiority).
THERAPIST:	(After a moment.) Perhaps the idea of her leaving triggers not only anger but also this feeling.
CLIENT:	Well... maybe that is possible. (Takes a long breath, then exhales, looking down.)

Let us add that even with an Inflated Self, of course, our goal in therapy is not to uncover some unchanging "narcissistic traits." Here, too, we aim to reveal particular *processes* taking place in the client's body and mind (cf. Edershile & Wright, 2022; Krizan & Herlache, 2018). For here, too, mindful awareness and compassionate understanding of these feelings can be healing. However, we will delve deeper into the healing process in Chapter 10.

TABLE 5 The Inflated Self

Attachment style:	• dismissing-avoidant
Life position:	• I'm OK, you're not OK.
Young's schemas:	• entitlement/grandiosity
	• insufficient self-control/self-discipline

EXERCISE 9
Descending from the pedestal of superiority[10]

To heal the Wounded Self and to develop the Authentic Self, one must learn, among other things, to mindfully recognize arrogance and contempt. Do you have the courage to explore what lies behind your superiority? If so, try the following exercise. Recall a situation where you felt offended or boasted in front of someone. Perhaps you were thinking something like: "This is beneath me," "I don't need this," "That person is impossible," "What does he think of himself?" or "I have more important things to do than this."

Now, observe for a moment how quickly your mind creates a dramatic story from that situation and how stubbornly it clings to it (see also Chapter 12). The mind doesn't want to let go of the story at all. Can you mindfully observe this clinging? Interesting, isn't it? Also, mindfully notice how your experience has changed as you recall that situation. What does your state of mind look like now? What color could it be? What other qualities does an inflated mind like this have? And what do you feel in your body? What emotions arise when you observe the proud mind? Try repeatedly stepping back first from the entire dramatic thought storm, the clinging, then from the state of your mind, and instead, observe how you feel. Do you feel resistance? Fear? Sadness?

Abandonment? Pain? Then, look at your bodily feelings with gentle eyes as if you want to caress or embrace them. Although challenging, don't avoid these feelings; stay with them until they dissolve. Only then, redirect your attention to your breathing. Be aware of your body's position. Listen to the sounds coming from your surroundings here and now. Notice what you see around you. Bring your full attention back to the present moment. Take a moment to rest. Continue the exercise only when the "drama" of your memory stops engulfing you.

Then, recall a situation that triggered conceit or disdain within you. Remember all the people involved in this situation. Gradually bring each participant to mind and let these memories touch your heart. Repeat the following phrases in your mind: "This person, just like me, desires to be happy and free from suffering. Just like me, they want to feel safe and loved. Just like me, they act in confusion and make mistakes. Just like me, deep down, they often feel vulnerable and unsupported." Develop phrases that would sincerely connect or reconcile you with these people. Notice how you feel during this process.

Finally, let your mind rest in your body for a while. Be consciously in touch with all bodily feelings. Observe how conceit sometimes arises within you and influences your thinking. When this happens, first observe the thoughts, then directly observe the proud mind, and then the painful feeling. Repeat letting this feeling dissolve. Watch how the mind keeps getting "entangled" in thinking and redirect your attention back to the body each time. Can you distinguish what is happening in your experience during thinking and mindful observation of bodily feelings? How do you feel now?

NOTES

1 This refers to a widely recognized and utilized typology of parenting styles, the validity of which is confirmed by current research on maladaptive schemas (see Louis, 2022).
2 In this chapter, I refrain from using the term narcissism to denote narcissistic personality disorder (as per DSM-5) but rather understand it more broadly as a more or less pronounced personality trait.
3 Some psychologists in recent years have discussed an increased prevalence of narcissistic traits in the current younger generation (Twenge & Campbell, 2009; cf. also Lasch, 2018). It is possible that the "narcissism epidemic" is influenced by the overly liberal parenting style of contemporary parents.
4 See also Jung's concept of "ego inflation" (Jung, 2011, 2017).
5 If you, as parents, are seeking inspiration on how to set limits for your children effectively, I recommend the books *No-drama discipline* (Siegel & Payne-Bryson, 2016) and *Mindful discipline: A loving approach to setting limits and raising an emotionally intelligent child* (Shapiro & White, 2014).
6 Individuals with narcissistic traits often struggle with any form of physical contact. They are reluctant to engage in hugs, and closeness frightens them.

7 The sense of entitlement leads us to automatically claim privileges that, in reality, do not belong to us. It offends us when we have to wait in line like everyone else at the cashier, and we find it natural not to listen to others and only talk about ourselves, etc.
8 By the way, so-called highly sensitive people (see Aron, 2020), according to some authors, strikingly resemble a vulnerable form of narcissism (see Jauk et al., 2023).
9 Inflated Self is typically encountered, for example, in clients during the manic phase of bipolar disorder. However, narcissistic traits commonly appear in anxiety, depression, addictions, obsessive-compulsive disorder, post-traumatic stress disorder, mental anorexia, etc. (cf., e.g., Yakeley, 2018).
10 The exercise was inspired by the book *From mindfulness to insight* (Nairn et al., 2019).

CHAPTER TEN

Healing the Wounded Self

In Chapters 6–9, we have demonstrated that a fundamental building block of all maladaptive schemas consists of three variations of the traumatic feeling of core pain: existential dread, sad loneliness, and the feeling of inferiority (shame).[1] These are reflective self-conscious emotions (cf. Benda, 2019) arising from our *subjective interpretation* of reality and conditioned by our negative core beliefs. However, both core beliefs and the feelings of core pain are relatively challenging to capture through mindfulness because they often occur very briefly (sometimes just fractions of a second). When they do emerge in our experience, they are typically immediately "replaced" by defense mechanisms and subsequently by a state of narrowed consciousness, which we can perceive as an archaic ego state (see Chapter 3). However, these two secondary, reactive elements of maladaptive schemas usually persist longer, making them substantially easier to mindfully notice.

EGO STATES

Mindful awareness of the narrowed state of consciousness (archaic ego state) can be one of the initial steps in therapy. Suppose the client becomes aware of a specific state of mind and labels this state with the therapist's assistance (see note 2 on pages 54–55). In that case, they gain experiential distance (see so-called disidentification) and a new *perspective* on themselves. There is a surprisingly significant difference between a client experiencing, for instance, depressive rumination and mindfully observing depression as an interesting state of mind (cf., e.g., Guendelman et al., 2017; Heppner et al., 2015). Just this step alone can bring some relief.

DEFENSE MECHANISMS

Even more exciting shifts in experience result from mindfully acknowledging defense mechanisms and changing one's *attitude* toward them. In Mindfulness-Informed Integrative Psychotherapy, we use the experiential technique of "Taming the Demons Within" (see Benda, 2019; cf. also Allione, 2009; Goldin et al., 2023) to work with defense mechanisms. This technique personifies the defense mechanism as an imaginary "demon" with whom the client engages in a dialogue.[2] In five steps, the client gradually gets to know the "demon" and experiences a transformation from the initial aversion to *compassion* and *acceptance*. Due to the changed attitude, maladaptive defense transforms into a more adaptive response, transforming the entire maladaptive schema. However, the core of psychotherapeutic change lies in working with core pain.

CORE PAIN AND MEMORY RECONSOLIDATION

While cognitive interventions can be utilized for changing core beliefs (see further), transforming core pain requires experiential techniques. These techniques mediate a *corrective emotional (relational) experience* for the client (cf. also Castonguay & Hill, 2012), which includes a *compassionate attitude* toward core pain (cf. Simione et al., 2021). The client typically cannot imagine such an *attitude* until they experience it in therapy, having a "blind spot" in this area. Therefore, the therapist's task is to guide the client toward such an *attitude* through experiential interventions. When successful, this leads to a noticeable shift in the client, often manifested by the sudden (and sometimes somewhat mysterious to the client) disappearance of some symptoms. How is this possible?

In psychotherapy, positive changes and the elimination of psychopathological symptoms sometimes occur gradually (see, e.g., Langkaas et al., 2018) and sometimes suddenly (e.g., Singh et al., 2021). Research on the trajectory of psychotherapeutic change has shown that gradual changes are often unstable. Symptoms temporarily recede and later reappear. However, sudden changes are sometimes surprisingly enduring (Ecker & Vaz, 2022). Is it possible that entirely different mechanisms condition gradual and sudden changes? Moreover, how can one explain the fact that after some interventions, psychopathological symptoms cease to appear without conscious effort? The scientific explanation for sudden and enduring changes, a phenomenon therapists have always encountered, has only recently been made possible by the discovery of *memory reconsolidation* (Nader et al., 2013; Pedreira et al., 2004; cf. Stevens, 2019). For the first time in history, this groundbreaking discovery elucidates *why* experiential and psychodynamic therapies work and the *neurobiological mechanism* underlying psychotherapeutic change (Ecker & Bridges, 2020; Ecker & Vaz, 2022). It is closely related to maladaptive schemas.

Maladaptive schemas are stored in our brains in the so-called implicit semantic memory. And that is what the *reconsolidation* process changes. Unlike episodic memory, which contains memories of specific events, semantic memory includes (1) our *general ideas* and *interpretations* (core beliefs, mental models) about how the world behaves, (2) our *expectations* based on these ideas, (3) *general rules* we follow, (4) *roles* we fulfill, and (5) *self-protective tactics* (Ecker & Vaz, 2022). These general patterns are not easily accessible for retraining, as attempted by traditional cognitive-behavioral therapy. To unlock the relevant neural synapses in the brain, it is necessary first to activate these memory structures (maladaptive schemas), i.e., evoke the *re-experiencing* of core pain (not just talk about these feelings!).[3] Then, the therapist must provide the client with a new and surprising experience that contradicts the original expectation (a mismatch or prediction error). These two successive steps can initiate the *reconsolidation* process, during which the maladaptive schema is canceled (erased) or replaced with an adaptive schema. If *reconsolidation* occurs, the same triggers that previously activated the maladaptive schema begin to evoke a completely different emotional response. Moreover, this happens entirely automatically, without any conscious effort on the client's part (cf. Benda, 2019; Žvelc & Žvelc, 2021).

In the dialogue with clients Peter (Chapter 7), Daniel (Chapter 8), and Martin (see further Chapter 13), the re-experiencing of core pain is denoted by the letter (A), and the new corrective emotional experience by the letter (B). Distinguishing the type of "Wounded Self" enables the therapist to tailor the corrective experience to the specific unmet needs of the client. Whether the client describes their conscious feeling of core pain more as (1) a feeling of paralyzing horror, (2) a feeling of cosmic loneliness, or (3) a feeling of personal inadequacy will guide us in focusing on fulfilling (1) the need for protection and safety, (2) the need for care and nurture, and the need for place, or (3) the need for support and the need for limits (see Chapters 6–9). However, it is only when the client in therapy truly *feels* what it is like to have his or her need fulfilled that the maladaptive schema can be *reconsolidated* (cf. Greenberg, 2021). The client then internalizes the new experience and learns to have compassion toward themselves.

CORE BELIEFS

Each type of maladaptive schema carries a specific kind of emotional vulnerability (Timuľák & Keogh, 2021) or heightened emotional reactivity (McLaughlin et al., 2020; Weissman et al., 2019). Individuals with a "Lost Self" are hypersensitive to stimuli related to responsibility, guilt, or any threat. Those with an "Abandoned Self" excessively intensify experiences of farewells, breakups, or losses. People with an "Inferior" or "Inflated Self" react disproportionately strongly to any evaluation, criticism, or humiliation. Suppose we have a schema of a particular "Wounded Self" stored in our limbic system and encounter a typical stimulus (trigger). In that case, our perception (interpretation) of the situation begins to be influenced by core beliefs, such as "I am too weak and vulnerable, I must not alienate others," "no one can love me," or "I am worse than others." At that moment, we feel helpless like children despite our conscious efforts to prevent it. The problem is that we are unaware that we perceive the situation from the position of a dependent Child. At that moment, we believe our profoundly ingrained belief corresponds to reality. For some people, maladaptive schemas activate only exceptionally and usually only in close relationships, while for others, the maladaptive schema is active almost permanently.

Chapters 6–9 delved into how our core beliefs originate in early interactions with our caregivers (parents). When a young boy frequently gets the *impression*, "Dad does not love me," he concludes from this relational experience, "I must not be worthy of love; no one can love me." Thus, an excessively generalizing core belief emerges. The difficulty lies precisely in this overgeneralization. Core beliefs are always too "black and white," abstract, and rigid. They correspond to the perception of a young child and are a bit like fairy tales (see Chapter 12). They have an absolute, total, and global nature (cf. Moore et al., 2017). When verbalized, they often begin with words like "never," "nobody," "always," "everyone," and "forever". If they concern ourselves, core beliefs also stem from the naive childhood assumption that there is an unchangeable Self with essential, once-and-for-all given qualities, and it is either entirely good or bad. A healthy adult can view things from multiple perspectives and is not dependent on others as a small child is. They can assess what they have achieved and what they have not without overevaluating their entire existence. They might say, for example: "It seems this person does not like me. However, some of my close ones do. Moreover, after all, I love myself. So, it is not the end of the world. Maybe that person did not like *something specific* I did or did not do. However, that can be different next time. Things change." It looks different, though, when our perception is (unconsciously) dominated by the narrative of the "Wounded Self." At that moment, deep down, we again believe our childhood convictions, such as "I am unacceptable." The question then is whether we can see through the nonsense of the core belief and maintain a balanced adult perspective.

While, chronologically, core beliefs stand at the inception of the activated maladaptive process (see Chapter 3), in therapy, their mindful awareness and cognitive reappraisal usually come into play only when the client is capable of noticing the feelings of core pain without automatically responding with secondary defense mechanisms. This occurs when the client can adopt a somewhat *compassionate attitude* toward emotional pain and has some understanding of how the entire maladaptive schema developed in their childhood (see client Ryan, Chapter 3). Attempting to address core beliefs earlier could risk inundating the client with feelings of core pain, making it difficult for them to observe core beliefs with a certain detachment. Instead, they might completely *identify* with these beliefs (cf. Beck, 2021).

In contrast to traditional cognitive-behavioral therapy, cognitive reappraisal is used only as a complementary strategy that can (thanks to the client's conscious understanding) support the transformation of maladaptive schemas.[4] However, we do not rely solely on cognitive interventions to lead to *memory reconsolidation*.[5] As explained in Chapter 5, maladaptive *emotional* schemas are addressed *within relationships*. Corrective experiences are always lived *in a relational context*, whether with the therapist or an imagined "ideal parent." Purely rational cognitive reappraisal, which would compel the client to change their *relationship* with themselves without prior corrective *relational* experience, would likely not trigger *reconsolidation*. It would require the client to reappraise core beliefs *each time* maladaptive schemas are activated, regardless of their current emotional state. *Memory reconsolidation*, however, does not demand such repeated conscious efforts from the client. The *compassionate attitude* is automatically activated after *reconsolidation*. Nevertheless, cognition can help clients understand their inner processes and support their conscious efforts toward change. Cognitive change complements emotional change effectively.

How does one achieve mindful awareness of core beliefs? If a client experiences thought rumination during the activation of maladaptive schemas—repetitive, cyclical automatic thoughts about the same themes[6]—we can assist in uncovering the hidden common denominators (central themes) of these thoughts or images and their concealed *personal significance*. These automatic thoughts often fall into three categories: First, there are excessively self-critical and self-blaming thoughts (where a person evaluates not specific actions but their entire personality or character). Second, there are notions about what a person "should" or "must" do (usually essentially demanding absolute perfection). Third, there are catastrophic visions of a threatening future for the individual (disregarding the fact that what happens and how we cope with it are separate matters). With self-critical thoughts, the point is to discover what all the criticism means when expressed in one sentence, e.g., "I am worthless." Regarding ideas about what a person should be, it is crucial to uncover what emerges in the client's mind when they fail to achieve perfection, for example, "I am weak; I am not a man." Concerning catastrophic visions, the aim is to reveal the subjective significance the most extreme possible catastrophe would have for the individual, like "I will be alone; everyone will abandon me."

To mindfully notice that all repetitive thoughts covertly stem from one deeply ingrained idea (belief), such as "I do not deserve love," means to see through (gain insight into) the fact that it is merely an idea, not reality. When such awareness occurs, the idea completely loses its power. As mentioned before, conditions often need to be prepared for such awareness in therapy. First, guiding the client to recognize the feeling of core pain mindfully. Second, by exploring together when in their past they experienced this traumatic feeling and what they genuinely needed (and lacked) at that time. Compassion for the experienced pain facilitates later mindful awareness and reappraisal of the core belief. When this happens, our Narrative Self, our conception of who we are, transforms.

I find it fascinating that the historical Buddha (*Siddhattha Gotama*), over two and a half millennia ago, extensively explored what constitutes our identity, distinguishing five sets of phenomena with which we typically identify (*pañca-upādāna-kkhandha* in Pali; see Armstrong, 2017; Bodhi, 2005; Bradford, 2021; Harris, 2019a). He mindfully noticed that we identify (1) with our *body*, (2) with our *feelings*, (3) with our *consciousness*, but also (4) with the typical way we *perceive* and interpret ourselves and the world (see core beliefs), and (5) with typical *patterns* by which we react, i.e., with our (maladaptive) schemas. The transformation of maladaptive schemas discussed in this chapter thus challenges our self-concept. When entering therapy, we should likely ask ourselves: Are we ready to set aside a part of our old identity? Many clients during therapy doubt and say, "If I learn to react differently in those problematic situations, then it will not be me at all!" And even though it sounds somewhat comical, it is true. Healing the Wounded Self indeed brings about a significant change in functioning. Moreover, a decision needs to be made. Do we want to change? Do we want to heal? It is, of course, up to us. Another question, however, is what our life can then be like. How can it look when rigid childhood traumatic patterns no longer define our perceptions, experiences, and actions? What can our "Authentic Self" be like? If these questions interest you, let us contemplate them in the book's third part.

EXERCISE 10

Your core belief on a billboard

Have you ever experienced that you couldn't "get unpleasant thoughts or images out of your head" for a long time and kept coming back to them in your mind? If you want to explore your core beliefs, take a notepad and jot down these thoughts in a few points. What specific thoughts or images were running through your mind at that time?

Read through the points again and realize whether you were thinking more about yourself or someone else back then. Were you thinking generally about the world, life, or people? Did your thoughts look toward the future? Were these thoughts evaluative or generalizing? Were you afraid of something? What were your thoughts primarily about? Briefly note down their central themes.

Now, imagine what it would mean for you if these unpleasant thoughts or images were true. What consequences would it have for you? What would be the worst part for you? What would bother or frighten you the most about it? What would it mean for your future? How would you feel? Give space to the darkest visions.

If your thoughts were about the world or other people, focus more on yourself and ask again: How does this all relate to me? What does it say about me? What worst traits of my personality or character could be revealed by this? And try to imagine for a moment what your inner critic, judge, or (false) prophet whispers to you in this context. What does it say about yourself? (You can draw inspiration from the beliefs mentioned in Chapters 6–9.) Try to formulate it as precisely as possible and write down the most concise sentence.

Consider the sentence that expresses some of your hidden core beliefs. Can you imagine where this belief might have originated in your childhood? What circumstances contributed to the formation of this belief back then? Do you still believe that your conviction is true?

In any case, imagine that you had to design a billboard with your belief. What colors would you use? What background? What photo or illustration could be on the billboard? If you feel like it, you can draw the billboard. Imagine (or draw) other versions as well. How would your billboard look with a pink background? What would it look like in retro style, in the style of communist propaganda, or the art deco style? How would a heavy metal version or a disco-style version look? Which version do you find visually appealing? And how do you feel when you imagine it?

NOTES

1 The eminent cognitive-behavioral therapist Judith S. Beck, incidentally, has outlined three categories of negative core beliefs—beliefs expressing (1) helplessness, (2) unlovability, and (3) worthlessness (Beck, 2021). This classification naturally corresponds roughly to (1) the Lost Self, (2) the Abandoned Self, and (3) the Inferior Self, and we can readily associate with it the three variations of the experience of core pain described above.
2 Core beliefs can be personified as the metaphorical voice of the "inner critic," "judge," "scarer," or "false prophet," while the defense mechanisms themselves can be embodied as incarnate "vices" or "sinful thoughts."
3 When the maladaptive schema is activated (manifesting as visible emotional arousal), it is possible to "update" this schema with a new corrective experience for a period of 5–6 hours (the so-called *reconsolidation window*). After that, the relevant synapses "lock" again, and *reconsolidation* is no longer possible (see Ecker & Vaz, 2022; Schiller et al., 2010).

4 From a psychological perspective rooted in Abhidhamma, working with core pain involves interrupting the 12-link chain of dependent origination between the members of feeling (*vedanā*) and craving (*taṇhā*). Subsequent work with core beliefs disrupts the cycle of dependent origination between the elements of aging-death of ego state (*jarā–maraṇa*) and ignorance (*avijjā*, cf., e.g., Brewer, 2017; Burbea, 2014; Frýba, 1989, 2008; Hájek & Benda, 2008).
5 The results of research on sudden positive changes after cognitive interventions are currently inconsistent (see Aderka & Shalom, 2021). Perhaps this is because traditional cognitive-behavioral approaches do not emphasize the necessary emotional arousal, a crucial condition for *memory reconsolidation*. Additionally, they do not intentionally mediate corrective relational experiences.
6 In meditation slang, such thoughts are referred to as "sticky thoughts."

PART III

The Authentic Self

As mentioned above, we need a narrative identity for a healthy, satisfying life in relationships with others. Our Narrative Self, or mental representation of ourselves, allows us to understand the continuity of our lives, attribute subjective meaning to the events we have experienced, and find purpose in life (see, e.g., McAdams & McLean, 2013). The Narrative Self makes us human (McAdams et al., 2021). It provides a unique perspective from which we perceive and interpret our inner experiences, external events, and the world around us. Unlike a range of psychological traits and personality features that manifest in our behavior and can often be observed and evaluated using objective scientific methods, the Narrative Self is known only to ourselves. Only we know how we understand ourselves, interpret events in our lives, what values we adhere to, and where we are heading in life. Others can recognize our Narrative Self only when we decide to reveal our "story" to them (e.g., by telling it; cf. McAdams et al., 2021).

For example, I can introduce myself to you, the readers, as follows: "I am a psychologist and therapist. I am the father of a fifteen-year-old daughter. I am fascinated by Vipassanā meditation and altered states of consciousness. I enjoy lecturing and writing articles about mindfulness, compassion, psychotherapy, and spirituality. I also love traveling and experiencing different cultures." Such self-presentation, of course, reveals only a tiny part of my self-concept. In ordinary social interaction, however, it will give you at least a basic idea of how I perceive myself and what you can expect from me. Self-concept and self-presentation are, of course, influenced by the extent and depth of our self-awareness and our willingness or courage. In other words, our readiness to truthfully admit to ourselves and others what we truly feel, believe, what goals, values, motives, etc., we have. Some people significantly embellish their self-image, while others are sometimes overly critical of themselves. On May 8, 2013, Donald Trump tweeted about himself: "My IQ is one of the highest." Socrates declared about himself: "I, in front of myself, neither know nor think I know" (Plato, 2022). Our self-image can be realistic but also entirely false if we deceive ourselves about something. We can behave authentically, in harmony with what we are truly experiencing, or we can present to others only a mask that is more intended to conceal our genuine attitude and real feelings. Sometimes, we pretend something entirely consciously and intentionally. However, fear sometimes dominates us, preventing us from expressing ourselves sincerely.

The significance of authenticity, self-actualization, and self-determination for mental health and personal well-being has been emphasized primarily by humanistically oriented authors, such as Carl Rogers (2021, 2022), Fritz Perls (1992), or Abraham Maslow (1987).[1] However, psychodynamically oriented therapists, such as Donald Winnicott (2018a) or Heinz Kohut (2014; Kohut & Wolf, 1978), also differentiated between the "true" (nuclear) and "false" (damaged) Self. Carl Gustav Jung spoke in this context about a lifelong process of becoming a unique human being (the process of *individuation*), which involves gradually becoming aware of and integrating previously unconscious contents and processes occurring in our minds (see, e.g., Edinger, 1992). Thus, he hinted already at the path from the Authentic Self (in this part) to the Transcendent Self (Part IV). However, in this part, we will focus on the fundamental levels of self-awareness and authenticity in relationships and communication with our close ones. Only when we can indeed be ourselves in relationships with others, that is, when we can be sufficiently independent, flexible, resilient, honest, assertive, initiative, spontaneous, creative, but also consciously vulnerable (see Chapter 15), does it make sense, in my opinion, to pay attention to transpersonal experiences and spiritual development.

According to Olga R. Sohmer, a psychologist from the California Institute of Integral Studies, we are authentic if, at any given moment, we can (1) be present and simply curiously and attentively perceive what is happening right now, without constant overthinking; (2) be consciously connected with our own experience, i.e., with the bodily feelings occurring within us; (3) have the courage to be genuinely open in communication, honestly and truthfully sharing with others what we are currently feeling and experiencing; (4) be willing and able to acknowledge and integrate painful or unpleasant feelings, thoughts, and images, as well as other contents and processes happening within us; (5) be aware of our innermost values while simultaneously admitting all conflicting impulses and urges that may be at odds with our values; and (6) be fully aware that our experience is constantly changing depending on ever-changing external and internal conditions, is dynamic, and occurs within relationships (Sohmer, 2020). However, can such assumptions be realized?

You may have noticed that to be authentic, we need a considerable dose of mindfulness and self-compassion. The more we develop these two abilities, the more likely we can be authentic. In the following chapters, we will see that mindfulness will enable us to create an authentic and realistic Narrative Self that is both sufficiently flexible and dynamic on the one hand and anchored in our innermost values on the other hand (cf. Žvelc & Žvelc, 2021). Mindfulness and self-compassion allow us to (1) "dissolve" or transform all our pathologies and (2) humbly accept "ordinary human unhappiness" (see Freud, 1952), which life inevitably brings. They enable us to discover that it is not external events themselves but rather our *attitude* toward what we experience that decisively influences the extent of our suffering. Perhaps, then, we will gradually find the courage for independence as well as the courage to be close (see Chapter 15) and start understanding and embracing life's struggles and troubles as opportunities for growth rather than as "evidence" that we deserve nothing else based on who we are (cf. McAdams & McLean, 2013; McLean et al., 2020).

In our everyday life, our self-perception changes depending on our current mood or the state of our mind. When things are going well and we are in a good mood, our view of ourselves is optimistic. For instance, we might think, "I am a handy woman, and I look good." However, this can change quite rapidly if a maladaptive schema is activated. At that moment, our mind is dominated by a traumatic childhood narrative, such as, "I will never achieve anything. I am incapable." Trying to convince ourselves that it is not true usually does not help much. Eric Berne, the founder of transactional analysis, categorized states of mind into three categories: Parent, Adult, and Child (e.g., Berne, 1957, 2022). The Child ego state activates patterns of thinking, feeling, and behaving that we experienced in childhood. These patterns can be associated with spontaneity and creativity, which may be fine. However, they can also be traumatic patterns linked to negative core beliefs, maladaptive defense mechanisms, and learned helplessness, which poses a problem (cf., e.g., "enraged Child" or "spoiled Child" in Table 1 on pages 52–53). Similarly, the Parent ego state activates patterns of thinking, feeling, and behaving that are internalized from our relationships with caregivers during childhood. The Parent ego state can sometimes be helpful, such as providing a model of loving care. However, at other times, it can be highly destructive, activating schemas associated with insensitive and excessive criticism (cf., e.g., "punitive Parent" or "suspicious overcontroller" in Table 1 on pages 52–53). According to Berne, only the Adult ego state can be considered exclusively healthy since it represents the adult's ability to process information realistically and regulate emotions and behavior. The Adult ego state allows us to adapt our actions flexibly to the current external and internal situation. In contrast, the Child and Parent ego states may compel us to act in a stereotyped manner according to a long-fixed script.

Maša and Gregor Žvelc, integrative psychotherapists from Ljubljana, Slovenia, have pointed out that in maladaptive Child and Parent ego states, we always feel threatened. The level of our physiological arousal is either disproportionately high (agitation, mobilization, referred to as hyperarousal) or disproportionately low (freezing, immobilization, referred to as hypoarousal). According to them, consciousness is narrowed in these ego states (cf. Žvelc & Žvelc, 2021). However, how do we function in the Adult ego state? Eric Berne (2022) described the Adult ego state as a state in which we can rationally process information and constructively solve problems. However, Žvelc (2010) emphasized that the Adult ego state not only encompasses the ability to act effectively (the doing mode) but also the ability to simply be (the being mode) and *accept* our experiences as they are (cf. Deikman, 1982; Segal et al., 2013). He thus distinguished an exceptional level of the Adult ego state, which he termed the "mindful Adult" (cf. also Xiao et al., 2017). The mindful Adult can consciously be in contact with unpleasant and painful feelings without automatically avoiding or being overwhelmed by them. He or she can use mindfulness to recognize that a traumatic core belief has emerged in consciousness and discern that it is just a thought, not an objective reality. He can notice defense mechanisms such as conceit, hatred, or detached apathy and wisely rise above them or prevent them from influencing his behavior. Therefore, he can act authentically without being controlled by maladaptive schemas. Note that this does not mean he has no maladaptive schemas; he is just aware of the individual elements of the activated maladaptive schema and shows self-compassion.

As Gabor Maté, a renowned expert on child development and trauma, pointed out, we live in a toxic culture (Maté & Maté, 2022). Consequently, we all have more or less Wounded Selves. Core pain is a universal human experience (cf. also Epstein, 2014; Levine, 2012). However, in the following chapters, we will see that the Authentic Self emerges precisely through the conscious healing of childhood emotional injuries. We will discover that trauma has transformative potential and can make us more compassionate and wiser. Healing the Wounded Self will also alter our self-image, our Narrative Self. Then, we will be ready to explore the Transcendent Self.

NOTE

1 Compare also the self-determination theory by Edward L. Deci and Richard Ryan (e.g., Ryan & Deci, 2017).

CHAPTER ELEVEN

The Mindful Adult

In the original Buddhist context, the cultivation of mindfulness is employed as part of training aimed at realizing absolute, unconditional reality and liberation from all forms of suffering. This training encompasses eight practices (see the Noble Eightfold Path) and leads to the gradual "purification of the mind" from all pathology.[1] In addition to mindfulness, followers of Buddha's teachings also develop "right understanding," "right intention," "right speech," "right action," "right livelihood," "right effort," and "right concentration" (see, e.g., Frýba, 2008). Mindfulness by itself is not the only panacea! Buddha clearly distinguished between right mindfulness (*sammā-sati* in Pali) and wrong mindfulness (*micchā-sati* in Pali), considering whether mindfulness is utilized in harmony with the equally crucial aspects of the Eightfold Path (cf., e.g., Greenberg & Mitra, 2015; Stanley et al., 2018). If we omit seven aspects of the eight, it would be difficult to expect the training to lead us to the desired goal. However, many contemporary mindfulness enthusiasts seem to have no clue about this.

When Jon Kabat-Zinn published the book *Full catastrophe living* in 1990 (revised edition in 2013), he characterized mindfulness somewhat imprecisely as "paying attention… non-judgmentally." He meant awareness "without rejection (aversion)," that is, awareness combined with the *acceptance* of inner experiences.[2] However, some present-day mindfulness enthusiasts mistakenly believe that non-judgment means we should not *distinguish* whether the phenomena we observe are beneficial (*kusala* in Pali) or harmful (*akusala* in Pali) in their consequences.[3] And that is a cardinal error (cf., e.g., Bodhi, 2011; Dreyfus, 2011; Gethin, 2011; Grossman, 2015; Monteiro et al., 2015; Walpola et al., 2022)! The opposite is, in fact, the truth. In the Pali language, mindfulness meditation is termed *vipassanā-bhāvanā*, literally translated as the *cultivation of insight* or the development of cognitive understanding! Ongoing *evaluation* of experiences gained through mindfulness is a logical and necessary condition for liberating ourselves from the constant arising of further suffering (cf., e.g., Mahāsi, 2014). When we observe through mindfulness how our suffering arises, we naturally draw conclusions from such acquired experience (*vipassanā-paññā* in Pali). Therefore, accepting does not mean not evaluating.

Mindfulness allows us, among other things, to directly observe the psychological consequences of craving (*taṇhā* in Pali), clinging (*upādāna* in Pali), or exaggerated "personality-belief" (*sakkāya-diṭṭhi* in Pali). It enables us to understand critical ethical-psychological connections in our experience (see "right understanding," cf. Benda, 2019; Frýba, 2008; Sevinc & Lazar, 2019) and, for instance, to see through defense mechanisms like desire, hatred, apathy, conceit, endless doubt, or cyclic remorse and worries (see Table 1 on pages 52–53), which are inherently unpleasant (or destructive, cf. Goleman, 2004) and, moreover, only divert attention from genuinely important feelings indicating what we currently need. For example, when we feel fear, we may need protection and safety. When experiencing sadness, we may need closeness and understanding. However, if we automatically suppress fear or sadness just because they are unpleasant, it is challenging to attend to fulfilling the corresponding need.

Without mindfulness, our minds are governed by primitive mechanisms that Freud (1940, 1945) associated with the id, describing them as the pleasure principle (*Lustprinzip* in German) and the unpleasure principle (*Unlustprinzip* in German). We instinctively resist anything unpleasant and cling to everything pleasant (cf. Ng et al., 2017; Weber, 2017). However, through the cultivation of mindfulness, we learn to *accept* all internal phenomena. Therefore, if we mindfully notice, for example, hatred arising in our minds, we *accept* it as a fact and inquire about the primary feeling that triggered the emergence of hatred and the need hidden within that primary feeling (see self-compassion). We do not condemn ourselves for the presence of hatred in our minds (this is precisely what Kabat-Zinn meant). On the contrary, we can be glad that we have mindfully noticed it. Thanks to such mindful awareness and clear understanding (*sati-sampajañña* in Pali; see, e.g., Anālayo, 2020) that actions motivated by hatred always cause further suffering (not only to others but also to ourselves), we can "wisely consider" (*yoniso-manasikāra* in Pali) our next steps (cf. Kang & Whittingham, 2010). We can consciously decide not to let hatred influence our behavior. Instead, we can act with compassion (see "right intention," "right speech," and "right action"). Note that this does not automatically mean doing nothing externally (see Chapter 19, cf. Choi et al., 2021)! If necessary, we can reasonably assert ourselves. However, assertion motivated by compassion has an entirely different impact on our subsequent experiences (and usually on other people) than assertion motivated by hatred (see further Chapter 14). We can illustrate this with the example of the client, Oliver.

In a phone conversation with his girlfriend Samantha, Oliver shared his joy about successfully persuading his boss to sponsor a local children's home. At that moment, he felt genuinely proud that he managed to secure support for the children. He mentioned it to Samantha during their conversation, expecting her to share his joy and appreciate his engagement. However, Samantha did not react; she remained silent on the phone. This seemed unusual to Oliver. Initially, he, too, fell into an awkward silence. However, a maladaptive schema activated within him at that moment. Oliver felt as if he were sinking into an endless black hole. Despite being aware that he was tired and that the silence "unnerved" him suspiciously intensely, he couldn't prevent a thousand automatic thoughts about betrayal, injustice, and humiliation from gradually filling his mind (see the drama triangle, Chapter 12). He was engulfed in a mood of cosmic sadness, occasionally punctuated by flashes of hateful thoughts. "I can't handle this," he thought. "If I've upset her, why doesn't she tell me? Does she hate me? Does she despise me? Is she jealous of those children, perhaps?" He felt like a "wounded jaguar" or, if you will, a "victimized/abused Child" (Child ego state). The conversation with Samantha ended, but the defeated mood lingered with Oliver overnight and into the next day.

As Oliver had been through therapy before, he understood that he would need mindfulness and self-compassion to start feeling like an Adult again and potentially communicate constructively with Samantha about what was happening within him. He knew that in such a state, it made no sense to make significant decisions (such as breaking up with her) or let significantly clouded thinking to weave catastrophic visions of the future. He, therefore, directed mindful attention to his mind. He knew he didn't feel like an Adult. What kind of peculiar state was this? "I feel like a hurt little Olly," he suddenly realized. He had to smile bitterly at that label. What else was happening within him? Oliver tried to identify what he was feeling exactly. "Suspiciously intense fear and flashes of hatred," he observed after a while. "Aha, those are probably defense mechanisms," he realized. However, Oliver didn't want to act out of hatred (see "right intention"). He knew from experience that it wouldn't help much. But what primary feeling of core pain was driving this whole inner drama of his? "A feeling of inferiority? That I'm not good enough for her?" he pondered initially. "No, that doesn't fit. Or loneliness, abandonment?" When he posed that question to himself, something shifted within him. "Yes, cosmic childhood loneliness. That's it. That's what I feel," he realized (see "Abandoned Self").

This awareness already brought Oliver some relief. "I know that if I don't abandon myself, it won't be that bad," he comforted himself. "But it's just sad that I probably will never find someone who truly cares about me and won't kick me away when I need something." *Oliver continued to contemplate this way.* "Hmm... I must not need anything because no one ever... What? That's a core belief, like stitched in! Good Lord!" *When Oliver realized it, tears of emotion sparkled in his eyes. He smiled with relief.* "Yes. It's just a traumatic childhood fantasy. It's not reality," *Oliver now clearly understood.* "Sometimes Samantha and I get closer, and sometimes we drift apart. No 'never' or 'forever' exists. It's just the archaic idea of a little boy who once depended on his parents. In reality, everything is constantly changing in every moment. Ah!" *Finally, Oliver felt like an Adult again. The childhood traumatic ego state was gone. So was the hatred and fear. And the feeling of abandonment. Now Oliver was genuinely ready to talk to Samantha about how her lack of response to his joy and pride affected him. He was curious, of course, about what was going on with her. Would she be able to recall it? Would she be willing to tell him? Oliver remained curious. But he knew he probably wouldn't feel like a "hurt little Olly" anymore, whether he found out anything or not.*

This episode from Oliver's life illustrates that mindful exploration of maladaptive schemas and more precise recognition of their four main elements (see Figure 1 on page 25) enables us to interrupt our automatic, compulsive, habitual behavior patterns and consciously choose how we will respond. Conscious decision-making naturally involves *assessing* various options and estimating their consequences, including *evaluating* specific phenomena we notice. It could be destructive to judge *oneself* at that moment (one's Narrative Self, e.g., "If I experience hatred, it means *I am bad*"). On the contrary, recognizing the unhelpfulness of hatred is essential for the constructive handling of the situation. Oliver handled it excellently. When he mindfully noticed the emergence of hatred in his experience, he did not react with resistance or an attempt to suppress it. He *accepted* the fact that hatred arose in his mind. Based on past life experiences, however, he concluded that expressing this hatred outwardly would not be beneficial. So, he preferred to spend more time exploring the primary feeling that generated the hatred. Once Oliver realized that his perception and experience stemmed from an unrealistic childhood belief that "no one will ever love him," he was subsequently able to "protect" himself adequately. In an Adult manner, he told Samantha that her silence had saddened him.

In general, it can be stated that the more we are mindful of what is happening within us in each moment, the better we can then, based on this gained experience, *assess* which of our impulses and motives will lead to a pleasant experience in the long run and which, conversely, will lead to an unpleasant one ("right understanding," cf., e.g., Monteiro et al., 2015; Walpola et al., 2022). This relatively simple evaluative criterion allows us to make decisions and act by principles and *values* that make sense to us as adults (cf. LeJeune & Luoma, 2019; Žvelc & Žvelc, 2021). While the pleasure principle (automatic clinging) and the unpleasure principle (automatic resistance) take us back to archaic ego states of the Child or internalized Parent, mindfulness enables us to act authentically and simultaneously as Adults, considering the long-term impacts of our actions. We could say that every time we start noticing what is happening within us, we return to the Adult ego state. In the Child or Parent ego states, we may think but not mindfully notice. As soon as we engage mindfulness, we are suddenly outside the Child and Parent ego states.

When we genuinely start to be mindful in detail of what is happening within us in moments when some maladaptive schema is activated, sooner or later, we will find a path to skillfully manage both our own experiences and the given external situation. Gradually, we cease to fear our emotional vulnerability (cf. Brown, 2015, 2017). Situations we once perceived as betrayals, injustices, or crises become interesting and almost welcome opportunities for further self-discovery and growth. That is the Adult perspective. However, it does not end there. Developed mindfulness also teaches us not to overly identify with some unnecessarily narrow and specific description of ourselves (conceptual, Narrative Self, cf., e.g., Whitehead et al., 2018). It instructs us to understand our existence more as a fascinating and constantly changing stream of experiences and a challenge for continuous self-discovery. This does not just mean that our traumatic childhood core belief, such as "I am inadequate," changes to another belief, like "I am OK." What changes primarily is our relationship to any story we tell about ourselves (see Hayes et al., 2016; McHugh et al., 2019). We comprehend that, just like the world around us, we are constantly evolving, and any definition of our identity is always relative and very, very simplifying. We stop taking any self-concept too seriously (see further in Part IV of this book). Then, we can act as mindful Adults.

EXERCISE 11

Who am I?[4]

Many spiritual traditions guide their followers to deeply contemplate the question, "Who am I?". However, in the following exercise, the goal is not to find a specific rational answer to this question. It is more about fully realizing the conceptual nature of our Narrative Self. We can explore this essence by repeatedly asking, "Who am I?" and mindfully observing the feeling this question evokes. We experience that we cannot find a satisfying answer to this question. Take a few minutes and ask yourself, "Who am I?" If you find this exercise intriguing, you can then pose the following questions:

- I have a name. However, am I the name my parents gave to me?
- I have a gender identity. However, am I the gender that was assigned to me?
- I belong to a specific age category (e.g., in my 40s, a teenager). However, am I the age category society tells me I am?
- I have some education. However, am I my level of education?
- I have a profession. However, am I the job that I work at?
- I play various social roles (e.g., mother, father, spouse, daughter, son, someone's friend). However, am I the social roles that I play?
- I identify with various groups and institutions (e.g., Czechs, heavy metal fans, volleyball players, environmental activists). However, am I the group or institution I identify with?
- Am I the reputation I have in society?
- Am I the intelligence attributed to me by society?
- Am I the body through which others perceive me?
- Am I the thoughts in my head?
- Am I the memories I remember?
- Am I the preferences I usually have? Am I what I like?
- Am I my desires?
- Am I my emotions?
- Am I my beliefs?
- Am I my typical reactions?
- Am I my expectations?
- Am I the ideas playing out in my mind?
- Am I a mystery?
- Who am I?

NOTES

1. The gradual "purification of the mind" is intricately described in the classic and still widely used meditation manual *Visuddhi-magga*, also known as *The Path of Purification*, dating back to the fifth century (Buddhaghosa, 2020).
2. There is no doubt that Kabat-Zinn is well aware of the need to distinguish in meditation practice which mindfully noticed phenomena are "beneficial" and which are "harmful." This is evidenced by many later works by this author and the dialogue he has engaged in recent years with Buddhist scholars (see, e.g., Williams & Kabat-Zinn, 2013).
3. Precise "investigation of phenomena" (*dhamma-vicaya* in Pali) is considered in Buddha's teachings as one of the seven crucial factors leading to awakening *bojjhaṅga* in Pali; see, e.g., Nyanatiloka, 2019; Rhys Davids, 2016).
4. The exercise was inspired by Chris Niebauer's book *No self, no problem* (Niebauer, 2019).

CHAPTER TWELVE

The Drama Triangle and How to Get Out of It?

While in Part I and Part II of this book, we primarily focused on how maladaptive schemas manifest in our inner world—our perception, thinking, and experience—in the third part, we will also explore how these maladaptive schemas manifest externally, affecting our behavior, *relationships*, and communication. I find it crucial and valuable to realize that each maladaptive schema represents a prototype of a relational event. It compels us to repeatedly stage and reenact the same scenarios (cf. Röhr, 2022a; Žvelc & Žvelc, 2021).[1] Typically, though, we are not consciously aware that this is happening. We continue to act in the same way, unaware that core traumatic beliefs, core pain, and automatic defense mechanisms are controlling us. The drama we experienced in childhood thus continues to unfold in our lives incessantly.

GAMES

Eric Berne referred to these stereotypically repeating "dramas" as so-called games (cf. also life scripts). In his now-classic book *Games People Play*, he described 36 such games and thoroughly explained how the archaic ego states of Child and Parent contribute to the creation of these games (Berne, 2022). For it is precisely in these maladaptive ego states that we "play games." Instead of authentic adult openness and honesty, we pretend, "play games." While some games may be relatively functional and harmless in social interaction, others can be highly destructive in their consequences. Why do we play them, then? Maladaptive schemas compel us to do so, along with the characteristic internal conflicts they contain.

On the one hand, each type of Wounded Self has a hypertrophied longing to fulfill a need not adequately met in childhood. However, the traumatic core beliefs, on the other hand, obstruct the actual fulfillment of that need. A person with a "Lost Self," for instance, desperately yearns for relational safety and certainty on the one hand. Simultaneously, they may think, "Having personal feelings or needs is extremely dangerous." Can they then feel safe in any relationship? No. Their convictions keep them in a state of almost permanent threat in every relationship. They can never truly express themselves. Safety is only achieved when they are "invisible." The same is true for the other three types of Wounded Self. A person with an "Abandoned Self" deeply craves closeness and understanding in their soul. However, they may think, for example, "I must be completely independent. Needing anything from others is a sign of weakness." A person with an "Inferior Self" avidly hungers for appreciation and acknowledgment. Nevertheless, they may think, "If people discovered who I truly am, they would reject me." Finally, someone with an "Inflated Self" subconsciously yearns for loving *limits*. However, they are convinced that "no one is competent enough to assess or correct their uniqueness in any way." Maladaptive schemas make us akin to "hungry ghosts," as depicted in Buddhist cosmology, beings with immense hunger and thirst but mouths and throats too small to satisfy themselves (see Epstein, 2013b; cf. also, e.g., Maté, 2018).

When communicating with others, if we "play out" a game deep down, we usually expect a reward, such as reassurance, closeness, or appreciation. However, because negative core beliefs compel us not to reveal our Authentic Self, this genuine connection can never actually occur. The game tends to reinforce the confirmation of our Wounded Narrative Self (e.g., "I truly do not matter") and solidify our "life position" (e.g., I am not OK, you are OK; see Harris, 2012). Let us consider a brief example. Thomas asks his wife, Lena, "Have you seen my woolen socks anywhere, please?" And Lena responds, "Me? Am I your servant to keep track of your socks?" This could be the beginning of one of the games that Berne (2022) aptly called, for instance, "Kick Me," "Now, I have got you, you son of a bitch," "See what you made me do," "Look how hard I have tried," "If it were not for you," "I am only trying to help you," "Yes, but…," or "Frigid woman." What is the problem? Lena has entered the Parent ego state and started communicating with Thomas as a Parent to a Child. If Thomas were to react as a Parent (e.g., "Are you a bit irritable, huh?") or as a Child (e.g., "Can't I ask a normal question?"), the game could begin. However, let us suggest how Lena could communicate as a mindful Adult. If she mindfully noticed her painful feeling of childhood inadequacy and had compassion for herself, she could respond to Thomas' question, for example: "No, I have not seen your socks. Moreover, you know, Thomas, when you repeatedly ask me such things, I feel like I cannot handle anything, that I am not a good enough wife, and I get upset with you. I would need you to be more involved in household chores and take more responsibility." This way, Lena would communicate with Thomas as an Adult to an Adult. If Thomas also communicated as an Adult, they wouldn't play destructive games but would cultivate mutual closeness and collaboration.

THE DRAMA TRIANGLE

Let us go back to the mechanism of immature games often played in relationships. Transactional analyst Stephen Karpman (1968), identified and described three complementary roles that consistently appear in relational and communication games (Karpman, 1968). These roles are the Victim, Persecutor, and Rescuer. They are roles found in every drama or fairy tale (cf. also with mythology). In a fairy tale, the Victim is typically portrayed as an innocent person pursued by the Persecutor. Despite the Victim's earnest efforts to handle the situation, they are usually utterly powerless against the Persecutor. They cannot help themselves and depend on the Rescuer for assistance. The Persecutor is usually depicted as arrogant, authoritarian, evil, cruel, and heartless, a villain who torments, humiliates, abuses, and intimidates the Victim. The Rescuer is then described as a kind, noble, and brave being who selflessly helps the Victim. It is a classic! We all enjoy reading or watching such stories. However, there is one catch. In real life, we do not live in a fairy tale.

When, in our everyday lives, we begin to perceive real situations through the lens of the drama triangle, we can be sure that we are not in an Adult ego state. In such a moment, we are under the influence of our maladaptive schema. It does not matter which role we feel we are in then. All three roles contain something childishly naive and immature (cf., e.g., Petitcollin, 2020). Maladaptive schemas always compel us to perceive things in an exaggeratedly black-and-white manner and radically "split" the world around us into things and people who are either good (Victims and Rescuers) or evil (Persecutors)—nothing in between. However, splitting corresponds to the mental age of a toddler (Weinhold & Weinhold, 2013; cf. Klein, 2017). Experience shows that when we start perceiving situations or other people through the lens of the drama triangle, we usually gradually "rotate" from one role to another. Our Narrative Self then transforms in an equally black-and-white manner.

In our story about Thomas and Lena, the sentence "Am I your servant?" could activate Thomas' Lost Self and evoke in him a feeling of existential dread and, secondarily, a feeling of omnipotent guilt. If Thomas automatically took responsibility for Lena's irritation, he could start playing the Rescuer (Parent ego state) role and try to take better care of Lena. In his zealous efforts, however, he would likely do many things Lena does not desire. Lena's irritation would thus gradually increase, and Thomas himself would start feeling like a Victim (rotation within the triangle). On the other hand, he might stop seeing Lena as a Victim and perceive her as a Persecutor. "She is so ungrateful," he might think. "I do so much for her. I try so hard. However, it is never enough for her!" Eventually, he might start verbally undermining and humiliating Lena because he would feel entitled. That would put him in the role of the Persecutor (another rotation in the drama triangle). However, all roles in the drama triangle are pathological.

Dysfunctional social games based on the drama triangle externalize our maladaptive schemas. Every time maladaptive schemas catapult our minds into archaic ego states of Parent or Child, we begin to perceive ourselves and others through our negative core beliefs, behaving as Victims, Persecutors, or Rescuers. However, in none of these roles are we authentic and sincere. Instead of explicitly expressing our needs, we resort to manipulation and conceal our true motivations. Why do we do this? Because we fear rejection or abandonment as if we were still toddlers unable to survive without the help of others (see Chapter 15). Due to such inadequate fear, we keep revolving in the vicious cycle of the drama triangle!

THE RESPONSIBILITY ISSUE

The Rescuer automatically takes responsibility for the feelings and needs of other people (cf. the Lost Self) while disregarding or outright denying their feelings and needs ("I do not need anything. I do not want anything. I do not expect anything. Nothing bothers me. I am not angry at all"). Outwardly, the Rescuer appears as a kind of superhuman or savior. They excessively sacrifice themselves without being asked (believing they know best what others need). Simultaneously, they covertly attempt to evoke a feeling of obligation or debt in others (manipulation). The Rescuer expects others to naturally "reciprocate" by fulfilling his own needs, even though he does not express them and is often not even aware of them. Ultimately, they always feel exploited and resent others for not meeting their needs (usually followed by rotations within the triangle; see Glover, 2004; Lue, 2023; Schmidbauer, 2007; von Franz, 2000).

The responsibility issue, however, also affects the Victim. The Victim avoids responsibility for personal decisions by simply refraining from making any decisions. When the Victim refrains from deciding anything on their own, they cannot make any mistakes, can they? This way, they maintain the illusion of their innocence and perfection (see the Narrative Self). However, delegating all responsibility for their feelings and needs to others logically makes them feel utterly powerless and dependent on others. When the Victim does not feel well, they seek someone to blame outside themselves ("I feel bad because of you. Poor me. I am not responsible for anything. What kind of life could I have if it were not for you?"). In other people, the Victim always sees either a Persecutor or a Rescuer (see splitting). Through their self-presentation, the Victim often elicits pity from others, portraying themselves as martyrs. By making others responsible for their feelings, the Victim manipulates and abuses them covertly. The Victim always needs both a Persecutor and a Rescuer.

Ultimately, we can state that even the Persecutor blames their troubles on others. However, for perceived wrongs and injustices, they openly seek revenge and "teach others a lesson." They feel they are merely defending themselves, that they are correct, and only "administering justice" (cf. the Inflated Self). The Persecutor typically assumes an authoritative and superior stance. They enjoy escalating conflicts and express their supposedly righteous anger in them. The Persecutor criticizes and accuses others, attempting to control them. Without moral scruples, they use any "coercive means" for this purpose. They humiliate and shame, insult, apply "derogatory labels," intimidate, bring up old matters, and exploit their social status, money, or sex to control others, and so on. However, the Persecutor also, understandably, rotates within the triangle and quickly shifts alternately into the Victim role (cf. Petitcollin, 2020; Weinhold & Weinhold, 2013).

HOW TO BREAK FREE OF THE DRAMA TRIANGLE?

We engage in games based on the drama triangle in moments when specific maladaptive patterns govern our perception, thinking, and experience. These are times when we do not notice what is happening within us but identify with archaic black-and-white thinking, corresponding either to the Child ego state (the Victim role) or the Parent ego state (both the Persecutor and Rescuer roles). How, then, can we liberate ourselves from the drama triangle? The key to stopping these games lies again in mindfulness, which reliably brings us back to the mindful Adult ego state at any moment (see Oliver in Chapter 11). When, during the game, we start to notice what is taking place within us mindfully, we might realize, for example, that we are unusually agitated (hyperarousal) or, conversely, immobilized (hypoarousal) and that the drama of our inner experience does not correspond to the mundane external situation (see the example with the socks). These are signs of narrowed consciousness. Exploring and verbally naming this awareness is then advisable (cf. also note 2 on pages 54–55). If, in the given example, Lena mindfully noticed the state of her mind, she could label this state as, for instance, the ego state of the "abused poor thing." In the ego state he found himself in after Lena's accusation, Thomas could label it as a "caught monster," perhaps. Both could also mindfully observe the automatic thoughts and images swirling through their minds in this narrowed state of consciousness, labeling them as "black-and-white thinking" or "cruel sock drama," gaining distance from these thoughts. That would be a good start.

However, as we know, three additional elements contribute to the emergence of each maladaptive ego state: core beliefs, core pain, and defense mechanisms (see Figure 1 on page 25). If we genuinely want to deactivate the maladaptive schema and interrupt the triangle game effectively, we must also be mindful of these elements. Lena and Thomas could mindfully notice, for example, the emergence of conceit, shamelessness, hatred, endless doubt, or cyclical remorse and worries in their minds (see Table 1 on pages 52–53).[2] However, the most crucial aspect is for them to mindfully notice the painful feelings of inadequacy (Lena) and existential dread (Thomas). If Lena and Thomas, with the help of mindfulness, captured this hidden core pain they are experiencing, they could adopt a *compassionate attitude* toward it (self-compassion).[3] Only through this would the activated maladaptive schemas be definitively "dissolved." The core pain would disappear. Then, they could finally mindfully notice the core beliefs that trigger feelings of inadequacy and existential dread. Lena might capture her hidden belief: "If I do not know where Thomas has his socks, it means I am completely incapable and despicable." Thomas would capture his belief: "I have no right to ask anything from anyone. I should not exist at all." Moreover, if both realized these beliefs were absurd, they could smile at them (cognitive reappraisal). After that, they would not have to play any more games.

In general, it can be stated that when we start to be mindful in detail of what is happening within us in moments when some maladaptive schema is activated, sooner or later, we will observe that the most painful feelings are not directly caused by other people, or at least not directly. We will notice that the most painful feelings arise in our minds due to our core beliefs. We will understand that only ourselves can influence the emergence (and disappearance) of these feelings. This is how we can liberate ourselves from the drama triangle. When we learn to recognize our feelings and understand the needs that individual feelings signal (cf. also Benda, 2019), we can take full responsibility for regulating our emotions and fulfilling our needs. That is how we truly become adults. At the same time, it is essential to understand that, as adults, we are not entitled to expect others to recognize and fulfill our needs automatically. It is up to us to express our feelings and needs adequately, clearly, and openly. However, if we, through mindfulness, rid ourselves of the childish fear of rejection or abandonment, it should no longer pose any problem.

Let us add that once we grasp that core pain arises from identifying with negative core beliefs, we find the boundary where the responsibility of others regarding our experience ends and our responsibility begins. The relieving aspect is that, at the same time, we understand that we are not automatically responsible for the feelings of core pain experienced by someone else. We can thus definitively rid ourselves of feelings of inadequate (omnipotent) guilt. If someone who perceives themselves as a Victim considers us "selfish and evil Persecutors," simply because we do not automatically take responsibility for their feelings and problems that they refuse to address, it may make us sad. However, there is no reason to feel guilty. We will delve more into the boundaries of our responsibility in Chapter 13.

EXERCISE 12

Transcending the drama triangle[4]

Recall an emotionally unpleasant relationship situation in which you felt thrown off balance or had the impression that you were at the mercy of other people or events beyond your control. Based on this specific situation, try to answer the following questions from the *Victim's* perspective. Beware, even if you are not used to feeling sorry for yourself, make an exception this time and try deliberately thinking like a "sulking Child" or a "punitive Parent" for a moment. To achieve the goals of this exercise, you first need to embrace the role of the Victim in all its fullness. Try to genuinely feel "innocent" and "hurt" by others.

- What happened to you?
- Who is to blame? (Who wronged you?)
- What did they do wrong? (What was unfair about what they did to you?)
- What should they have done instead?
- What should they do now to make amends?
- What punishment do they deserve? (What would satisfy you? How would the fearless protector in a fairy tale punish the persecutor?)

Only go on when the idea of punishment gives you a feeling of justice. Only then, in your thoughts, return to the same situation. This time, however, answer from the perspective of the "mindful Adult" who takes full responsibility for their emotions and actions.

- What *challenge* did you face?
- How did your actions, or lack thereof, contribute to creating this situation?
- How did you feel when it happened?
- How did you *decide to react* when it happened?
- Could you have acted more effectively?
- Could you have better prepared?
- What can you do now to help minimize or rectify the damage?
- What *lessons* can you take from this?
- How do you feel about it now?

NOTES

1 Compare also Freud's concept of the "compulsion to repeat" (*Wiederholungszwang* in German, Freud, 1940, 1946).
2 More detailed explanations of defense mechanisms can be found in the book *Mindfulness and self-compassion* (Benda, 2019).
3 As we mentioned in Chapter 4, adopting a compassionate attitude toward the feelings of core pain is challenging for many clients and is typically achievable only after experiencing corrective emotional experiences within the therapeutic relationship (cf., e.g., Greenberg, 2021). Therefore, if you are attempting to navigate out of the drama triangle on your own and find that this step proves challenging, do not hesitate to seek the assistance of a professional therapist (see note 2 in Chapter 5 on page 50).
4 The exercise was inspired by Fred Kofman's book *Conscious Business* (2013).

CHAPTER THIRTEEN

Adult Responsibility and Its Limits

Are we responsible for our experience? Furthermore, are we responsible for the experience of other people? We must answer these questions if we want to establish healthy personal boundaries and function in close relationships. However, what is the experience exactly? When we mindfully observe our experience, we can verify that it is a constantly occurring *process* of the emergence and disappearance of various bodily and mental phenomena that interact with each other (see Hájek, 2002, 2012; cf., Herma & Greve, 2024). Experiencing includes processes of sensory perception, thinking, imagining, volitional processes, as well as feelings and states of mind. Some feelings arise automatically (inevitably) with our perception and interpretation of reality (see appraisal, e.g., Moors, 2014; cf., Levenson, 1999, 2011). Others result from our thinking and imagination (see reflective emotions, Benda, 2019; cf., McRae et al., 2012).[1] The crucial point is that we *can influence* our experience of both types of feelings. For reflective, self-conscious emotions, such as shame, we, for instance, can become aware of and cognitively reappraise our unrealistic core beliefs on which shame is based (see Dahl et al., 2015; Vago & Silbersweig, 2012). Above all, however, we can always influence the course of automatic and reflective emotions with our *attitude* toward a particular feeling (see Greenberg, 2021). In short, if we can consciously *mindfully notice* any feeling and *accept* it with understanding, the feeling will dissipate (for a more detailed explanation of this mechanism, see Benda, 2019; see also, e.g., Coffey et al., 2010; Kotsou et al., 2018; Lindsay & Creswell, 2017, 2019). However, since the course of our experience depends significantly on our ability or inability to *notice* and *accept* our feelings *mindfully*, we can also say that only we are responsible for the course of our experience. Of course, we cannot always influence external circumstances or control whether some (primary) feeling arises within us. However, we are always responsible for internally *responding* to our feelings. This depends solely on us! Until we start *mindfully noticing* what is happening within us and *being compassionate* with ourselves, no one else can do it for us. Therefore, no one else is directly responsible for our experience either.[2]

For the sake of completeness, let us note that Robert Leahy (2019, 2022), the author of emotional schema therapy, has pointed out in his approach that even the *attitude* we automatically adopt toward our feelings can be influenced by our negative core beliefs. Just as we have unconscious core beliefs about ourselves, others, or the world, we can internalize general core beliefs about emotions, including possibilities and "correct" ways of regulating emotions, the causes and consequences of emotions, or the influence of emotions on our identity.[3] According to Leahy, irrational negative core beliefs about emotions arise as a result of our early traumatic experiences. Understandably, they covertly influence whether we *approach* our (especially unpleasant) emotions with trust, interest, understanding, and *compassion*, or conversely, with mistrust, disdain, and an automatic attempt to suppress emotions (cf., e.g., Mitmansgruber et al., 2009). I can confirm that many clients, based on their childhood traumatic experiences, are convinced that emotions are essentially uncontrollable yet entirely meaningless, useless, unnecessary, irrational, invalid, shameful, and/or even damaging (cf., Manser et al., 2012).[4] They hold maladaptive core beliefs such as: "Emotions are dangerous, they must always be suppressed, and one should rely solely on reason," "Experiencing emotions is just a manifestation of personal weakness," "When I am emotionally upset, it means I am failing," "If I feel angry, it means I am fundamentally a bad person," and "When I feel angry, it can harm others" (cf. also Leahy, 2016; Veilleux et al., 2021). Fortunately, however, corrective emotional (relational) experience and subsequent cognitive reappraisal of dysfunctional core beliefs also lead these clients to change their rejecting *attitude* toward their feelings and, consequently, toward themselves (see further). However, let us return to the topic of responsibility.

According to the ancient introspective phenomenological psychology of Abhidhamma, the psychological consequences of our actions (*kamma-vipāka* in Pali) are determined by the intention (*cetanā* in Pali) with which we act (Frýba, 1989, 2008), and not the action itself. As it is well known, "when two do the same, it is not the same." For instance, when communicating criticism to someone, there is a difference between doing it to help them (well-intended constructive feedback) and doing it to belittle or embarrass them. If, deep down, I know that I intended to hurt the other person verbally, I will inevitably experience an adequate feeling of guilt (I can suppress this feeling, but I cannot prevent its emergence).

However, suppose I am sure[5] that I intended to help the other person. In that case, there will be no feeling of guilt within me, even if the other person explicitly accuses me later (e.g., "You got me! Because of your criticism, I did not sleep the entire weekend! I feel like a complete fool!"). Manipulative, unjust accusations and shifting responsibility (see the drama triangle in Chapter 12) can, however, evoke a feeling of inadequate (omnipotent) guilt in us if it activates some of our maladaptive schemas or our traumatic negative core beliefs about ourselves (our Wounded Self). However, how do we distinguish between adequate and inadequate guilt?

Both emotions manifest in our bodies quite differently, and it is possible to learn to distinguish them based on distinct bodily cues (cf., Gendlin, 2003; Weiser Cornell, 1996). However, both are also associated with significantly different states of mind, making it possible to differentiate them through mindfulness at this level. While we experience an adequate (adaptive) feeling of guilt in the Adult ego state, an inadequate (omnipotent, maladaptive) feeling of guilt is linked to the Child ego state. We can easily recognize this by the noticeably high or, conversely, low levels of our physiological arousal (hyperarousal or hypoarousal). Therefore, if we feel threatened like small children, it is likely that we are experiencing omnipotent guilt (cf., Gazzillo et al., 2017, 2020).[6]

The adequate (adaptive) feeling of guilt alerts us that we have made a specific *mistake* or engaged in some wrong, inappropriate *action*. It urges us to become aware of this *mistake*, learn from it for the future, and attempt to mend relationships with others if our error has damaged those connections. When we take responsibility for the consequences of our mistakes, we can subsequently forgive ourselves for the adequate guilt (Benda, 2019). However, when we mentally associate the *specific mistake* we made with the notion of some supposedly *permanent identity*, that is, with our Narrative Self (e.g., "I am an inherently bad, selfish person"), we primarily experience some variation of the core pain (existential dread, desperate abandonment, or shame), and secondarily, omnipotent guilt arises in us as a maladaptive defense mechanism (cf., Bush, 2005; Leary & Tangney, 2012; Tangney, 2015; Tracy & Robins, 2006).[7] Forgiving oneself for omnipotent guilt is impossible, however. If we want to rid ourselves of this feeling, we must thoroughly understand that, in reality, we have not committed any wrongdoing.

In my experience, clients with a Lost Self (see Amy in Chapter 4, Kate in Chapter 6, and Thomas in Chapter 12) are particularly prone to feelings of inadequate (omnipotent) guilt. These clients are often aware that they struggle to perceive their personal boundaries, to refuse, or to say no. They recognize their unhealthy tendency to take responsibility for the experiences of others. Moreover, they are conscious that they experience a feeling of (omnipotent) guilt when they try to resist this compulsive tendency. However, they are unaware of the feeling of existential threat from which the compulsion to assume responsibility for others usually arises. Additionally, they cannot take a *compassionate attitude* toward this feeling of core pain. To learn this, they first need to undergo a new, corrective emotional experience, as was the case with the client Martin.

> Martin grew up without a father, only with his mother and younger brother. When Martin was about five, his grandfather (his mother's father) passed away, and Martin's mother struggled deeply with this loss. For many years, she seemed lifeless, submerged in her grief to the point where she didn't hesitate to repeatedly talk to young Martin about how she found no joy in living. She even spoke of suicide, which terrified Martin to death. He vividly remembers the anxiety he felt, often waiting anxiously by the window for his mother to return from work or shopping. He would look impatiently out the window. And if his mother were slightly late, he would imagine scenarios where she had been hit by a car or, worse, had taken her own life. It was hell. In his childhood, Martin did everything he could to ensure his mother felt well. He was very independent and an exemplary student, meticulously organizing his toys. His thoughts were always focused on how to bring joy to his mother. The idea that he might have his own needs didn't even cross his mind.
>
> As Martin gradually matured, he became an even more outstanding support for his mother, and he took pride in that role. He felt strong and believed that being a supporter suited him well (see the Rescuer role in Chapter 12). Moreover, Martin often played the "wise advisor" role to his peers. It pleased him that others turned to him for guidance. It was something he was accustomed to. When he got married after college, he naturally adopted the same protective attitude toward his wife. His wife became the center of his life, and he would go to great lengths to make her happy. He rejoiced when she was pleased and felt troubled when she was even slightly upset. It took many years for Martin to realize that he was living solely for others, that he was exhausted, and that his well-being depended entirely on his wife's happiness. He essentially had no personal life. This realization led him to therapy.

To initiate therapeutic change in Martin's case, he needed to understand that his compulsion to automatically take responsibility for others' experiences was connected to the traumatic experiences he had as a child in his relationship with his mother. He had to mindfully notice the feeling of existential dread from which this compulsion originated and learn to approach this painful feeling with adult understanding and compassion. To initiate a corrective experience, we repeatedly employed the Ideal Parents Technique (Benda, 2019; cf., Brown & Elliott, 2016; Jencius & Duba, 2003). Within this framework, Martin first needed to create an image of an "ideal mommy" who would love life, enjoy her own life, and be happy. It is worth noting that even such an imagination brought Martin a certain relief. When he imagined how he might have felt if he had an "ideal mommy" in his childhood—someone who laughed frequently sang throughout the day, and danced around the house—he initially felt sadness about not having had such a mother back then. However, when encouraged to accept this sadness, Martin delved deeper into the imagination and breathed a sigh of relief, saying, "Oh! I would not have to worry about such an ideal mommy!" The following session then featured this dialogue[8]:

THERAPIST: If your ideal mommy, when you were five, had her father (your grandfather) pass away, she'd probably say to you, "I feel sad that I won't see Grandpa again, you know? Having such a dad was great for me. But my tears right now express my love for Grandpa, which I still feel in my heart. Adults sometimes cry out of love." She'd smile. "But that doesn't mean I can't handle it. I love life. I'm so glad to have you, your little brother, and (the ideal) dad, and I still have plenty of love for myself and all of you. You don't have to worry about my tears at all!" Then, your ideal mommy would probably warmly hug you and kiss you on the head.

CLIENT: (Looks at me. Appears to be a mix of sadness and a certain hope.)

THERAPIST: Then your ideal mommy would focus on you. What did you like when you were five? What interested or amused you back then?

CLIENT: Me? (Pauses, looking surprised.) God, I don't remember ...

THERAPIST: If you had ideal parents, they would be very interested in what you liked and found interesting. They would show you the various games and entertainment that life offers.

CLIENT: Games? (Shakes his head in confusion.)

THERAPIST: They might paint with you, read children's books, sing songs, build with building blocks ... Go outside, on trips, to the playground, to the water ...

CLIENT: I don't know any of that. I was mainly just at home in my room. When I had a moment, I usually imagined I was a diver. We had an aquarium, and beside it, I would dream about the underwater world.

THERAPIST: Ah! Ideal parents would surely notice that. Would you like to go somewhere with ideal parents to a pond, a lake, or maybe the sea?

CLIENT: What would we do there? (Asks in confusion.)

THERAPIST: Well, play, of course! Splash around, squirt water at each other with water pistols, be silly, dive...

CLIENT: (Smiles.) And ideal parents would have time for that?

THERAPIST: Absolutely! Ideal parents would love life and their children. They would enjoy your childlike joy. They'd gladly buy you diving goggles, fins, and a snorkel. They would dive with you.

CLIENT: (Imagines fighting his sadness. His eyes become moist.) (A)

THERAPIST: Ideal parents would be proud to have a son who enjoys exploring the underwater realm. They might jokingly say something like, "You're quite the diver! Completely immersed in the watery element!" But most importantly, they'd be happy about your happiness. They might say something like, "We had so much fun! We love playing with you! What shall we do tomorrow?" And as you dried off on a beach towel, you could all chat, gaze up at the sky, and touch each other's hands. Parents might say, "Life is wonderful!"

CLIENT: (Smiles.)

THERAPIST: How do you feel now?

CLIENT: It's a beautiful imagination. So relaxed! I feel good. (B)

THERAPIST: Allow yourself to experience that feeling fully. Feel free to close your eyes and stay in that fantasy for a while. Take your time. (After a moment.) Hmm, you really needed that back then. The feeling that someone sees you, that someone cares about you, and that you can enjoy life's pleasures carefree ...

We had to gradually create a series of such fantasies with Martin during several therapeutic sessions. In these visualizations, ideal parents consistently set firm and loving *limits* on his tendencies to automatically assume responsibility for the emotions of others ("You don't have to worry about my tears at all!"), while simultaneously "addressing" his feelings of *invisibility* and *existential dread*. After a few of these experiential sessions, Martin, however, discovered that the experience of the omnipotent guilt altogether ceased in his emotional experience (*memory reconsolidation*). He became more aware of his emotions (such as protective anger) and better understood what he needed. He realized that it was okay to take care of his own needs. He understood that self-compassion did not mean self-denial. He stopped automatically taking responsibility for the emotions of others (boundaries of responsibility). And he ceased entangling himself in the drama triangle (see Chapter 12). It could be said that Martin discovered a self-attitude that Erich Fromm (1939) or Abraham Maslow (1996) referred to as "healthy selfishness." However, a *corrective emotional experience* played a significant role in Martin's transformation. I want to emphasize that, in my opinion, this experience taught Martin to approach the feelings of core pain with compassion and allowed him to establish healthy personal boundaries. It is a question of whether Martin could have learned this on his own without this experience *in* the therapeutic *relationship*.

EXERCISE 13
Learning to understand your warning lights

The syndrome of omnipotent guilt associated with our Wounded Self (see, e.g., Chapter 6) urgently compels us to (1) *automatically* assume responsibility for the feelings and needs of others and (2) simultaneously wholly disregard *our* feelings and needs. When afflicted by this syndrome, we take care of others regardless of our limits and naively expect that others will (of course) reciprocally care for us boundlessly without clearly expressing our needs. However, this never happens. In reality, it is entirely up to us to learn (1) to notice our feelings, (2) to recognize what we need, and (3) to communicate that to others. As adults, we should also learn (4) to fulfill our needs at least partially.

Our bodily feelings could be likened to the indicators in a car. Each feeling signals a specific need. Just as a dashboard light illuminates when the vehicle needs fuel, oil, or coolant, our body produces feelings to signal that we need something. It is not wise to ignore these indicators or expect someone else to monitor them on our behalf!

Suppose you have already tried exercise 6 on pages 62–63. In that case, it is likely that, in certain situations that previously triggered feelings of omnipotent responsibility and existential fear, you will gradually start experiencing anger or disgust (see Benda, 2019; cf. also exercise 14 on pages 127–128). These are emotions you probably couldn't afford in your childhood, and their emergence is a sign that your Wounded Self is beginning to heal. Anger signals that you should protest against something. In contrast, disgust signals that you should distance yourself from something (e.g., explicitly reject responsibility that someone is covertly trying to transfer onto you). However, if you want to learn to understand other "indicators" (emotions), let's try the following exercise.[9]

Recall an emotionally charged situation you recently experienced. Bring back the memory with all the details. What evokes the strongest emotions in you about this situation? Can you recall the situation vividly enough to start re-experiencing some feelings on a bodily level? If so, stop thinking about this situation now and observe what you feel *in your body*. Transfer your full attention to your body. Where *in your body* does the feeling arise? What kind of feeling is it? Can you name it? Does any word come to mind that could capture the essence of the feeling? Take a moment (several minutes) to find the most accurate name for this feeling. And every time a word comes to mind, immediately focus back on your body. Has anything changed in your body when you mentally uttered that particular word? If not, the word doesn't capture the feeling. In that case, try to find other words. Be patient. After all, you are learning to understand your "indicators" and, therefore, yourself.

After several minutes of trying to accurately name the feeling, transition to the next phase and ask yourself: What need does my emotion signal? What do I *need* when I recall this situation? You can ask yourself the following questions: Do I need protection? Do I need to assert myself? Do I need someone's closeness and understanding? Do I need to share what I feel with someone? Do I need to distance myself from something? Do I need to forgive myself for something? What do I need?

Once you understand what you need in relation to the situation, realize that fulfilling any need starts with adopting a compassionate attitude toward that need within yourself. Fully admit that you have this need. Allow yourself to have it and refrain from suppressing it. Accept it with understanding and compassion for yourself. Then ask yourself: What can I do to fulfill this need? Don't be deceived by learned helplessness telling you you can't do anything. What can you do for yourself?

Finally, imagine what it would be like to *express* that feeling and need to the people it affects. What if you told them, "You know, in this situation, I *feel*... (insert a specific feeling) and I *need*... (insert a specific need) right now." Is it difficult or impossible for you to imagine such a scenario? If you doubt that expressing your feelings and needs to the people you're addressing would have any impact, realize that expressing your emotions and needs would affect you regardless. A significant difference exists between keeping your feelings to yourself and telling them. You can also imagine what it would be like to have an assertive advocate who would articulate it for you. They might say something like, "In this situation, my client feels... (insert a specific feeling) and needs... (insert a specific need)." Would that be a relief for you? Or does such a thought frighten you? Explore the emotions that such thoughts evoke in you for a moment, and don't resist them. Accept them. How do you feel now?

NOTES

1 Neuroscience, in this sense, discusses the genesis of emotion as either "bottom-up" or "top-down" (cf., e.g., Brandmeyer & Delorme, 2021; Kendler & Woodward, 2021).
2 Please note that these statements apply exclusively to adults! In the parent-child relationship, I believe there is a greater responsibility on our part to recognize what our child needs and take care of fulfilling those needs.
3 Leahy (2022) says it is essentially about an "implicit theory of emotions."
4 The reader will find the importance of selected basic and self-conscious emotions in our lives in the book *Mindfulness and self-compassion* (Benda, 2019). A detailed

explanation of the significance of 87 emotions can be found in the new book by the famous author and researcher Brené Brown, *Atlas of the Heart* (Brown, 2021).
5 Please note that it is crucial to be completely honest with oneself! One's conscience cannot be deceived.
6 By the way, it is possible to differentiate between feelings of adequate guilt and toxic shame based on their distinct neural signatures in our brains. This is supported by a meta-analysis of 34 neuroimaging studies recently published by Piretti et al. (2023).
7 In the Abhidhammic typology of defense mechanisms, omnipotent guilt corresponds to restlessness and cyclical, endless remorse (*uddhacca-kukkucca* in Pali; see Table 1 on pages 52–53).
8 The sample dialogue has been shortened and is presented here only to capture the most relevant moments for *memory reconsolidation*. In reality, the visualization of "ideal parents" typically takes 20–30 minutes.
9 The messages conveyed by individual basic emotions can be found in the book *Mindfulness and self-compassion* (Benda, 2019). A detailed explanation of the significance of 87 emotions is provided by Brown (2021) in the book *Atlas of the heart*.

CHAPTER FOURTEEN

Self-Compassion and Protective Anger

The number of scientific publications on self-compassion in the past 20 years has dramatically increased.[1] Numerous studies have documented that higher levels of self-compassion are associated with greater well-being, life satisfaction, resilience, creativity, social connectedness, and emotion regulation skills (see, e.g., Benda, 2020a; Inwood & Ferrari, 2018; Zessin et al., 2015). Additionally, several studies have established a link between a lack of self-compassion and the prevalence of psychopathology (see, e.g., MacBeth & Gumley, 2012; Marsh et al., 2018; Muris & Petrocchi, 2017).[2] However, is self-compassion compatible with experiencing and expressing anger? Yes, it is, but it depends on the type of anger. Emotion-Focused Therapy distinguishes between two types: reactive anger and protective anger (Timuľák, 2015; Timuľák & Keogh, 2021). Reactive anger aligns with the attitude described in Abhidhamma as aversion or hatred (*dosa* in Pali). This attitude is generally unhelpful in its consequences. On the other hand, there is protective anger, known in the Mahayana and Vajrayana traditions as compassionate wrath (see Masters, 2000), often associated with fierce compassion (see, e.g., Jinpa, 2016; Lama, 2019; Neff, 2021). It is an adaptive emotion that provides strength to assert or defend ourselves when confronted with threats, harm, or injury to us or our loved ones. Thus, it is an essential component of both self-compassion and compassion toward others.

To distinguish between both types of anger, it is helpful first to understand that both are secondary emotions (see Greenberg, 2015, 2017). When we are genuinely mindful of what is happening within us, we can always mindfully notice that anger is preceded by some other feeling, even if that feeling lasts only a fraction of a second (see exercise 1 on pages 15–16). This primary feeling is often some variant of core pain. It could also be humiliation, disappointment, a feeling of injustice, and so forth.[3] Reactive anger is, in any case, a maladaptive defensive reaction that conceals this primary feeling. It blinds us (see the phenomenon of tunnel vision) and outwardly masks our vulnerability. In contrast, compassionate anger arises from a clear awareness of this primary feeling and the corresponding need. Unlike reactive anger, it does not control us but allows us to "consider wisely" (*yoniso-manasikāra* in Pali) whether and how to react outwardly. However, both types of anger also differ in the *intention* they contain.[4] If we *intend* to harm others, to emotionally or physically hurt them, or to cause damage, our motivation is undoubtedly hatred or reactive anger. However, if our *intention* is solely to protect ourselves or others and to stop someone's harmful *behavior*, it is compassionate anger.

Perhaps the easiest way to illustrate compassionate anger is with an example involving a young child. Imagine a two-year-old who is rapidly running toward a busy road. Upon seeing this, we might be startled by the impending danger (fear, the need for safety) in the first fraction of a second. However, shortly afterward, we firmly shout, "Stop! Where are you going? Come back!" We might feel upset that the child did not respect our safety instructions, but it is undoubtedly not hatred toward the *child*. On the contrary, our anger stems from our love for the child. Our intention is solely to prevent their potentially dangerous *actions*. Compassionate anger can serve a similarly significant function in our relationships with adults. We might intervene physically when our drunken friend is about to get behind the wheel. We might even end up in a scuffle! However, is this an expression of our uncontrolled aggression? Not at all. Such a brawl may stem from a very "wise consideration" of the potential consequences of drunk driving. It comes from compassion for a friend who cannot realistically assess his actions due to his intoxication and from compassion for ourselves. After all, we do not want to lose a friend!

Appearance can be deceiving. If we treat others nicely only because we want to maintain a good "image" or fear rejection (see omnipotent responsibility), it is not a virtue but rather hypocrisy. On the other hand, compassion for oneself and others does not always outwardly manifest as gentleness or even submissiveness (cf., Catarino et al., 2014; Quaglia, 2023). It has an angry face, too. Moreover, it does not matter whether the expressions of compassionate anger are pleasant for others. An intoxicated friend may not be thrilled when we remove their car keys. However, the compassion of our actions is determined by internal motivation, not external appearances. We may feel sadness when confronted with someone else's already committed destructive act. However, experiencing compassionate anger is entirely appropriate if the destructive behavior *continues*. Sadness would not help us at that moment. Compassionate anger gives us the strength and energy needed for (self)defense and to stop the destructive actions of others (cf., McRae, 2015).

Mindfully noticing what is happening within us when experiencing anger is, in any case, a fantastic opportunity to study our conceptual, narrative identity, and maladaptive schemas (see Makransky, 2016; Masters, 2000). In the case of hatred, clinging to our Wounded Narrative Self often plays a significant role (*sakkāya-diṭṭhi* in Pali, see "ego" in a negative sense). Let us recall the drama triangle (Chapter 12)! When people behave hatefully, they typically see themselves as Victims, perceiving their victims as "evil Persecutors." However, their behavior is a reaction to this black-and-white *story* they have created in their mind (interpretation of reality), not to the factual reality. When we are angry, we can ask ourselves: Does our anger evoke some *story*, or is it related to a *specific behavior*, a specific thing? Are we angry *at the person* for whom we think they *are* (selfish, tyrant, cruel), or are we angry because of their specific *actions* and specific *wrongdoings*? And if we find that our anger is triggered by a *story* we have created, it is good to be aware of it and redirect our attention to the facts. However, the most crucial step that allows us to handle the situation skillfully is recognizing the *primary feeling* from which our anger springs—what touched us (cf., Greenberg, 2015, 2017).

Only when we can mindfully notice the specific *primary feeling* that *always* precedes anger can we understand what we need at that moment and, therefore, have compassion for ourselves.[5] The ability to have compassion for any feelings of core pain (see Chapters 5 and 10) is a prerequisite for compassionate anger. Interestingly, compassion for oneself and others develops automatically in parallel. When we mindfully study our maladaptive schemas, we are inevitably confronted with our greed, hatred, conceit, and recklessness (see Table 1 on pages 52–53; cf., Benda, 2019). We realize that we, too, have the potential to harm. At the same time, however, we discover that we also have the potential for change. As we become mindful, we change. Moreover, such an experience gradually changes our view of others. We know that when someone behaves arrogantly, hatefully, or insensitively, it is not because they *are* unchangeably *like that*. They, too, can change. We can then set firm boundaries with compassionate anger toward their destructive *behavior* without elevating ourselves above such a person or harboring hatred toward them. That is compassionate, protective anger.

Outbursts of reactive anger are typically present in individuals with an Inflated Self. On the other hand, people with a Lost Self typically completely suppress anger and struggle to acknowledge it (cf., e.g., Grecucci et al., 2023; Leahy, 2022). However, for skillfully managing life and maintaining healthy relationships, it is essential in any case to (1) learn to *accept* feelings of anger with understanding and (2) learn to express anger in an appropriate way (set boundaries). This means learning to explicitly talk about one's feelings (ideally, even the primary ones) and needs, and when it comes to another person, focusing on constructive criticism of their *behavior* rather than their presumed *personality*. Let us recall, for example, the case of the client Peter and his issue with the dish sponge (Chapter 1). The prerequisite for handling Peter's explosive reactive anger was becoming aware of the primary feeling of childhood abandonment that triggered his anger. When Peter learned to adopt a compassionate attitude toward this painful, traumatic feeling, his experience changed. He could then tell his wife, for instance: "Cris, the fact that you repeatedly leave the wet sponge in the sink angers me. I'm genuinely upset. Maybe it doesn't seem that important to you, but for me, it is a matter of principle. When you promise me that you'll be careful and then forget about it again, it means that I can't rely on you or trust you. And then I feel alone in everything. I know I'm sensitive about it, but I don't want to feel alone anymore. Moreover, I don't want to treat you like a Parent to a Child and scold you for it. I want to trust you and feel like an Adult with an Adult. I love you and appreciate how you take care of our household overall. However, it would help me if you paid attention to the sponge. Thank you." Once Peter learns to communicate like this, he won't have to reproach himself for outbursts of reactive anger because they will not occur. Moreover, of course, Cristina's reaction is also likely to be different than before.

The notion that the wiser always yields is a myth. Compassionate anger is a crucial element of skillful life management. Even Jesus drove merchants and money changers out of the Jerusalem temple when they behaved disrespectfully (see Holy Bible, 2022, e.g., Mt 21:12–17), not to mention numerous examples of compassionate, wise, yet ruthless Mahayana and Vajrayana masters (see Jinpa, 2016; Lama, 2019; Masters, 2000). If we want to bid farewell to the childish Victim role (see the drama triangle), we must learn the art of assertively confronting others when they behave destructively. This requires compassion for ourselves and others, which also means having the courage to acknowledge our vulnerability, needs, and limits. We will delve more into courage in Chapter 15.

EXERCISE 14

Anger as a guardian animal

Anger is one of the basic emotions, and it's natural to appear in our experience. It is a guardian of our personal boundaries (cf., Benda, 2019). Long-term efforts to ignore or suppress anger can be highly destructive for us. The real challenge is to learn how to express anger appropriately and use it for self-protection without unnecessary aggression or hatred toward others. However, to learn to express anger in a measured and constructive manner, we must first learn to *be aware* of it (recognize it) and *accept* it with understanding. We need to learn to take a compassionate attitude toward anger. The concept of anger as a guardian animal can help us with this.

Throughout history, people have utilized various animals to help protect their privacy and alert them to potential intruders. A typical guardian animal is a dog, but in some cultures, this role is also fulfilled, for example, by geese or peacocks. The warning call of these territorial birds can alert a person that someone has crossed boundaries and entered the private property—similar to how a jay serves as a guardian of the forest in European woods or monkeys signal the presence of a predator in Asian jungles.

Imagine, then, what kind of animal could personify your anger. What animal guardian and protector would you like? Could it be a dog? And would you prefer a wolf or a chihuahua? Or would you fancy a bear? A jaguar? A squirrel? Or perhaps a dragon? Tyrannosaurus rex? An eagle? A gorilla? A hippo? In your imagination, find an animal that will symbolize your inner protector.

Now, envision what would happen if you had such a protective animal on your property and you completely ignored it. You wouldn't feed it, wouldn't take care of it, or you'd keep it permanently chained and even beat it. That could be pretty dangerous. When you lovingly care for your animal and raise it, it's much more likely to serve and protect you faithfully.

So, learn to develop a loving attitude toward your anger. When you feel anger, you can imagine that inside you, your guard dog is barking or your inner dragon is breathing fire, alerting you that it's necessary to protect yourself. However, don't just try to silence your guardian animal. Thank it lovingly for guarding your boundaries. Scratch it behind the ears. Could you give it a treat, perhaps? And then, make it clear that you're aware of the boundary violator, and you'll now handle the situation maturely and assertively. You can start by saying something like, "I don't like this," or "I'm furious right now." And if you're afraid to say something like that, imagine that you have your protective animal by your side. Your guardian animal (your anger) doesn't want anyone to hurt you or take advantage of you. So, use the idea of a guardian animal to find the strength and courage not to stay silent but to assertively express your *feelings*. When you try this, you will realize how much better you feel Unexpressed anger harms you. Protective anger is, in fact, an essential part of self-compassion.

NOTES

1 At the beginning of 2003, the scientific database *Web of Science* recorded three scholarly publications mentioning self-compassion. Today, in December 2023, it documents 4855 such publications.
2 Benda (2020a) published a comprehensive overview of 19 research studies demonstrating the correlation between early childhood experiences and later levels of self-compassion.
3 Feelings such as humiliation or disappointment can be appropriate and adaptive in certain situations. On the other hand, feelings of core pain are *always* maladaptive, and their intensity is *always* disproportionate. Mindful awareness and compassionate acceptance of feelings of core pain are, therefore, more challenging than with some other (adaptive) emotions. However, in both cases, recognizing the primary emotion is a prerequisite for compassionate anger.

4 According to the psychology of Abhidhamma, every state of mind, or consciousness (*citta* in Pali), contains some intention (*cetanā* in Pali). Advanced meditators distinguish a total of 89 different types of consciousness, among which 21 are considered beneficial, 12 as detrimental, and 56 as neutral (see, e.g., Barendregt, 2006; Narada, 1987; Nyanatiloka, 2019; cf. Bodhi, 2007, 2021; Epstein, 2013b). However, for our purposes, we will suffice by distinguishing two detrimental ego states (Parent, Child) and one beneficial ego state (the mindful Adult; see Berne, 1957, 2022; Žvelc & Žvelc, 2021). This, in my opinion, should be sufficient for skillful life management (see also note 2 on pages 54–55).
5 Examples of revealing primary feelings that preceded reactive anger have been observed, for instance, in the cases of clients like Peter (Chapter 1), Daniel, Simon, Veronica (Chapter 4), Oliver (Chapter 11), and Thomas (Chapter 12).

CHAPTER FIFTEEN

Courage to Separate and Courage to Be Close

In a famous performance, Czech stand-up comedian Jiří Charvát likened a man to a "lonely pickled cucumber in his private preserving jar" (see also Charvát, 2017). Regarding interpersonal relationships within this metaphor, he declared, "We clink our glasses against each other as hard as we can, but we never touch cucumber to cucumber." Is it so, however? Personally, I am not as skeptical in this regard because my subjective experience is different. In my opinion, experiencing a profound feeling of mutual closeness and understanding in a relationship with another person is possible. However, only on the condition that we are mindful, have an intimate, kind, and empathetic relationship with our own experiences, and are willing and able to talk to others about our experiences. Only when we dare to reveal our vulnerability (see Authentic Self), can we experience true closeness. However, why is expressing our emotions and needs in relationships sometimes so challenging?

ATTACHMENT ANXIETY AND ATTACHMENT AVOIDANCE

John Bowlby, followed by Mary Ainsworth, Cindy Hazan, Phillip Shaver, Mario Mikulincer, and other authors, explained this in the 1980s within the framework of attachment theory. Early traumatic experiences (see Chapters 2, 6, 7, 8, and 9), according to this theory, lead to the development of powerful defense tendencies referred to as "attachment anxiety" or "attachment avoidance." Both tendencies persist in us from childhood to adulthood and negatively impact our ability to be aware of and express feelings and needs, hindering the formation of genuinely *close relationships* (see Mikulincer & Shaver, 2016, 2019; cf. Caldwell & Shaver, 2012; Gardner et al., 2020; Hesse & Floyd,

2011; Winterheld, 2015). Interestingly, attachment theory is gaining support in recent findings in neuroscience.

Research confirms that newborns do not yet have developed brain structures collectively referred to as the so-called social brain (see also the so-called attachment system, cf., e.g., salient network, default mode network), and the development of these structures occurs during early interactions between parents (caregivers) and the child. Furthermore, the contact of empathetic, caring parents with the child stimulates the release of endogenous opioids and neurotransmitters such as oxytocin and dopamine (happiness hormones) in the child. These substances help the child endure painful feelings and, at the same time, teach the child to seek the closeness of other people as a means of *co-regulating* their own emotions (see, e.g., Siegel, 2020; cf. also Atzil et al., 2018; Callaghan & Tottenham, 2016; Feldman, 2017; Long et al., 2020). Meeting basic developmental needs (see Figure 9 on page 54) in early interactions with our caregivers undoubtedly stimulates the development of specific functional and structural neural connections in our brains. It is essential to realize that the Wounded Self (or maladaptive schemas) can thus be indirectly identified through objective neuroimaging methods.

From a phenomenological perspective, we can observe that the developing mind of a young child gradually internalizes the typical caregiver's *attitude* toward the child's needs, as well as the caregiver's *mental state* as a prototype for the child's later own *attitude* toward these needs and their *mental state* in similar situations (see Long et al., 2020; Siegel, 2020). When our needs are met, our *resilience* to unpleasant feelings gradually increases, and our *dependence* on our caregivers decreases. Experiencing a "secure attachment," we gradually learn to understand our needs and cultivate self-compassion (see, e.g., Homan, 2018; Pepping et al., 2015; Shaver et al., 2017). On the other hand, we also gain *trust* and positive expectations *in* our *relationships* with others (see core beliefs, internal working models, or mental scripts, cf., e.g., Thompson et al., 2021). However, what happens when our needs are chronically unmet?

According to researchers studying attachment, children whose parents are inconsistent in meeting the basic developmental needs of the child develop what is known as attachment anxiety. Children with attachment anxiety constantly *fear abandonment* (or emotional detachment from the caregiver), and their level of physiological arousal remains disproportionately high even in the presence of caregivers (hyperactivation, hyperarousal). These children are highly sensitive to any negative signals from the caregiver, and they react tumultuously to even the slightest perceived threat of abandonment (or emotional separation) from the caregiver. They cry, demand attention, and seek repeated reassurance that the caregiver will stay close. However, they do not develop the necessary resilience to frustration. They fail to learn to recognize their own needs. The problem is that, even in adulthood, they remain disproportionately *dependent* on others (see, e.g., the Lost Self, cf. Röhr, 2015).

People with so-called attachment avoidance face the opposite challenge. If a caregiver is predominantly emotionally unavailable to a child,[1] the child will stop expecting the fulfillment of its basic developmental needs from them. It loses *trust* in others and even develops a *fear of closeness* because the anticipation of closeness becomes a source of frustration (or feelings of loneliness and shame) and repeated disappointment (Bartholomew, 1990; Hazan & Shaver, 1987). In response to the physical presence of caregivers, such a child exhibits emotional detachment (deactivation, hypoarousal) and suppresses or denies its vulnerability and the need for closeness. However, such an avoidant strategy manifests as difficulties in establishing and maintaining genuinely close relationships in adulthood. Adults with attachment avoidance harbor deep *mistrust* toward others. Even in close relationships, they automatically maintain emotional distance and struggle to acknowledge and express their feelings toward others. They are emotionally distant, fear relationship commitments, and strive for complete *independence*. Interestingly, these individuals are often unaware of their inner isolation and may even consider it an advantage. Their loneliness, therefore, is not outwardly apparent (see, e.g., the Inflated Self, cf. Röhr's "inner prison"—Mikulincer et al., 2021; Röhr, 2022b).

Hundreds of studies have consistently demonstrated that individuals with attachment anxiety and avoidance generally feel less satisfied in romantic relationships than those with secure attachment (Mikulincer & Shaver, 2016). People with attachment anxiety experience intimate relationships intensely but have excessively high (childish) expectations in their interactions with others (see the role of the Victim in Chapter 12). Despite transferring full responsibility for meeting their needs to their partners, they struggle to articulate these needs clearly and communicate as adults. Consequently, they repeatedly feel misunderstood, unloved, rejected, or dismissed. On the other hand, individuals with attachment avoidance approach their partners much like colleagues at work. They do not expect any deeper emotional understanding from their partners. They share thoughts but not feelings with their counterparts, showcasing their abilities, competitiveness, and strength while refraining from expressing emotions (except for sexuality), which they consider a weakness. When partners share emotions, they react reservedly and feel uncomfortable, irritated, or bored. The prospect of closeness and the possibility of revealing their hidden vulnerability terrifies them. Despite this, they lack emotional connection with their loved ones. Deep down, they sense that their relationships are somewhat empty, but they struggle to reveal themselves to others and thus draw closer.

NARRATIVE SELF IN INSECURE ATTACHMENT

The Narrative Self of individuals with attachment anxiety and avoidance is incoherent and inauthentic (Emery et al., 2018; Mikulincer et al., 2021) for two main reasons. First, the narrative fluctuates based on whether a person is in the Adult ego state or, during the activation of some maladaptive schema, finds themselves in the archaic ego states of Parent or Child (Wounded Self; see note 2 on pages 54–55).[2] However, it is consistently influenced by the fact that individuals with attachment anxiety and avoidance are not in conscious contact with their experiences and struggle to clearly distinguish their emotions and needs (see, e.g., Ferraro & Taylor, 2021; Schimmenti & Caretti, 2018). Consequently, they cannot be authentic (cf. Sohmer, 2020). Let us delve more into the social aspects of our narrative identity here.

According to social psychologists Nathan Cheek and Jonathan Cheek from Princeton University, we can distinguish four dimensions of our Narrative Self, influencing our relationships with others: the individual Self, relational Self, public Self, and collective Self (Cheek & Cheek, 2018). It is essential to recognize that even though we vary greatly in the significance we assign to our social status, our self-concept is invariably shaped within relationships. Our relational Self primarily influences close relationships ("I am a caring mother," "reliable partner," "faithful spouse," "honest friend"). The public Self affects aspects such as our reputation, societal standing, and physical attractiveness ("I am an attractive woman," "social outsider," "troublemaker," "rebel"). The collective Self shapes our affiliations with various groups or institutions ("I am a New Yorker," "Democrat," "New York Yankees fan," "Texan," "Caucasian," "Buddhist"). The individual Self impacts our feelings, perceptions, opinions, values, dreams, and goals ("I am a sensitive," "independent," "honest" person, "temperamental," "exceptional," or "ordinary" woman). However, creating a well-functioning *individual* Narrative Self still requires the presence of others.

Self-awareness and self-reflection evolve in the context of our relationships with others from the moment of our birth. Creating an Authentic and flexible Narrative Self requires being "self-verified" by others (Emery et al., 2018). This means that in childhood, we need to experience that we can reveal our innermost feelings, thoughts, and desires to others. Additionally, we must experience parental mirroring and feel unconditionally accepted and lovingly *limited* (see Fonagy et al., 2018). However, individuals with insecure attachment lack such experiences. Adults with attachment anxiety tend to overly identify with their relational, public, and collective Selves.[3] They become hyper conformist, striving to adapt and fit in, highly concerned about how others perceive them. However, their self-perception is *solely* through the lens of others. The *fear of abandonment* or rejection by others controls them so much that they do not express their true feelings, thoughts, and desires and often remain unaware of them. On the other hand, individuals with attachment avoidance are not much better off. Due to a deeply rooted *fear of intimacy*, they do not acknowledge their true feelings or needs. They function like efficient machines, maintaining the illusion of independence. They do not reveal themselves to others but, consequently, lack the necessary feedback (cf. Scigala et al., 2021). Their self-awareness is limited, and their self-concept often contradicts how their close ones perceive them. They are alienated from themselves (cf., e.g., Asper, 2018; Sierra-Siegert & Jay, 2020). The relational dimension of their lives largely eludes them.

MALADAPTIVE EMOTION REGULATION STRATEGIES

In recent years, numerous studies have sought to uncover specific correlations between different attachment styles and distinct emotion regulation strategies. Existing research has demonstrated that individuals with secure attachments generally possess better emotion regulation abilities than those with insecure attachments. However, individuals with secure attachment not only exhibit superior regulation capabilities but also employ more adaptive emotion regulation strategies, such as problem-solving, seeking social support, or cognitive reappraisal. Conversely, individuals with attachment anxiety often resort to maladaptive emotion regulation strategies, including suppression or rumination (see cyclic self-criticism or the creation of catastrophic scenarios), which, unfortunately, intensify their unpleasant emotional experiences. Those with attachment avoidance tendencies attempt to regulate emotions by completely denying the need for closeness and intimacy. In addition to emotion suppression or external expression, they utilize strategies like redirecting attention elsewhere (cf. dissociation), avoiding thoughts about the matter, and so forth (see Caldwell & Shaver, 2012; Gardner et al., 2020; Stuart-Parrigon et al., 2015; Velotti et al., 2016; Winterheld, 2015).

Research has also demonstrated that individuals with secure attachments are generally more adept at *recognizing* and articulating their emotions than those with insecure attachments. People with attachment anxiety or avoidance, however, struggle considerably with emotional awareness, recognition, and verbal expression (see Besharat & Khajavi, 2013; Goodall et al., 2012; Stevens, 2014). In comparison to individuals with attachment avoidance and those with secure attachment, individuals with attachment anxiety tend to be more emotionally reactive, and their emotional responses are more intense (e.g., Wei et al., 2005, 2007). Nevertheless, they struggle to respond to emotions maturely (reacting impulsively) and become completely overwhelmed.

From the perspective of mindful diagnosis, both attachment anxiety and attachment avoidance manifest in our experience through 11 specific defense or coping mechanisms (see Table 1 on pages 52–53, cf. Benda, 2019), which, through mindfulness, we can learn to discern clearly. However, as we begin to notice these defense mechanisms, feelings of core pain gradually penetrate our consciousness, signifying *fear of abandonment* and *fear of intimacy*.[4] Conscious confrontation with these traumatic childhood fears is an inevitable part of healing the rigid, Wounded Self (see Chapter 10) and cultivating a flexible, Authentic Self. Carl Gustav Jung (2021a) once wrote to his acquaintance Warner McCullen: "Where your fear is, there is your task." One of the tasks of a mindful Adult is to learn to have conscious compassion with core pain (cf. Masters, 2009).

From a mindfulness perspective, the *fear of abandonment* is the fear of confronting the feeling of traumatic childhood abandonment that we might experience when being abandoned by someone close. If we suffer from this fear, we need to recognize that securing someone's constant closeness and unconditional acceptance is not the only option to eliminate this fear in adulthood. In fact, it is not feasible in adulthood. We need to learn to transform feelings of annihilation anxiety and desperate childhood abandonment through mindfulness and self-compassion. A corrective emotional (relational) experience can assist us in this process (see further, cf., Chapters 5 and 10). Similar principles apply to the *fear of closeness*. To overcome this deeply rooted feeling, we need to realize that in adulthood, we are not as vulnerable as we were in childhood. As adults, we can open ourselves to closeness with less risk. We can learn to withstand potential disappointment, rejection, or abandonment. It is crucial to understand that when someone rejects us, it does not mean that, in an absolute sense, "we are not good enough" (shame) or that "no one can ever love us" (core beliefs). No rejection can reveal permanent and *objectively unacceptable* qualities of our Self, first because every rejection is *subjective*; second, because we have no enduring and unchangeable essential qualities.

HEALING SHARING OF EMOTIONS AND NEEDS

Because individuals with attachment anxiety struggle to have compassion with themselves, they often remain as emotionally dependent in adult relationships as they were in childhood (cf., e.g., the Lost Self). On the other hand, individuals with attachment avoidance strive to maintain an illusion of *independence*, even at the cost of giving up the opportunity to establish a genuinely close relationship with someone (cf. the Inflated Self). However, what is the adult attitude toward our dependence on others? If we want to function healthily in relationships, we should acknowledge that we are not independent (a childish illusion), need close relationships, and have feelings for people. On the other hand, we should also learn to endure separations, breakups, or misunderstandings and rely on our relationship with ourselves in such moments (cf., e.g., Faustino et al., 2020). It means balancing dependence and independence and consciously creating relationships that Sue Johnson (2019) calls "constructive dependency."

Close relationships bring us the most opportunities to study our maladaptive schemas. They evoke the most emotions in us and stir up our old traumas. At the same time, they offer us the chance to learn to *express* and *share* emotions and needs. This is a condition for creating emotional closeness and understanding in a relationship with others (see, e.g., Falconier et al., 2015; Marroquín et al., 2017). Genuine disclosure of emotions and needs in a close relationship can also bring us corrective emotional experiences (cf. Baylin & Winnette, 2016; Greenberg, 2015, 2017; Johnson, 2019; Stevens, 2021). It can heal our maladaptive schemas (Wounded Self). However, revealing our vulnerability often requires more courage than fighting an enemy in a wartime conflict (cf., e.g., Brown, 2015, 2017).

It is peculiar, but if we suffer from the Inflated Self syndrome, it can be challenging to realize and admit that we were looking forward to seeing our partner. It becomes even more challenging to express it when meeting her or him. To tightly embrace her or him and say, "I was looking forward to seeing you," "I'm glad I'm with you now," "I love you." It means finding the courage to consciously feel and acknowledge our vulnerability (cf. Masters, 2013; Preece, 2009). If we suffer from the Lost Self syndrome, it can be just as challenging for us to say, for example, "I'm angry with you," "I don't like this," or "I don't want to watch this movie right now." For some, expressing anger is much easier than love or sadness; for others, it is the opposite. In any case, our early experience comes into play, where revealing our emotions and needs was threatening, dangerous, or frustrating for us in childhood (see developmental trauma, Chapter 2, and Part II).

It is essential to understand that maladaptive schemas no longer protect us in adulthood; instead, they hinder us from forming close connections with others, compelling us to experience traumatic relational patterns repeatedly. However, if we start to *be mindful* of what we genuinely experience in close relationships, we can gradually build an intimate and compassionate relationship with our emotions and suppressed needs. This provides us a new opportunity to experience closeness and understanding in relationships with our closest ones. It depends on whether we find the courage to consciously confront core pain and take adult responsibility for *expressing* our emotions and fulfilling our needs. Without *sharing*, healing our traumas is impossible; meditation or other transpersonal experiences may not assist in this regard (cf. Otway & Carnelley, 2013; Welwood, 2002).

EXERCISE 15

Open your heart in relation to others

Close, especially intimate, relationships offer us many opportunities to explore the feelings of core pain and develop self-compassion. So, in this exercise, let's use the relational experience to heal our Wounded Selves. By doing so, we benefit both ourselves and our close relationships. However, first, estimate whether you lean more toward the fear of revealing your vulnerability or the fear of abandonment. Do you find it more challenging to express love or assert yourself and say something the other person might not like? Would you feel more uneasy if you had to genuinely speak to your partner, "I *love* you" or "I'm *upset* with you"?

If you already know the answers to the previous questions, find a quiet place to dedicate at least 20 minutes to yourself. Sit comfortably and observe your breath for a moment. Try to relax a bit. Watch how your body naturally inhales and exhales. Nothing more. When you feel ready, try to imagine how you would feel if you had to genuinely say that sentence to your partner ("I *love* you" or "I'm *upset* with you"). Then stop thinking and observe what is happening in your body, pelvic area, abdomen, stomach, throat, face, and around your heart. If you feel tension anywhere in your body, acknowledge it. Accept this tension. You can feel it. It's completely fine. What feeling do you have in your heart? If your heart is tight, allow it to be. Try placing both palms in the middle of your chest as if you wanted to protect your heart. How is it now? Observe your heart until you feel it starting to relax.

Revealing one's feelings in close relationships requires more courage than one might think. Of course, no one can force you to express your emotions. However, it can also be fascinating and adventurous. So, if the idea of sincere emotional sharing starts to appeal to you, you can use the previous exercise repeatedly as preparation for real future "action." But I have another preparatory variation for you. Before you go into actual "action," you can imagine what it would be like if your "ideal therapist" said the sentence for you. Picture how it would be for you if you had some "ideal couples therapist." How would it be for you if the therapist, instead of you, would say to your partner, "You know, (your name) *loves* you a lot," or "You know, (your name) is *upset* with you." That would be nice, right? How do you feel when you imagine this version? Feel free to visualize it repeatedly until you desire to say it for real and on your own. I'll be rooting for you!

NOTES

1 Daniel Siegel (2020) states that a secure attachment is formed when the child "feels felt by the parent." The mere physical proximity of the parent is not enough to establish a secure attachment. Also crucial is the parent's ability to empathize with

the child (or the parent's compassion with the child). However, an anxious or emotionally detached parent cannot empathize with the child.
2 Of course, maladaptive schemas activate most often within close relationships.
3 Jung referred to this identification as "identification with the persona" (e.g., Jung, 2021b). Winnicott spoke about creating the "false self" (Winnicott, 2017, 2018a, b, c).
4 While the fear of abandonment is most commonly encountered with the Lost Self and the fear of closeness with the Inflated Self, no specific variant of the core pain is unequivocally linked to a particular defense mechanism. Practice shows that existential dread, loneliness, and shame can initiate any of the 11 defense mechanisms within the framework of maladaptive schemas. The *phenomenological model of maladaptive schemas* (see Figure 1 on page 25) allows for a more specific mapping of these schemas than theoretical concepts of attachment anxiety and avoidance.

CHAPTER SIXTEEN

Meditation, Psychedelics, and Their Pitfalls

Transpersonal psychology has, for decades, explored dimensions of human consciousness that were until recently marginalized in mainstream scientific research. The rapidly growing interest in studying long-term meditators (see, e.g., Baminiwatta & Solangaarachchi, 2021; Luders & Kurth, 2019) and the renaissance of psychedelic research (see, e.g., Hadar et al., 2022; Kelly et al., 2022) have started to reshape this landscape in recent years. Both of these research streams now investigate *altered states of consciousness* using the most cutting-edge methods, gaining increasing respect and attention from experts in psychology, psychiatry, and neuroscience (e.g., Millière et al., 2018; Winter et al., 2020). New horizons are thus opening up for transpersonal psychology. It is anticipated that in several Western countries, psychedelics[1] will be made accessible for therapeutic purposes within the next five years.[2] Public interest in meditation is also rising (see, e.g., Cramer, 2019; Simonsson et al., 2021). However, meditation and psychedelics can likely aid in the treatment of mental disorders *only* if the meditative or psychedelic experiences are subsequently processed in a therapeutic context (see, e.g., Alper, 2016; Winkelman & Sessa, 2019; cf. Chapter 18). The expectation that the experience of altered states of consciousness *alone* would be sufficient for therapeutic change seems unrealistic. Because both meditative and psychedelic experiences can be pretty stressful and destabilizing, we caution against some pitfalls in meditation and psychedelics in this chapter (cf., e.g., Bender & Hellerstein, 2022; Farias et al., 2020; Goldberg et al., 2022; Lambert et al., 2021; Lindahl et al., 2017, 2019; Schlag et al., 2022; Schlosser et al., 2019; Thomas & Malcolm, 2021).

Transpersonal psychologists Roberto Assagioli and Ken Wilber asserted many years ago that individuals can evolve in two distinct dimensions throughout their lives, labeled by these authors as personal (horizontal) and

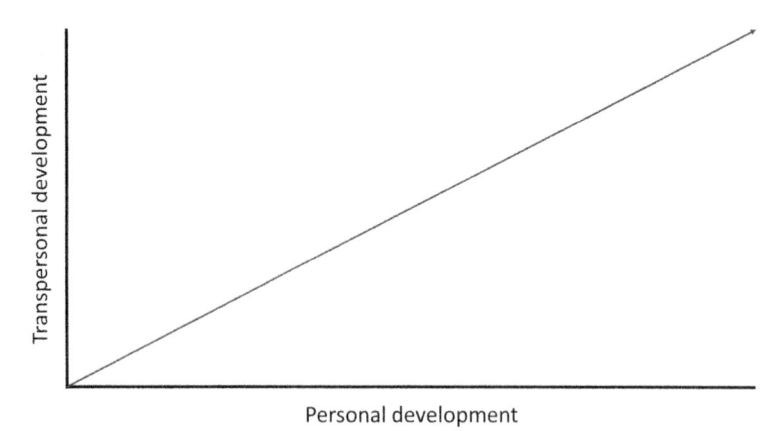

FIGURE 10 Personal and transpersonal development

transpersonal (vertical) (see Figure 10, Assagioli, 1993, 2007; Firman & Vargiu, 1977, 1996; Wilber, 2006, 2016). Development in both dimensions can complement each other well. However, intensive meditation and psychedelic experiences primarily stimulate transpersonal development. Therefore, they may not *automatically* foster personal development (cf. Engler, 1984, 2003). Throughout history, people have utilized meditation and psychedelics as part of spiritual practices aimed at expanding consciousness, exploring more profound levels of reality, and connecting with something beyond ourselves (see Benda, 2007). Many contemporary enthusiasts of meditation or psychedelics, however, anticipate that transpersonal experiences will help them heal childhood wounds and cope with specific challenges they face in everyday life. Can expanded states of consciousness assist us in this direction? Yes, but only indirectly and in combination with other procedures.

In order to cope skillfully with everyday life and thrive in our relationships with others, we need to gradually acquire a range of knowledge and practical skills throughout our lives (cf. Chapters 11–15). We learn, for instance, to recognize and fulfill our needs, regulate emotions, communicate effectively, assert ourselves, collaborate with others, and handle potentially conflictual situations. Contemporary interpersonal neurobiology is increasingly revealing other people's crucial role in our *personal development*. Our brain requires the influence of others to evolve (see, e.g., Siegel & Solomon, 2013; Siegel et al., 2021). To make our Authentic Narrative Self function, being mindful of what is happening within us is not enough. For healthy functioning in everyday life, we must skillfully interpret, express, and integrate our experiences into a coherent life story (cf., e.g., Watts & Luoma, 2020). However, this requires a particular understanding of the external world around us and the people in it (cf. Siegel, 2010a, b, 2020). Even in adulthood, our needs for safety, love and belonging, recognition, and appreciation are fulfilled through *relationships* with others (cf. Maslow, 1987, 2014). Our *personal development* (see Figure 10 on page 140) demands the gradual healing of our maladaptive schemas, especially *within* our *relationships* with others. Nevertheless, neither meditation nor psychedelics enable us to achieve complete independence from others (cf. attachment avoidance, Chapter 15). They also do not teach us how to express our feelings and needs in relationships. Transpersonal development cannot replace personal development (cf. Masters, 2010). However, the distinction in how we deal with emotions in meditation versus everyday life can help us understand the difference between the personal and transpersonal dimensions of development.

In advanced mindfulness and insight meditation (*vipassanā* in Pali), among other things, we learn to be mindful of the most subtle bodily feelings. However, we deliberately do not differentiate their psychological and interpersonal significance (see, e.g., Gendlin, 2003).[3] It is not about whether we are experiencing feelings of joy, surprise, disappointment, disgust, or feelings of inferiority or loneliness (cf. also, e.g., Benda, 2019; Brown, 2021). We *intentionally* leave aside the connection of a particular feeling with our life situation or personal story. In meditation, our primary focus is observing our automatic reactions to pleasant and unpleasant feelings. We discover that our natural resistance to unpleasant feelings and "clinging" to pleasant feelings leads to even greater suffering (see Ng et al., 2017; Weber, 2017). We also realize that every feeling is inherently transient and unsatisfactory and that feelings emerge beyond our control. However, we simultaneously discover that we can influence how we *respond* to these feelings. Gradually, we learn to *accept* all feelings (see Barendregt, 2011; Nyanaponika, 2014; Sujiva, 2000). Such a skill undoubtedly proves valuable in everyday life. However, being able to *accept* our feelings does not mean we will stop expressing them in relationships with others (see Mindful Zombie, Chapter 19). *Expressing* our feelings and needs is necessary for healthy and meaningful relationships with others. However, understanding the specific needs underlying our feelings, expressing them effectively in words, and ensuring the fulfillment of those needs *in relationships* with others are skills that meditation does not teach. Mindfulness and insight meditation aim to gain experiences far beyond our everyday concerns (cf. Engler, 1984, 2003). The same applies to psychedelics.

When the pioneers of psychedelic research, Timothy Leary, Ralph Metzner, and Richard Alpert (Ram Dass), published the now classic guide *The Psychedelic Experience* in 1964 (latest edition 2022), they likened individual psychedelic experiences to states of mind described in *The Tibetan Book of the Dead*.[4] For each type of psychedelic experience, they provided recommendations on how one should navigate the psychedelic journey to avoid unpleasant or potentially traumatizing outcomes, commonly known as a "bad trip." Their instructions for different psychedelic states, however, share several common denominators. One should remain relaxed under all circumstances, learn to observe any unusual experiences with trust, refrain from attempting to control or intellectually grasp these experiences, and passively accept everything, opening oneself to all incoming emotions, etc. (see Leary et al., 2022). Thus, psychedelic experiences teach us to consciously observe all the phenomena we undergo and *accept* them. However, what we take away from these experiences to everyday life is a different matter and, in fact, the only thing that truly matters.

Experienced Western meditation teachers and psychonauts[5] consistently caution that integrating transpersonal experiences into everyday life typically requires additional conscious effort (see, e.g., Coder, 2017; Kornfield, 2001; cf. Bathje et al., 2022). Activation of maladaptive schemas seems to occur even in individuals who have devoted years to meditation practices or have participated in traditional psychedelic ceremonies. Thus, it appears that the healing of maladaptive schemas does not *automatically* coincide with transpersonal development (see Figure 10 on page 140). Based on my experiences, addressing maladaptive schemas necessitates undergoing a corrective emotional (relational) experience, likely achievable only through interaction with another person. However, can such an experience occur during a traditional psychedelic ceremony or meditation retreat? Perhaps, at times. However, it seems to happen outside the actual meditation or psychedelic experience itself.

In August 2007, I participated in a meditation retreat in the Eagle Mountains led by the Buddhist monk Bhante Sujiva. Following his instructions, I meditated from morning till evening, alternating between sitting and walking meditation. I observed phenomena in my body and mind, and my mindfulness gradually increased. However, after about a week, a feeling of cosmic childhood abandonment emerged in my experience, coupled with a feeling of helplessness, and I found myself completely stuck in this state. All my efforts to accept this state of mind seemed in vain; nothing was helping. That is until I encountered the venerable Sujiva. We crossed paths on a forest trail leading to the retreat house. As we passed, I paused momentarily to bow to the venerable Sujiva. Then it happened. Sujiva suddenly embraced me tightly, and the world spun around me. It must have been only a second or two, but I completely lost track of time. I only remember that Sujiva's kindness and compassion deeply touched me, and my loneliness disappeared. Today, I would say that Bhante Sujiva provided me with a corrective emotional (relational) experience in this way. An experience that served as an antidote to my childhood loneliness and helplessness. Later, when I had several more similar experiences, the maladaptive schema of the Abandoned Self ceased to appear in my experience. Hence, I am grateful to Bhante Sujiva for his embrace to this day.

Hundreds of studies examining the effectiveness of psychotherapy over the past decades have shown that the therapeutic *relationship* and variables on the therapist's side have a more significant impact on the outcome of psychotherapy than the techniques employed (see, e.g., Flückiger et al., 2018; Wampold & Imel, 2015). The therapist's authenticity, or congruence, empathy toward the client and the ability for unconditional acceptance (positive regard) significantly influence psychotherapeutic change (see Castonguay & Hill, 2017; Norcross & Lambert, 2019).[6] In other words, it is not about *what* the therapist does with the client but *how* he does it (Norcross & Lambert, 2018). For the alteration of maladaptive schemas in a client, how the client *feels in* the therapeutic *relationship* when a specific maladaptive schema is activated (unlocked) is crucial. An unanswered question remains whether, for example, the psychedelic experience itself, during which a person feels accepted by God, the universe, nature, angels, or other supernatural beings, can replace the experience of interpersonal *relationships* (cf. Cherniak et al., 2022).

Traditional healing psychedelic ceremonies have always taken place under the guidance of an experienced shaman and often with the participation of the entire community (see, e.g., Metzner, 1998). Besides the psychedelic experience itself, these ceremonies have consistently involved close interactions with other people, and it is possible that these interactions played a significant role in achieving the resulting therapeutic effect (cf. Kettner et al., 2021). Similarly, contemporary psychedelic-assisted psychotherapy always includes preparation for the psychedelic experience and its subsequent integration in the therapeutic *relationship* (see, e.g., Garcia-Romeu & Richards, 2018). It is, therefore, a combination of psychotherapeutic procedures and psychedelic experience. Studies are confirming the positive impact of psychedelic experiences on changing negative core beliefs or maladaptive schemas (e.g., Amada et al., 2020; Healy et al., 2021; Zeifman et al., 2023a). However, it is not clear from them whether these changes were caused by the psychedelics themselves or the subsequent therapeutic processing of the psychedelic experience in the therapeutic *relationship* (cf. Amada & Shane, 2022; Cherniak et al., 2022; Gukasyan & Nayak, 2022).[7]

Contemporary researchers are, however, well aware of the significance of these so-called extra-pharmacological factors, and they strive to understand how the *preparation* for a psychedelic experience and the subsequent *integration* of that experience influence the overall therapeutic effect of the psychedelic encounter (e.g., Carhart-Harris et al., 2018). For instance, Roberta Murphy from the Imperial College London and her team recently examined the impact of the therapist-client relationship on the efficacy of psilocybin in depressive patients. They found that the strength of the therapeutic alliance before administering psilocybin positively influenced the power of emotional breakthroughs during psilocybin sessions and the degree of subsequent reduction in depression among these patients (Murphy et al., 2022). The question of whether psychedelic experiences can aid in the healing of the "Wounded Self" (see Part II) may also be addressed by research exploring the influence of psychedelics on attachment.

Experts on attachment presume that individuals with a secure attachment are well-prepared to trustingly surrender themselves to psychedelic experiences, as recommended by seasoned psychonauts (see Cherniak et al., 2022; cf. Aday et al., 2021; Leary et al., 2022). Therefore, they can seamlessly harness psychedelic experiences for their transpersonal development. However, individuals with attachment anxiety (cf. Lost Self) may undergo enticing connections with an archetypal parental "Rescuer" during a psychedelic experience without subsequently transferring this compassionate experience into their everyday lives and learning to have compassion with themselves (cf. Aixalà, 2022). Such transfer (internalization) likely requires additional integrative work in *relation* to a real person (therapist). On the other hand, individuals with attachment avoidance (cf. Inflated Self) who typically suppress all unpleasant feelings may encounter significant difficulties in losing control during a psychedelic experience. It may bring to their awareness those feelings and contents they attempted to suppress in everyday life. Consequently, the experience can be challenging for them. To utilize it for their benefit, they once again require subsequent therapeutic work.

Christopher Stauffer from the University of California, San Francisco, and his team recently investigated whether group therapy consisting of eight to ten sessions and one individual session with psilocybin would impact attachment anxiety and attachment avoidance in a group of AIDS patients. The research revealed that attachment anxiety was associated with a more significant number of mystical experiences, while attachment avoidance was linked to a higher frequency of challenging and stressful experiences. Attachment anxiety significantly decreased in study participants after completing the program. However, attachment avoidance remained unchanged. It appears that the combination of psychedelic experience and psychotherapy holds the potential to alleviate attachment anxiety. Nevertheless, attachment avoidance is a somewhat "tougher nut to crack" for brief psychedelic-assisted psychotherapy (see Stauffer et al., 2021).

Insights gained through transpersonal experiences can influence our self-concept (Narrative Self) and *attitude* toward ourselves and others. They can inspire us. However, whether our everyday functioning and how we handle the activation of maladaptive schemas will change depends on our conscious *commitment* to overcoming defense mechanisms, specifically the fear of abandonment and the fear of intimacy *in relationships*. Such a change, however, does not happen automatically. Relying on the belief that a transpersonal experience alone will solve our everyday personal and relational problems is naive (Benda, 2012). The genuine healing of our rigid Wounded Self occurs only *after* meditation or psychedelic experience (see Kornfield, 2001). Only when our altered perspective on ourselves and others begins to manifest in our specific decisions, actions, and communication can we speak of developing a healthy, flexible, Authentic Self. Nevertheless, an Authentic Self always evolves *in relationships* with others. In the following, the fourth part of this book will further illustrate how transpersonal development can stimulate personal development. However, meditation or psychedelics cannot replace *relational* experiences. In the treatment of maladaptive schemas, psychotherapy is undoubtedly more effective than transpersonal experiences alone. I wanted to emphasize this before we start discussing the Transcendent Self.

EXERCISE 16

Do I Have a Healthy Functioning Authentic Self?

If you want to find out whether you have a healthy, functioning, Authentic Self, complete the following quiz. Circle the answer T (true) or F (false) for each item. If you can't decide, circle T.

1. When someone close to me has a problem, I am very tempted to try to solve it for them. T/F
2. I never prioritize my own needs over the needs of others. That would be selfish. T/F
3. The thought that I might unintentionally hurt someone emotionally scares me. T/F
4. It is difficult for me to ask someone for help. I usually try to handle everything on my own. T/F
5. I feel so exposed when I make a mistake that I would rather disappear. T/F
6. I feel significant uncertainty about others' opinions of me. T/F
7. I feel indifferent to others when I come to a celebration and am not welcomed by everyone at the entrance. T/F
8. If someone at school or work performs a task better than me, I feel like a complete failure. T/F
9. I often feel ashamed of my family members' behavior. T/F
10. The fewer mistakes I make, the more people will like me. T/F
11. It is often challenging for me to admit what I truly feel. T/F
12. I believe that expressing emotions is a sign of weakness. T/F
13. I try not to bother others. T/F
14. I never fully trust other people. T/F
15. When I truly need someone, they are usually unavailable. T/F
16. Sometimes, I feel like an actor who is constantly playing a role. T/F
17. In general, it is difficult for me to say no to people. T/F
18. Various "tricks" exist for persuasion. I often use them. T/F
19. I'm afraid to criticize and tell other people what I think. T/F
20. Average people are dull and uninteresting, so I avoid them. T/F

Evaluation

The items in this quiz aimed to capture some typical manifestations of the Wounded Self. The more often you choose the answer F (false), the healthier your Authentic Self functions. The more often you choose the answer T (true), the more the Wounded Self influences you. If you did not choose T at all, you are well-prepared to engage in transpersonal development in your life. If you decide T only once to five times, it is likely sufficient for you to draw some inspiration from Chapters 11–15 and be mindful of your feelings in situations that pose challenges. However, if you choose T more frequently, you should focus on cultivating kindness and compassion toward yourself. Review Chapters 6–10 again. Reflect on which need in your childhood was unfulfilled (see Figure 9 on page 54). Try talking about your old wounds with someone close who won't give you advice but will listen with understanding. Sharing is healing. Then, firmly decide that now, as an adult, you will carefully and determinedly attend to your needs. What can you do for yourself today? Any (even small) expression of love and compassion toward yourself can help initiate the healing process of your Wounded Self.

NOTES

1 Psychedelics are psychoactive substances belonging to the hallucinogen group. When ingested, they induce significant alterations in perception, mood, and consciousness. Among the most researched psychedelics currently are psilocybin, mescaline, lysergic acid diethylamide (LSD), dimethyltryptamine (DMT), 3,4-methylenedioxymethamphetamine (MDMA), ketamine, ibogaine, and mebufotenin (5 McO DMT).
2 As of July 1, 2023, Australia has permitted psychiatrists to prescribe MDMA for patients with post-traumatic stress disorder and psilocybin for patients with depression (Commonwealth of Australia, 2023). In the United States and Canada, psychedelics are legally utilized for treatment in certain states (see, e.g., Siegel et al., 2023). In the Czech Republic, legal research on the effects of psychedelic substances is being conducted at the National Institute of Mental Health (see, e.g., Postránecká et al., 2019).
3 In meditation, we typically categorize feelings into pleasant, unpleasant, and neutral, occasionally distinguishing between "bodily" and "mental" feelings as well (e.g., Vedanā Samyutta, SN, IV, 36—see Bodhi, 2005).
4 *The Tibetan Book of the Dead* (Padmasambhava, 2008) describes a total of 31 levels through which our consciousness purportedly passes after the death of the physical body. Leary et al. (2022) interpret these levels as states of mind that one can also experience within the context of a psychedelic journey (cf. also Epstein, 2013b).
5 The term psychonaut is used here to refer to an individual who deliberately explores their mind and altered states of consciousness through psychedelic substances (see Grof, 2019).

6 In a special edition of the *Psychotherapy* Journal from 2018, three extensive meta-analyses were published, demonstrating the impact of these three classic Rogerian variables on the outcome of psychotherapy (see Elliott et al., 2018; Farber et al., 2018; Kolden et al., 2018).

7 It is interesting that several days to weeks after the use of psychedelics, individuals typically exhibit heightened emotional openness and a willingness to form close relationships. Researchers suggest that the effect of psychotherapeutic interventions during this period, known as the afterglow period, is more pronounced than at other times (see Evens et al., 2023; Majić et al., 2015). Therefore, it is not ruled out that psychedelics might significantly extend the so-called *reconsolidation window*, during which maladaptive schemas can be influenced by corrective relational experiences (cf. Ecker & Vaz, 2022; Schiller et al., 2010).

PART IV

The Transcendent Self

When cultivating mindfulness, we begin to understand early on that our thoughts and imaginations are something different than the reality we experience in the present moment. We learn to pay more attention to what we *perceive* and *feel* here and now. Such focus on present sensations and bodily feelings often brings considerable relief from the stress that arises when we imagine what might be or endlessly revisit something that was. However, merely experiencing present sensations and feelings without prolonged escapades into thoughts and imaginations does not yet constitute true mindfulness but only what is called "bare attention," a kind of preliminary stage of right mindfulness (see Čopelj, 2022; Nyanaponika, 2014). Right mindfulness comes into play only after we distinctly realize "there is perception happening in consciousness right now" or "there is feeling happening in the body right now" (Anālayo, 2019a; Barendregt, 2011; Rapgay & Bystrisky, 2009; Tejaniya, 2014). Contemporary psychological literature associates mindfulness with the abilities of so-called decentering, disidentification, or "meta-awareness" (see, e.g., Hanley et al., 2020). All these terms relate to the ability of an individual to view their own experience from the *perspective* of an external observer.[1] Psychologist Amit Bernstein from the University of Haifa and his team described meta-awareness as an awareness of *processes* occurring in our consciousness (such as processes of perception, thinking, or feeling). Simply put, looking at the sunset without critically thinking about it is bare attention. However, once we realize that visual perception is happening in our consciousness right now, it becomes meta-awareness (and thus mindful noticing; see Bernstein et al., 2015).

It is interesting that under normal circumstances, we usually automatically associate all phenomena that arise in our consciousness with our Narrative Self. So, when a thought emerges in our consciousness, we automatically identify with it, assuming, "This is what I think." If a gloomy state of mind arises in our experience, we automatically declare, for example, "I am feeling down." However, meta-awareness allows us to maintain a certain distance from our experience and not necessarily link the processes we notice with our concept of Self. We can then observe our perceptions, feelings, thoughts, and states of mind impartially, like observers or witnesses (see disidentification). While, without mindfulness, our brain responds to our thoughts and ideas as it does to actual facts, meta-awareness also reduces our emotional reactivity to mental content. When imagining an unpleasant conversation with the boss, our body reacts as if this conversation were actually taking place. However, our emotional response diminishes once we clearly recognize that we are merely imagining this conversation (meta-awareness) (Bernstein et al., 2015).

Meta-awareness thus enables disidentification and the reduction of emotional reactivity to mental contents. All three of these processes collectively lead to what is known as *decentering*, allowing us to view our experiences from the *perspective* of an observer. The observer perspective is crucial for transpersonal development (see Chapter 16). In this part, we will refer to this perspective as the Observing or Transcendent Self (see Assagioli, 1993; Deikman, 1982; Žvelc & Žvelc, 2021). However, since the entire book has focused primarily on various forms of the *Narrative* Self, let us first organize all the mentioned Selves (see Figure 11 on page 150).

"The father of American psychology," William James (2019), distinguished in the late nineteenth century between two fundamental forms of the Self: the *I* as subject and the *me* as object. This fundamental distinction was more or less adopted by figures like Carl Rogers (2021), who spoke of the "organismic self" (~*I*) and the "conceptual self" (~*me*). It also aligns with Shaun Gallagher's (2000) conceptualization, where he differentiated the so-called Minimal Self (~*I*)

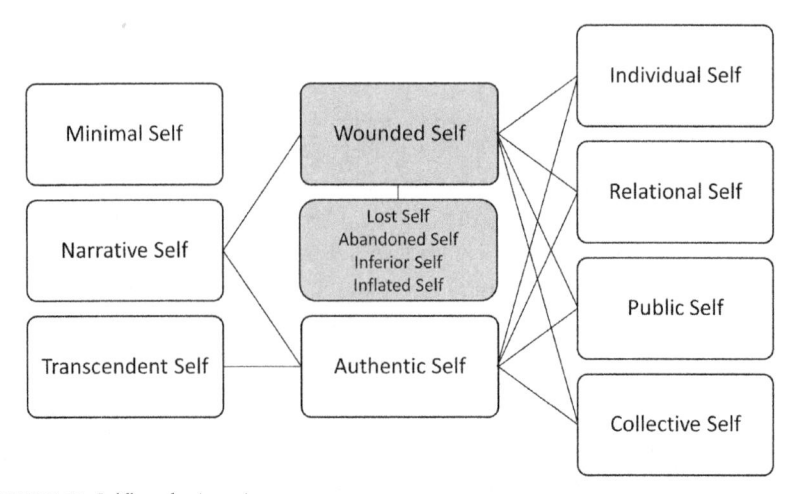

FIGURE 11 Selfhood triumvirate

and the Narrative Self (~*me*). The Minimal Self is the *perspective* of a person who experiences individual sensory and mental phenomena here and now (see bare attention). It is a simple awareness that I am experiencing present sensations, feelings, moods, and thoughts (cf. Benda, 2019). It is the Self present even before the conceptualization of the experience. However, it allows us to interpret and attribute subjective meaning to the experience (Brown & Leary, 2017a). The Narrative (also autobiographical) Self emerges based on our thinking and imagination. It is our *conception* of ourselves, our "story of the Self."

In the book's second part, we delved into four types of rigid "Wounded" Narrative Selves that influence our perception, thinking, experience, and behavior when any maladaptive schema is activated (see Figure 11). At such a moment, our Narrative Self is defined by some core beliefs, such as "I am weak, unlovable, worthless, or, conversely, perfect." In the book's third part, we hinted at the emergence of a flexible, Authentic Narrative Self, accessible to us if we can *be mindful* of what is happening within us moment by moment while understanding that the flow of experience is constantly changing.[2] The Wounded Narrative Self, briefly put, stems from the implicit childhood assumption that our identity has some unchangeable, inherent qualities, such as "helplessness," "unacceptability," "worthlessness," or, conversely, "irresistibility." On the other hand, the flexible, Authentic Self arises from the understanding that every evaluation is subjective and relative and from the realization that we can develop, change, and learn from our mistakes.

The transformation from a rigid, Wounded Self to a flexible, Authentic Self is at the core of psychotherapeutic change and, simultaneously, a part of personal development. Even for this transformation, we need at least essential *momentary* mindfulness and compassion towards ourselves. However, in this part, we will explain that the intensive cultivation of *constant* mindfulness in meditation leads to further developing the Observing, Transcendent Self and subsequently to achieving the so-called non-dual awareness (see Chapter 17). This is the goal of mysticism in all world religions (see Benda, 2007; Underhill, 2019) and also becomes the subject of interest in contemporary science (see, e.g., Cooper et al., 2022; Josipovic, 2019; Millière, 2020; Winter et al., 2020). Psychiatrist Arthur Deikman, who dedicated a significant part of his professional life to the exploration of mystical experiences, once stated in the book *The observing self* that "the principal aim of meditation is to enhance the observing self until its reality is without question and the meditator totally identifies with it" (Deikman, 1982).[3] However, non-dual awareness *itself* is not an automatic panacea for our Wounded Self. It is also impossible to simultaneously experience non-dual awareness, make decisions, and solve everyday matters. The goal of mindfulness and insight meditation is not identical to the goal of psychotherapy. Moreover, skillful life management always requires a Narrative Self (see Chapters 16, 18, and 19).

The Minimal, Narrative, and Transcendent Selves represent distinct *perspectives* on self-perception.[4] The Minimal Self observes lived experiences from within. The Narrative Self provides an external view, regarding itself either as a more or less unchanging object (Wounded Self) or as a dynamic and constantly evolving stream of experiences (Authentic Self). However, the Transcendent Self does not identify with the contents of our experience. It identifies with pure awareness without content. It is as if the figure and the background switched places. Metaphorically, the Transcendent Self does not identify with the water in the river but with the empty riverbed through which the river flows.[5] Buddhist monk and scholar Nagarjuna, who lived at the turn of the second and third centuries, declared in his work *The precious garland*: "Emptiness is the womb of compassion" (Nagarjuna, 2007). We can assert that we need the Observing Transcendent Self (or at least a certain degree of mindfulness) to have compassion with ourselves and others (cf. McHugh, 2015). However, as we will see in Chapters 17–20, the Transcendent Self and the Authentic Narrative Self should develop hand in hand (see Figure 10 on page 140). Transpersonal development, by itself, will not solve our personal and relational problems, even though it provides suitable conditions for addressing them.

NOTES

1 Daniel Siegel (2010a) introduced the term "mindsight" to describe this perspective. Mindsight refers to meta-awareness associated with gaining insight into the functioning of one's mind and acquiring knowledge that can be utilized in relationships with others.
2 For completeness, let us add that all four social dimensions of our narrative Self, as mentioned in Chapter 15 (individual Self, relational Self, public Self, and collective Self), can stem from both the wounded childhood narrative (e.g., Wounded relational Self) and the flexible authentic narrative (e.g., Authentic relational Self; see Figure 11 on page 150, cf. Cheek & Cheek, 2018).
3 The verb identifies used in this sentence may be somewhat misleading. After all, in non-dual awareness, there is no consciousness of the self, just as there is no consciousness of time or space (cf., e.g., Wittmann, 2018).
4 Finnish neuroscientists Andrew Fingelkurts, Alexander Fingelkurts, and philosopher Tarja Kallio-Tamminen, by the way, recently distinguished three different ways of experiencing the Self at the level of distinct activity of the so-called default mode network, demonstrating that each of these three Selves has a unique neurophenomenological profile (Fingelkurts et al., 2020, 2022; cf. Farb et al., 2007). However, their definition of the three distinct Selves differs slightly from the concept presented here.
5 For comparison, contextual behavioral science (CBS), which underlies Acceptance and Commitment Therapy (ACT), uses the term "Self as Process" for the minimal Self, "Self as Content" for the Narrative Self, and "Self as Context" for the Transcendent Self (Moran et al., 2018). This conceptualization in contextual behavioral science is consistent with our understanding.

CHAPTER SEVENTEEN

Non-Dual Awareness

As we venture into the upcoming chapters exploring transpersonal development, it is essential to clarify that mindfulness and insight meditation (*vipassanā* in Pali) yield different effects based on whether we engage in them in our daily lives, perhaps for 30 or 60 minutes each day, and different effects when we go on a meditation retreat where we meditate intensively 10, 12, or more hours daily for several weeks or months (see King et al., 2019).[1] While in everyday life, meditation can assist in relaxation, finding inner calm, and tending to ongoing mental hygiene, on a retreat, meditation sometimes serves as a gateway to altered states of consciousness and profound insights into the functioning of our minds and the very essence of our existence (Brown & Engler, 1980; Walsh & Vaughan, 1993; Welwood, 1996; Zanesco et al., 2023). However, achieving such insights requires the cultivation of *constant* mindfulness.[2] Are you interested in learning more about it?

Imagine yourself sitting on a meditation cushion in the living room at home. You are meditating, observing the inhalation and exhalation, and a blaring ambulance passes by your windows. Perhaps the thought crosses your mind: What happened? Where might that ambulance be headed? After some time, you will likely mindfully notice that you have developed some mental imagery. You return to observing your breath. However, after a week of intensive meditation on a retreat, in such a situation, you can mindfully notice in much more detail what is going on inside you. You mindfully notice, for example, the process of hearing. In the first fraction of a second, you distinctly realize, "Now, in consciousness, hearing is occurring." Next, you mindfully notice that the heard sound triggers a slightly unpleasant bodily feeling. You become aware that "now, in the body, an unpleasant feeling is occurring." Then, you mindfully notice that your mind has created an image of the passing ambulance. You realize that "now, in the mind, an image has appeared." In each moment, you similarly mindfully notice several different processes occurring within you. Now, now, now, now, now .... When intentionally mindfully observing what is happening within you moment by moment from morning to evening during a retreat, mindfulness gradually develops in such a way that it is almost unstoppable. It automatically monitors everything that is going on inside you. Moreover, over time, you become capable of noticing how individual processes (such as hearing, feeling, and thinking) arise in your consciousness, persist for a while, and then fade away. And then, things indeed start happening (see Mahāsi, 2014; Ñāṇārāma, 2010)!

While our consciousness typically appears as continuous under ordinary circumstances, Abhidhamma psychology explains that the stream of consciousness actually consists of discrete moments of awareness (*citta-kkhaṇa*) in Pali) that alternate so rapidly as to create an illusion of continuity.[3] This resembles individual frames in a movie, producing the illusion of continuous motion (see Barendregt, 2006). However, what happens when, in intensive meditation, we cultivate *constant* mindfulness that allows us not to identify with anything transpiring within us but merely to observe the constant arising and ceasing of various bodily and mental phenomena from morning to evening? The perspective of the uninvolved observer (Transcendent Self) will eventually enable us to realize that all the phenomena we mindfully observe share something in common: They are impermanent, fundamentally unsatisfactory, and devoid of any unchanging self (see *sammasana-ñāṇa* in Pali, cf. Grabovac et al., 2011). Coming to terms with such direct knowledge is not easy (cf. Barendregt, 2011).

If you have thus far believed that mindfulness and insight meditation should be pleasant, please note that intensive Vipassanā meditation is, in fact, no walk in the park. It includes phases that the Saint John of the Cross (2003) referred to as the dark night of the soul, and meditation manuals label them as the "knowledge of fearfulness" (*bhaja-ñāṇa* in Pali), the "knowledge of misery" (*ādīnava-ñāṇa* in Pali), and the "knowledge of disenchantment/disgust" (*nibbidā-ñāṇa* in Pali; see Grabovac, 2015; Mahāsi, 2014; Ñāṇārāma, 2010). The point is that once we start "seeing" everything we previously considered reality consists of fleeting and inevitably constantly disintegrating atoms of consciousness, it often makes us uncomfortable. In this phase of meditation, we are typically confronted with extreme existential fear and existential nausea (see Anālayo, 2019b; Buddhaghosa, 2020; cf. Lindahl et al., 2022).[4] Our consciousness resists accepting this phenomenological reality. We fear absolute "loss of control" and often react with irritability, panic, or succumb to despair and hopelessness.[5] However, if we cease to be mindful of what is happening within us at this stage, we expose ourselves to the risk of developing more prolonged psychological issues (see Chapter 18).

In the professional literature concerning intensive meditation retreats, cases of meditators who, after struggling with these demanding meditation experiences, developed depression, experienced suicidal thoughts, or even had a psychotic episode have been documented (see, e.g., Epstein & Lieff, 1981; Kuijpers et al., 2007; Lomas et al., 2015; Schlosser et al., 2019). Similarly, re-experiencing traumatic experiences sometimes occurs (see, e.g., Lindahl et al., 2017; Miller, 1993; cf. Chapter 16). In advanced meditation, it is, therefore, crucial to continue mindfully noting everything that is happening within us during such moments. We must learn to mindfully observe existential fear, which is just as transient a phenomenon as any other. If we have the support of an experienced meditation teacher, we gradually progress to the stage of "knowledge of equanimity about formations" (saṅkhāra-upekkhā-ñāṇa in Pali). And that is when we are already out of the worst.[6]

New York psychiatrist Mark Epstein (2013a) likens advanced mindfulness and insight meditation to gradually train oneself "to go to pieces without falling apart." Dutch mathematician and meditation teacher Henk Barendregt (2011) speaks of a gradual "taming" of existential fear (cf. also, e.g., Dokic, 2022). In each case, as we learn to observe the unceasing stream of our inner experience with nonattached mindfulness, we have the chance to experience non-dual or content-free awareness (nibbāna in Pali).[7] The decentralized perspective (1) combined with a clear discernment of all experienced phenomena (2), an accepting attitude toward these phenomena (3), concentration (4), a firm commitment to persevere in meditation (5), rapture (6), and tranquility (7) together constitute the so-called seven factors of awakening (satta sambojjhaṅgā in Pali; see, e.g., Goldstein, 2017). Developing these seven qualities guides us toward achieving non-dual, empty consciousness, in which the observer's perspective (Transcendent Self) completely disappears at some point (see, e.g., Costines et al., 2021; Welwood, 1996). In non-dual awareness, there is no awareness of time or space. There is no distinction between the external and internal worlds. There are no boundaries in it (Ataria et al., 2015; Josipovic, 2019, 2021; Josipovic & Miskovic, 2020; Millière et al., 2018; Srinivasan, 2020; Winter et al., 2020; Wittmann, 2018). However, why is achieving such a state considered desirable in Buddha's teachings?

The attainment of *nibbāna*, which itself lasts only a brief moment, leads, according to Abhidhamma, to lasting *subsequent* changes in the meditator's perception, experience, and behavior. The first-hand realization that there is no unchanging Self separate from everything else *subsequently* permanently eliminates self-referential processing, including maladaptive schemas, among other things (see Niebauer, 2019; Smith, 2010; cf. Chapter 3). However, there is a catch. Abhidhamma distinguishes four levels of awakening (Amaro, 2019; Sirimane, 2016) and describes, in addition to the "attachment to the idea of an unchanging Self" (*sakkāya-diṭṭhi* in Pali), nine other "attachments" (*saṃyojana* in Pali) that keep a person in the cycle of continuous arising of suffering, and that the meditator *gradually* sheds (see Barua, 2018; cf. also the concept of *kilesa*, Benda, 2019). Only at the fourth stage of awakening (*arahatta-magga-phala* in Pali) does the meditator *permanently* free themselves from all ten fetters. Only the fourth level of awakening, therefore, leads to the *complete* elimination of maladaptive schemes.[8] Because achieving this level is undoubtedly rare among contemporary Western meditators, it cannot be reliably assumed that intensive meditation will completely heal our Wounded Self. However, this does not mean that intensive meditation does not impact maladaptive schemas at all.

Maladaptive schemas initially manifest as a relatively challenging obstacle to more pronounced meditation progress in intensive meditation practices (see, e.g., Goldberg et al., 2022; VanderKooi, 1997; Walsh & Roche, 1979; cf. also Chapter 16). However, meditators may succeed in *temporarily* overcoming these schemas. Usually, though, it is not a permanent overcoming. Even highly advanced meditators commonly face maladaptive schemas in their everyday lives (see Kornfield, 1993). Nevertheless, it is likely that transpersonal experiences *gradually* weaken our core beliefs (Dahl et al., 2015). Unfortunately, existing research has so far only focused on verifying the occurrence of non-dual awareness or "ego dissolution" during meditation itself or during a psychedelic experience (see Gamma & Metzinger, 2021; Hanley et al., 2018; Nour et al., 2016). They have not examined *subsequent*, long-term reductions in "attachment" to the rigid Narrative Self in everyday life. However, since questionnaires measuring this characteristic already exist (see, e.g., Whitehead et al., 2018; Czech version by Benda, 2020b),[9] we can assume that future research on the influence of transpersonal experiences on the degree of "attachment" to the Narrative Self will soon help clarify this aspect.

Existing studies have indicated that meditative insights *gradually* alter how we understand ourselves (see Shireen et al., 2022; van Gordon et al., 2019; cf. Giles, 2019). They guide meditators toward a deeper understanding of the interdependence of each individual on others and the surrounding environment (cf. Kałużna et al., 2022), fostering a non-self-centered perspective on oneself, others, and the world. Long-term intensive meditation practice reduces the tendency for self-prioritization among meditators (Shi & He, 2020; see also Chapter 3). A selfless perspective also mitigates blind hedonic tendencies to cling to pleasant experiences and avoid unpleasant ones (cf. the pleasure principle and the unpleasure principle, Chapter 11). It also gradually eliminates all ego-defense mechanisms (cf., e.g., Wheeler et al., 2017). According to Michael Dambrun (2017) from the University of Clermont Auvergne, selflessness is even the foundation of authentic-durable happiness (cf. Dambrun & Ricard, 2011). It definitely proves to be an essential factor influencing mental health (Moore et al., 2017).

While mental disorders are characterized by considerable *rigidity* in self-concept (see Chapter 4), in long-term meditators, self-concept is typically much more *flexible* (Dominguez et al., 2022; Giommi et al., 2023; Xiao et al., 2017). It does not rely on a fixed idea we have about ourselves but respects the continuously changing stream of our experiences. Sometimes, for instance, we wish to be alone, and at other times, we feel like being with people. However, suppose our decision-making automatically leans on an unchanging definition of ourselves (e.g., "I am an introvert"). In that case, it can easily happen that we do not mindfully notice the current desire to socialize. We then ignore our own needs. When we fail to cultivate mindfulness and the "Transcendent Self," our *concept* of who we are (Narrative Self) can become overly rigid. However, when we can observe our experiences with a mindful perspective from the outside (Transcendent Self), we have the opportunity not to let various learned automatic responses control us. We do not have to act based on an unchanging definition of ourselves. Moreover, we can at least partially free ourselves from obsessive self-centered tendencies that compel us to constantly think about ourselves, self-critically evaluate, and compare ourselves to others (see Chapter 4).[10]

While episodic experiences of non-dual awareness may not completely rid us of maladaptive schemas, they undeniably strengthen our Transcendent Self and transform our Narrative Self. It is worth noting that psychedelic experiences yield a similar effect. Psychedelic experiences also teach psychonauts to observe their own experiences from an external observer's standpoint (cf. Letheby & Gerrans, 2017) and reassess rigid self-conceptions (see, e.g., Amada et al., 2020; Franquesa et al., 2018; Hayes et al., 2020; Smigielski et al., 2019). Nevertheless, the question remains: What additional factors, besides transpersonal experiences themselves, contribute to enabling psychonauts and meditators to adopt an observing perspective toward their experiences, even in everyday situations where maladaptive schemas are activated?

As we know, in psychotherapy, the treatment of maladaptive schemas and the "Wounded Self" involves not only cognitive reappraisal of core beliefs but also corrective emotional experiences *within* the therapeutic *relationship* (see Chapter 10). These experiences teach clients to *accept* feelings of core pain. Even though some experts suggest that psychedelic experiences and intensive meditation may also lead to the *reconsolidation* of maladaptive schemas (see, e.g., Dominguez et al., 2022; Grigsby, 2021), it is possible that the corrective emotional experience does not actually occur in isolation within the transpersonal experience itself, it likely takes place *in* the *relationship* with a psychedelic experience guide (sitter), a meditation teacher, or *in relationships* with other members of a supportive community (saṅgha in Pali). In both psychedelic experiences and intensive meditation, a close *relationship* with an experienced and compassionate guide assists psychonauts and meditators in navigating potentially challenging phases of the transpersonal experience. This relationship can positively impact the course of the transpersonal experience and its subsequent integration. However, since the experience of non-dual awareness also seems to contribute to the further development of self-compassion and compassion toward others (cf., e.g., Kałużna et al., 2022; van Gordon et al., 2019), the long-term impacts of this experience should, in turn, reflect in interpersonal relationships. *Close relationships* are a litmus test for personal development (see Figure 10 on page 140, cf. Chapter 15). If our transpersonal development does not subsequently manifest in close relationships, we might become mere "Enlightened Nerds" (see Chapter 19). However, the practical application of transpersonal insights in everyday situations usually requires further learning (cf., e.g., Dahl & Davidson, 2019; Kornfield, 2001; Masters, 2010).

EXERCISE 17
Transpersonal disidentification[11]

Take a comfortable and relaxed seated position. Direct your attention to your body. And state: I have a body, but I am not this body. This body may be healthy or may have various difficulties or illnesses. It can be rested and full of energy or tired. However, this has nothing to do with me. I can observe the body, but it is not my Self. This body is a precious instrument that enables me to have all kinds of experiences and perform all types of deeds in the outer world, but it is just an instrument. I take good care of it, striving to keep it healthy and in good condition, but it is not my Self. I have this body at my disposal, but I am not this body.

Now, mindfully notice the bodily feelings. Realize: I am experiencing various feelings and emotions, but I am not these feelings or emotions. I go through countless emotions, sometimes contradictory and constantly changing. Hope, despair, joy, sadness, excitement, and calm. I can observe them, whether they are pleasant or unpleasant. I can accept, understand, judge, regulate, express, and use them. However, it is evident that these emotions are not my Self. I experience emotions, but I am not these emotions.

Now, become aware of your thoughts, reflections, imaginations, opinions, and intellectual attitudes. Acknowledge: I can think and contemplate or create various ideas. I can take positions. However, I am not these thoughts, imaginations, or positions. Some thoughts and ideas are highly developed and detailed, while others are vague. The mind can be undisciplined yet creative. Through thinking, I can solve problems and face challenges in the external and internal world. However, these thoughts, ideas, and opinions are not the Self.

Furthermore, realize that various desires, compulsions, habitual tendencies, impulses, and future intentions can be recognized in the mind. And consider the following fact: I have multiple desires, aversions, wishes, habits, and plans. However, I am not these inclinations or intentions. Desires, aversions, wishes, habits, and plans change. Sometimes, they are contradictory. They emerge and disappear. I experience various desires and aversions, but I am not these desires or aversions.

Finally, become aware of consciousness itself, which is aware of all sensory perceptions, feelings, thoughts, and desires. And for a moment, observe this consciousness. Notice that this consciousness sometimes identifies with an impulse, thought, feeling, or sensation; sometimes, it does not. However, this consciousness is no specific thought, sensation, or feeling. It can be aware of itself. Perhaps fleetingly, you may catch a glimpse of empty consciousness without content. Does some Self hide in this consciousness?

NOTES

1 In Theravāda Buddhist countries such as Sri Lanka, Burma, or Thailand, monks traditionally meditate intensively during the three-month rainy season retreat (*vassa* in Pali).
2 When we guide a client in psychotherapy to be mindful of what is happening in their body and mind during the activation of maladaptive schemas, it involves momentary, in-the-moment mindfulness. This mindfulness allows the client to regulate emotions in that particular situation. However, it typically does not lead to the transpersonal insights addressed in this chapter.
3 Contemporary neuroscience and cognitive science still debate whether consciousness is continuous or consists of discrete moments of awareness. However, many recent models describe consciousness similarly to Abhidhamma, portraying it as a stream composed of discontinuous flashes of awareness (see Fleming, 2020; Herzog et al., 2020; Lundqvist & Wutz, 2022; Raffone, 2021; Yurchenko, 2022, cf. Herma & Greve, 2024).
4 Some contemporary thinkers, influenced by new insights from cognitive science and neuroscience, incidentally, question the existence of free will and moral responsibility (cf. determinism, e.g., Caruso, 2013; Seth, 2021). However, Buddhist psychology, specifically Abhidhamma, is not as radical in this regard (cf. compatibilism). It argues that even though there is no independent Self, at the conventional level of reality, we can make decisions freely and liberate ourselves from the dependent arising of suffering. In doing so, Abhidhamma places great emphasis on ethics (see, e.g., Meyers, 2014; Repetti, 2017).
5 During this phase of meditation, practitioners teeter on the edge between psychotic disintegration and "mindful disintegration" (Schoenberg & Barendregt, 2016; cf. Deane et al., 2020; Lindahl & Britton, 2019).
6 In Buddha's teachings, reliance on close *relationships* within the community is considered one of the so-called three refuges (*ti-saraṇa* in Pali; see Bodhi, 2009; Nyanaponika, 2008). Additionally, loving-kindness meditation (*mettā-bhāvanā* in Pali) and compassion meditation (*karuṇā-bhāvanā* in Pali) can assist meditators in confronting existential fear.
7 Abhidhamma psychology describes not only *nibbāna* but also a variety of other mystical experiences (see, e.g., the so-called *jhānas*). However, unlike *nibbāna*,

these experiences involve the presence of the Observing, Transcendent Self (see, e.g., Costines et al., 2021; Dennison, 2022).
8 How the attainment of different levels of awakening affects the personality of advanced meditators was investigated as early as the 1980s in Burma and India by Jack Engler (1983; cf. also Brown & Engler, 1980).
9 Existing research has shown that psychedelic experiences contribute to the development of mindfulness (Radakovic et al., 2022) and self-compassion (e.g., Kamboj et al., 2018; Ruffell et al., 2021; Sampedro et al., 2017; van der Kolk et al., 2024). However, no study has yet confirmed the potential impact of psychedelics or intensive meditation on nonattachment to the Narrative Self. In psychedelic research, only the similarly focused Quiet Ego Scale has been used so far (Wayment et al., 2015; see, e.g., Brasher et al., 2023; St. Arnaud & Sharpe, 2023).
10 Several neuroscience studies in recent years have documented corresponding functional and structural brain changes in individuals engaged in long-term meditation (see, e.g., Feruglio et al., 2021; Weder, 2022).
11 The exercise was inspired by Roberto Assagioli's book *Psychosynthesi"* (Assagioli, 1993).

CHAPTER EIGHTEEN

Integration of Transpersonal Experiences

The altered states of consciousness induced by psychedelics or through techniques such as Holotropic or Maitri Breathwork are tremendously diverse in terms of sensory perceptions, thoughts, and imagery experienced. However, in terms of emotional experiences, they share many similarities with the experiences of advanced meditators in intensive meditation (see, e.g., Letheby, 2022; Millière et al., 2018; Scheidegger, 2021).[1] What do these experiences have in comon? Both intensive meditation and psychedelic experiences *temporarily* weaken our defense mechanisms, allowing us to *consciously* confront feelings of core pain or vulnerability (cf. internal exposure). They provide us with the opportunity to (1) better understand our deep, not always clearly conscious needs (see Figure 9 on page 54) and (2) possibly even *temporarily* overcome our learned helplessness (see Tiwari et al., 2023), and discover what happens when we completely let go of trying to control our experience and instead fully open ourselves to it, *accepting* it with compassion (see Wolff et al., 2020). In both meditation and psychedelic experiences, we learn to simply observe all experienced phenomena (see the Transcendent Self). Gradually, we gain *insights* into the mechanisms underlying our suffering. We discover possibilities for reducing or transforming our suffering. We also gain a new perspective on ourselves, others, and the world around us. Typically, we gradually *reappraise* our *core beliefs* and fundamental life values and priorities (see, e.g., Kähönen, 2023; cf. Sloshower et al., 2020; Watts & Luoma, 2020).[2]

Research on psychedelics has thus far demonstrated that psychedelic experiences enhance our social connectivity (see Forstmann et al., 2020; Griffiths et al., 2018; Watts et al., 2017), our openness, and prosocial behavior (e.g., Bouso et al., 2018; Knudsen, 2023; Schmid & Liechti, 2018), and also deepen our connection to nature and the environment (e.g., Forstmann & Sagioglou,

2017; Kettner et al., 2019; Nour et al., 2017). However, it is important to note once again that the development of a new *relationship* with ourselves, with others, and with the world likely significantly involves *corrective relational experiences* that we undergo *in relationships* with our guides, therapists, or community members during psychedelic experiences (cf., e.g., Cherniak et al., 2022; Villiger, 2022).

A professional guide in psychedelic-assisted psychotherapy should be capable of creating a safe and supportive environment (setting) for the client. Ideally, the guide should temporarily become an externalized representation of mindfulness and compassion in relation to the client (cf. Benda, 2019). The guide's experience-based trust that it is possible to completely relinquish control in a protected environment, to "go to pieces without falling apart" (see Epstein, 2013a), can help clients experience what is known as an *emotional breakthrough* and subsequent relief (see Roseman et al., 2019). If an *emotional breakthrough* occurs during the psychedelic experience, core pain is replaced by a highly positive experience. The pervasive feeling of unconditional love can heal our Lost Self (existential dread). The feeling of connection and closeness with others, nature, and the universe can heal our Abandoned Self (loneliness). The feeling of universal unity can heal our Inferior Self (shame) and the feeling of numinosity and awe our Inflated Self. In the most profound cases, one may even experience non-dual awareness or a "mystic death and rebirth" (Grof, 2001; cf. Benda, 2007; Underhill, 2019). However, it is not only about how the guide can facilitate these experiences but also how the guide can help ensure that these experiences positively impact our everyday lives. In this regard, *sharing* is of utmost importance (see further).

Participants in intensive meditation retreats can *share* and discuss all their meditation experiences with an experienced meditation teacher. This teacher usually possesses rich personal experience with challenging meditation insights (cf. Grabovac, 2015)[3] and can *empathize* with the meditators' experiences. The *relationship* with a compassionate and understanding teacher can thus become a crucial emotional anchor for the meditator and, at times, even a remedy for their Wounded Self. However, that is not all. Another significant benefit for meditators is the teacher's knowledge of Buddha's teaching. The theory of Buddha's teaching (including Abhidhamma psychology) offers meditators a *conceptual framework* through which they can *understand* or find *meaning* in unpleasant or frightening meditation experiences. The meditation teacher has access to a wide range of methods, tools, and techniques that allow *processing* demanding meditation insights and subsequently *applying* them wisely in everyday life (cf., e.g., "right understanding," "right intention," "right livelihood," etc., see Chapter 11). Yet, even intensive meditation has risks (cf., e.g., Compson, 2018; Lindahl & Britton, 2019; Schoenberg & Barendregt, 2016; VanderKooi, 1997).

About a year ago, Caleb met a Czech-born Theravada Buddhist monk who lectured on the unsatisfactory nature of a materialistic way of life. It seemed that the monk had answers to many of Caleb's questions. Even more promising were the monk's teachings on meditation! It didn't take long for Caleb to decide to fly to Sri Lanka, where he would undergo an intensive meditation retreat in a mountain hermitage. And so it happened. Caleb had significant motivation and high expectations. Initially, he diligently meditated from morning till evening, day after day. However, after a few weeks, Caleb began to observe in meditation how all phenomena he noticed in his body and mind inevitably disintegrated immediately after being aware of them (see the so-called knowledge of dissolution, bhaṅga-ñāṇa in Pali). This began to frighten him.

In this stage of meditation, Caleb felt like he was losing all certainties of life. He saw only complete decay and chaos everywhere. He found nothing to rely on. It was a nightmare! Caleb experienced immense fear of losing his sanity. He panicked and became paranoid. He quickly lost trust in the Czech monk and in meditation itself. Where had it led him? Until then, Caleb had no idea that advanced meditation could involve such experiences. He felt that meditation had led him precisely into the state from which he wanted to liberate himself through meditation. Nothing made sense to him. The world seemed unreal to him (so-called derealization). He felt unreal. He was alienated from himself (so-called depersonalization). He felt utterly lost.

Caleb was unaware that he had experienced similar feelings as a little boy when his parents were indifferent to his emotions, and he felt invisible (see the Abandoned Self). However, the maladaptive schema of the Abandoned Self compelled him to unknowingly repeat the old childhood script – not trusting anyone (see the fear of closeness, Chapter 15) and figuring things out on his own. Caleb stopped communicating with the monk and returned to the Czech Republic. He was prescribed antidepressants and "struggled" with the absence of life's meaning (cyclical thought rumination). Thus, the Abandoned Self "halted" his transpersonal development, and it took several months before Caleb decided to address his condition with the help of therapy.

It is challenging to speculate on what would have happened if Caleb hadn't quickly lost trust in the Czech monk and stopped *sharing* his meditation experiences with him. Would the monk have been able to *empathize* with Caleb's state of mind and respond *with compassion*? Could the monk have helped Caleb *understand* what he was currently experiencing in meditation? Would he have advised him on how to proceed? Naturally, several factors come into play. On one side, there's the teacher's mindfulness, compassion, and wisdom (expertise). On the other side, there's the trust and openness of the meditator (see therapeutic *relationship*). However, these factors also play a crucial role in integrating psychedelic experiences.

It should be noted that psychedelic therapists currently do not have nearly as much knowledge about altered states of consciousness as Buddhist meditation teachers do (see, e.g., Buddhaghosa, 2020; cf. Dennison, 2022). The entire Abhidhamma is, in fact, a psychology of the Transcendent Self. Abhidhamma intricately describes all meditation experiences, explaining the mechanisms through which we rid ourselves of "delusion" (see Bodhi, 2007; Burbea, 2014; Frýba, 2008; Narada, 1987). It provides teachers and meditators with a reliable *cognitive map*. Such a map can be invaluable for meditators facing unknown experiences (see Grabovac, 2015). Moreover, new psychedelic-assisted psychotherapy will need such a map (cf., e.g., Millière, 2020; Millière et al., 2018). For therapeutic work with psychedelics, it will be necessary to clarify not only the pharmacological and neurocognitive mechanisms of their effects but also the psychological mechanisms of their impact. A detailed phenomenological map of altered states of consciousness will be required (see also, e.g., Yaden & Newberg, 2022), along with the development of a theory of personal and transpersonal development (see Assagioli, 1993, 2007; Wilber, 2006, 2016; cf. e.g., Forman, 2010). In the future, psychedelic research (and research of long-term meditators) may stimulate the emergence of secular spirituality (see Walach, 2015) and secular ethics (cf. Greenberg & Mitra, 2015; Monteiro et al., 2015). Only such a broader theoretical framework can serve as a reliable guide for the effective use of psychedelics in the treatment of mental disorders.

Current psychotherapists typically do not aspire to support clients in their transpersonal development. The guidance of intensive meditation retreats is left to meditation teachers (see King et al., 2019). Moreover, psychedelic experiences are predominantly utilized "only" for therapeutic purposes (see, e.g., Grob & Grigsby, 2021; Winkelman & Sessa, 2019). The transpersonal dimension of development is thus discovered somewhat incidentally in contemporary research (see, e.g., Letheby & Gerrans, 2017). However, for psychedelic therapists to distinguish "healthy" personal and transpersonal development from the activation of maladaptive schemas (see client Caleb in this chapter) or from "spiritual bypassing" (see Chapter 19), they will soon need to form some understanding of transpersonal development (cf. Welwood, 1996, 2002). For now, we can assume that maladaptive schemas undoubtedly influence our meditation and psychedelic experiences (see Cherniak et al., 2022; Engler, 1984). And if, as therapists, we encounter clients in whom the activation of maladaptive schemas occurred within any transpersonal experience, we can naturally use similar approaches to those in regular psychotherapy when working with them (see Part II, cf. Benda, 2019). If the transpersonal experience also includes positive and potentially corrective emotional experiences or insights into the mechanisms underlying our suffering, we can help clients transfer these *insights* and newly discovered *attitudes* into everyday life. However, this already brings us to therapeutic approaches in integrating transpersonal experiences.

The recent surge in interest in the therapeutic use of psychedelics in recent years has led to the development of various experimental models for integrating psychedelic experiences (see Bathje et al., 2022).[4] Because our *Transdiagnostic Theory of the Wounded Self* offers a unique perspective on mental disorders and their treatment, we will outline our model for the integration of transpersonal experiences in the following paragraphs. The Compassion-Comprehension-Commitment model (abbreviated as CCC)[5] can be applied when working with a client who has undergone any meditative, holotropic, or psychedelic experience. Integration, in this context, is understood as a process during which the client emotionally processes and conceptualizes the lived experience, attributes subjective meaning to it, and seeks ways to apply newly gained insights and attitudes in everyday life and relationships with others (cf. Earleywine et al., 2022). The CCC model represents three phases of *dialogue* between the therapist and the client. To utilize any transpersonal experience not only for transpersonal development but also for *healing the Wounded Self*, it is necessary to *share* this experience within a confidential (therapeutic) *relationship* (Wolfson, 2023).

THE COMPASSION-COMPREHENSION-COMMITMENT MODEL

Before we introduce the Compassion-Comprehension-Commitment model, let us recall that mindful therapists should be able to adopt a *compassionate attitude* toward their own feelings of core pain. This competence is a crucial prerequisite for the therapist to *empathize* with a client experiencing existential dread, profound traumatic loneliness, or inadequacy (see Figure 9 on page 54). The therapist should be capable of resonating emotionally with the client, meaning genuinely *feeling* what the client is going through (cf. Timmermann et al., 2022). This is only possible when the therapist can empathetically *accept* these feelings within their own being. It is noteworthy that, despite the vast diversity of altered states of consciousness, these states do not contain any more extreme negative feelings than these three well-known variations of core pain. The good news is that if we can *accept* them compassionately, we should not be fundamentally surprised in our integrative work with the client. Therefore, I would like to emphasize that although personal experiences with altered states of consciousness are undoubtedly an advantage for us as therapists (cf., e.g., Phelps, 2017), the essential prerequisites for the successful integration of transpersonal experiences are our mindful presence and compassion toward the client (cf. Thal et al., 2022). The therapist's responsibility primarily lies in these two variables. The CCC model provides a rough structure for proceeding during the debriefing process.

Compassion

In the first phase of the integration process, we guide the client toward mindful *reflection* of their lived transpersonal experience (see Benda, 2019). We assist the client in becoming aware of, naming, and expressing primarily the *feelings* and *emotional states* they went through. Special attention is devoted to feelings of *core pain*. We can utilize the method of interpersonal focusing (Gendlin, 2003; Hájek, 2012; Weiser Cornell, 1996) or various options for artistic *expression of emotions* (e.g., mandala drawing). Explicitly, we also convey an understanding of the client's *needs* (cf. Figure 9 on page 54 and Part II). In this phase of the integration process, the client should *feel* that we *co-experience* their emotions with them (see emotional resonance) and simultaneously adopt a *compassionate attitude* toward them. They should "feel felt" (cf. Siegel, 2020). During the reflection, if the client re-experiences core pain, such relational experience may have a similar *corrective effect* as the Ideal Parents Technique or dialogue with an empty chair in psychotherapy (see *memory reconsolidation*, Chapter 10). This authentic experience in the therapeutic relationship can strengthen a potential *emotional breakthrough* (see Roseman et al., 2019). If the client gets "stuck" in core pain, it can replace an *emotional breakthrough*. In any case, the therapist's compassion should help the client internalize it and develop *self-compassion*. This is the goal of the compassion phase.

Let us add that if the transpersonal experience the client shares includes pleasant experiences of sacred awe, pervasive love, interconnectedness, and closeness with others or nature, experiences of universal unity, etc. (see, e.g., Barrett & Griffiths, 2018; Zanesco et al., 2023), we, of course, help the client express and share this experience as well. Symbolic (artistic) or verbal expression and sharing of positive mystical or ecstatic experiences also assist the client in "discovering" and "activating" their inner potential for compassion and other "divine attitudes" (Benda, 2019). From the perspective of healing the Wounded Self, the development of *self-compassion* is more crucial than the cognitive reappraisal of rigid core beliefs. Mindful and self-compassion processing of experienced emotions is more important than any potential rational interpretation of transpersonal experiences (cf. Žvelc & Žvelc, 2021).

We should, therefore, always emphasize this initial phase of the integration process, mainly when we aim for the subsequent utilization of transpersonal experiences in everyday life.

Comprehension

Only when we have successfully helped the client compassionately accept the emotionally challenging aspects of the transpersonal experience can we progress to the second phase of the integration process, which is cognitive. Transpersonal experiences often challenge our self-concept and general worldview (cf., e.g., Carhart-Harris & Friston, 2019; Kähönen, 2023). It is, therefore, appropriate to give due attention to the cognitive apprehension of the lived experience. As research findings demonstrate, deep meditative, holotropic, or psychedelic experiences and insights can significantly shake our materialistic view of the world in some cases (see, e.g., Nayak et al., 2023). They can induce an "ontological shock" (e.g., Timmermann et al., 2021). On the other hand, they can also lead to the formation of false or maladaptive beliefs (see Timmermann et al., 2022). Dialogue with an experienced therapist should, therefore, help the client find individual meaning in the lived experience and potentially understand its autobiographical context. It should assist the client in using the "ontological shock" to see through the unreality and limiting rigidity of their negative core beliefs (cf. Amada & Shane, 2022; Amada et al., 2020; Gashi et al., 2021; Nayak & Johnson, 2021). It should also help them humbly accept that we cannot explain and comprehend every transpersonal experience in detail. After all, healing the Wounded Self does not involve replacing it with a new but equally rigid notion. It is instead healed through the direct realization that the very nature of our existence is transpersonal and far surpasses all our concepts.

We already know that, for daily content functioning, we must create stories about ourselves that give meaning to our lives (Authentic Narrative Self, see Part III). All our emotional experiences can be internally integrated and subsequently shared with others essentially only when we can meaningfully place them in the context of our private story (Greenberg, 2021). However, the Authentic Narrative Self is a dynamic tale of our continuous self-discovery, learning, and *transformations* that we constantly undergo. It does not represent any static idea of an unchanging identity (see the rigid Wounded Self). The integration of transpersonal experiences should involve *understanding* the causal connections of our distress and the mechanisms of therapeutic change. Such *insights* allow us to create a dynamic story of our personal *transformation* (flexible Authentic Self). The goal of a mindful therapist in the understanding phase is to help the client capture and articulate their insights.

I do not consider it a mistake when a therapist offers their interpretation of the transpersonal experience, conceptual framework, or a "cognitive map" (cf. Compson, 2018; Grabovac, 2015; Lindahl et al., 2017). However, the purpose of such an interpretation should be the "normalization" of the transpersonal experience and reassuring the client that any experience can be integrated and utilized for their benefit. If the client can verbalize the lived experience to some extent and simultaneously understand it as meaningful, they are ready for the third phase of the integration process.

Commitment

A positive transpersonal experience can serve as a long-term tool for healing maladaptive schemas (the Wounded Self) if the client intentionally recalls insights, feelings, and attitudes from these experiences in typical everyday situations where maladaptive schemas are activated. In the commitment phase, we assist the client in identifying such situations (triggers). Subsequently, we help them prepare a strategy that *deliberately* uses the recalled transpersonal experience or specific insight as an "antidote" to a particular core belief and the feeling of core pain. For example, suppose a client mindfully notices in daily life that they are experiencing a feeling of existential dread. In that case, they can mentally recall the feeling of all-encompassing, unconditional love they experienced during a psychedelic session. When they become mindful of a core belief like "I am unwanted, I do not belong anywhere," they can mentally recall an experience where they felt that "We are all part of one whole" (cf. Kałużna et al., 2022). The narrowed awareness of maladaptive archaic ego states (see Figure 1 on page 25) can be influenced and "reverted" to the mindful Adult ego state by recalling the perspective of expanded consciousness (cf. Chapters 11 and 20). However, it is crucial to be *mindfully aware* of what is happening within us and to have the *intention* to actively work with maladaptive schemas (cf. Simonds, 2023). Therefore, the third phase of the integration process is directed toward creating such an *intention*.

EXERCISE 18

Saving a feeling of wonder and gratitude in your inner database

Meditative and psychedelic experiences are, of course, not the only paths to expanded states of consciousness. Moments of profound awe and gratitude or the feeling of touching something transcendent can also be experienced in everyday life. Let us recall such experiences in this exercise so that we can later use the memories of them in situations when our consciousness, on the contrary, narrows. This is also one of the paths to healing the Wounded Self.

Find a quiet place where you can dedicate at least 20 minutes solely to yourself. Sit comfortably. Begin by focusing your attention on your breath, observing how your body inhales and exhales. Then, try to recall moments in the past when you experienced a sense of awe, gratitude, a feeling of deep connection with others, or the feeling of touching something that transcends you. Perhaps it was in nature while observing a scenic landscape, mountainous terrain, icy plains, a desert, a sunset over the ocean, a rainforest, or the starry sky above you. Maybe similar feelings were evoked by an artistic work, a film, a painting, a ballet performance, or a rock concert. Perhaps you attended a historical or extraordinary event where people suddenly came together and "pulled in the same direction." Maybe you experienced such feelings when in love or present at the birth of your child. Try to recall such an experience and visualize it with all the details. Who was there with you? Can you also recall the bodily feeling you experienced at that time?

If you can recall such a feeling, realize that this feeling has healing power. Do you feel how you relaxed during that memory? Do you feel happy or grateful again for a moment? Stay with this feeling for a while, and store the image that reminded you of this feeling. You can use this image in moments when you feel contracted, scared, lonely, or inadequate. Whatever you are going through in your life, no one can take this memory away from you, and you can use it whenever you need to gather strength. So, the next time one of your maladaptive schemas is activated, and you find yourself reliving the core pain of childhood, recall this moment of awe and gratitude for a moment. Observe how your pain dissolves. You might be surprised that you are not as powerless against your pain as it may seem.

NOTES

1 It appears that psychedelic experiences and experiences from intensive mindfulness and insight meditation may complement each other well in clinical applications. In recent years, efforts have emerged to combine psychedelic-assisted psychotherapy with the cultivation of mindfulness (see, e.g., Payne et al., 2021).
2 Currently, numerous theories are attempting to elucidate the mechanisms of the psychedelic effects (see Girn et al., 2023; van Elk & Yaden, 2022). While many theories presuppose that the significant contribution to positive therapeutic change involves the *reappraisal of core beliefs* (e.g., Amada et al., 2020; Carhart-Harris & Friston, 2019; Gattuso et al., 2023; Cherniak et al., 2022), some theories emphasize the importance of *acceptance* (e.g., Wolff et al., 2020; Zeifman et al., 2023b). However, there are also considerations that psychedelic experiences trigger the process of *memory reconsolidation* (e.g., Grigsby, 2021).

3 In the Burmese meditation tradition (see Mahāsi, 2014), which underlies the current surge of interest in mindfulness in psychology, attaining the first stage of awakening (called *sotāpatti-magga-phala* in Pali) is typically considered one of the prerequisites for someone to become a meditation teacher.
4 Our approach aligns with models of psychedelic integration based on Acceptance and Commitment Therapy (see Gorman et al., 2021; Sloshower et al., 2020; Watts & Luoma, 2020).
5 The CCC model can be applied both in therapeutic and ontological integration (cf. Aixalà, 2022). However, considering the therapeutic context of this book, this chapter will specifically focus on using this model in therapeutic integration.

CHAPTER NINETEEN

Mindful Zombie, Spiritual Narcissist, and Enlightened Nerd

Evelyn Underhill is undoubtedly among the first Western authors to systematically map mystics' personal and transpersonal development across various world religions. In her monumental and now-classic work *Mysticism: A study in the nature and development of man's spiritual consciousness* (Underhill, 2019), she proposed a schema of five stages through which mystics typically progress. Underhill noted that ecstatic periods filled with peak experiences in the lives of mystics are usually followed by challenging periods she termed "purification" and the "dark night of the soul" (cf. John of the Cross, 2003). In her case studies, we can discern that the mystic's progress in transpersonal development is consistently interspersed with new challenges in personal growth (see Fig. 10 on page 140). Even achieving the stage of "enlightenment" does not signify the end of the mystic's personal development, as affirmed by the classic meditation guide *The path of purification* (Buddhaghosa, 2020). It asserts that the initial experience of content-free awareness (*nibbāna* in Pali), referred to as the so-called stream-entry (*sotāpatti-magga-phala* in Pali), does not lead to the permanent elimination of all psychopathologies (cf. Mahāsi, 2014; Ñāṇārāma, 2010). The same holds for other mystical experiences known as "jhānas" (cf. Dennison, 2022). According to Buddha's teachings, developing wisdom and ethical conduct is equally vital as meditation practice within the Noble Eightfold Path (cf. Struhl, 2020). Imagining that, thanks to a single or repeated experience of nondual awareness, one can avoid dealing with the challenges of *personal* development would, therefore, be naive (cf. Chapter 16).

Nevertheless, such an idea is widespread among contemporary Western meditators and psychonauts. Hence, we dedicate a separate chapter to it. However, do you know what such an idea is called? Transpersonal psychologist and Buddhist therapist John Welwood (2002) introduced the term "spiritual bypassing" to describe the attempt to avoid addressing our relationship issues and healing our emotional wounds through spiritual practices (see also Masters, 2010). In this chapter, we will explore three of the most common types of "spiritual bypassing," namely the "Mindful Zombie" syndrome, the "Spiritual Narcissist" syndrome, and the "Enlightened Nerd" syndrome. As we will see, these are essentially three common errors on the spiritual path (cf. Caplan, 2015), three different variations of avoiding adult responsibility (cf. Chapter 13), and relational closeness (cf. Chapter 15). To avoid falling into these traps and help our clients navigate them, we should be able to recognize them.

MINDFUL ZOMBIE

The cultivation of mindfulness leads us, among other things, to a progressively more precise awareness of all our feelings (*vedanānupassanā* in Pali), which are one of the so-called four foundations (*satipaṭṭhāna* in Pali) of right mindfulness (see, e.g., Goldstein, 2017). However, besides mere awareness, we also learn to adopt a compassionate or accepting attitude toward all our feelings (cf., e.g., Simione et al., 2021). This means understanding that each feeling signals some *need* to us (see Benda, 2019). And this is something that the Mindful Zombie struggles with. The (Pseudo)mindful Zombie *unconsciously* utilizes the development of *bare attention* to distance themselves even faster and more effectively from their feelings than before. They are unaware that by doing so, they deepen their internal isolation and increase their self-alienation (see Kaufmann et al., 2021). From the perspective of Buddha's teachings, this constitutes a "wrong understanding" (*micchādiṭṭhi* in Pali) of spiritual practice (cf. Fuller, 2012; Vörös, 2016). Genuine selflessness should not lead to dissociation or even depersonalization (cf. Deane et al., 2020).

The Mindful Zombie syndrome is a consequence of developmental trauma (see Chapter 2). An Abandoned, Inferior, or Inflated Self, coupled with attachment avoidance (see Chapter 15), leads the Mindful Zombie to approach their emotions as meaningless and unimportant phenomena that do not really concern them. The Mindful Zombie uses meditation-cultivated *bare attention* to maintain emotional distance. They categorically deny *needing* anything from others and expect the same in return. However, such an approach inevitably results in a disaster in close relationships. The Mindful Zombie typically regards people who visibly experience emotions and express their needs with concealed condescension. They (incorrectly) consider their perfected dissociation ability as a sign of emotional maturity or even spiritual progress.

We can break free from the Mindful Zombie syndrome by becoming mindful of our conceit and fear of genuine closeness (cf., e.g., Chefetz, 2015; Preece, 2009). Once we start to be mindful of what *truly* goes on within us when someone close expresses positive or negative emotions, sooner or later, we typically uncover feelings of core pain and, along with them, our unmet needs (see Fig. 9 on page 54). In this regard, our close relationships provide an excellent opportunity for mindfully studying maladaptive schemas (see Fig. 1 on page 25) and simultaneously serve as indicators of our personal development (see Kornfield, 1993, 2001; Masters, 2009, 2010, 2013; Welwood, 2002). They offer us an invaluable chance to learn compassion for ourselves and others, thus healing our Wounded Selves. It is simple. When we consciously open up to core pain, we cease to behave like Mindful Zombies. Only then can we cultivate the right mindfulness and begin to develop genuine close relationships with others. However, transpersonal development still conceals additional challenges.

SPIRITUAL NARCISSIST

Meditation courses, psychedelic ceremonies, and various esoteric (New Age) workshops attract our Wounded Selves like streetlights in the night draw in insects. The hope that "instant (weekend) spirituality" will quickly and painlessly rid us of our personal and relational issues seems to be a significant allure for our Wounded Selves. Thus, another typical dead-end in transpersonal development is the syndrome of Spiritual Narcissist (cf., e.g., Aixalà, 2022; Vonk & Visser, 2021; Walach, 2008). The danger of "inflating" our Wounded Selves when encountering transpersonal experiences was already emphasized by Carl Gustav Jung (see "ego inflation"—Jung, 2011, 2017). This syndrome has been vividly and thoroughly described by Tibetan meditation teacher Chögyam Trungpa (2002), who referred to it as "spiritual materialism." What does this involve?

As we know, the hidden feeling of inferiority can be compensated for by an Inflated Self with a false, idealized self-image (see Chapter 9). This self-image is based on the belief in one's exceptionalism and can rely on any presumed qualities. We may delude ourselves into thinking that we are superior to others due to our intelligence (as illustrated by Donald Trump in the introduction to Part III), physical attractiveness, wealth, power, or even our transpersonal experiences.[1]

> *Hannah was a prominent member of the spiritual community. She personally connected with indigenous shamans from Peru, Brazil, and Ecuador, having visited these countries multiple times. She participated in dozens of ceremonies involving ayahuasca, San Pedro cactus, and the secretion of the Kambô frog. She led self-development workshops and worked as a counselor and healer. Despite being surrounded by people, she had virtually no close relationships. Years ago, Hannah experienced*

a passionate relationship with a young Peruvian shaman. However, it turned out that he had relationships with many other "apprentices," leading Hannah to end things with him. Since then, she had no one, not even a close friend, to whom she could be herself, free from the "amazing healer Hannah" facade, and share her doubts and loneliness.

Everyone admired and considered Hannah a strong and independent woman. However, for Hannah herself, this social role became a prison. She knew what lay beneath her polished "spiritual" mask. However, she doubted anyone would accept her if they knew "who she really was." Deep down, everyone around her seemed a bit foolish to Hannah. Moreover, she viewed men as self-centered and inconsiderate. "What could a man next door offer me?" she often asked herself. So it was only when Hannah noticed her arrogance and fear of self-disclosure that she started connecting with her "Wounded Self." She had to admit that even dozens of psychedelic ceremonies had not healed her Wounded Self. It was a bitter pill and a significant disappointment. However, who can know if the negative core beliefs about herself and the world would ever be uncovered without undergoing all those rituals? Perhaps she needed to take this "spiritual detour" through the Amazon before being ready to confront her core pain. In any case, Hannah began to understand that her extraordinary transpersonal experiences did not entitle her to believe she was more valuable than anyone else. Only this awareness started to bring her closer to others.

According to the psychology of Abhidhamma, a person completely rids themselves of conceit or arrogance (*māna* in Pali) only at the fourth stage of awakening (*arahatta-magga-phala* in Pali; see Amaro, 2019; Ñāṇamoli & Bodhi, 2005; Sirimane, 2016). Humility is, therefore, a relatively reliable indicator of genuine spiritual progress (see also Benda, 2007; Underhill, 2019). Conversely, a sense of superiority signifies that we still have a considerable way to go to achieve the highest spiritual goal. Conceit is one of the defense mechanisms (see Table 1 on pages 52–53) that divert our attention from the feelings of core pain (see Figure 1 on page 25), indirectly revealing the activation of some maladaptive schema. While transpersonal experiences unveil our interconnectedness with others (see, e.g., Kałużna, 2022), conceit separates us from others.

In fact, it is a paradox that contemporary Western mindfulness courses are often presented to enthusiasts as a means of self-development or "self-improvement" because such a presentation can lead people with an Inferior Self to an ultimately "wrong understanding" of meditation practice (see Giraldi, 2019; Joiner, 2017; Purser, 2019). Like any other spiritual path, the path of developing mindfulness should not make us feel increasingly perfect. Developing mindfulness is a journey of self-discovery, self-acceptance, and ultimately selfless self-transcendence. It is a path of humility. Mindfulness gradually deconstructs every aspect of our self-image, whether that self-image is Inflated, Wounded, or any other. Transpersonal development should lead us to experience a sense of belonging with others and cultivate compassion for ourselves and others. If we use any spiritual path to elevate ourselves above others or to feel exceptional, we are in a dead-end. We should understand that the goal is not to prove our (spiritual or otherwise) superiority to ourselves or the world but to accept our limitations, imperfections, and vulnerabilities (Brown, 2015, 2017; Masters, 2009, 2010, 2013). This is how we can overcome spiritual narcissism.

ENLIGHTENED NERD

Just as developmental psychologists describe individual stages of personal development (see, e.g., Erikson, 1998; Piaget, 2015; cf. Siegel, 2020), transpersonal psychologists distinguish typical phases and stages of transpersonal development (see, e.g., Vaughan, 1986; Wilber, 2016). However, development in both dimensions does not always progress evenly, as illustrated in Figure 10 on page 140. Sometimes, our personal development is faster than transpersonal development, and in such cases, we experience an existential crisis and seek deeper meaning in our lives (cf., e.g., Frankl, 2020). At other times, however, we may, conversely, "outrun" personal development in transpersonal development. In such cases, we undergo a "crisis of duality" (see Firman & Vargiu, 1996) and become "Enlightened Nerds" (see Wilber, 2016).

When engaging in intensive meditation retreats, psychedelic ceremonies, or any other spiritual practice, it can easily happen that we have profound transpersonal experiences even though we have not fully developed our Authentic Self and/or healed the Wounded Self. Meditative or other transpersonal experiences *alone* cannot replace psychotherapy or corrective relational experiences (cf., e.g., Benda, 2012; Compson, 2018; De Silva, 1984). In spiritual circles, we can find many well-known personalities who, despite their undeniable transpersonal experiences, are still under the influence of their maladaptive schemas. For instance, Sogyal Rinpoche, the author of the famous *Tibetan book of living and dying*, sexually molested and physically and psychologically abused his female students. Chögyam Trungpa was openly promiscuous, engaging in sexual relationships with many of his female students, and died at the age of 47 due to severe alcoholism (see Gleig, 2019; Zweig, 2023). Many similar cases can be found among indigenous psychedelic shamans (see, e.g., Peluso, 2014). So, how can one avoid becoming an Enlightened Nerd?

If we want to avoid the syndrome of the Enlightened Nerd, we should first clarify the difference between personal and transpersonal development (see Engler, 1984, 2003). We should understand that the realization of absolute reality, which occurs in advanced meditation or during psychedelic experiences, does not *automatically* encompass an understanding of the conventional, conditioned reality of our everyday lives (see Chapter 20, cf. also Gyamtso, 2016; Michalon, 2001; Ryan & Rigby, 2015; Siderits & Katsura, 2013). In other words, we should not expect transpersonal experiences to solve all our personal and relational problems *automatically*. Personal development requires us, among other things, to (1) cultivate mindfulness in everyday life and learn not to perceive relational situations through the childish lens of the drama triangle (see Chapter 12), (2) take full responsibility for regulating our own experiences (see Chapter 13), (3) establish healthy personal boundaries (see Chapter 14), and (4) learn to accept feelings of core pain and overcome our attachment anxiety or avoidance (see Chapter 15). Only through the conscious acceptance of all these challenges in our personal development can we effectively leverage our transpersonal experiences and "live an awakened life." When we grasp the difference between absolute and conventional reality, we can skillfully and flexibly utilize our Authentic Narrative Self and insights into the ethical-psychological connections of our own experiences in everyday life (see Benda, 2019). We will delve further into all of this in Chapter 20.

EXERCISE 19

What does life want from me?

Spiritual bypassing arises from a misguided understanding of the ultimate goal of any spiritual practice. Therefore, before embarking on a spiritual journey, we should always know what we want to gain from spiritual practice. Do we want to enhance somehow or strengthen our Narrative Self? Then we are likely to be disappointed. Transpersonal development brings about something else: a fundamental Copernican shift in our perspective on the world, our life, and ourselves. It aims at the realization of something much more significant than ourselves. It helps us shed all egocentric goals and find meaning in voluntary submission to something beyond us (see service, humility, ethics). It is related to finding the purpose of our existence and answers the question of why we are here.

In psychotherapy, the search for and discovery of life's meaning is addressed, for example, by logotherapy. Viktor Emil Frankl (e.g., 2020, 2021) guided his clients toward a similar shift in perspective on their lives as spirituality aims for. In the following exercise, let us draw inspiration from logotherapy and familiarize ourselves with this transpersonal perspective. Find a quiet place to dedicate at least 20 minutes to yourself. Prepare paper and a pencil. Pose the question: What is it that I want most right now? Ask this question and try to refrain from inventing an answer actively. Passively wait for the response that naturally emerges in your mind. Write down the answer. Then, proceed similarly, asking: What do I want most in the next five years? What do I want in the next 20 years? What do I want in my life?

Then ask yourself: What do I actually need most right now? Once again, passively wait for the answer to emerge in your mind. Please write it down.

And finally, completely change the perspective, asking yourself gradually: What does my current life situation demand from me right now? What is my life asking of me now, whether I like it or not? Can I do something in my life right now that has real meaning (according to me)? What could it be? How will I feel when I take this step? And how will I feel if I don't take this step?

If you wish, take a moment to reflect on your life and ask: Which of my past life steps, goals, or decisions retrospectively seem most meaningful to me? Which relationships seem most meaningful to me? Which activities to which I dedicated myself in the past absorbed me so much that I forgot about time and everything else while doing them? What gave me strength and courage to move forward during difficult times in the past? And what meaningful opportunities do I have in my life now? What can I do to ensure that what I do makes sense?

Once you have your answers written down, take a short break. After a while, compare how you feel when you realize what you want. How do you feel when you recognize what you need? And how do you feel when you contemplate what life demands from you or what gives you the most tremendous sense of meaning? Do you now feel like changing something in your current life? What exactly? And what concrete steps can you take toward that?

NOTE

1 Spiritual narcissism is often associated with "spiritual gluttony" (*la gula espiritual* in Spanish) or the craving for more and more extraordinary spiritual experiences (see John of the Cross, 2003). The Spiritual Narcissist "consumes" these experiences without understanding what they should take away for their everyday life. Essentially, they live two parallel lives, and their real personal life remains somewhat separate from their "spiritual" life.

CHAPTER TWENTY

Master of the Two Worlds

The practice of intensive mindfulness and insight meditation, as well as psychedelic experiences, assists us in developing the ability to observe our inner experiences from a decentered perspective of the uninvolved observer (= Transcendent Self). Once we learn to actively employ this mindful and compassionate perspective in our everyday lives, it allows us, among other things, to recognize the "untruthfulness" or at least the "misleading inaccuracy" of our core beliefs and to *accept* the feelings of core pain, which constitute the emotional core of our maladaptive schemas.[1] It could be said that through the cultivation of mindfulness (i.e., the Observing, Transcendent Self), we significantly reduce self-referential processing or the influence of a rigid Wounded Self (see, e.g., Wheeler et al., 2017; cf., e.g., Britton et al., 2021; Lin et al., 2018). However, to navigate daily life, make decisions, solve problems, and take action, we must utilize our flexible Authentic Self wisely. In the ego state of the mindful Adult (see Chapter 11), we continually "switch" between the passive, uninvolved, or receptive mode of mindful observation and being (~Transcendent Self) and the active, engaged mode of thinking and doing (~Authentic Self, cf. Deikman, 1982; Hayes et al., 2016; Segal et al., 2013).[2] Metaphorically speaking, we become the "masters of the two worlds" (see Campbell, 2008)—our inner (intrapersonal) world and the outer (interpersonal) world. We also learn to distinguish between the absolute, non-dual reality experienced through meditation and/or psychedelic experiences and the conventional, conditioned reality of our everyday life (cf. Gyamtso, 2016; Siderits & Katsura, 2013; Struhl, 2020).

In everyday life, it is evident that we cannot always "be in the present moment." We also need to think, remember, and plan. Therefore, it is about finding a balance between the mode of doing and the mode of being and extracting the best from the mode of being and, if applicable, from transpersonal experiences for daily life. Meditation and psychedelic experiences teach us to accept the inherent impermanence of all lived phenomena. Simultaneously, they guide us to regard our body (sensory experiences), thoughts, feelings, and states of consciousness (mind) with understanding and compassion. They instruct us not to cling to anything (see, e.g., Whitehead et al., 2018) and to let everything flow. However, how does such an attitude manifest in everyday life?

Suppose we can perceive our emotions as transient phenomena thanks to the decentered perspective of the Transcendent Self. In that case, it certainly does not mean we will cease to express them in our relationships with others (see Chapter 16). A selfless perspective does not imply self-denial. Understanding mutual interdependence and social interconnectedness (see Chapter 17) serves as a counterbalance to exaggerated self-importance. It enables us to see ourselves as part of a greater whole and thus simultaneously have compassion for ourselves and others. Through the lens of the Transcendent Self, our orientation shifts from competition toward collaboration, fostering harmonious relationships with others and the environment (cf., e.g., Dambrun & Ricard, 2011; Mitra & Greenberg, 2016). We strive to address our own needs while understanding the needs of others. With understanding, we accept the fact that we are all sentient beings. After all, even Buddha (*Siddhattha Gotama*) did not instruct his disciples to ignore their needs. He advocated the middle way between two extremes—asceticism and hedonism (see, e.g., *Dhammacakkappavattana sutta*, SN, V, 56.11—Bodhi, 2005; cf. also, e.g., Epstein, 1990; Thompson, 2014). Similarly, through mindfulness, we can avoid two extremes about our feelings—on the one hand, merging (fusion) or excessive identification with our emotions, and on the other hand, dissociation or maintaining excessive distance from them (see Žvelc & Žvelc, 2021). The being mode (~Transcendent Self) allows us to be kind and compassionate witnesses to our experiences. The doing mode (~Authentic Self) enables us to communicate assertively, express our needs, and generally function in relationships with others (see Part III of this book).

Let us add that, similarly to how transpersonal experiences and altered states of consciousness help us cultivate a balanced and compassionate attitude toward our own emotions, they can also assist us in developing a similar attitude toward our body and all other phenomena with which we may sometimes overly identify (see *pañca-upādāna-kkhandha* in Pali, cf. Armstrong, 2017). However, even in the case of the body, the point is not to distance oneself from the body. Out-of-body experiences, which commonly occur during meditation and after the use of psychedelics (see, e.g., Lindahl & Britton, 2019; Millière, 2020), can reveal that our consciousness can exist without bodily awareness. Nevertheless, it becomes evident that meditative and psychedelic experiences can help individuals with eating disorders accept their bodies (see, e.g., Calder et al., 2023; Sala et al., 2020). In this regard, it is also about finding a middle way between two extremes.

However, let us stop again at the metaphor of two worlds. According to Joseph Campbell (2008), who thoroughly examined the plot patterns of numerous mythological stories, the archetypal hero, after exploring their inner world and undergoing personal transformation, must return to the (outer) world of everyday life with a "life-altering trophy" (also known as an elixir). One of the hero's final tasks is to mediate their newly acquired *wisdom* to others and contribute to the renewal of the human community. However, what is this "trophy," "elixir," or wisdom? Suppose you closely examine Table 1 on pages 52–53. In that case, you may mindfully notice that most defense mechanisms, which we gradually shed during the healing of the Wounded Self and the development of the Authentic and Transcendent Self, have an unethical character.[3] The cultivation of mindfulness allows us to see through the consequences of greed, hatred, delusion, or conceit, revealing that they lead to more and more unpleasant experiences, prompting us to naturally let go of them (see Goleman, 2004). Meditative insights guide us toward more ethical conduct (see, e.g., Berryman et al., 2023; Greenberg & Mitra, 2015; Sevinc & Lazar, 2019; Varela, 1999). We can consider ethical purity, selflessness, and compassion typical trophies (symptoms) of our self-transcendence. However, does something similar occur in the case of psychedelic experiences?

Existing research on psychedelics strongly suggests that psychedelic experiences often lead to a shift in our life values toward self-transcendent values, such as altruism, tolerance, humility, and the pursuit of the "greater good" (see, e.g., Kähönen, 2023; Letheby, 2021).[4] However, the more significant impact lies in the specific long-term *behavioral* changes of psychonauts concerning themselves (see, e.g., Calleja-Conde et al., 2022), others (e.g., Schmid & Liechti, 2018), or the environment (e.g., Forstmann & Sagioglou, 2017; Paterniti et al., 2022). And even in this respect, the effects of psychedelics look promising. As the Bible states, a tree is known "by its fruit" (Holy Bible, 2022, e.g., Mt 7:15–20), and phases of personal and transpersonal development are best recognized by how we *behave* toward those close to us (see Coder, 2017; Kornfield, 2001; Masters, 2010). When great mystics reached the final "unification" stage, typically according to Evelyn Underhill (2019), they led active and socially engaged lives. After achieving *full awakening* at age 35, the historical Buddha (*Siddhattha Gotama*) lived for another 45 years. He taught, managed a large community of monks, and adeptly handled many everyday situations he encountered (see Ñāṇamoli, 2021). Similar examples of immense vitality, resilience, and "frustration tolerance" can be found in the lives of figures like Paul of Tarsus, Francis of Assisi, Ignatius of Loyola, or Teresa of Ávila (see Underhill, 2019).

If reaching transpersonal experiences typically requires a temporary withdrawal from social life, the subsequent "awakened life" guides us back to people. In the book *Ten oxherding pictures*, Zen Buddhist monk Kuòān Shīyuǎn (see Loori, 2002) states: "Entering the marketplace barefoot and unadorned. Blissfully smiling, though covered with dust and ragged of clothes. Using no supernatural power, you bring the withered trees spontaneously into bloom." Using poetic language, he describes an individual who, though internally receptive (mode of being), is externally active (mode of doing). He employs acquired wisdom and compassion in action, thus being the "master of two worlds." Buddha (*Siddhattha Gotama*) likened his entire teaching to a raft meant to carry us to the "other shore," signifying complete awakening. However, he cautioned against clinging to the raft (theoretical teachings) once we reach the "other shore" (see *Alagaddūpama sutta*, MN, III, 22—Ñāṇamoli & Bodhi, 2005). After attaining full awakening, we can actively live in the world and engage in relationships with others, flexibly utilizing the wisdom, humility, ethical purity, and compassion we have gained in our conscious actions. Yet, we need not cling to any theoretical concepts in the process. In fact, the lived experience of full awakening (mode of being) becomes our best support for decision-making and action (mode of doing). If, during our transpersonal development, we did not shy away from the challenges of personal growth (see Part III of this book and Chapter 19), we can utilize the developed Transcendent Self internally and manifest the Authentic Self externally. The Wounded Self remains in the past. However, we should not forget that the experience of healing the Wounded Self has equipped us with much-needed compassion for ourselves and others—a crucial part of the journey (see Epstein, 2014).

EXERCISE 20
Integrity of values

Self-discovery and developing an Authentic and Transcendent Self are closely linked to clarifying our most important life values. When maladaptive schemas cease to control us, we can gradually act more freely and make decisions in harmony with values that we truly believe in and make sense to us. Let's take a moment in the final exercise of this book to recall which values are currently at the top of our hierarchy. Clear awareness of cherished values can be a compass on our life journey.

Take a piece of paper and a pencil, and write down five to ten general values that are most important to you in life. Take time to reflect, noticing which values genuinely resonate with you and evoke a response in your bodily experience. If some values that come to mind don't elicit any physical reaction, put them in parentheses. You can draw inspiration from the following list: abundance, adventure, ambition, appreciation, comfort, consideration, consistency, creativity, credibility, compassion, cooperation, decency, diligence, enthusiasm, ethics, environment, faith, family, flexibility, freedom, friendship, generosity, genuineness, gratitude, harmony, health, honesty, humor, independence, integrity, joy, justice, love, loyalty, originality, openness, passion, peace, preparedness, professionalism, prosperity, reliability, respect, responsibility, safety, self-discipline, self-realization, service, simplicity, solidarity, stability, success, support, tolerance, trust, truthfulness, usefulness, versatility, and wisdom.

Once you have created your list, arrange the most essential values in order of importance. For the top five values, reflect on how these values manifest in your daily actions. How can others recognize that you live your life guided by these values? Make a note of at least one example for each value. If you find it challenging to identify specific examples of a particular value, consider how to ensure this value is more evident in your daily behavior. Are you inclined to make any changes in this regard? Make a concrete decision in this direction or reconsider your value hierarchy to better align with your current life situation. Values can evolve throughout life.

Last, share your value hierarchy with someone close, preferably your partner. Request their input. Does your partner feel that your daily life aligns with your values? Do they have any recommendations for you? Try to listen to the feedback humbly without defending yourself. Instead, reflect on what you've heard. What comes to mind now as you contemplate your values and your life?

NOTES

1 We have highlighted the potentially significant impact of corrective emotional (relational) experiences on the *reconsolidation* of maladaptive schemas within meditation training and psychedelic therapy in Chapters 16, 17, 18, and 19. In brief, learning to have compassion with oneself at the moment of maladaptive schema activation is challenging and typically achievable only after experiencing a corrective emotional event *in a relationship* with a meditation teacher, psychedelic guide, or community members. Suppose we aim to use transpersonal experiences for healing the Wounded Self. In that case, we should share them *in a relationship* with a competent and compassionate guide or integrate transpersonal experiences with psychotherapy.

2 Mindfulness in our everyday lives "switches" us from the conceptual, narrative, virtual reality of our thoughts and imaginings to the phenomenological (and possibly ontological) reality. Thinking or imagining then naturally "switches" us back again.

3 From the perspective of Abhidhamma, defense mechanisms (*kilesa* in Pali) stem from the so-called three unwholesome roots (*akusala-mūla* in Pali) of our motivation, namely greed, hatred, and delusion (see, e.g., Benda & Horák, 2008; Nyanaponika, 2009).

4 The resulting change in life values and priorities among psychonauts is likely influenced not only by the psychedelic experience itself but also by the inner disposition (set) and external context (setting) in which the psychedelic experience takes place (see Kähönen, 2023).

Conclusion

The history of psychotherapy has traditionally been associated with significant rivalry and a long-standing "cold war" between psychodynamic, cognitive-behavioral, and existential-humanistic approaches (Norcross & Goldfried, 2019). As recently as the 1950s and 1960s, these approaches offered entirely different and hardly reconcilable theories of the origin of mental disorders and their treatment. This, of course, did not contribute to the credibility of psychotherapy as a scientific discipline. However, the development did not stop, and in recent decades, there has been a real hyperinflation of new "brand-name" approaches (Prochaska & Norcross, 2018). Today, alongside each other, there are already hundreds of psychotherapeutic orientations and hundreds of alternative psychotherapeutic theories.[1] There are so many that no expert can know them all.[2] However, do they still have such incompatible ideas about the origin and treatment of mental disorders? I believe not. Although different approaches use different languages, in reality, individual psychotherapeutic theories are becoming more and more similar. Most (up to 99%) therapists today use procedures and techniques from various schools (see Rihacek & Roubal, 2017). Therefore, it seems that the time has come to seek a common consensus and attempt to create a universal, unified theory, explaining the etiology of mental disorders and the mechanisms of psychotherapeutic change (see, e.g., Gaines & Goldfried, 2021; Greenberg, 2021; Magnavita & Anchin, 2014; Marquis et al., 2021; Melchert, 2016).

The *Transdiagnostic Theory of the Wounded Self*, introduced in this book, aligns (similarly to various other theories) the onset of mental disorders with unmet basic developmental needs in childhood (cf., e.g., Williams, 2022a, 2022b). It elucidates the role of narrative identity and maladaptive schemas in shaping a broad spectrum of external symptoms of mental disorders (see Chapter 4) and emphasizing the significance of mindfulness and compassion (cf. Dunn et al., 2013; Goldberg, 2022; Greeson et al., 2014; Harrer & Weiss, 2016) along with corrective relational experiences in psychotherapeutic change (cf. Castonguay & Hill, 2012; Ecker & Bridges, 2020; Ecker & Vaz, 2022; Stevens, 2021). The original *phenomenological model of maladaptive schemas* presented in this book (see Figure 1 on page 25) integrates insights from psychodynamic, cognitive-behavioral, and neo-humanistic approaches, contributing to mutual understanding between therapeutic schools. This *phenomenological model of maladaptive schemas* reveals that behind the external symptoms of most mental disorders, remarkably similar maladaptive cognitive and affective *processes* can be recognized. As a result, it could contribute to a paradigm shift in diagnosing mental disorders (cf., e.g., Johnstone et al., 2018; Kotov et al., 2017).

Mindfulness research has shown that a mindful, phenomenological perspective on mental disorders allows for understanding psychopathological *processes* occurring in our brain at the biological level (see, e.g., Giommi et al., 2023; Guendelman et al., 2017; Vago & Silbersweig, 2012; Wielgosz et al., 2019; cf. Koban et al., 2021). The mindful perspective helps uncover intersections between the findings of neurophenomenology, affective neuroscience, interpersonal neurobiology, and psychotherapy, offering hope that biomarkers of mental disorders may finally be revealed (see, e.g., Faustino, 2022; Simon & Engström, 2015). Will the distinction between the Wounded, Authentic, and Transcendent Self help uncover these biomarkers? The *Transdiagnostic Theory of the Wounded Self* highlights the change in self-referential processing as one of the crucial mechanisms through which the development of mindfulness leads to mental health (cf., e.g., Britton et al., 2021; Lin et al., 2018; Wheeler et al., 2017). I hope this theory contributes to deepening the understanding between therapists and neuroscientists and, perhaps, helps streamline the practices and techniques of various therapeutic schools.

When William James heard a lecture on the Buddhist conception of the mind by Anagarika Dharmapala at Harvard in 1904, he reportedly stood up and declared to the entire audience, "Take my place. You are more competent to lecture on psychology than I am. This is the psychology everybody will be studying in twenty-five years from now" (cited, e.g., in Thompson, 2008). In terms of timing, James was mistaken. However, the current wave of psychologists' interest in incorporating mindfulness development into psychotherapy leads to an increased interest in Buddhist psychology per se. Moreover, it turns out that Abhidhamma certainly has much to offer us (see, e.g., Feldman & Kuyken, 2019; Germer & Siegel, 2012; Goodman, 2020; Harris, 2019a; Nairn et al., 2019; Shonin et al., 2015). Abhidhamma psychology is, to a significant extent, a psychology of the transpersonal. It meticulously describes altered states of consciousness, making it intriguing not only for the study of long-term meditators (see, e.g., Luders & Kurth, 2019), research on the nature of human consciousness (e.g., Winter et al., 2020), but also for research on the effects of psychedelics (see, e.g., Letheby, 2022; Millière et al., 2018; Scheidegger, 2021).

While Western psychology has long focused on treating mental disorders and developing human potential regarding personal growth, Abhidhamma primarily describes the possibilities of our transpersonal development (see Figure 10 on page 140). It can be assumed that, in the context of the therapeutic use of psychedelics, Western psychology will now be exploring transpersonal development. However, this book emphasizes that transpersonal development cannot replace personal development (see Engler, 1984, 2003; Firman & Vargiu, 1977, 1996), and meditation or psychedelics cannot replace *relational* experiences. Therefore, the differentiation of the Wounded, Authentic, and Transcendent Self may help us understand how to appropriately combine meditation, psychedelic experiences, and traditional psychotherapeutic approaches so that our transpersonal development can stimulate and complement our personal development. Egocentrism and individualism have brought us to the brink of a planetary crisis. Moreover, it seems that the entire West urgently needs to change its "culture of consciousness" to survive as a human race (see Metzinger, 2023). Let us use meditation and psychedelic experiences to become aware of our interconnectedness with others and the environment, fostering a selfless perspective on ourselves, others, and the world. When we heal our Wounded Selves, we can confidently embark not only on the path to self-realization but also on the path of self-transcendence.

NOTES

1 Vybíral et al. (2010) published a list of 227 recognized psychotherapeutic approaches. However, some sources suggest that there are now over 500 different approaches in psychotherapy (Pearsall, 2009; cf. Prochaska & Norcross, 2018).
2 Fifty-six experts recently released a joint estimate of the expected developments in psychotherapy over the next decade. The anticipation includes further growth and expansion of modern mindfulness-based therapies, including Acceptance and Commitment Therapy (ACT) and Dialectical Behavior Therapy (DBT). Emotion-Focused Therapy (EFT) and integrative psychotherapy are also highlighted in the top ten psychotherapeutic approaches. According to these experts, interest among professionals in traditional psychodynamic approaches (psychoanalysis, transactional analysis, Jungian therapy) and existential-humanistic approaches (gestalt therapy, person-centered approach) is expected to decline in the coming years (Norcross et al., 2022).

Recommended Reading

Baylin, J., & Winnette, P. (2016). *Working with traumatic memories to heal adults with unresolved childhood trauma: Neuroscience, attachment theory and Pesso Boyden System Psychomotor psychotherapy.* Jessica Kingsley Publishers.

Brown, D. P., & Elliott, D. S. (2016). *Attachment disturbances in adults: Treatment for comprehensive repair.* W. W. Norton & Company.

Castonguay, L. G., & Hill, C. E. (Eds.). (2017). *How and why are some therapists better than others? Understanding therapist effects.* American Psychological Association.

Germer, C. K., & Siegel, R. D. (Eds.). (2012). *Wisdom and compassion in psychotherapy: Deepening mindfulness in clinical practice.* Guilford Press.

Greenberg, L. (2021). *Changing emotion with emotion: A practitioner's guide.* American Psychological Association.

Johnson, S. M. (2019). *Attachment theory in practice: Emotionally focused therapy (EFT) with individuals, couples, and families.* Guilford Press.

Letheby, C. (2021). *Philosophy of psychedelics.* Oxford University Press.

Salvador, M. C. (2019). *Beyond the self: Healing emotional trauma and brainspotting.* Editorial Eleftheria.

Siegel, D. J. (2020). *The developing mind: How relationships and the brain interact to shape who we are* (3rd ed.). Guilford Press.

Stevens, F. L. (2021). *Affective neuroscience in psychotherapy: A clinician's guide for working with emotions.* Routledge.

Timuľák, L., & Keogh, D. (2021). *Transdiagnostic emotion-focused therapy: A clinical guide for transforming emotional pain.* American Psychological Association.

Treleaven, D. A. (2018). *Trauma-sensitive mindfulness: Practices for safe and transformative healing.* W. W. Norton & Company.

van der Wijngaart, R. (2021). *Imagery rescripting: Theory and practice.* Pavilion Publishing & Media.

Žvelc, G., & Žvelc, M. (2021). *Integrative psychotherapy: A mindfulness-and compassion-oriented approach.* Routledge.

References

Aafjes-van Doorn, K., Kamsteeg, C., & Silberschatz, G. (2020). Cognitive mediators of the relationship between adverse childhood experiences and adult psychopathology: A systematic review. *Development and Psychopathology, 32*(3), 1017–1029. https://doi.org/10.1017/S0954579419001317

Aafjes-van Doorn, K., McCollum, J., Silberschatz, G., Kealy, D., & Snyder, J. (2021). Perceived adverse parenting in childhood and psychological distress among psychotherapy patients: The mediating role of pathogenic beliefs. *Journal of Nervous and Mental Disease, 209*(3), 181–187. https://doi.org/10.1097/NMD.0000000000001274

Aardema, F., Radomsky, A. S., Moulding, R., Wong, S. F., Bourguignon, L., & Giraldo-O'Meara, M. (2021). Development and validation of the multidimensional version of the fear of self questionnaire: Corrupted, culpable and malformed feared possible selves in obsessive-compulsive and body-dysmorphic symptoms. *Clinical Psychology & Psychotherapy, 28*(5), 1160–1180. https://doi.org/10.1002/cpp.2565

Abramowitz, E. G., & Torem, M. S. (2018). The roots and evolution of ego-state theory and therapy. *International Journal of Clinical and Experimental Hypnosis, 66*(4), 353–370. https://doi.org/10.1080/00207144.2018.1494435

Aday, J. S., Davis, A. K., Mitzkovitz, C. M., Bloesch, E. K., & Davoli, C. C. (2021). Predicting reactions to psychedelic drugs: A systematic review of states and traits related to acute drug effects. *ACS Pharmacology & Translational Science, 4*(2), 424–435. https://doi.org/10.1021/acsptsci.1c00014

Aderka, I. M., & Shalom, J. G. (2021). A revised theory of sudden gains in psychological treatments. *Behaviour Research and Therapy, 139*, Article 103830. https://doi.org/10.1016/j.brat.2021.103830

Adler, A. (1964). *Individual psychology of Alfred Adler: A systematic presentation inselection from his writings*. Harper & Row.

REFERENCES

Adler, J. M., & Clark, L. A. (2019). Incorporating narrative identity into structural approaches to personality and psychopathology. *Journal of Research in Personality*, *82*, Article 103857. https://doi.org/10.1016/j.jrp.2019.103857

Agorastos, A., Pervanidou, P., Chrousos, G. P., & Baker, D. G. (2019). Developmental trajectories of early life stress and trauma: A narrative review on neurobiological aspects beyond stress system dysregulation. *Frontiers in Psychiatry*, *10*, Article 118. https://doi.org/10.3389/fpsyt.2019.00118

Ahern, C., & Kyrios, M. (2016). Self processes in obsessive-compulsive disorder. In M. Kyrios, R. Moulding, G. Doron, S. S. Bhar, M. Nedeljkovic, & M. Mikulincer (Eds.), *The self in understanding and treating psychological disorders*. Cambridge University Press. https://doi.org/10.1017/CBO9781139941297.013

Aixalà, M. (2022). *Psychedelic integration: Psychotherapy for non-ordinary states of consciousness*. Synergetic Press.

Akyunus, M., & Gençöz, T. (2020). The distinctive associations of interpersonal problems with personality beliefs within the framework of cognitive theory of personality disorders. *Journal of Rational-Emotive & Cognitive-Behavior Therapy*, *38*(1), 26–43. https://doi.org/10.1007/s10942-019-00322-6

Allione, T. (2009). *Feeding your demons: Ancient wisdom for resolving inner conflict*. Hay House UK.

Alper, S. A. (2016). *Mindfulness meditation in psychotherapy: An integrated model for clinicians*. New Harbinger Publications.

Amada, N., Lea, T., Letheby, C., & Shane, J. (2020). Psychedelic experience and the narrative self: An exploratory qualitative study. *Journal of Consciousness Studies*, *27*(9–10), 6–33.

Amada, N., & Shane, J. (2022). Self-actualization and the integration of psychedelic experience: The mediating role of perceived benefits to narrative self-functioning. *Journal of Humanistic Psychology*, Article 00221678221099680. https://doi.org/10.1177/00221678221099680

Amaro, A. (2019). Unshakeable well-being: Is the Buddhist concept of enlightenment a meaningful possibility in the current age. *Mindfulness*, *10*(9), 1952–1956. https://doi.org/10.1007/s12671-019-01179-7

American Psychiatric Association. (2013). *Diagnostic and statistical manual of mental disorders (DSM-5®)*. American Psychiatric Publishing. https://doi.org/10.1176/appi.books.9780890425596

Anālayo, B. (2020). Clear knowing and mindfulness. *Mindfulness*, *11*(4), 862–871. https://doi.org/10.1007/s12671-019-01283-8

Anālayo, B. (2019a). Adding historical depth to definitions of mindfulness. *Current Opinion in Psychology*, *28*, 11–14. https://doi.org/10.1016/j.copsyc.2018.09.013

Anālayo, B. (2019b). The insight knowledge of fear and adverse effects of mindfulness practices. *Mindfulness*, *10*(10), 2172–2185. https://doi.org/10.1007/s12671-019-01198-4

REFERENCES

Araujo, H. F., Kaplan, J., Damasio, H., & Damasio, A. (2015). Neural correlates of different self domains. *Brain and Behavior*, 5(12), Article e00409. https://doi.org/10.1002/brb3.409

Armstrong, G. (2017). *Emptiness: A practical guide for meditators*. Wisdom Publications.

Arntz, A., Rijkeboer, M., Chan, E., Fassbinder, E., Karaosmanoglu, A., Lee, C. W., & Panzeri, M. (2021). Towards a reformulated theory underlying schema therapy: Position paper of an international workgroup. *Cognitive Therapy and Research*, 45(6), 1007–1020. https://doi.org/10.1007/s10608-021-10209-5

Aron, E. N. (2020). *The highly sensitive person: How to thrive when the world overwhelms you*. Citadel Press.

Asper, K. (2018). *Verlassenheit und Selbstentfremdung: Zugänge zum therapeutischen Verständnis von Narzissmus*. Patmos.

Assagioli, R. (1993). *Psychosynthesis: A manual of principles and techniques*. HarperCollins Publishers.

Assagioli, R. (2007). *Transpersonal development: The dimension beyond psychosynthesis*. Smiling Wisdom.

Ataria, Y., Dor-Ziderman, Y., & Berkovich-Ohana, A. (2015). How does it feel to lack a sense of boundaries? A case study of a long-term mindfulness meditator. *Consciousness and Cognition*, 37, 133–147. https://doi.org/10.1016/j.concog.2015.09.002

Atzil, S., Gao, W., Fradkin, I., & Barrett, L. F. (2018). Growing a social brain. *Nature Human Behaviour*, 2(9), 624–636. https://doi.org/10.1038/s41562-018-0384-6

Bach, B., & Farrell, J. M. (2018). Schemas and modes in borderline personality disorder: The mistrustful, shameful, angry, impulsive, and unhappy child. *Psychiatry Research*, 259, 323–329. https://doi.org/10.1016/j.psychres.2017.10.039

Bach, B., Lockwood, G., & Young, J. E. (2018). A new look at the schema therapy model: Organization and role of early maladaptive schemas. *Cognitive Behaviour Therapy*, 47(4), 328–349. https://doi.org/10.1080/16506073.2017.1410566

Baminiwatta, A., & Solangaarachchi, I. (2021). Trends and developments in mindfulness research over 55 years: A bibliometric analysis of publications indexed in Web of Science. *Mindfulness*, 12(9), 2099–2116. https://doi.org/10.1007/s12671-021-01681-x

Bardone-Cone, A. M., Thompson, K. A., & Miller, A. J. (2020). The self and eating disorders. *Journal of Personality*, 88(1), 59–75. https://doi.org/10.1111/jopy.12448

Barendregt, H. (2006). The Abhidhamma model of consciousness AM0 and some of its consequences. In E. M. Kwee, K. J. Gergen, & F. Koshikawa (Eds.), *Horizons in Buddhist psychology: Practice, research & theory*. Taos Institute Publishing.

Barendregt, H. (2011). Mindfulness meditation: Deconditioning and changing view. In H. Walach, S. Schmidt, & W. B. Jonas (Eds.), *Neuroscience, consciousness and spirituality*. Springer. https://doi.org/10.1007/978-94-007-2079-4_12

Barrett, F. S., & Griffiths, R. R. (2018). Classic hallucinogens and mystical experiences: Phenomenology and neural correlates. In A. L. Halberstadt, F. X. Vollenweider, & D. E. Nichols (Eds.), *Behavioral neurobiology of psychedelic drugs*. Springer. https://doi.org/10.1007/7854_2017_474

Bartholomew, K. (1990). Avoidance of intimacy: An attachment perspective. *Journal of Social and Personal Relationships, 7*(2), 147–178. https://doi.org/10.1177/0265407590072001

Bartholomew, K., & Horowitz, L. M. (1991). Attachment styles among young adults: A test of a four-category model. *Journal of Personality and Social Psychology, 61*(2), 226–244. https://doi.org/10.1037/0022-3514.61.2.226

Barua, D. (2018). *The notion of fetter in early Buddhism*. Aditya Prakashan.

Basten, C., & Touyz, S. (2016). The self in eating disorders. In M. Kyrios, R. Moulding, G. Doron, S. S. Bhar, M. Nedeljkovic, & M. Mikulincer (Eds.), *The self in understanding and treating psychological disorders*. Cambridge University Press. https://doi.org/10.1017/CBO9781139941297.021

Bathje, G. J., Majeski, E., & Kudowor, M. (2022). Psychedelic integration: An analysis of the concept and its practice. *Frontiers in Psychology, 13*, Article 824077. https://doi.org/10.3389/fpsyg.2022.824077

Baumrind, D. (1971). Current patterns of parental authority. *Developmental Psychology, 4*(1, Pt.2), 1–103. https://doi.org/10.1037/h0030372

Baylin, J., & Winnette, P. (2016). *Working with traumatic memories to heal adults with unresolved childhood trauma: Neuroscience, attachment theory and Pesso Boyden System Psychomotor Psychotherapy*. Jessica Kingsley Publishers.

Beck, A. T. (2015). Theory of personality disorders. In A. T. Beck, D. D. Davis, & A. Freeman (Eds.), *Cognitive therapy of personality disorders*. Guilford Press.

Beck, J. S. (2021). *Cognitive behavior therapy: Basics and beyond*. Guilford Press.

Beck, A. T., & Haigh, E. A. (2014). Advances in cognitive theory and therapy: The generic cognitive model. *Annual Review of Clinical Psychology, 10*(1), 1–24. https://doi.org/10.1146/annurev-clinpsy-032813-153734

Beck, A. T., Wright, F. D., Newman, C. F., & Liese, B. S. (2001). *Cognitive therapy of substance abuse*. Guilford Press.

Benda, J. (2007). *Mystika a schizofrenie: Mystické zážitky jako předmět klinického zájmu*. Jan Benda.

Benda, J. (2019). *Všímavost a soucit se sebou: Proměna emocí v psychoterapii*. Portál.

Benda, J. (2011). Přínos meditace pro psychoterapeuty: Rozvíjení terapeutových kvalit pozitivně ovlivňujících výsledek psychoterapie. *Psychoterapie, 5*(1), 14–25. https://www.jan-benda.com/downloads/benda2011.pdf

Benda, J. (2012). Buddhismus a psychoterapie: Meditace není všelék. *Dingir, 15*(1), 12–15. https://www.jan-benda.com/downloads/benda2012.pdf

Benda, J. (2020a). *Soucit se sebou a jeho role v regulaci emocí, udržování duševního zdraví a osobní pohody: Disertační práce*. Univerzita Karlova.

Benda, J. (2020b). Škála nepřipoutanosti k Já (NTS-CZ): Pilotní studie české verze. *E-psychologie, 14*(4), 57–67. https://doi.org/10.29364/epsy.385

REFERENCES

Benda, J., & Horák, M. (2008). Moudrost abhidhammy v psychoterapii: Hojivé balzámy pro duši. *Psychoterapie*, 2(2), 85–93. https://www.jan-benda.com/downloads/benda_horak2008.pdf

Bender, D., & Hellerstein, D. J. (2022). Assessing the risk-benefit profile of classical psychedelics: A clinical review of second-wave psychedelic research. *Psychopharmacology*, 239(6), 1907–1932. https://doi.org/10.1007/s00213-021-06049-6

Benjet, C., Bromet, E., Karam, E. G., Kessler, R. C., McLaughlin, K. A., Ruscio, A. M., Shahly, V., Stein, D. J., Petukhova, M., Hill, E., Alonso, J., Atwoli, L., Bunting, B., Bruffaerts, R., Caldas-de-Almeida, J. M., de Girolamo, G., Florescu, S., Gureje, O., Y. Huang... & Koenen, K. C. (2016). The epidemiology of traumatic event exposure worldwide: Results from the World Mental Health Survey Consortium. *Psychological Medicine*, 46(2), 327–343. https://doi.org/10.1017/S0033291715001981

Berne, E. (1957). Ego states in psychotherapy. *American Journal of Psychotherapy*, 11(2), 293–309. https://doi.org/10.1080/1046171X.1989.12034356

Berne, E. (2021). *Transactional analysis in psychotherapy: A systematic individual and social psychiatry*. Mockingbird Press.

Berne, E. (2022). *Games people play*. Efinito.

Bernstein, A., Hadash, Y., Lichtash, Y., Tanay, G., Shepherd, K., & Fresco, D. M. (2015). Decentering and related constructs: A critical review and metacognitive processes model. *Perspectives on Psychological Science*, 10(5), 599–617. https://doi.org/10.1177/1745691615594577

Berryman, K., Lazar, S. W., & Hohwy, J. (2023). Do contemplative practices make us more moral? *Trends in Cognitive Sciences*, 27(10), 916–931. https://doi.org/10.1016/j.tics.2023.07.005

Besharat, M. A., & Khajavi, Z. (2013). The relationship between attachment styles and alexithymia: Mediating role of defense mechanisms. *Asian Journal of Psychiatry*, 6(6), 571–576. https://doi.org/10.1016/j.ajp.2013.09.003

Bodhi, B. (2005). *The connected discourses of the Buddha: A new translation of the Samyutta Nikaya*. Wisdom Publications.

Bodhi, B. (2007). *A comprehensive manual of Abhidhamma*. Buddhist Publication Society.

Bodhi, B. (2009). *Going for refuge & taking the precepts*. Buddhist Publication Society.

Bodhi, B. (2021). Abhidhamma dissects the mind. *Buddhadharma: The Practitioner's Quarterly*, 19(2), 14–27.

Bodhi, B. (2011). What does mindfulness really mean? *Contemporary Buddhism*, 12(1), 19–39. https://doi.org/10.1080/14639947.2011.564813

Borsboom, D., & Cramer, A. O. J. (2013). Network analysis: An integrative approach to the structure of psychopathology. *Annual Review of Clinical Psychology*, 9, 91–121. https://doi.org/10.1146/annurev-clinpsy-050212-185608

Borsboom, D., Cramer, A. O. J., & Kalis, A. (2019). Brain disorders? Not really: Why network structures block reductionism in psychopathology research. *Behavioral and Brain Sciences*, 42, Article e2. https://doi.org/10.1017/s0140525x17002266

REFERENCES

Bouso, J. C., dos Santos, R. G., Alcázar-Córcoles, M. Á., & Hallak, J. E. C. (2018). Serotonergic psychedelics and personality: A systematic review of contemporary research. *Neuroscience and Biobehavioral Reviews, 87*, 118–132. https://doi.org/10.1016/j.neubiorev.2018.02.004

Bowlby, J. (1976). *Separation: Anxiety and anger*. Basic Books.

Bowlby, J. (1982). *Loss: Sadness and depression*. Basic Books.

Bowlby, J. (1983). *Attachment: Attachment and loss* (2nd ed.). Basic Books.

Brach, T. (2004). *Radical acceptance: Embracing your life with the heart of a Buddha*. Bantam.

Bradford, K. (2021). Non-self psychology: The Buddhist phenomenology of self experience. *Existential Analysis: Journal of the Society for Existential Analysis, 32*(1), 101–112.

Brainstorm Consortium (2018). Analysis of shared heritability in common disorders of the brain. *Science, 360*(6395), Article eaap8757. https://doi.org/10.1126/science.aap8757

Brandmeyer, T., & Delorme, A. (2021). Meditation and the wandering mind: A theoretical framework of underlying neurocognitive mechanisms. *Perspectives on Psychological Science, 16*(1), 39–66. https://doi.org/10.1177/1745691620917340

Brasher, T., Rosen, D., & Spinella, M. (2023). Psychedelics and psychological strengths. *International Journal of Wellbeing, 13*(1), 1–35. https://doi.org/10.5502/ijw.v13i1.2325

Bretherton, I., & Munholland, K. A. (2016). Internal working model construct in light of contemporary neuroimaging research. In J. Cassidy & P. R. Shaver (Eds.), *Handbook of attachment: Theory, research, and clinical applications*. Guilford Press.

Brewer, J. (2017). *The craving mind: From cigarettes to smartphones to love? Why we get hooked and how we can break bad habits*. Yale University Press.

Britton, W. B., Desbordes, G., Acabchuk, R., Peters, S., Lindahl, J. R., Canby, N. K., Vago, D. R., Dumais, T., Lipsky, J., Kimmel, H., Sager, L., Rahrig, H., Cheaito, A., Acero, P., Scharf, J., Lazar, S. W., Schuman-Olivier, Z. Ferrer, R. & Moitra, E. (2021). From self-esteem to selflessness: An evidence (gap) map of self-related processes as mechanisms of mindfulness-based interventions. *Frontiers in Psychology, 12*, Article 730972. https://doi.org/10.3389/fpsyg.2021.730972

Brown, B. (2015). *Daring greatly: How the courage to be vulnerable transforms the way we live, love, parent, and lead*. Avery.

Brown, B. (2017). *Rising strong: How the ability to reset transforms the way we live, love, parent, and lead*. Random House.

Brown, B. (2021). *Atlas of the heart: Mapping meaningful connection and the language of human experience*. Random House.

Brown, D. P., & Elliott, D. S. (2016). *Attachment disturbances in adults: Treatment for comprehensive repair*. W. W. Norton & Company.

Brown, D. P., & Engler, J. (1980). The stages of mindfulness meditation: A validation study. *Journal of Transpersonal Psychology, 12*(2), 143–192. https://www.atpweb.org/jtparchive/trps-12-80-02-143.pdf

Brown, K. W., & Leary, M. R. (2017a). The emergence of scholarship and science on hypo-egoic phenomena. In K. W. Brown & M. R. Leary (Eds.), *The Oxford handbook of hypo-egoic phenomena*. Oxford University Press. https://doi.org/10.1093/oxfordhb/9780199328079.013.1

Brown, K. W., & Leary, M. R. (2017b). *The Oxford handbook of hypo-egoic phenomena*. Oxford University Press. https://doi.org/10.1093/oxfordhb/9780199328079.001.0001

Brummelman, E., & Sedikides, C. (2020). Raising children with high self-esteem (but not narcissism). *Child Development Perspectives, 14*(2), 83–89. https://doi.org/10.1111/cdep.12362

Brunoni, A. R. (2017). Beyond the DSM: Trends in psychiatry diagnoses. *Archives of Clinical Psychiatry (São Paulo), 44*, 154–158. https://doi.org/10.1590/0101-60830000000142

Buddhaghosa (2020). *The path of purification: Visuddhimagga*. Buddhist Publication Society.

Bulteau, S., Malo, R., Holland, Z., Laurin, A., & Sauvaget, A. (2023). The update of self-identity: Importance of assessing autobiographical memory in major depressive disorder. *Cognitive Science*, Article e1644. https://doi.org/10.1002/wcs.1644

Burbea, R. (2014). *Seeing that frees: Meditations on emptiness and dependent arising*. Troubador Publishing.

Bush, M. (2005). The role of unconscious guilt in psychopathology and in psychotherapy. In G. Silberschatz (Ed.), *Transformative relationships: The control-mastery theory of psychotherapy*. Routledge. https://doi.org/10.4324/9780203955963

Calder, A., Mock, S., Friedli, N., Pasi, P., & Hasler, G. (2023). Psychedelics in the treatment of eating disorders: Rationale and potential mechanisms. *European Neuropsychopharmacology, 75*, 1–14. https://doi.org/10.1016/j.euroneuro.2023.05.008

Caldwell, J. G., & Shaver, P. R. (2012). Exploring the cognitive-emotional pathways between adult attachment and ego-resiliency. *Individual Differences Research, 10*(3), 141–152.

Callaghan, B. L., & Tottenham, N. (2016). The neuro-environmental loop of plasticity: A cross-species analysis of parental effects on emotion circuitry development following typical and adverse caregiving. *Neuropsychopharmacology, 41*(1), 163–176. https://doi.org/10.1038/npp.2015.204

Calleja-Conde, J., Morales-García, J. A., Echeverry-Alzate, V., Bühler, K. M., Giné, E., & López-Moreno, J. A. (2022). Classic psychedelics and alcohol use disorders: A systematic review of human and animal studies. *Addiction Biology, 27*(6), Article e13229. https://doi.org/10.1111/adb.13229

Calvete, E., Orue, I., & Hankin, B. L. (2013). Early maladaptive schemas and social anxiety in adolescents: The mediating role of anxious automatic thoughts. *Journal of Anxiety Disorders, 27*(3), 278–288. https://doi.org/10.1016/j.janxdis.2013.02.011

Campbell, J. (2008). *The hero with a thousand faces*. New World Library.

Caplan, M. (2015). *Halfway up the mountain: The error of premature claims to enlightment*. Hohm Press.

REFERENCES

Carhart-Harris, R. L., & Friston, K. J. (2019). REBUS and the anarchic brain: Toward a unified model of the brain action of psychedelics. *Pharmacological Reviews*, 71(3), 316–344. https://doi.org/10.1124/pr.118.017160

Carhart-Harris, R. L., Roseman, L., Haijen, E., Erritzoe, D., Watts, R., Branchi, I., & Kaelen, M. (2018). Psychedelics and the essential importance of context. *Journal of Psychopharmacology*, 32(7), 725–731. https://doi.org/10.1177/0269881118754710

Carragher, N., Krueger, R. F., Eaton, N. R., & Slade, T. (2015). Disorders without borders: Current and future directions in the meta-structure of mental disorders. *Social Psychiatry and Psychiatric Epidemiology*, 50(3), 339–350. https://doi.org/10.1007/s00127-014-1004-z

Caruso, G. D. (Ed.). (2013). *Exploring the illusion of free will and moral responsibility*. Lexington Books.

Caspi, A., Houts, R. M., Belsky, D. W., Goldman-Mellor, S. J., Harrington, H., Israel, S., Meier, M. H., Ramrakha, S., Shalev, I., Poulton, R. & Moffitt, T. E. (2014). The p factor: One general psychopathology factor in the structure of psychiatric disorders? *Clinical Psychological Science*, 2(2), 119–137. https://doi.org/10.1177/2167702613497473

Cassidy, J., & Shaver, P. R. (Eds.). (2016). *Handbook of attachment: Theory, research, and clinical applications*. Guilford Press.

Castonguay, L. G., & Hill, C. E. (Eds.). (2012). *Transformation in psychotherapy: Corrective experiences across cognitive behavioral, humanistic, and psychodynamic approaches*. American Psychological Association. https://doi.org/10.1037/13747-000

Castonguay, L. G., & Hill, C. E. (Eds.). (2017). *How and why are some therapists better than others? Understanding therapist effects*. American Psychological Association. https://doi.org/10.1037/0000034-000

Catarino, F., Gilbert, P., McEwan, K., & Baião, R. (2014). Compassion motivations: Distinguishing submissive compassion from genuine compassion and its association with shame, submissive behavior, depression, anxiety and stress. *Journal of Social and Clinical Psychology*, 33(5), 399–412. https://doi.org/10.1521/jscp.2014.33.5.399

Charvát, J. (2017). *Eskejp: Na útěku z kanceláře*. Novela Bohemica.

Cheek, N. N., & Cheek, J. M. (2018). Aspects of identity: From the inner-outer metaphor to a tetrapartite model of the self. *Self and Identity*, 17(4), 467–482. https://doi.org/10.1080/15298868.2017.1412347

Chefetz, R. A. (2015). *Intensive psychotherapy for persistent dissociative processes: The fear of feeling real*. W. W. Norton & Company.

Cherniak, A. D., Gruneau Brulin, J., Mikulincer, M., Östlind, S., Carhart-Harris, R., & Granqvist, P. (2022). Psychedelic science of spirituality and religion: An attachment-informed agenda proposal. *The International Journal for the Psychology of Religion*, 33(4), 259–276. https://doi.org/10.1080/10508619.2022.2148061

Chodkiewicz, J., & Gruszczyńska, E. (2018). Maladaptive schemas among people addicted to alcohol: Heterogeneity but not specificity? *Alcohol and Alcoholism*, 53(6), 682–687. https://doi.org/10.1093/alcalc/agy047

Choi, E., Farb, N., Pogrebtsova, E., Gruman, J., & Grossmann, I. (2021). What do people mean when they talk about mindfulness? *Clinical Psychology Review*, 89, Article 102085. https://doi.org/10.1016/j.cpr.2021.102085

Clark, A. (2015). *Surfing uncertainty: Prediction, action, and the embodied mind.* Oxford University Press.

Cockram, D. M., Drummond, P. D., & Lee, C. W. (2010). Role and treatment of early maladaptive schemas in Vietnam veterans with PTSD. *Clinical Psychology & Psychotherapy: An International Journal of Theory & Practice*, 17(3), 165–182. https://doi.org/10.1002/cpp.690

Coder, K. (2017). *After the ceremony ends: A companion guide to help you integrate visionary plant medicine experiences.* Casa de Raices y Alas Books.

Coffey, K. A., Hartman, M., & Fredrickson, B. L. (2010). Deconstructing mindfulness and constructing mental health: Understanding mindfulness and its mechanisms of action. *Mindfulness*, 1(4), 235–253. https://doi.org/10.1007/s12671-010-0033-2

Commonwealth of Australia (2023, February 3). *Notice of final decisions to amend (or not amend) the current poisons standard in relation to psilocybine and MDMA.* Therapeutic Goods Administration. https://www.tga.gov.au/sites/default/files/2023-02/notice-of-final-decision-to-amend-or-not-amend-the-current-poisons-standard-june-2022-acms-38-psilocybine-and-mdma.pdf

Compson, J. (2018). Adverse meditation experiences: Navigating Buddhist and secular frameworks for addressing them. *Mindfulness*, 9(5), 1358–1369. https://doi.org/10.1007/s12671-017-0878-8

Cooper, A. C., Ventura, B., & Northoff, G. (2022). Beyond the veil of duality: Topographic reorganization model of meditation. *Neuroscience of Consciousness*, 8(1), Article niac013. https://doi.org/10.1093/nc/niac013

Čopelj, E. (2022). Mindfulness and attention: Towards a phenomenology of mindfulness as the feeling of being tuned in. *Asian Philosophy*, 32(2), 126–151. https://doi.org/10.1080/09552367.2022.2031015

Costines, C., Borghardt, T. L., & Wittmann, M. (2021). The phenomenology of "pure" consciousness as reported by an experienced meditator of the Tibetan Buddhist Karma Kagyu tradition. Analysis of interview content concerning different meditative states. *Philosophies*, 6(2), Article 50. https://doi.org/10.3390/philosophies6020050

Cowan, H. R., Mittal, V. A., & McAdams, D. P. (2021). Narrative identity in the psychosis spectrum: A systematic review and developmental model. *Clinical Psychology Review*, 88, Article 102067. https://doi.org/10.1016/j.cpr.2021.102067

Cowden Hindash, A. H., & Rottenberg, J. (2017). Turning quickly on myself: Automatic interpretation biases in dysphoria are self-referent. *Cognition and Emotion*, 31(2), 395–402. https://doi.org/10.1080/02699931.2015.1105792

Cozolino, L. (2014). *The neuroscience of human relationships: Attachment and the developing social brain* (2nd ed.). W. W. Norton & Company.

Craig, F., Tenuta, F., Rizzato, V., Costabile, A., Trabacca, A., & Montirosso, R. (2021). Attachment-related dimensions in the epigenetic era: A systematic review of the human research. *Neuroscience & Biobehavioral Reviews, 125,* 654–666. https://doi.org/10.1016/j.neubiorev.2021.03.006

Cramer, H. (2019). Meditation in Deutschland: Eine national repräsentative Umfrage. *Complementary Medicine Research, 26*(6), 382–389. https://doi.org/10.1159/000499900

Crouch, E., Probst, J. C., Radcliff, E., Bennett, K. J., & McKinney, S. H. (2019). Prevalence of adverse childhood experiences (ACEs) among US children. *Child Abuse & Neglect, 92,* 209–218. https://doi.org/10.1016/j.chiabu.2019.04.010

Cunningham, S. J., Brebner, J. L., Quinn, F., & Turk, D. J. (2014). The self-reference effect on memory in early childhood. *Child Development, 85*(2), 808–823. https://doi.org/10.1111/cdev.12144

Dahl, C. J., & Davidson, R. J. (2019). Mindfulness and the contemplative life: Pathways to connection, insight, and purpose. *Current Opinion in Psychology, 28,* 60–64. https://doi.org/10.1016/j.copsyc.2018.11.007

Dahl, C. J., Lutz, A., & Davidson, R. J. (2015). Reconstructing and deconstructing the self: Cognitive mechanisms in meditation practice. *Trends in Cognitive Sciences, 19,* 515–523. https://doi.org/10.1016/j.tics.2015.07.001

Dalgleish, T., Black, M., Johnston, D., & Bevan, A. (2020). Transdiagnostic approaches to mental health problems: Current status and future directions. *Journal of Consulting and Clinical Psychology, 88*(3), 179–195. https://doi.org/10.1037/ccp0000482

Damasio, A. (2000). *The feeling of what happens: Body, emotion and the making of consciousness.* Harcourt Brace.

Damasio, A. (2010). *Self comes to mind: Constructing the conscious brain.* Pantheon.

Dambrun, M. (2017). Self-centeredness and selflessness: Happiness correlates and mediating psychological processes. *PeerJ, 5,* Article e3306. https://doi.org/10.7717/peerj.3306

Dambrun, M., & Ricard, M. (2011). Self-centeredness and selflessness: A theory of self-based psychological functioning and its consequences for happiness. *Review of General Psychology, 15*(2), 138–157. https://doi.org/10.1037/a0023059

Davey, C. G., & Harrison, B. J. (2022). The self on its axis: A framework for understanding depression. *Translational Psychiatry, 12*(1), Article 23. https://doi.org/10.1038/s41398-022-01790-8

Davey, C. G., Pujol, J., & Harrison, B. J. (2016). Mapping the self in the brain's default mode network. *NeuroImage, 132,* 390–397. https://doi.org/10.1016/j.neuroimage.2016.02.022

De Silva, P. (1984). Buddhism and behaviour modification. *Behaviour Research and Therapy, 22*(6), 661–678. https://doi.org/10.1016/0005-7967(84)90129-3

Deane, G., Miller, M., & Wilkinson, S. (2020). Losing ourselves: Active inference, depersonalization, and meditation. *Frontiers in Psychology, 11,* Article 539726. https://doi.org/10.3389/fpsyg.2020.539726

Deikman, A. J. (1982). *The observing self: Mysticism and psychotherapy.* Beacon Press.

Dennison, P. (2022). *Jhana consciousness: Buddhist meditation in the age of neuroscience*. Shambhala.

Dokic, J. (2022). Variations on familiarity in self-transcendent experiences. *Metodo: International Studies in Phenomenology and Philosophy, 10*(1), 19–48. https://doi.org/10.19079/metodo.10.1.19

Dominguez, E., Casagrande, M., & Raffone, A. (2022). Autobiographical memory and mindfulness: A critical review with a systematic search. *Mindfulness, 13*(7), 1614–1651. https://doi.org/10.1007/s12671-022-01902-x

Dreyfus, G. (2011). Is mindfulness present-centred and non-judgmental? A discussion of the cognitive dimensions of mindfulness. *Contemporary Buddhism, 12*(1), 41–54. https://doi.org/10.1080/14639947.2011.564815

Dückers, M. L., Alisic, E., & Brewin, C. R. (2016). A vulnerability paradox in the cross-national prevalence of post-traumatic stress disorder. *The British Journal of Psychiatry, 209*(4), 300–305. https://doi.org/10.1192/bjp.bp.115.176628

Dunn, R., Callahan, J. L., & Swift, J. K. (2013). Mindfulness as a transtheoretical clinical process. *Psychotherapy, 50*(3), 312–315. https://doi.org/10.1037/a0032153

Earleywine, M., Low, F., Lau, C., & De Leo, J. (2022). Integration in psychedelic-assisted treatments: Recurring themes in current providers' definitions, challenges, and concerns. *Journal of Humanistic Psychology*, Article 00221678221085800. https://doi.org/10.1177/00221678221085800

Ecker, B. (2018). Clinical translation of memory reconsolidation research: Therapeutic methodology for transformational change by erasing implicit emotional learnings driving symptom production. *International Journal of Neuropsychotherapy, 6*(1), 1–92. https://doi.org/10.12744/ijnpt.2018.0001-0092

Ecker, B., & Bridges, S. K. (2020). How the science of memory reconsolidation advances the effectiveness and unification of psychotherapy. *Clinical Social Work Journal, 48*(3), 287–300. https://doi.org/10.1007/s10615-020-00754-z

Ecker, B., & Vaz, A. (2022). Memory reconsolidation and the crisis of mechanism in psychotherapy. *New Ideas in Psychology, 66*, Article 100945. https://doi.org/10.1016/j.newideapsych.2022.100945

Edershile, E. A., & Wright, A. G. C. (2021). Fluctuations in grandiose and vulnerable narcissistic states: A momentary perspective. *Journal of Personality and Social Psychology, 120*(5), 1386–1414. https://doi.org/10.1037/pspp0000370

Edershile, E. A., & Wright, A. G. C. (2022). Narcissism dynamics. *Social and Personality Psychology Compass, 16*(1), Article e12649. https://doi.org/10.1111/spc3.12649

Edinger, E. F. (1992). *Ego and archetype: Individuation and the religious function of the psyche*. Shambhala.

Ein-Dor, T., Mikulincer, M., & Shaver, P. R. (2011). Attachment insecurities and the processing of threat-related information: Studying the schemas involved in insecure people's coping strategies. *Journal of Personality and Social Psychology, 101*(1), 78–93. https://doi.org/10.1037/a0022503

REFERENCES

Elliott, R., Bohart, A. C., Watson, J. C., & Murphy, D. (2018). Therapist empathy and client outcome: An updated meta-analysis. *Psychotherapy*, 55(4), 399–410. https://doi.org/10.1037/pst0000175

Emery, L. F., Gardner, W. L., Carswell, K. L., & Finkel, E. J. (2018). You can't see the real me: Attachment avoidance, self-verification, and self-concept clarity. *Personality and Social Psychology Bulletin*, 44(8), 1133–1146. https://doi.org/10.1177/0146167218760799

Engel, G. L. (1977). The need for a new medical model: A challenge for biomedicine. *Science*, 196(4286), 129–136. https://doi.org/10.1126/science.847460

Engler, J. (1983). *Theravada Buddhist insight meditation and an object-relational model of therapeutic-developmental change (Dissertation)*. University of Chicago.

Engler, J. (1984). Therapeutic aims in psychotherapy and meditation: Developmental stages in the representation of self. *Journal of Transpersonal Psychology*, 16(1), 25–61. https://www.atpweb.org/jtparchive/trps-16-84-01-025.pdf

Engler, J. (2003). Being somebody and being nobody: A reexamination of the understanding of self in psychoanalysis and Buddhism. In J. D. Safran (Ed.), *Psychoanalysis and Buddhism: An unfolding dialogue*. Wisdom Publications.

Epstein, M. (1990). Psychodynamics of meditation: Pitfalls on the spiritual path. *Journal of Transpersonal Psychology*, 22(1), 17–34. https://www.atpweb.org/jtparchive/trps-22-90-01-017.pdf

Epstein, M. (2014). *The trauma of everyday life*. Hay House UK.

Epstein, M. (2013a). *Going to pieces without falling apart: A Buddhist perspective on wholeness*. Broadway Books.

Epstein, M. (2013b). *Thoughts without a thinker: Psychotherapy from a Buddhist perspective*. Basic Books.

Epstein, O. B. (2022). Primary shame: Needing you and the economy of affects. In O. B. Epstein (Ed.), *Shame matters: Attachment and relational perspectives for psychotherapists*. Routledge. https://doi.org/10.4324/9781003175612

Epstein, M. D., & Lieff, J. D. (1981). Psychiatric complications of meditation practice. *Journal of Transpersonal Psychology*, 13(2), 137–147. https://www.atpweb.org/jtparchive/trps-13-81-02-137.pdf

Erikson, E. (1998). *The life cycle completed*. W. W. Norton & Company.

Evans, J., & Read, T. (2020). *Breaking open: Finding a way through spiritual emergencies*. Aeon Books.

Evens, R., Schmidt, M. E., Majić, T., & Schmidt, T. T. (2023). The psychedelic afterglow phenomenon: A systematic review of subacute effects of classic serotonergic psychedelics. *Therapeutic Advances in Psychopharmacology*, 13, 1–20. https://doi.org/10.1177/20451253231172254

Everaert, J., Podina, I. R., & Koster, E. H. (2017). A comprehensive meta-analysis of interpretation biases in depression. *Clinical Psychology Review*, 58, 33–48. https://doi.org/10.1016/j.cpr.2017.09.005

Fairbairn, W. R. D. (2013). *Psychoanalytic studies of the personality*. Routledge.

Falconier, M. K., Jackson, J., Hilpert, J., & Bodenmann, G. (2015). Dyadic coping and relationship satisfaction: A meta-analysis. *Clinical Psychology Review*, 42, 28–46. https://doi.org/10.1016/j.cpr.2015.07.002

Farber, B. A., Suzuki, J. Y., & Lynch, D. A. (2018). Positive regard and psychotherapy outcome: A meta-analytic review. *Psychotherapy*, 55(4), 411–423. https://doi.org/10.1037/pst0000171

Farb, N. A., Segal, Z. V., Mayberg, H., Bean, J., McKeon, D., Fatima, Z., & Anderson, A. K. (2007). Attending to the present: Mindfulness meditation reveals distinct neural modes of self-reference. *Social Cognitive and Affective Neuroscience*, 2(4), 313–322. https://doi.org/10.1093/scan/nsm030

Farias, M., Maraldi, E., Wallenkampf, K. C., & Lucchetti, G. (2020). Adverse events in meditation practices and meditation-based therapies: A systematic review. *Acta Psychiatrica Scandinavica*, 142(5), 374–393. https://doi.org/10.1111/acps.13225

Faustino, B. (2022). Minding my brain: Fourteen neuroscience-based principles to enhance psychotherapy responsiveness. *Clinical Psychology & Psychotherapy*, 29(4), 1254–1275. https://doi.org/10.1002/cpp.2719

Faustino, B., Vasco, A. B., Silva, A. N., & Marques, T. (2020). Relationships between emotional schemas, mindfulness, self-compassion and unconditional self-acceptance on the regulation of psychological needs. *Research in Psychotherapy: Psychopathology, Process, and Outcome*, 23(2), 442–442. https://doi.org/10.4081/ripppo.2020.442

Feldman, R. (2017). The neurobiology of human attachments. *Trends in Cognitive Sciences*, 21(2), 80–99. https://doi.org/10.1016/j.tics.2016.11.007

Feldman, C., & Kuyken, W. (2019). *Mindfulness: Ancient wisdom meets modern psychology*. Guilford Press.

Ferraro, I. K., & Taylor, A. M. (2021). Adult attachment styles and emotional regulation: The role of interoceptive awareness and alexithymia. *Personality and Individual Differences*, 173, Article 110641. https://doi.org/10.1016/j.paid.2021.110641

Feruglio, S., Matiz, A., Pagnoni, G., Fabbro, F., & Crescentini, C. (2021). The impact of mindfulness meditation on the wandering mind: A systematic review. *Neuroscience and Biobehavioral Reviews*, 131, 313–330. https://doi.org/10.1016/j.neubiorev.2021.09.032

Fingelkurts, A. A., Fingelkurts, A. A., & Kallio-Tamminen, T. (2020). Selfhood triumvirate: From phenomenology to brain activity and back again. *Consciousness and Cognition*, 86, Article 103031. https://doi.org/10.1016/j.concog.2020.103031

Fingelkurts, A. A., Fingelkurts, A. A., & Kallio-Tamminen, T. (2022). Self, me and I in the repertoire of spontaneously occurring altered states of selfhood: Eight neurophenomenological case study reports. *Cognitive Neurodynamics*, 16, 255–282. https://doi.org/10.1007/s11571-021-09719-5

Firman, J., & Vargiu, J. (1977). Dimensions of growth. *Synthesis*, 3(4), 60–120.

Firman, J., & Vargiu, J. (1996). Personal and transpersonal growth: The perspective of psychosynthesis. In S. Boorstein (Ed.), *Transpersonal psychotherapy*. Science and Behavior Books.

Fleming, S. M. (2020). Awareness as inference in a higher-order state space. *Neuroscience of Consciousness*, 6(1), Article niz020. https://doi.org/10.1093/nc/niz020

REFERENCES

Flückiger, C., Del Re, A. C., Wampold, B. E., & Horvath, A. O. (2018). The alliance in adult psychotherapy: A meta-analytic synthesis. *Psychotherapy, 55*(4), 316–340. https://doi.org/10.1037/pst0000172

Fonagy, P., Gergely, G., Jurist, E. L., & Target, M. (2018). *Affect regulation, mentalization, and the development of the self.* Routledge. https://doi.org/10.4324/9780429471643

Forman, M. D. (2010). *A guide to integral psychotherapy: Complexity, integration, and spirituality in practice.* Suny Press.

Forstmann, M., & Sagioglou, C. (2017). Lifetime experience with (classic) psychedelics predicts pro-environmental behavior through an increase in nature relatedness. *Journal of Psychopharmacology, 31*(8), 975–988. https://doi.org/10.1177/0269881117714049

Forstmann, M., Yudkin, D. A., Prosser, A. M. B., Heller, S. M., & Crockett, M. J. (2020). Transformative experience and social connectedness mediate the mood-enhancing effects of psychedelic use in naturalistic settings. *PNAS Proceedings of the National Academy of Sciences of the United States of America, 117*(5), 2338–2346. https://doi.org/10.1073/pnas.1918477117

Frankl, V. E. (2020). *The will to meaning.* Nourabooks.

Frankl, V. E. (2021). *Man's search for meaning: Classic editions.* Rider.

Franquesa, A., Sainz-Cort, A., Gandy, S., Soler, J., Alcázar-Córcoles, M., & Bouso, J. C. (2018). Psychological variables implied in the therapeutic effect of ayahuasca: A contextual approach. *Psychiatry Research, 264,* 334–339. https://doi.org/10.1016/j.psychres.2018.04.012

Freud, A. (2019). *The ego and the mechanisms of defence.* Routledge.

Freud, S. (1940). *Jenseits des Lustprinzips/Massenpsychologie und Ich-Analyse/Das Ich und das Es/Und andere Werke aus den Jahren 1920–1924.* S. Fischer.

Freud, S. (1942). *Werke aus den Jahren 1904–1905.* S. Fischer.

Freud, S. (1945). *Die Traumdeutung/Über den Traum.* S. Fischer.

Freud, S. (1946). *Werke aus den Jahren 1913–1917.* S. Fischer.

Freud, S. (1952). *Werke aus den Jahren 1892–1899.* S. Fischer.

Frewen, P., Schroeter, M. L., Riva, G., Cipresso, P., Fairfield, B., Padulo, C., Kemp, A. H., Palaniyappan, L., Owolabi, M., Kusi-Mensah, K., Polyakova, M., Fehertoi, N., D'Andrea, W., Lowe, L., & Polyakova, M. (2020). Neuroimaging the consciousness of self: Review, and conceptual-methodological framework. *Neuroscience and Biobehavioral Reviews, 112,* 164–212. https://doi.org/10.1016/j.neubiorev.2020.01.023

Freyd, J., & Birrell, P. (2013). *Blind to betrayal: Why we fool ourselves we aren't being fooled.* John Wiley & Sons.

Fromm, E. (1939). Selfishness and self-love. *Psychiatry: Journal for the Study of Interpersonal Processes, 2,* 507–523.

Frýba, M. (1989). *The art of happiness: Teachings of Buddhist psychology.* Shambhala.

Frýba, M. (2008). *Psychologie zvládání života: Aplikace metody Abhidhamma.* Albert.

Fuller, P. (2012). *The notion of diṭṭhi in Theravāda Buddhism: The point of view.* Routledge.

REFERENCES

Gaines, A. N., & Goldfried, M. R. (2021). Consensus in psychotherapy: Are we there yet? *Clinical Psychology: Science and Practice*, *28*(3), 267–276. https://doi.org/10.1037/cps0000026

Gallagher, S. (2000). Philosophical conceptions of the self: Implications for cognitive science. *Trends in Cognitive Sciences*, *4*, 12–21. https://doi.org/10.1016/S1364-6613(99)01417-5

Gallagher, S., Raffone, A., Berkovich-Ohana, A., Barendregt, H. P., Bauer, P. R., Brown, K. W., Giommi, F., Nyklíček, I., Ostafin, B. D., Slagter, H. Trautwein, F. M., & Vago, D. R. (2024). The self-pattern and Buddhist psychology. *Mindfulness*, *15*(4), 795–803. https://doi.org/10.1007/s12671-023-02118-3

Gamma, A., & Metzinger, T. (2021). The minimal phenomenal experience questionnaire (MPE-92M): Towards a phenomenological profile of "pure awareness" experiences in meditators. *PLoS ONE*, *16*(7), 1–39. https://doi.org/10.1371/journal.pone.0253694

Garcia-Romeu, A., & Richards, W. A. (2018). Current perspectives on psychedelic therapy: Use of serotonergic hallucinogens in clinical interventions. *International Review of Psychiatry*, *30*(4), 291–316. https://doi.org/10.1080/09540261.2018.1486289

Gardner, A. A., Zimmer-Gembeck, M. J., & Campbell, S. M. (2020). Attachment and emotion regulation: A person-centred examination and relations with coping with rejection, friendship closeness, and emotional adjustment. *British Journal of Developmental Psychology*, *38*(1), 125–143. https://doi.org/10.1111/bjdp.12310

Gashi, L., Sandberg, S., & Pedersen, W. (2021). Making "bad trips" good: How users of psychedelics narratively transform challenging trips into valuable experiences. *International Journal of Drug Policy*, *87*, Article 102997. https://doi.org/10.1016/j.drugpo.2020.102997

Gattuso, J. J., Perkins, D., Ruffell, S., Lawrence, A. J., Hoyer, D., Jacobson, L. H., Timmermann, Ch., Castle, D., Rossell, S. L., Downey, L. A., Pagni, B. A., Galvão-Coelho, N. L., Nutt, D., & Sarris, J. (2023). Default mode network modulation by psychedelics: A systematic review. *International Journal of Neuropsychopharmacology*, *26*(3), 155–188. https://doi.org/10.1093/ijnp/pyac074

Gazzillo, F., Fimiani, R., De Luca, E., Dazzi, N., Curtis, J. T., & Bush, M. (2020). New developments in understanding morality: Between evolutionary psychology, developmental psychology, and control-mastery theory. *Psychoanalytic Psychology*, *37*(1), 37–49. https://doi.org/10.1037/pap0000235

Gazzillo, F., Gorman, B., Bush, M., Silberschatz, G., Mazza, C., Faccini, F., Crisafulli, V., Alesiani, R., & De Luca, E. (2017). Reliability and validity of the Interpersonal Guilt Rating Scale-15: A new clinician-reporting tool for assessing interpersonal guilt according to Control-Mastery Theory. *Psychodynamic Psychiatry*, *45*(3), 362–384. https://doi.org/10.1521/pdps.2017.45.3.362

Geller, S. M., & Greenberg, L. S. (2012). *Therapeutic presence: A mindful approach to effective therapy*. American Psychological Association. https://doi.org/10.1037/13485-000

Gendlin, T. E. (2003). *Focusing: How to gain direct access to your body's knowledge*. Rider.

REFERENCES

Germer, C. K. (2013). Mindfulness: What is it? What does it matter? In Ch. K. Germer, R. D. Siegel, & P. R. Fulton (Eds.), *Mindfulness and psychotherapy* (2nd ed.). Guilford Press.

Germer, C. K., & Siegel, R. D. (Eds.). (2012). *Wisdom and compassion in psychotherapy: Deepening mindfulness in clinical practice.* Guilford Press.

Gethin, R. (2011). On some definitions of mindfulness. *Contemporary Buddhism*, 12(1), 263–279. https://doi.org/10.1080/14639947.2011.564843

Giano, Z., Wheeler, D. L., & Hubach, R. D. (2020). The frequencies and disparities of adverse childhood experiences in the US. *BMC Public Health*, 20(1). https://doi.org/10.1186/s12889-020-09411-z

Gilboa, A., & Marlatte, H. (2017). Neurobiology of schemas and schema-mediated memory. *Trends in Cognitive Sciences*, 21(8), 618–631. https://doi.org/10.1016/j.tics.2017.04.013

Gilboa-Schechtman, E., Keshet, H., Peschard, V., & Azoulay, R. (2020). Self and identity in social anxiety disorder. *Journal of Personality*, 88(1), 106–121. https://doi.org/10.1111/jopy.12455

Giles, J. (2019). Relevance of the no-self theory in contemporary mindfulness. *Current Opinion in Psychology*, 28, 298–301. https://doi.org/10.1016/j.copsyc.2019.03.016

Gillath, O., & Karantzas, G. (2019). Attachment security priming: A systematic review. *Current Opinion in Psychology*, 25, 86–95. https://doi.org/10.1016/j.copsyc.2018.03.001

Giommi, F., Bauer, P. R., Berkovich-Ohana, A., Barendregt, H., Brown, K. W., Gallagher, S., Nyklíček, I., Ostafin, B., Raffone, A., Slagter, H. A., Trautwein, F. M., & Vago, D. R. (2023). The (in)flexible self: Psychopathology, mindfulness, and neuroscience. *International Journal of Clinical and Health Psychology*, 23(4), Article 100381. https://doi.org/10.1016/j.ijchp.2023.100381

Giraldi, T. (2019). *Psychotherapy, mindfulness and Buddhist meditation.* Springer. https://doi.org/10.1007/978-3-030-29003-0

Girn, M., Rosas, F. E., Daws, R. E., Gallen, C. L., Gazzaley, A., & Carhart-Harris, R. L. (2023). A complex systems perspective on psychedelic brain action. *Trends in Cognitive Sciences*, 27(5), 433–445. https://doi.org/10.1016/j.tics.2023.01.003

Gleig, A. (2019). *American dharma: Buddhism beyond modernity.* Yale University Press.

Glover, R. (2004). *No more Mr. Nice Guy: A proven plan for getting what you want in love, sex and life.* Running Press.

Goldberg, S. B. (2022). A common factors perspective on mindfulness-based interventions. *Nature Reviews Psychology*, 1(10), 605–619. https://doi.org/10.1038/s44159-022-00090-8

Goldberg, S. B., Lam, S. U., Britton, W. B., & Davidson, R. J. (2022). Prevalence of meditation-related adverse effects in a population-based sample in the United States. *Psychotherapy Research*, 32(3), 291–305. https://doi.org/10.1080/10503307.2021.1933646

Goldin, P. R., Braun, A., Ekman, E., Simons, V., Flora, T., Easton, C., & Allione, T. (2023). Randomized controlled trial of the Tibetan Buddhist feeding your demons contemplative process in meditation practitioners. *Journal of Emotion and Psychopathology, 1*(1), 90–103. https://doi.org/10.55913/joep.v1i1.11

Goldman, R. N., & Greenberg, L. S. (2015). *Case formulation in emotion-focused therapy: Co-creating clinical maps for change.* American Psychological Association. https://doi.org/10.1037/14523-000

Goldstein, J. (2017). *The experience of insight: A simple and direct guide to Buddhist meditation.* Shambhala.

Gold, E. K., & Zahm, S. G. (2018). *Buddhist psychology & gestalt therapy integrated: Psychotherapy for the 21st century.* Metta Press.

Goleman, D. (Ed.). (2004). *Destructive emotions: A scientific dialogue with the Dalai Lama.* Bantam.

Gong, Q., Scarpazza, C., Dai, J., He, M., Xu, X., Shi, Y., Zhou, B., Vieira, S., McCrory, F., Ai, Y., Yang, Ch., Zhang, F., Lui, S., & Mechelli, A. (2019). A transdiagnostic neuroanatomical signature of psychiatric illness. *Neuropsychopharmacology, 44*(5), 869–875. https://doi.org/10.1038/s41386-018-0175-9

Goodall, K., Trejnowska, A., & Darling, S. (2012). The relationship between dispositional mindfulness, attachment security and emotion regulation. *Personality and Individual Differences, 52*(5), 622–626. https://doi.org/10.1016/j.paid.2011.12.008

Goodkind, M., Eickhoff, S. B., Oathes, D. J., Jiang, Y., Chang, A., Jones-Hagata, L. B., Brissa N.Ortega, B. N., Zaiko, Y. V., Roach, E. L., Korgaonkar, M. S., Grieve, S. M., Galatzer-Levy, I., Fox, P. T., & Etkin, A. (2015). Identification of a common neurobiological substrate for mental illness. *JAMA Psychiatry, 72*(4), 305–315. https://doi.org/10.1001/jamapsychiatry.2014.2206

Goodman, S. D. (2020). *The Buddhist psychology of awakening: An in-depth guide to Abhidharma.* Shambhala.

Gorman, I., Nielson, E. M., Molinar, A., Cassidy, K., & Sabbagh, J. (2021). Psychedelic harm reduction and integration: A transtheoretical model for clinical practice. *Frontiers in Psychology, 12*, Article 645246. https://doi.org/10.3389/fpsyg.2021.645246

Grabovac, A. (2015). The stages of insight: Clinical relevance for mindfulness-based interventions. *Mindfulness, 6*(3), 589–600. https://doi.org/10.1007/s12671-014-0294-2

Grabovac, A. D., Lau, M. A., & Willett, B. R. (2011). Mechanisms of mindfulness: A Buddhist psychological model. *Mindfulness, 2*(3), 154–166. https://doi.org/10.1007/s12671-011-0054-5

Grecucci, A., Sorella, S., & Consolini, J. (2023). Decoding individual differences in expressing and suppressing anger from structural brain networks: A supervised machine learning approach. *Behavioural Brain Research, 439*, Article 114245. https://doi.org/10.1016/j.bbr.2022.114245

Greenberg, L. S. (2015). *Emotion-focused therapy: Coaching clients to work through their feelings* (2nd ed.). American Psychological Association. https://doi.org/10.1037/14692-000

Greenberg, L. S. (2017). *Emotion-focused therapy: Revised edition*. American Psychological Association. https://doi.org/10.1037/15971-000

Greenberg, L. S. (2021). *Changing emotion with emotion: A practitioner's guide*. American Psychological Association. https://doi.org/10.1037/0000248-000

Greenberg, M. T., & Mitra, J. L. (2015). From mindfulness to right mindfulness: The intersection of awareness and ethics. *Mindfulness*, 6(1), 74–78. https://doi.org/10.1007/s12671-014-0384-1

Greenberg, L. S., & Paivio, S. C. (2003). *Working with emotions in psychotherapy*. Guilford Press.

Greeson, J., Garland, E. L., & Black, D. (2014). Mindfulness: A transtherapeutic approach for transdiagnostic mental processes. In A. Ie, C. T. Ngnoumen, & E. J. Langer (Eds.), *The Wiley Blackwell handbook of mindfulness*. Wiley-Blackwell. https://doi.org/10.1002/9781118294895

Gregory, B., Peters, L., & Rapee, R. M. (2016). The self in social anxiety. In M. Kyrios, R. Moulding, G. Doron, S. S. Bhar, M. Nedeljkovic, & M. Mikulincer (Eds.), *The self in understanding and treating psychological disorders*. Cambridge University Press. https://doi.org/10.1017/CBO9781139941297.011

Griffiths, R. R., Johnson, M. W., Richards, W. A., Richards, B. D., Jesse, R., MacLean, K. A., Barrett, F. S., Cosimano, M. P., & Klinedinst, M. A. (2018). Psilocybin-occasioned mystical-type experience in combination with meditation and other spiritual practices produces enduring positive changes in psychological functioning and in trait measures of prosocial attitudes and behaviors. *Journal of Psychopharmacology*, 32(1), 49–69. https://doi.org/10.1177/0269881117731279

Grigsby, J. (2021). Memory reconsolidation in psycholytic psychotherapy. In C. S. Grob & J. Grigsby (Eds.), *Handbook of medical hallucinogens*. Guilford Press.

Grob, C. S., & Grigsby, J. (Eds.). (2021). *Handbook of medical hallucinogens*. Guilford Press.

Grof, S. (1988). *The adventure of self-discovery: Dimensions of consciousness and new perspectives in psychotherapy and inner exploration*. State University of New York Press.

Grof, S. (2001). *LSD psychotherapy: The healing potential of psychedelic medicine*. Multidisciplinary Association for Psychedelic Studies.

Grof, S. (2019). *The way of the psychonaut: Encyclopedia for inner journeys*. Multidisciplinary Association for Psychedelic Studies.

Grof, S. (2021). *Realms of the human unconscious: Observations from LSD research*. Souvenir Press.

Grossman, P. (2015). Mindfulness: Awareness informed by an embodied ethic. *Mindfulness*, 6(1), 17–22. https://doi.org/10.1007/s12671-014-0372-5

Grotzinger, A. (2021). Shared genetic architecture across psychiatric disorders. *Psychological Medicine*, 51(13), 2210–2216. https://doi.org/10.1017/s0033291721000829

Guendelman, S., Medeiros, S., & Rampes, H. (2017). Mindfulness and emotion regulation: Insights from neurobiological, psychological, and clinical studies. *Frontiers in Psychology*, 8, Article 220. https://doi.org/10.3389/fpsyg.2017.00220

Gukasyan, N., & Nayak, S. M. (2022). Psychedelics, placebo effects, and set and setting: Insights from common factors theory of psychotherapy. *Transcultural Psychiatry*, 59(5), 652–664. https://doi.org/10.1177/1363461520983684

Gyamtso, K. T. (2016). *Progressive stages of meditation on emptiness*. Shrimala Trust.

Hadar, A., David, J., Shalit, N., Roseman, L., Gross, R., Sessa, B., & Lev-Ran, S. (2022). The psychedelic renaissance in clinical research: A bibliometric analysis of three decades of human studies with psychedelics. *Journal of Psychoactive Drugs*, 55(1), 1–10. https://doi.org/10.1080/02791072.2021.2022254

Hájek, K. (2002). *Tělesně zakotvené prožívání*. Karolinum.

Hájek, K. (2012). *Práce s emocemi pro pomáhající profese: Tělesně zakotvené prožívání*. Portál.

Hájek, K., & Benda, J. (2008). Podmíněné vznikání: Cestou abhidhammy z bludného kruhu neurózy. *Psychoterapie*, 2(3–4), 151–160. https://www.jan-benda.com/downloads/hajek_benda2008.pdf

Hanley, A. W., Dorjee, D., & Garland, E. L. (2020). Mindfulness training encourages self-transcendent states via decentering. *Psychology of Consciousness: Theory, Research, and Practice*. Advance online publication. https://doi.org/10.1037/cns0000262

Hanley, A. W., Nakamura, Y., & Garland, E. L. (2018). The Nondual Awareness Dimensional Assessment (NADA): New tools to assess nondual traits and states of consciousness occurring within and beyond the context of meditation. *Psychological Assessment*, 30(12), 1625–1639. https://doi.org/10.1037/pas0000615

Harlow, H. F. (1958). The nature of love. *American Psychologist*, 13(12), 673–685. https://doi.org/10.1037/h0047884

Harlow, H. F., & Suomi, S. J. (1971). Social recovery by isolation-reared monkeys. *Proceedings of the National Academy of Sciences*, 68(7), 1534–1538. https://doi.org/10.1073/pnas.68.7.1534

Harrer, M. E., & Weiss, H. (2016). *Wirkfaktoren der Achtsamkeit: Wie sie die Psychotherapie verändern und bereichern*. Schattauer.

Harris, J. S. (2019a). *Zen beyond mindfulness: Using Buddhist and modern psychology for transformational practice*. Shambhala.

Harris, R. (2019b). *ACT made simple: An easy-to-read primer on acceptance and commitment therapy (second edition, revised)*. New Harbinger Publications.

Harris, T. A. (2012). *I'm ok, You're ok*. Arrow.

Hasson-Ohayon, I., & Lysaker, P. H. (Eds.). (2021). *The recovery of the self in psychosis: Contributions from metacognitive and mentalization based oriented psychotherapy*. Routledge. https://doi.org/10.4324/9780429486500

Hatoum, A. H., Burton, A. L., & Abbott, M. J. (2022). Assessing negative core beliefs in eating disorders: Revision of the eating disorder core beliefs questionnaire. *Journal of Eating Disorders*, 10(1), Article 18. https://doi.org/10.1186/s40337-022-00542-9

REFERENCES

Hayes, S. C., Law, S., Malady, M., Zhu, Z., & Bai, X. (2020). The centrality of sense of self in psychological flexibility processes: What the neurobiological and psychological correlates of psychedelics suggest. *Journal of Contextual Behavioral Science, 15*, 30–38. https://doi.org/10.1016/j.jcbs.2019.11.005

Hayes, S. C., Strosahl, K. D., & Wilson, K. G. (2016). *Acceptance and commitment therapy: The process and practice of mindful change.* Guilford Press.

Hazan, C., & Shaver, P. (1987). Romantic love conceptualized as an attachment process. *Journal of Personality and Social Psychology, 52*(3), 511–524. https://doi.org/10.1037/0022-3514.52.3.511

Healy, C. J., Lee, K. A., & D'Andrea, W. (2021). Using psychedelics with therapeutic intent is associated with lower shame and complex trauma symptoms in adults with histories of child maltreatment. *Chronic Stress, 5*, Article 24705470211029881. https://doi.org/10.1177/24705470211029881

Heppner, W. L., Spears, C. A., Vidrine, J. I., & Wetter, D. W. (2015). Mindfulness and emotion regulation. In B. D. Ostafin, M. D. Robinson, & B. P. Meier (Eds.), *Handbook of mindfulness and self-regulation.* Springer. https://doi.org/10.1007/978-1-4939-2263-5_9

Herma, H., & Greve, W. (2024). A processed processor: The processual nature of the self. *Review of General Psychology, 28*(1), 30–46. https://doi.org/10.1177/10892680231197805

Herzog, M. H., Drissi-Daoudi, L., & Doerig, A. (2020). All in good time: Long-lasting postdictive effects reveal discrete perception. *Trends in Cognitive Sciences, 24*(10), 826–837. https://doi.org/10.1016/j.tics.2020.07.001

Hesse, C., & Floyd, K. (2011). Affection mediates the impact of alexithymia on relationships. *Personality and Individual Differences, 50*(4), 451–456. https://doi.org/10.1016/j.paid.2010.11.004

Hobfoll, S. E., Gaffey, A. E., & Wagner, L. M. (2020). PTSD and the influence of context: The self as a social mirror. *Journal of Personality, 88*(1), 76–87. https://doi.org/10.1111/jopy.12439

Hohwy, J. (2016). The self-evidencing brain. *Noûs, 50*(2), 259–285. https://doi.org/10.1111/nous.12062

Holy Bible (2022). *New revised standard version, updated edition.* Zondervan.

Homan, K. J. (2018). Secure attachment and eudaimonic well-being in late adulthood: The mediating role of self-compassion. *Aging & Mental Health, 22*(3), 363–370. https://doi.org/10.1080/13607863.2016.1254597

Horowitz, M. J., & Sicilia, M. A. (2016). The self in posttraumatic stress disorder. In M. Kyrios, R. Moulding, G. Doron, S. S. Bhar, M. Nedeljkovic, & M. Mikulincer (Eds.), *The self in understanding and treating psychological disorders.* Cambridge University Press. https://doi.org/10.1017/CBO9781139941297.012

Hughes, K., Bellis, M. A., Hardcastle, K. A., Sethi, D., Butchart, A., Mikton, C., Jones, L., & Dunne, M. P. (2017). The effect of multiple adverse childhood experiences on health: A systematic review and meta-analysis. *Lancet Public Health, 2*(8), e356–e366. https://doi.org/10.1016/S2468-2667(17)30118-4

Hughes, K., Ford, K., Bellis, M. A., Glendinning, F., Harrison, E., & Passmore, J. (2021). Health and financial costs of adverse childhood experiences in 28 European countries: A systematic review and meta-analysis. *Lancet Public Health*, 6(11), e848–e857. https://doi.org/10.1016/S2468-2667(21)00232-2

Hurvich, M. (2018). New developments in the theory and clinical application of the annihilation anxiety concept. In A. B. Druck, C. S. Ellman, N. Freedman, & A. Thaler (Eds.), *A new Freudian synthesis: Clinical process in the next generation*. Routledge. https://doi.org/10.4324/9780429471391

Husserl, E. (2012). *Cartesianische Meditationen*. Meiner.

Huxley, E., & Bizumic, B. (2017). Parental invalidation and the development of narcissism. *The Journal of Psychology*, 151(2), 130–147. https://doi.org/10.1080/00223980.2016.1248807

Insel, T., Cuthbert, B., Garvey, M., Heinssen, R., Pine, D. S., Quinn, K., Sanislow, Ch., & Wang, P. (2010). Research domain criteria (RDoC): Toward a new classification framework for research on mental disorders. *American Journal of Psychiatry*, 167(7), 748–751. https://doi.org/10.1176/appi.ajp.2010.09091379

Inwood, E., & Ferrari, M. (2018). Mechanisms of change in the relationship between self-compassion, emotion regulation, and mental health: A systematic review. *Applied Psychology: Health and Well-Being*, 10(2), 215–235. https://doi.org/10.1111/aphw.12127

Jacobs, I., Lenz, L., Wollny, A., & Horsch, A. (2020). The higher-order structure of schema modes. *Journal of Personality Disorders*, 34(3), 348–376. https://doi.org/10.1521/pedi_2018_32_401

James, W. (2019). *The principles of psychology*. Wentworth Press.

Jauk, E., & Kanske, P. (2021). Can neuroscience help to understand narcissism? A systematic review of an emerging field. *Personality Neuroscience*, 4, Article e3. https://doi.org/10.1017/pen.2021.1

Jauk, E., Knödler, M., Frenzel, J., & Kanske, P. (2023). Do highly sensitive persons display hypersensitive narcissism? Similarities and differences in the nomological networks of sensory processing sensitivity and vulnerable narcissism. *Journal of Clinical Psychology*, 79(1), 228–254. https://doi.org/10.1002/jclp.23406

Jencius, M., & Duba, J. D. (2003). Searching for the ideal parents: An interview with Al Pesso and Diane Boyden. *The Family Journal*, 11(1), 89–97. https://doi.org/10.1177/1066480702238478

Jinpa, T. (2016). *A fearless heart: How the courage to be compassionate can transform our lives*. Avery.

John of the Cross (2003). *The dark night of the soul*. Dover Publications.

Johnson, S. M. (2019). *Attachment theory in practice: Emotionally focused therapy (EFT) with individuals, couples, and families*. Guilford Press.

Johnstone, L., Boyle, M., With Cromby, J., Dillon, J., Harper, D., Kinderman, P., Longden, E., Pilgrim, D., & Read, J. (2018). *The power threat meaning framework: Towards the identification of patterns in emotional distress, unusual experiences and troubled or troubling behaviour, as an alternative to functional psychiatric diagnosis*. British Psychological Society.

Joiner, T. (2017). *Mindlessness: The corruption of mindfulness in a culture of narcissism*. Oxford University Press.

Josipovic, Z. (2019). Nondual awareness: Consciousness-as-such as non-representational reflexivity. *Progress in Brain Research, 244*, 273–298. https://doi.org/10.1016/bs.pbr.2018.10.021

Josipovic, Z. (2021). Implicit-explicit gradient of nondual awareness or consciousness as such. *Neuroscience of Consciousness, 7*(2), Article niab031. https://doi.org/10.1093/nc/niab031

Josipovic, Z., & Miskovic, V. (2020). Nondual awareness and minimal phenomenal experience. *Frontiers in Psychology, 11*, Article 2087. https://doi.org/10.3389/fpsyg.2020.02087

Jung, C. G. (2011). *Psychogenese der Geisteskrankheiten: Gesammelte Werke 3*. Patmos.

Jung, C. G. (2017). *Die Archetypen und das kollektive Unbewusste: Gesammelte Werke 9/1*. Patmos.

Jung, C. G. (2021a). *C. G. Jung letters, volume 2: 1951–1961*. Princeton University Press. https://doi.org/10.2307/j.ctv1qgnq5k

Jung, C. G. (2021b). *Zwei Schriften über Analytische Psychologie: Gesammelte Werke 7*. Patmos.

Kabat-Zinn, J. (2013). *Full catastrophe living: Using the wisdom of your body and mind to face stress, pain, and illness*. Bantam.

Kähönen, J. (2023). Psychedelic unselfing: Self-transcendence and change of values in psychedelic experiences. *Frontiers in Psychology, 14*, Article 1104627. https://doi.org/10.3389/fpsyg.2023.1104627

Kałużna, A., Schlosser, M., Craste, E. G., Stroud, J., & Cooke, J. (2022). Being no one, being one: The role of ego-dissolution and connectedness in the therapeutic effects of psychedelic experience. *Journal of Psychedelic Studies, 6*(2), 111–136. https://doi.org/10.1556/2054.2022.00199

Kamboj, S. K., Walldén, Y. S. E., Falconer, C. J., Alotaibi, M. R., Blagbrough, I. S., Husbands, S. M., & Freeman, T. P. (2018). Additive effects of 3,4-methylenedioxymethamphetamine (MDMA) and compassionate imagery on self-compassion in recreational users of ecstasy. *Mindfulness, 9*(4), 1134–1145. https://doi.org/10.1007/s12671-017-0849-0

Kang, C., & Whittingham, K. (2010). Mindfulness: A dialogue between Buddhism and clinical psychology. *Mindfulness, 1*(3), 161–173. https://doi.org/10.1007/s12671-010-0018-1

Karatzias, T., Jowett, S., Begley, A., & Deas, S. (2016). Early maladaptive schemas in adult survivors of interpersonal trauma: Foundations for a cognitive theory of psychopathology. *European Journal of Psychotraumatology, 7*, Article 30713. https://doi.org/10.3402/ejpt.v7.30713

Karpman, S. (1968). Fairy tales and script drama analysis. *Transactional Analysis Bulletin, 7*(26), 39–43.

Kaufmann, M., Rosing, K., & Baumann, N. (2021). Being mindful does not always benefit everyone: Mindfulness-based practices may promote alienation among psychologically vulnerable people. *Cognition and Emotion*, 35(2), 241–255. https://doi.org/10.1080/02699931.2020.1825337

Kelly, J. R., Baker, A., Babiker, M., Burke, L., Brennan, C., & O'Keane, V. (2022). The psychedelic renaissance: The next trip for psychiatry? *Irish Journal of Psychological Medicine*, 39(4), 335–339. https://doi.org/10.1017/ipm.2019.39

Kelly, J. R., Gillan, C. M., Prenderville, J., Kelly, C., Harkin, A., Clarke, G., & O'Keane, V. (2021). Psychedelic therapy's transdiagnostic effects: A Research Domain Criteria (RDoC) perspective. *Frontiers in Psychiatry*, 12, Article 800072. https://doi.org/10.3389/fpsyt.2021.800072

Kendler, K. S. (2014). The structure of psychiatric science. *American Journal of Psychiatry*, 171(9), 931–938. https://doi.org/10.1176/appi.ajp.2014.13111539

Kendler, K. S., & Woodward, J. (2021). Top-down causation in psychiatric disorders: A clinical-philosophical inquiry. *Psychological Medicine*, 51(11), 1783–1788. https://doi.org/10.1017/S0033291721001811

Kernberg, O. F. (2000). *Borderline conditions and pathological narcissism*. Jason Aronson.

Kersten, T. (2012). Schema therapy for personality disorders and addiction. In M. van Vreeswijk, J. Broersen, & M. Nadort (Eds.), *The Wiley-Blackwell handbook of schema therapy: Theory, research and practice*. John Wiley & Sons. https://doi.org/10.1002/9781119962830.ch31

Kettner, H., Gandy, S., Haijen, E. C., & Carhart-Harris, R. L. (2019). From egoism to ecoism: Psychedelics increase nature relatedness in a state-mediated and context-dependent manner. *International Journal of Environmental Research and Public Health*, 16(24), Article 5147. https://doi.org/10.3390/ijerph16245147

Kettner, H., Rosas, F. E., Timmermann, C., Kärtner, L., Carhart-Harris, R. L., & Roseman, L. (2021). Psychedelic communitas: Intersubjective experience during psychedelic group sessions predicts enduring changes in psychological wellbeing and social connectedness. *Frontiers in Pharmacology*, 12, Article 623985. https://doi.org/10.3389/fphar.2021.623985

Kılıçkaya, S., Uçar, N., & Denizci Nazlıgül, M. (2021). A systematic review of the association between parenting styles and narcissism in young adults: From Baumrind's perspective. *Psychological Reports*, 126(2), 620–640. https://doi.org/10.1177/00332941211041010

King, B. G., Conklin, Q. A., Zanesco, A. P., & Saron, C. D. (2019). Residential meditation retreats: Their role in contemplative practice and significance for psychological research. *Current Opinion in Psychology*, 28, 238–244. https://doi.org/10.1016/j.copsyc.2018.12.021

Klein, M. (2017). *The psychoanalysis of children*. Andesite Press.

Knapík, P., & Slancová, K. (2020). Core beliefs: Schemas and coping styles in addictions. *Cognitive Remediation Journal*, 9(3), 9–19. https://doi.org/10.5507/crj.2020.003

Knudsen, G. M. (2023). Sustained effects of single doses of classical psychedelics in humans. *Neuropsychopharmacology*, 48(1), 145–150. https://doi.org/10.1038/s41386-022-01361-x

REFERENCES

Koban, L., Gianaros, P. J., Kober, H., & Wager, T. D. (2021). The self in context: Brain systems linking mental and physical health. *Nature Reviews Neuroscience*, 22(5), 309–322. https://doi.org/10.1038/s41583-021-00446-8

Kofman, F. (2013). *Conscious business: How to build value through values*. Sounds True.

Kohut, H. (2009). *The analysis of the self: A systematic approach to the psychoanalytic treatment of narcissistic personality disorders*. University of Chicago Press.

Kohut, H. (2014). *The restoration of the self*. University of Chicago Press.

Kohut, H., & Wolf, E. S. (1978). The disorders of the self and their treatment: An outline. *International Journal of Psycho-Analysis*, 59, 413–425.

Kolden, G. G., Wang, C.-C., Austin, S. B., Chang, Y., & Klein, M. H. (2018). Congruence/genuineness: A meta-analysis. *Psychotherapy*, 55(4), 424–433. https://doi.org/10.1037/pst0000162

Kopala-Sibley, D. C., & Zuroff, D. C. (2020). The self and depression: Four psychological theories and their potential neural correlates. *Journal of Personality*, 88(1), 14–30. https://doi.org/10.1111/jopy.12456

Kornfield, J. (1993). Even the best meditators have old wounds to heal: Combining meditation and psychotherapy. In R. Walsh & F. Vaughan (Eds.), *Paths beyond ego: The transpersonal vision*. Tarcher/Penguin.

Kornfield, J. (2001). *After the ecstasy, the laundry: How the heart grows wise on the spiritual path*. Bantam.

Kotov, R., Krueger, R. F., Watson, D., Achenbach, T. M., Althoff, R. R., Bagby, R. M., Brown, T. A., Carpenter, W. T., Caspi, A., Clark, L. A., Eaton, N. R., Forbes, M. K., Forbush, K. T., Goldberg, D., Hasin, D., Hyman, S. E., Ivanova, M. Y., Lynam, D. R., Markon, K., ... & Zimmerman, M. (2017). The Hierarchical Taxonomy of Psychopathology (HiTOP): A dimensional alternative to traditional nosologies. *Journal of Abnormal Psychology*, 126(4), 454–477. https://doi.org/10.1037/abn0000258

Kotsou, I., Leys, C., & Fossion, P. (2018). Acceptance alone is a better predictor of psychopathology and well-being than emotional competence, emotion regulation and mindfulness. *Journal of Affective Disorders*, 226, 142–145. https://doi.org/10.1016/j.jad.2017.09.047

Kraepelin, E. (1920). Die Erscheinungsformen des Irreseins. *Zeitschrift für die gesamte Neurologie und Psychiatrie*, 62(1), 1–29. https://doi.org/10.1177/0957154X9200301208

Kramer, U., Pascual-Leone, A., Rohde, K. B., & Sachse, R. (2018). The role of shame and self-compassion in psychotherapy for narcissistic personality disorder: An exploratory study. *Clinical Psychology & Psychotherapy*, 25(2), 272–282. https://doi.org/10.1002/cpp.2160

Krizan, Z., & Herlache, A. D. (2018). The narcissism spectrum model: A synthetic view of narcissistic personality. *Personality and Social Psychology Review*, 22(1), 3–31. https://doi.org/10.1177/1088868316685018

Krueger, R. F., & Eaton, N. R. (2015). Transdiagnostic factors of mental disorders. *World Psychiatry*, 14(1), 27–29. https://doi.org/10.1002/wps.20175

Kuijpers, H. J., van der Heijden, F. M. M. A., Tuinier, S., & Verhoeven, W. M. A. (2007). Meditation-induced psychosis. *Psychopathology, 40*(6), 461–464. https://doi.org/10.1159/000108125

Kurak, M. (2003). The relevance of the Buddhist theory of dependent co-origination to cognitive science. *Brain and Mind, 4*(3), 341–351. https://doi.org/10.1023/B:BRAM.0000005468.95009.86

Kyrios, M., Moulding, R., Bhar, S. S., Doron, G., Nedeljkovic, M., & Mikulincer, M. (2016a). Future directions in examining the self in psychological disorders. In M. Kyrios, R. Moulding, G. Doron, S. S. Bhar, M. Nedeljkovic, & M. Mikulincer (Eds.), *The self in understanding and treating psychological disorders*. Cambridge University Press. https://doi.org/10.1017/CBO9781139941297.024

Kyrios, M., Moulding, R., Doron, G., Bhar, S. S., Nedeljkovic, M., & Mikulincer, M. (2016b). *The self in understanding and treating psychological disorders*. Cambridge University Press. https://doi.org/10.1017/CBO9781139941297

Laing, R. D. (2010). *The divided self: An existential study in sanity and madness*. Penguin Books.

Lama, D. XIV. (2019). *Be angry*. Hampton Roads Publishing.

Lama, D., & Ekman, P. (2008). *Emotional awareness: Overcoming the obstacles to psychological balance and compassion*. Henry Holt and Company.

Lambert, D., van den Berg, N. H., & Mendrek, A. (2021). Adverse effects of meditation: A review of observational, experimental and case studies. *Current Psychology, 42*, 1112–1125. https://doi.org/10.1007/s12144-021-01503-2

Lancer, D. (2015). *Codependency for dummies*. John Wiley & Sons.

Lane, R. D., Lee, R., Nadel, L., & Greenberg, L. (2015). Memory reconsolidation, emotional arousal, and the process of change in psychotherapy: New insights from brain science. *Behavioral and Brain Sciences, 38*, Article e1. https://doi.org/10.1017/S0140525X14000041

Langkaas, T. F., Wampold, B. E., & Hoffart, A. (2018). Five types of clinical difference to monitor in practice. *Psychotherapy, 55*(3), 241–254. https://doi.org/10.1037/pst0000194

Lasch, C. (2018). *The culture of narcissism: American life in an age of diminishing expectations*. W. W. Norton & Company.

Leahy, R. L. (2015). *Emotional schema therapy*. Guilford Press.

Leahy, R. L. (2016). Emotional schema therapy: A meta-experiential model. *Australian Psychologist, 51*(2), 82–88. https://doi.org/10.1111/ap.12142

Leahy, R. L. (2019). *Emotional schema therapy: Distinctive features*. Routledge. https://doi.org/10.4324/9780203711095

Leahy, R. L. (2022). Emotional schemas. *Cognitive and Behavioral Practice, 29*(3), 575–580. https://doi.org/10.1016/j.cbpra.2022.02.004

Lear, W. P. (2019). The Icarus complex and the trauma of falling forever. In T. McBride & M. Murphy (Eds.), *Trauma and the destructive-transformative struggle*. Routledge. https://doi.org/10.4324/9780429319587

Leary, T., Metzner, R., & Alpert, R. (2022). *The psychedelic experience: A manual based on the Tibetan book of the dead*. Kensington.

Leary, M., & Tangney, J. P. (Eds.). (2012). *Handbook of self and identity* (2nd ed.). Guilford Press.

Lee, P. H., Anttila, V., Won, H., Feng, Y. C. A., Rosenthal, J., Zhu, Z., Tucker-Drob, E. M., Nivard, M. G., Grotzinger, A. D., Posthuma, D., Wang, M. M. J., Yu, D., Stahl, E. A., Walters, R. K., Anney, R. J. L., Duncan, L. E., Ge, T., Adolfsson, R., Banaschewski, T., & Smoller, J. W. (2019). Genomic relationships, novel loci, and pleiotropic mechanisms across eight psychiatric disorders. *Cell, 179*(7), 1469–1482. https://doi.org/10.1016/j.cell.2019.11.020

Lehrhaupt, L., & Meibert, P. (2010). *Stress bewältigen mit Achtsamkeit: Zu innerer Ruhe kommen durch MBSR*. Kösel.

LeJeune, J., & Luoma, J. B. (2019). *Values in therapy: A clinician's guide to helping clients explore values, increase psychological flexibility, and live a more meaningful life*. New Harbinger Publications.

Lepow, L., Morishita, H., & Yehuda, R. (2021). Critical period plasticity as a framework for psychedelic-assisted psychotherapy. *Frontiers in Neuroscience, 15*, 710004–710004. https://doi.org/10.3389/fnins.2021.710004

Letheby, C. (2021). *Philosophy of psychedelics*. Oxford University Press. https://doi.org/10.1093/med/9780198843122.001.0001

Letheby, C. (2022). Psychedelics and meditation: A neurophilosophical perspective. In R. Repetti (Ed.), *Routledge handbook on the philosophy of meditation*. Routledge.

Letheby, C., & Gerrans, P. (2017). Self unbound: Ego dissolution in psychedelic experience. *Neuroscience of Consciousness, 3*(1), Article nix016. https://doi.org/10.1093/nc/nix016

Levenson, R. W. (1999). The intrapersonal functions of emotion. *Cognition & Emotion, 13*(5), 481–504. https://doi.org/10.1080/026999399379159

Levenson, R. W. (2011). Basic emotion questions. *Emotion Review, 3*(4), 379–386. https://doi.org/10.1177/1754073911410743

Levine, P. A. (2012). *Healing trauma: A pioneering program for restoring the wisdom of your body*. ReadHowYouWant.

Levine, P. A. (2015). *Trauma and memory: Brain and body in a search for the living past*. North Atlantic Books.

Levine, P. A., & Frederick, A. (1997). *Waking the tiger: Healing trauma*. North Atlantic Books.

Liese, B. S., & Beck, A. T. (2022). *Cognitive-behavioral therapy of addictive disorders*. Guilford Press.

Lin, Y., Callahan, C. P., & Moser, J. S. (2018). A mind full of self: Self-referential processing as a mechanism underlying the therapeutic effects of mindfulness training on internalizing disorders. *Neuroscience and Biobehavioral Reviews, 92*, 172–186. https://doi.org/10.1016/j.neubiorev.2018.06.007

Lind, M., Adler, J. M., & Clark, L. A. (2020). Narrative identity and personality disorder: An empirical and conceptual review. *Current Psychiatry Reports, 22*(12), 1–11. https://doi.org/10.1007/s11920-020-01187-8

Lindahl, J. R., & Britton, W. B. (2019). "I have this feeling of not really being here": Buddhist meditation and changes in sense of self. *Journal of Consciousness Studies, 26*(7–8), 157–183.

Lindahl, J. R., Britton, W. B., Cooper, D. J., & Kirmayer, L. J. (2019). Challenging and adverse meditation experiences: Toward a person-centered approach. In M. Farias, D. Brazier, & M. Lalljee (Eds.), *The Oxford handbook of meditation*. Oxford University Press. https://doi.org/10.1093/oxfordhb/9780198808640.013.51

Lindahl, J. R., Britton, W. B., & Cooper, D. J. (2022). Fear and terror in Buddhist meditation: A cognitive model for meditation-related changes in arousal and affect. *Journal of Cognitive Historiography*, 7(1–2), 147–170. https://doi.org/10.1558/jch.22807

Lindahl, J. R., Fisher, N. E., Cooper, D. J., Rosen, R. K., & Britton, W. B. (2017). The varieties of contemplative experience: A mixed-methods study of meditation-related challenges in Western Buddhists. *PLoS ONE*, 12(5), Article e0176239. https://doi.org/10.1371/journal.pone.0176239

Lindsay, E. K., & Creswell, J. D. (2017). Mechanisms of mindfulness training: Monitor and acceptance theory (MAT). *Clinical Psychology Review*, 51, 48–59. https://doi.org/10.1016/j.cpr.2016.10.011

Lindsay, E. K., & Creswell, J. D. (2019). Mindfulness, acceptance, and emotion regulation: Perspectives from monitor and acceptance theory (MAT). *Current Opinion in Psychology*, 28, 120–125. https://doi.org/10.1016/j.copsyc.2018.12.004

Linehan, M. M. (1993). *Cognitive-behavioral treatment of borderline personality disorder*. Guilford Press.

Liotti, G., & Farina, B. (2016). Painful incoherence: The self in borderline personality disorder. In M. Kyrios, R. Moulding, G. Doron, S. S. Bhar, M. Nedeljkovic, & M. Mikulincer (Eds.), *The self in understanding and treating psychological disorders*. Cambridge University Press. https://doi.org/10.1017/CBO9781139941297.018

Lomas, T., Cartwright, T., Edginton, T., & Ridge, D. (2015). A qualitative analysis of experiential challenges associated with meditation practice. *Mindfulness*, 6(4), 848–860. https://doi.org/10.1007/s12671-014-0329-8

Long, M., Verbeke, W., Ein-Dor, T., & Vrtička, P. (2020). A functional neuroanatomical model of human attachment (NAMA): Insights from first- and second-person social neuroscience. *Cortex*, 126, 281–321. https://doi.org/10.1016/j.cortex.2020.01.010

Loori, J. D. (2002). *Riding the ox home: Stages on the path of enlightenment*. Shambhala.

LoSavio, S. T., Dillon, K. H., & Resick, P. A. (2017). Cognitive factors in the development, maintenance, and treatment of post-traumatic stress disorder. *Current Opinion in Psychology*, 14, 18–22. https://doi.org/10.1016/j.copsyc.2016.09.006

Louis, J. P. (2022). The young parenting inventory (YPI-R3), and the Baumrind, Maccoby and Martin parenting model: Finding common ground. *Children*, 9(2), Article 159. https://doi.org/10.3390/children9020159

Luders, E., & Kurth, F. (2019). The neuroanatomy of long-term meditators. *Current Opinion in Psychology*, 28, 172–178. https://doi.org/10.1016/j.copsyc.2018.12.013

REFERENCES

Lue, N. (2023). *The joy of saying no: A simple plan to stop people-pleasing, reclaim your boundaries, and say yes to the life you want.* Harper Horizon.

Lukáč, J., & Popelková, M. (2020). The relationship between early maladaptive schemas and attachment. *Pomáhajúce profesie, 3*(1), 5–19. https://doi.org/10.1016/j.sbspro.2011.10.101

Lundqvist, M., & Wutz, A. (2022). New methods for oscillation analyses push new theories of discrete cognition. *Psychophysiology, 59*(5), 1–16. https://doi.org/10.1111/psyp.13827

Luoma, J. B., Chwyl, C., & Kaplan, J. (2019). Substance use and shame: A systematic and meta-analytic review. *Clinical Psychology Review, 70*, 1–12. https://doi.org/10.1016/j.cpr.2019.03.002

Luyten, P., Campbell, C., & Fonagy, P. (2020). Borderline personality disorder, complex trauma, and problems with self and identity: A social-communicative approach. *Journal of Personality, 88*(1), 88–105. https://doi.org/10.1111/jopy.12483

Luyten, P., & Fonagy, P. (2016). The self in depression. In M. Kyrios, R. Moulding, G. Doron, S. S. Bhar, M. Nedeljkovic, & M. Mikulincer (Eds.), *The self in understanding and treating psychological disorders.* Cambridge University Press. https://doi.org/10.1017/CBO9781139941297.009

MacBeth, A., & Gumley, A. (2012). Exploring compassion: A meta-analysis of the association between self-compassion and psychopathology. *Clinical Psychology Review, 32*(6), 545–552. https://doi.org/10.1016/j.cpr.2012.06.003

Magnavita, J. J., & Anchin, J. C. (2014). *Unifying psychotherapy: Principles, methods, and evidence from clinical science.* Springer Publishing Company.

Mahāsi, S. (2014). *The progress of insight: A modern pali treatise on Buddhist Satipatthana meditation.* Buddhist Publication Society.

Majić, T., Schmidt, T. T., & Gallinat, J. (2015). Peak experiences and the afterglow phenomenon: When and how do therapeutic effects of hallucinogens depend on psychedelic experiences? *Journal of Psychopharmacology, 29*(3), 241–253. https://doi.org/10.1177/0269881114568040

Makransky, J. (2016). Confronting the "sin" out of love for the "sinner": Fierce compassion as a force for social change. *Buddhist-Christian Studies, 36*(1), 87–96. https://doi.org/10.1353/bcs.2016.0009

Mancini, A., & Mancini, F. (2018). Rescripting memory, redefining the self: A meta-emotional perspective on the hypothesized mechanism (s) of imagery rescripting. *Frontiers in Psychology, 9*, Article 581. https://doi.org/10.3389/fpsyg.2018.00581

Manser, R., Cooper, M., & Trefusis, J. (2012). Beliefs about emotions as a metacognitive construct: Initial development of a self-report questionnaire measure and preliminary investigation in relation to emotion regulation. *Clinical Psychology & Psychotherapy, 19*(3), 235–246. https://doi.org/10.1002/cpp.745

Marquis, A., Henriques, G., Anchin, J., Critchfield, K., Harris, J., Ingram, B., Magnavita, J., & Osborn, K. (2021). Unification: The fifth pathway to psychotherapy integration. *Journal of Contemporary Psychotherapy, 51*(4), 285–294. https://doi.org/10.1007/s10879-021-09506-7

REFERENCES

Marraffa, M., Di Francesco, M., & Paternoster, A. (2016). *The self and its defenses: From psychodynamics to cognitive science*. Springer. https://doi.org/10.1057/978-1-137-57385-8

Marroquín, B., Tennen, H., & Stanton, A. L. (2017). Coping, emotion regulation, and well-being: Intrapersonal and interpersonal processes. In M. D. Robinson & M. Eid (Eds.), *The happy mind: Cognitive contributions to well-being*. Springer. https://doi.org/10.1007/978-3-319-58763-9_14

Marsh, I. C., Chan, S. W., & MacBeth, A. (2018). Self-compassion and psychological distress in adolescents: A meta-analysis. *Mindfulness*, 9(4), 1011–1027. https://doi.org/10.1007/s12671-017-0850-7

Maslow, A. H. (1987). *Motivation and personality*. Longman.

Maslow, A. H. (1996). Is human nature basically selfish? In E. Hoffman (Ed.), *Future visions: The unpublished papers of Abraham Maslow*. Sage Publications.

Maslow, A. H. (2014). *Religions, values, and peak-experiences*. Important Books.

Masters, R. A. (2000). Compassionate wrath: Transpersonal approaches to anger. *Journal of Transpersonal Psychology*, 32(1), 31–52. https://www.atpweb.org/pdf/masters.pdf

Masters, R. A. (2009). *Meeting the dragon: Ending our suffering by entering our pain*. Tehmenos Press.

Masters, R. A. (2010). *Spiritual bypassing: When spirituality disconnects us from what really matters*. North Atlantic Books.

Masters, R. A. (2013). *Emotional intimacy: A comprehensive guide for connecting with the power of your emotions*. Sounds True.

Maté, G. (2018). *In the realm of hungry ghosts: Close encounters with addiction*. Vermilion.

Maté, G., & Maté, D. (2022). *The myth of normal: Trauma, illness, and healing in a toxic culture*. Avery.

May, T., Younan, R., & Pilkington, P. D. (2022). Adolescent maladaptive schemas and childhood abuse and neglect: A systematic review and meta-analysis. *Clinical Psychology & Psychotherapy*, 29(4), 1159–1171. https://doi.org/10.1002/cpp.2712

McAdams, D. P., & McLean, K. C. (2013). Narrative identity. *Current Directions in Psychological Science*, 22(3), 233–238. https://doi.org/10.1177/0963721413475622

McAdams, D., Trzesniewski, K., Lilgendahl, J., Benet-Martinez, V., & Robins, R. W. (2021). Self and identity in personality psychology. *Personality Science*, 2, Article e6035. https://doi.org/10.5964/ps.6035

McGrath, J. J., Lim, C. C. W., Plana-Ripoll, O., Holtz, Y., Agerbo, E., Momen, N. C., Mortensen, P. B., Pedersen, C. B., Abdulmalik, J., Aguilar-Gaxiola, S., Al-Hamzawi, A., Alonso, J., Bromet, E. J., Bruffaerts, R., Bunting, B., de Almeida, J. M. C., de Girolamo, G., De Vries, Y A., Florescu, S., ... & De Jonge, P. (2020). Comorbidity within mental disorders: A comprehensive analysis based on 145 990 survey respondents from 27 countries. *Epidemiology and Psychiatric Sciences*, 29, e153, 1–9. https://doi.org/10.1017/S2045796020000633

McHugh, L. (2015). A contextual behavioural science approach to the self and perspective taking. *Current Opinion in Psychology*, 2, 6–10. https://doi.org/10.1016/j.copsyc.2014.12.030

REFERENCES

McHugh, L., Stewart, I., & Almada, P. (2019). *A contextual behavioral guide to the self: Theory and practice.* New Harbinger Publications.

McLaughlin, K. A., Colich, N. L., Rodman, A. M., & Weissman, D. G. (2020). Mechanisms linking childhood trauma exposure and psychopathology: A transdiagnostic model of risk and resilience. *BMC Medicine, 18*(1), Article 96. https://doi.org/10.1186/s12916-020-01561-6

McLaughlin, K. A., & Sheridan, M. A. (2016). Beyond cumulative risk: A dimensional approach to childhood adversity. *Current Directions in Psychological Science, 25*(4), 239–245. https://doi.org/10.1177/0963721416655883

McLaughlin, K. A., Weissman, D., & Bitrán, D. (2019). Childhood adversity and neural development: A systematic review. *Annual Review of Developmental Psychology, 1*, 277–312. https://doi.org/10.1146/annurev-devpsych-121318-084950

McLean, K. C., Syed, M., Pasupathi, M., Adler, J. M., Dunlop, W. L., Drustrup, D., Fivush, R., Graci, M. E., Lilgendahl, J. P., Lodi-Smith, J., McAdams, D. P., & McCoy, T. P. (2020). The empirical structure of narrative identity: The initial big three. *Journal of Personality and Social Psychology, 119*(4), 920–944. https://doi.org/10.1037/pspp0000247

McRae, E. (2015). Metabolizing anger: A tantric Buddhist solution to the problem of moral anger. *Philosophy East and West, 65*(2), 466–484. https://doi.org/10.1353/pew.2015.0041

McRae, K., Misra, S., Prasad, A. K., Pereira, S. C., & Gross, J. J. (2012). Bottom-Up and top-down emotion generation: Implications for emotion regulation. *Social Cognitive & Affective Neuroscience, 7*(3), 253–262. https://doi.org/10.1093/scan/nsq103

McTeague, L. M., Rosenberg, B. M., Lopez, J. W., Carreon, D. M., Huemer, J., Jiang, Y., ... & Etkin, A. (2020). Identification of common neural circuit disruptions in emotional processing across psychiatric disorders. *American Journal of Psychiatry, 177*(5), 411–421. https://doi.org/10.1176/appi.ajp.2019.18111271

McWilliams, N. (2020). *Psychoanalytic diagnosis: Understanding personality structure in the clinical process* (2nd ed.). Guilford Press.

Melchert, T. P. (2016). Leaving behind our preparadigmatic past: Professional psychology as a unified clinical science. *American Psychologist, 71*(6), 486–496. https://doi.org/10.1037/a0040227

Menon, V. (2023). 20 years of the default mode network: A review and synthesis. *Neuron, 111*(16), 2469–2487. https://doi.org/10.1016/j.neuron.2023.04.023

Merrick, M. T., Ford, D. C., Ports, K. A., & Guinn, A. S. (2018). Prevalence of adverse childhood experiences from the 2011–2014 behavioral risk factor surveillance system in 23 states. *JAMA Pediatrics, 172*(11), 1038–1044. https://doi.org/10.1001/jamapediatrics.2018.2537

Metzinger, T. (2023). *Bewusstseinskultur: Spiritualität, intellektuelle Redlichkeit und die planetare Krise.* Berlin Verlag.

Metzner, R. (1998). Hallucinogenic drugs and plants in psychotherapy and shamanism. *Journal of Psychoactive Drugs, 30*(4), 333–341. https://doi.org/10.1080/02791072.1998.10399709

Meyers, K. (2014). Free persons, empty selves. In M. R. Dasti & E. F. Bryant (Eds.), *Free will, agency, and selfhood in Indian philosophy*. Oxford University Press. https://doi.org/10.1093/acprof:oso/9780199922734.003.0003

Michalon, M. (2001). "Selflessness" in the service of the ego: Contributions, limitations and dangers of Buddhist psychology for Western psychotherapy. *American Journal of Psychotherapy*, 55(2), 202–218. https://doi.org/10.1176/appi.psychotherapy.2001.55.2.202

Michelini, G., Palumbo, I. M., DeYoung, C. G., Latzman, R. D., & Kotov, R. (2021). Linking RDoC and HiTOP: A new interface for advancing psychiatric nosology and neuroscience. *Clinical Psychology Review*, 86, Article 102025. https://doi.org/10.1016/j.cpr.2021.102025

Mikulincer, M., & Shaver, P. R. (2016). *Attachment in adulthood: Structure, dynamics, and change* (2nd ed.). Guilford Press.

Mikulincer, M., & Shaver, P. R. (2019). Attachment orientations and emotion regulation. *Current Opinion in Psychology*, 25, 6–10. https://doi.org/10.1016/j.copsyc.2018.02.006

Mikulincer, M., Shaver, P. R., & Gal, I. (2021). An attachment perspective on solitude and loneliness. In R. J. Coplan, J. C. Bowker, & L. J. Nelson (Eds.), *The handbook of solitude: Psychological perspectives on social isolation, social withdrawal, and being alone*. Wiley-Blackwell. https://doi.org/10.1002/9781119576457.ch3

Miller, J. J. (1993). The unveiling of traumatic memories and emotions through mindfulness and concentration meditation: Clinical implications and three case reports. *Journal of Transpersonal Psychology*, 25(2), 169–180.

Miller, J. D., Lynam, D. R., Hyatt, C. S., & Campbell, W. K. (2017). Controversies in narcissism. *Annual Review of Clinical Psychology*, 13(1), 291–315. https://doi.org/10.1146/annurev-clinpsy-032816-045244

Millière, R. (2020). The varieties of selflessness. *Philosophy and the Mind Sciences*, 1(I), 1–41. https://doi.org/10.33735/phimisci.2020.1.48

Millière, R., Carhart-Harris, R. L., Roseman, L., Trautwein, F.-M., & Berkovich-Ohana, A. (2018). Psychedelics, meditation, and self-consciousness. *Frontiers in Psychology*, 9, Article 1475. https://doi.org/10.3389/fpsyg.2018.01475

Minami, F., Zohar, J., Suzuki, T., Koizumi, T., Mimura, M., Yagi, G., & Uchida, H. (2019). Discrepancies between nomenclature and indications of psychotropics. *Pharmacopsychiatry*, 52(04), 175–179. https://doi.org/10.1055/a-0626-7135

Mitmansgruber, H., Beck, T. N., Höfer, S., & Schüßler, G. (2009). When you don't like what you feel: Experiential avoidance, mindfulness and meta-emotion in emotion regulation. *Personality and Individual Differences*, 46(4), 448–453. https://doi.org/10.1016/j.paid.2008.11.013

Mitra, J. L., & Greenberg, M. T. (2016). The curriculum of right mindfulness: The relational self and the capacity for compassion. In R. E. Purser, D. Forbes, & A. Burke (Eds.), *Handbook of mindfulness: Culture, context, and social engagement*. Springer. https://doi.org/10.1007/978-3-319-44019-4_27

Monteiro, L. M., Musten, R. F., & Compson, J. (2015). Traditional and contemporary mindfulness: Finding the middle path in the tangle of concerns. *Mindfulness*, 6(1), 1–13. https://doi.org/10.1007/s12671-014-0301-7

REFERENCES

Moore, R. L. (2003). *Facing the dragon: Confronting personal and spiritual grandiosity*. Chiron Publications.

Moore, K. E., Christian, M. A., Boren, E. A., & Tangney, J. P. (2017). A clinical psychological perspective on hyper- and hypo-egoicism: Symptoms, treatment, and therapist characteristics. In K. W. Brown & M. R. Leary (Eds.), *The Oxford handbook of hypo-egoic phenomena*. Oxford University Press. https://doi.org/10.1093/oxfordhb/9780199328079.013.7

Moors, A. (2014). Flavors of appraisal theories of emotion. *Emotion Review*, 6(4), 303–307. https://doi.org/10.1177/1754073914534477

Moran, O., Almada, P., & McHugh, L. (2018). An investigation into the relationship between the three selves (self-as-content, self-as-process and self-as-context) and mental health in adolescents. *Journal of Contextual Behavioral Science*, 7, 55–62. https://doi.org/10.1016/j.jcbs.2018.01.002

Muris, P., & Petrocchi, N. (2017). Protection or vulnerability? A meta-analysis of the relations between the positive and negative components of self-compassion and psychopathology. *Clinical Psychology & Psychotherapy*, 24(2), 373–383. https://doi.org/10.1002/cpp.2005

Murphy, R., Kettner, H., Zeifman, R., Giribaldi, B., Kartner, L., Martell, J., Read, T., Murphy-Beiner, A., Baker-Jones, M., Nutt, D., Erritzoe, D., Watts, R., & Carhart-Harris, R. (2022). Therapeutic alliance and rapport modulate responses to psilocybin assisted therapy for depression. *Frontiers in Pharmacology*, 12, Article 788155. https://doi.org/10.3389/fphar.2021.788155

Nader, K., Hardt, O., & Lanius, R. (2013). Memory as a new therapeutic target. *Dialogues in Clinical Neuroscience*, 15(4), 475–486. https://doi.org/10.31887/DCNS.2013.15.4/knader

Nagarjuna (2007). *Nagarjuna's precious garland: Buddhist advice for living and liberation*. Snow Lion.

Nairn, R., Choden, & Regan-Addis, H. (2019). *From mindfulness to insight: Meditations to release your habitual thinking and activate your inherent wisdom*. Shambhala.

Ñāṇamoli, B. (2021). *The life of the Buddha: According to the Pali Canon*. Pariyatti Publishing.

Ñāṇamoli, B., & Bodhi, B. (2005). *The middle length discourses of the Buddha: A translation of the Majjhima Nikaya*. Wisdom Publications.

Ñāṇārāma, M. S. (2010). *The seven stages of purification and the insight knowledge: A guide to the progressive stages of Buddhist meditation*. Buddhist Publication Society.

Narada, M. (1987). *A manual of Abhidhamma*. Buddhist Missionary Society.

Nasrallah, H. A. (2021). Re-inventing the DSM as a transdiagnostic model: Psychiatric disorders are extensively interconnected. *Annals of Clinical Psychiatry*, 33(3), 148–150. https://doi.org/10.12788/acp.0037

Nayak, S., & Johnson, M. W. (2021). Psychedelics and psychotherapy. *Pharmacopsychiatry*, 54(4), 167–175. https://doi.org/10.1055/a-1312-7297

Nayak, S. M., Singh, M., Yaden, D. B., & Griffiths, R. R. (2023). Belief changes associated with psychedelic use. *Journal of Psychopharmacology*, 37(1), 80–92. https://doi.org/10.1177/02698811221131989

Neff, K. (2021). *Fierce self-compassion: How women can harness kindness to speak up, claim their power, and thrive.* Harper Wave.

Nelson, C. A., & Gabard-Durnam, L. J. (2020). Early adversity and critical periods: Neurodevelopmental consequences of violating the expectable environment. *Trends in Neurosciences, 43*(3), 133–143. https://doi.org/10.1016/j.tins.2020.01.002

Nemeroff, C. B. (2016). Paradise lost: The neurobiological and clinical consequences of child abuse and neglect. *Neuron, 89*(5), 892–909. https://doi.org/10.1016/j.neuron.2016.01.019

Newson, J. J., Pastukh, V., & Thiagarajan, T. C. (2021). Poor separation of clinical symptom profiles by DSM-5 disorder criteria. *Frontiers in Psychiatry, 12*, Article 775762. https://doi.org/10.3389/fpsyt.2021.775762

Ng, S. M., Chow, K. W., Lau, H. P., & Wang, Q. (2017). Awareness versus un-clinging: Which matters in mindfulness? *Contemporary Buddhism, 18*(2), 277–291. https://doi.org/10.1080/14639947.2017.1374326

Nguyen, K. T., & Shaw, L. (2020). The aetiology of non-clinical narcissism: Clarifying the role of adverse childhood experiences and parental overvaluation. *Personality and Individual Differences, 154*, Article 109615. https://doi.org/10.1016/j.paid.2019.109615

Niebauer, C. (2019). *No self, no problem: How neuropsychology is catching up to Buddhism.* Hierophant Publishing.

Nieto, I., Robles, E., & Vazquez, C. (2020). Self-reported cognitive biases in depression: A meta-analysis. *Clinical Psychology Review, 82*, Article 101934. https://doi.org/10.1016/j.cpr.2020.101934

Nolen-Hoeksema, S., Wisco, B. E., & Lyubomirsky, S. (2008). Rethinking rumination. *Perspectives on Psychological Science, 3*(5), 400–424. https://doi.org/10.1111/j.1745-6924.2008.00088.x

Norcross, J. C., & Goldfried, M. R. (Eds.). (2019). *Handbook of psychotherapy integration: Third edition.* Oxford University Press. https://doi.org/10.1093/med-psych/9780190690465.001.0001

Norcross, J. C., & Lambert, M. J. (Eds.). (2019). *Psychotherapy relationships that work: Volume 1: Evidence-based therapist contributions.* Oxford University Press. https://doi.org/10.1093/med-psych/9780190843953.001.0001

Norcross, J. C., & Lambert, M. J. (2018). Psychotherapy relationships that work III. *Psychotherapy, 55*(4), 303–315. http://dx.doi.org/10.1037/pst0000193

Norcross, J. C., Pfund, R. A., & Cook, D. M. (2022). The predicted future of psychotherapy: A decennial e-Delphi poll. *Professional Psychology: Research and Practice, 53*(2), 109–115. https://doi.org/10.1037/pro0000431

Norton, A. R., Penney, E. S., & Abbott, M. J. (2022). Schema modes in social anxiety disorder: Empirical findings and case conceptualisation. *Journal of Clinical Psychology, 21*(1), 34–47. https://doi.org/10.1177/15346501211027866

Nour, M. M., Evans, L., & Carhart-Harris, R. L. (2017). Psychedelics, personality and political perspectives. *Journal of Psychoactive Drugs, 49*(3), 182–191. https://doi.org/10.1080/02791072.2017.1312643

Nour, M. M., Evans, L., Nutt, D., & Carhart-Harris, R. L. (2016). Ego-dissolution and psychedelics: Validation of the ego-dissolution inventory (EDI). *Frontiers in Human Neuroscience, 10,* Article 269. https://doi.org/10.3389/fnhum.2016.00269

Nyanaponika, T. (2008). *The threefold refuge.* Buddhist Publication Society.

Nyanaponika, T. (2009). *Roots of good and evil.* Buddhist Publication Society.

Nyanaponika, T. (2014). *The heart of Buddhist meditation: The Buddha's way of mindfulness.* Weiser Books.

Nyanatiloka, T. (2019). *Buddhist dictionary: Manual of Buddhist terms and doctrines.* BPS Pariyatti Editions.

O'Connor, L. E., Berry, J. W., & Weiss, J. (1999). Interpersonal guilt, shame, and psychological problems. *Journal of Social and Clinical Psychology, 18*(2), 181–203. https://doi.org/10.1521/jscp.1999.18.2.181

Oakley, B. A. (2013). Concepts and implications of altruism bias and pathological altruism. *Proceedings of the National Academy of Sciences, 110*(supplement_2), 10408–10415. https://doi.org/10.1073/pnas.1302547110

Olatunji, B. O., Christian, C., Brosof, L., Tolin, D. F., & Levinson, C. A. (2019). What is at the core of OCD? A network analysis of selected obsessive-compulsive symptoms and beliefs. *Journal of Affective Disorders, 257,* 45–54. https://doi.org/10.1016/j.jad.2019.06.064

Otani, K., Suzuki, A., Matsumoto, Y., & Shirata, T. (2018). Marked differences in core beliefs about self and others, between sociotropy and autonomy: Personality vulnerabilities in the cognitive model of depression. *Neuropsychiatric Disease and Treatment, 14,* 863–866. https://doi.org/10.2147/ndt.s161541

Otway, L. J., & Carnelley, K. B. (2013). Exploring the associations between adult attachment security and self-actualization and self-transcendence. *Self and Identity, 12*(2), 217–230. https://doi.org/10.1080/15298868.2012.667570

Padmasambhava (2008). *The Tibetan book of the dead.* Penguin Classics.

Parkes, L., Moore, T. M., Calkins, M. E., Cook, P. A., Cieslak, M., Roalf, D. R., Wolf, D. H., Gur, R. C., Gur, R. E., Satterthwaite, T. D., & Bassett, D. S. (2021). Transdiagnostic dimensions of psychopathology explain individuals' unique deviations from normative neurodevelopment in brain structure. *Translational Psychiatry, 11*(1), Article 232. https://doi.org/10.1038/s41398-021-01342-6

Paterniti, K., Bright, S., & Gringart, E. (2022). The relationship between psychedelic use, mystical experiences, and pro-environmental behaviors. *Journal of Humanistic Psychology,* Article 00221678221111024. https://doi.org/10.1177/00221678221111024

Payne, J. E., Chambers, R., & Liknaitzky, P. (2021). Combining psychedelic and mindfulness interventions: Synergies to inform clinical practice. *ACS Pharmacology & Translational Science, 4*(2), 416–423. https://doi.org/10.1021/acsptsci.1c00034

Pearsall, P. (2009). *500 therapies: Discovering a science for everyday living.* W. W. Norton & Company.

Pedreira, M. E., Pérez-Cuesta, L. M., & Maldonado, H. (2004). Mismatch between what is expected and what actually occurs triggers memory reconsolidation or extinction. *Learning & Memory, 11*(5), 579–585. https://doi.org/10.1101/lm.76904

Peluso, D. (2014). Ayahuasca's attractions and distractions: Examining sexual seduction in shaman-participant interactions. In B. Caiuby Labate & C. Cavnar (Eds.), *Ayahuasca shamanism in the Amazon and beyond*. Oxford University Press. https://doi.org/10.1093/acprof:oso/9780199341191.003.0011

Pepping, C. A., Davis, P. J., O'Donovan, A., & Pal, J. (2015). Individual differences in self-compassion: The role of attachment and experiences of parenting in childhood. *Self and Identity*, *14*(1), 104–117. https://doi.org/10.1080/15298868.2014.955050

Perls, F. S. (1992). *Gestalt therapy verbatim* (2nd revised ed.). Gestalt Journal Press.

Perquin, L. (2004). Issues of narcissism and omnipotence treated by the use of physical limits with a symbolic meaning in Pesso Boyden System Psychomotor. *European Psychotherapy*, *5*(1), 85–101.

Perry, J. W. (2020). *The far side of madness*. Spring Publications.

Pesso, A. (2013). *Presentations & lectures by Albert Pesso on Pesso Boyden System Psychomotor therapy (1984–2012)*. Kindle Edition.

Petitcollin, C. (2020). *Victime, bourreau ou sauveur: Comment sortir du piège?* Jouvence.

Phelps, J. (2017). Developing guidelines and competencies for the training of psychedelic therapists. *Journal of Humanistic Psychology*, *57*(5), 450–487. https://doi.org/10.1177/0022167817711304

Piaget, J. (2015). *The psychology of intelligence*. Routledge.

Pilkington, P. D., Bishop, A., & Younan, R. (2021). Adverse childhood experiences and early maladaptive schemas in adulthood: A systematic review and meta-analysis. *Clinical Psychology & Psychotherapy*, *28*(3), 569–584. https://doi.org/10.1002/cpp.2533

Pincus, A. L., Cain, N. M., & Wright, A. G. C. (2014). Narcissistic grandiosity and narcissistic vulnerability in psychotherapy. *Personality Disorders: Theory, Research, and Treatment*, *5*(4), 439–443. https://doi.org/10.1037/per0000031

Pinto-Gouveia, J., Castilho, P., Galhardo, A., & Cunha, M. (2006). Early maladaptive schemas and social phobia. *Cognitive Therapy and Research*, *30*(5), 571–584. https://doi.org/10.1007/s10608-006-9027-8

Piretti, L., Pappaianni, E., Garbin, C., Rumiati, R. I., Job, R., & Grecucci, A. (2023). The neural signatures of shame, embarrassment, and guilt: A voxel-based meta-analysis on functional neuroimaging studies. *Brain Sciences*, *13*(4), Article 559. https://doi.org/10.3390/brainsci13040559

Plato (2022). *The apology of Socrates*. Legare Street Press.

Pollak, S., Pedulla, T., & Siegel, R. D. (2014). *Sitting together: Essential skills for mindfulness-based psychotherapy*. Guilford Press.

Postránecká, Z., Vejmola, Č., & Tylš, F. (2019). Psychedelic therapy in the Czech Republic: A theoretical concept or a realistic goal? *Journal of Psychedelic Studies*, *3*(1), 19–31. https://doi.org/10.1556/2054.2019.003

Preece, R. (2009). *The courage to feel: Buddhist practices for opening to others*. Snow Lion.

Price, M., Albaugh, M., Hahn, S., Juliano, A. C., Fani, N., Brier, Z. M., Legrand, A. C., van Stolk-Cooke, K., Chaarani, B., Potter, A., Peck, K., Allgaier, N., Banaschewski, T., Bokde, A. L. W., Quinlan, E. B., Desrivières, S., Flor, H.,

Grigis, A., Gowland, P., ... & Garavan, H. (2021). Examination of the association between exposure to childhood maltreatment and brain structure in young adults: A machine learning analysis. *Neuropsychopharmacology*, 46(11), 1888–1894. https://doi.org/10.1038/s41386-021-00987-7

Price, C. J., & Hooven, C. (2018). Interoceptive awareness skills for emotion regulation: Theory and approach of mindful awareness in body-oriented therapy (MABT). *Frontiers in Psychology*, 9, Article 798. https://doi.org/10.3389/fpsyg.2018.00798

Prochaska, J. O., & Norcross, J. C. (2018). *Systems of psychotherapy: A transtheoretical analysis* (9th ed.). Oxford University Press.

Purser, R. (2019). *McMindfulness: How mindfulness became the new capitalist spirituality*. Repeater.

Quaglia, J. T. (2023). One compassion, many means: A big two analysis of compassionate behavior. *Mindfulness*, 14(10), 2430–2442. https://doi.org/10.1007/s12671-022-01895-7

Radakovic, C., Radakovic, R., Peryer, G., & Geere, J. A. (2022). Psychedelics and mindfulness: A systematic review and meta-analysis. *Journal of Psychedelic Studies*, 6(2), 137–153. https://doi.org/10.1556/2054.2022.00218

Raffone, A. (2021). Grand challenges in consciousness research across perception, cognition, self, and emotion. *Frontiers in Psychology*, 12, Article 5507. https://doi.org/10.3389/fpsyg.2021.770360

Rapgay, L., & Bystrisky, A. (2009). Classical mindfulness: An introduction to its theory and practice for clinical application. *Annals of the New York Academy of Sciences*, 1172(1), 148–162. https://doi.org/10.1111/j.1749-6632.2009.04405.x

Repetti, R. (2017). *Buddhist perspectives on free will: Agentless agency?* Routledge. https://doi.org/10.4324/9781315668765

Rhys Davids, T. W. (2016). *A Buddhist manual of psychological ethics*. Pali Text Society.

Riegel, K., Kalina, K., & Pěč, O. (2020). *Poruchy osobnosti v 21. století: Diagnostika v teorii a praxi*. Portál.

Rihacek, T., & Roubal, J. (2017). The proportion of integrationists among Czech psychotherapists and counselors: A comparison of multiple criteria. *Journal of Psychotherapy Integration*, 27(1), 13–22. https://doi.org/10.1037/int0000069

Riskind, J. H., & Calvete, E. (2020). Anxiety and the dynamic self as defined by the prospection and mental simulation of looming future threats. *Journal of Personality*, 88(1), 31–44. https://doi.org/10.1111/jopy.12465

Rogers, C. R. (2021). *Client centered therapy*. Robinson.

Rogers, C. R. (2022). *Becoming a person*. Mockingbird Press.

Röhr, H. P. (2015). *Wege aus der Abhängigkeit: Belastende Beziehungen überwinden*. Patmos.

Röhr, H. P. (2022a). *Die Kunst, sich wertzuschätzen: Angst und Depression überwinden – Selbstsicherheit gewinnen*. Patmos.

Röhr, H. P. (2022b). *Narzissmus: Dem inneren Gefängnis entfliehen*. Patmos.

Röhr, H. P. (2022c). *Wie Sie Ihr Selbstwertgefühl stärken: Die geheimen Programme der Seele entschlüsseln*. Patmos.

Roseman, L., Haijen, E., Idialu-Ikato, K., Kaelen, M., Watts, R., & Carhart-Harris, R. (2019). emotional breakthrough and psychedelics: Validation of the emotional breakthrough inventory. *Journal of Psychopharmacology*, 33(9), 1076–1087. https://doi.org/10.1177/0269881119855974

Ruffell, S. G., Netzband, N., Tsang, W., Davies, M., Butler, M., Rucker, J. J., Tófoli, L. F., Dempster, E. L., Young, A. H., & Morgan, C. J. (2021). Ceremonial ayahuasca in Amazonian retreats: Mental health and epigenetic outcomes from a six-month naturalistic study. *Frontiers in Psychiatry*, 12, Article 687615. https://doi.org/10.3389/fpsyt.2021.687615

Ryan, R. M., & Deci, E. L. (2017). *Self-determination theory: Basic psychological needs in motivation, development, and wellness*. Guilford Press.

Ryan, R., & Rigby, C. (2015). Did the Buddha have a self? No-self, self, and mindfulness in Buddhist thought and western psychologies. In K. Brown, J. Creswell, & R. Ryan (Eds.), *Handbook of mindfulness: Theory, research and practice*. Guilford Press.

Sacks, V., & Murphey, D. (2018). The prevalence of adverse childhood experiences, nationally, by state, and by race or ethnicity. *Child Trends*, Article 2018-03. http://hdl.handle.net/20.500.11990/1142

Sala, M., Shankar Ram, S., Vanzhula, I. A., & Levinson, C. A. (2020). Mindfulness and eating disorder psychopathology: A meta-analysis. *International Journal of Eating Disorders*, 53(6), 834–851. https://doi.org/10.1002/eat.23247

Sampedro, F., de la Fuente Revenga, M., Valle, M., Roberto, N., Domínguez-Clavé, E., Elices, M., Luna, L. E., Crippa, J. A. S., Hallak, J. E. C., de Araujo, D. B., Friedlander, P., Barker, S. A., Álvarez, E., Soler, J., Pascual, J. C., Feilding, A., & Riba, J. (2017). Assessing the psychedelic "after-glow" in ayahuasca users: Post-acute neurometabolic and functional connectivity changes are associated with enhanced mindfulness capacities. *International Journal of Neuropsychopharmacology*, 20(9), 698–711. https://doi.org/10.1093/ijnp/pyx036

Sass, L., Borda, J. P., Madeira, L., Pienkos, E., & Nelson, B. (2018). Varieties of self disorder: A bio-pheno-social model of schizophrenia. *Schizophrenia Bulletin*, 44(4), 720–727. https://doi.org/10.1093/schbul/sby001

Scheidegger, M. (2021). Comparative phenomenology and neurobiology of meditative and psychedelic states of consciousness: Implications for psychedelic-assisted therapy. In C. S. Grob & J. Grigsby (Eds.), *Handbook of medical hallucinogens*. Guilford Press.

Schiller, D., Monfils, M. H., Raio, C. M., Johnson, D. C., LeDoux, J. E., & Phelps, E. A. (2010). Preventing the return of fear in humans using reconsolidation update mechanisms. *Nature*, 463(7277), 49–53. https://doi.org/10.1038/nature08637

Schimmenti, A., & Caretti, V. (2018). Attachment, trauma, and alexithymia. In O. Luminet, R. M. Bagby, & G. J. Taylor (Eds.), *Alexithymia: Advances in research, theory, and clinical practice*. Cambridge University Press.

Schlag, A. K., Aday, J., Salam, I., Neill, J. C., & Nutt, D. J. (2022). Adverse effects of psychedelics: From anecdotes and misinformation to systematic science.

Journal of Psychopharmacology, 36(3), 258–272. https://doi.org/10.1177/02698811211069100

Schlosser, M., Sparby, T., Vörös, S., Jones, R., & Marchant, N. L. (2019). Unpleasant meditation-related experiences in regular meditators: Prevalence, predictors, and conceptual considerations. *PLoS ONE, 14*(5), Article e0216643. https://doi.org/10.1371/journal.pone.0216643

Schmidbauer, W. (2007). *Das Helfer-syndrom: Hilfe für Helfer.* Rowohlt.

Schmid, Y., & Liechti, M. E. (2018). Long-lasting subjective effects of LSD in normal subjects. *Psychopharmacology, 235*(2), 535–545. https://doi.org/10.1007/s00213-017-4733-3

Schoeller, F. (2023). Existential priors: Top-down cognition in rostral prefrontal cortex. *PsyArXiv.* https://doi.org/10.31234/osf.io/fye2m

Schoenberg, P. L. A., & Barendregt, H. P. (2016). Mindful disintegration and the decomposition of self in healthy populations: Conception and preliminary study. *Psychological Studies, 61*(4), 307–320. https://doi.org/10.1007/s12646-016-0374-6

Scigala, D. K., Fabris, M. A., Badenes-Ribera, L., Zdankiewicz-Scigala, E., & Longobardi, C. (2021). Alexithymia and self differentiation: The role of fear of intimacy and insecure adult attachment. *Contemporary Family Therapy, 43,* 165–176. https://doi.org/10.1007/s10591-021-09567-9

Segal, Z. V., Williams, M., & Teasdale, J. (2013). *Mindfulness-based cognitive therapy for depression* (2nd ed.). Guilford Press.

Seligman, M. E. (2005). *Helplessness: On depression, development and death.* W. H. Freeman & Co.

Selzam, S., Coleman, J. R., Caspi, A., Moffitt, T. E., & Plomin, R. (2018). A polygenic p factor for major psychiatric disorders. *Translational Psychiatry, 8*(1), 1–9. https://doi.org/10.1038/s41398-018-0217-4

Seth, A. (2021). *Being you: A new science of consciousness.* Faber & Faber.

Sevinc, G., & Lazar, S. W. (2019). How does mindfulness training improve moral cognition: A theoretical and experimental framework for the study of embodied ethics. *Current Opinion in Psychology, 28,* 268–272. https://doi.org/10.1016/j.copsyc.2019.02.006

Shahar, G., Noyman, G., Schnidel-Allon, I., & Gilboa-Schechtman, E. (2013). Do PTSD symptoms and trauma-related cognitions about the self constitute a vicious cycle? Evidence for both cognitive vulnerability and scarring models. *Psychiatry Research, 205*(1–2), 79–84. https://doi.org/10.1016/j.psychres.2012.07.053

Shalit, E. (2002). *Complex: Path of transformation from archetype to ego.* City Books.

Shapiro, S., & White, C. (2014). *Mindful discipline: A loving approach to setting limits and raising an emotionally intelligent child.* New Harbinger Publications.

Shaver, P. R., Mikulincer, M., Sahdra, B. K., & Gross, J. T. (2017). Attachment security as a foundation for kindness toward self and others. In K. W. Brown & M. R. Leary (Eds.), *The Oxford handbook of hypo-egoic phenomena.* Oxford University Press. https://doi.org/10.1093/oxfordhb/9780199328079.013.15

Shepherd, G. (2020). "Normally I'd get really agitated, but I just laughed!": What do participants reflect upon in a transactional analysis/mindfulness based anger management programme? *British Journal of Guidance & Counselling*, 48(4), 537–551. https://doi.org/10.1080/03069885.2020.1730303

Sheridan, M. A., & McLaughlin, K. A. (2014). Dimensions of early experience and neural development: Deprivation and threat. *Trends in Cognitive Sciences*, 18(11), 580–585. https://doi.org/10.1016/j.tics.2014.09.001

Shi, Z., & He, L. (2020). Mindfulness: Attenuating self-referential processing and strengthening other-referential processing. *Mindfulness*, 11(3), 599–605. https://doi.org/10.1007/s12671-019-01271-y

Shireen, H., Khanyari, S., Vance, A., Johannesson, H., Preissner, C., Dor-Ziderman, Y., Khoury, B., & Knauper, B. (2022). Paying attention to the self: A systematic review of the study of the self in mindfulness research. *Mindfulness*, 13(6), 1373–1386. https://doi.org/10.1007/s12671-022-01844-4

Shonin, E., van Gordon, W., & Griffiths, M. D. (2016). Ontological addiction: Classification, etiology, and treatment. *Mindfulness*, 7(3), 660–671. https://doi.org/10.1007/s12671-016-0501-4

Shonin, E., van Gordon, W., & Singh, N. N. (Eds.). (2015). *Buddhist foundations of mindfulness*. Springer. https://doi.org/10.1007/978-3-319-18591-0

Siderits, M., & Katsura, S. (2013). *Nagarjuna's middle way: Mulamadhyamakakarika*. Wisdom Publications.

Siegel, D. J. (2010a). *Mindsight: The new science of personal transformation*. Bantam.

Siegel, D. J. (2010b). *The mindful therapist: A clinician's guide to mindsight and neural integration*. W. W. Norton & Company.

Siegel, D. J. (2020). *The developing mind: How relationships and the brain interact to shape who we are* (3rd ed.). Guilford Press.

Siegel, J. S., Daily, J. E., Perry, D. A., & Nicol, G. E. (2023). Psychedelic drug legislative reform and legalization in the US. *JAMA Psychiatry*, 80(1), 77–83. https://doi.org/10.1001/jamapsychiatry.2022.4101

Siegel, D. J., & Payne-Bryson, T. (2016). *No-drama discipline: The whole-brain way to calm the chaos and nurture your child's developing mind*. Bantam.

Siegel, D. J., Schore, A. N., & Cozolino, L. (2021). *Interpersonal neurobiology and clinical practice*. W. W. Norton & Company.

Siegel, D. J., & Solomon, M. F. (Eds.). (2013). *Healing moments in psychotherapy*. W. W. Norton & Company.

Sierra-Siegert, M., & Jay, E.-L. (2020). Reducing oneself to a body, a thought, or an emotion: A measure of identification with mind contents. *Psychology of Consciousness: Theory, Research, and Practice*, 7(3), 218–237. https://doi.org/10.1037/cns0000233

Simeon, D., & Abugel, J. (2023). *Feeling unreal: Depersonalization and the loss of the self*. Oxford University Press.

Simione, L., Raffone, A., & Mirolli, M. (2021). Acceptance, and not its interaction with attention monitoring, increases psychological well-being: Testing

REFERENCES

the monitor and acceptance theory of mindfulness. *Mindfulness*, *12*(6), 1398–1411. https://doi.org/10.1007/s12671-021-01607-7

Simonds, C. H. (2023). View, meditation, action: A Tibetan framework to inform psychedelic-assisted therapy. *Journal of Psychedelic Studies*, *7*(1), 58–68. https://doi.org/10.1556/2054.2023.00255

Simon, R., & Engström, M. (2015). The default mode network as a biomarker for monitoring the therapeutic effects of meditation. *Frontiers in Psychology*, *6*, Article 776. https://doi.org/10.3389/fpsyg.2015.00776

Simonsson, O., Fisher, S., & Martin, M. (2021). Awareness and experience of mindfulness in Britain. *Sociological Research Online*, *26*(4), 833–852. https://doi.org/10.1177/1360780420980761

Singh, T., Pascual-Leone, A., Morrison, O. P., & Greenberg, L. (2021). Working with emotion predicts sudden gains during experiential therapy for depression. *Psychotherapy Research*, *31*(7), 895–908. https://doi.org/10.1080/10503307.2020.1866784

Sirimane, Y. (2016). *Entering the stream to enlightenment, experiences of the stages of the Buddhist path in contemporary Sri Lanka*. Equinox Publishing.

Sloshower, J., Guss, J., Krause, R., Wallace, R. M., Williams, M. T., Reed, S., & Skinta, M. D. (2020). Psilocybin-assisted therapy of major depressive disorder using acceptance and commitment therapy as a therapeutic frame. *Journal of Contextual Behavioral Science*, *15*, 12–19. https://doi.org/10.1016/j.jcbs.2019.11.002

Smigielski, L., Scheidegger, M., Kometer, M., & Vollenweider, F. X. (2019). Psilocybin-assisted mindfulness training modulates self-consciousness and brain default mode network connectivity with lasting effects. *NeuroImage*, *196*, 207–215. https://doi.org/10.1016/j.neuroimage.2019.04.009

Smith, R. (2010). *Stepping out of self-deception: The Buddha's liberating teaching of no-self*. Shambhala.

Smith, K. E., Mason, T. B., & Lavender, J. M. (2018). Rumination and eating disorder psychopathology: A meta-analysis. *Clinical Psychology Review*, *61*, 9–23. https://doi.org/10.1016/j.cpr.2018.03.004

Smoller, J. W., Andreassen, O. A., Edenberg, H. J., Faraone, S. V., Glatt, S. J., & Kendler, K. S. (2019). Psychiatric genetics and the structure of psychopathology. *Molecular Psychiatry*, *24*(3), 409–420. https://doi.org/10.1038/s41380-017-0010-4

Sohmer, O. R. (2020). The experience of the authentic self: A cooperative inquiry. *Journal of Humanistic Psychology*, Article 0022167820952339. https://doi.org/10.1177/0022167820952339

Spalletta, G., Janiri, D., Piras, F., & Sani, G. (Eds.). (2020). *Childhood trauma in mental disorders: A comprehensive approach*. Springer. https://doi.org/10.1007/978-3-030-49414-8

Spinazzola, J., Van der Kolk, B., & Ford, J. D. (2018). When nowhere is safe: Interpersonal trauma and attachment adversity as antecedents of posttraumatic stress disorder and developmental trauma disorder. *Journal of Traumatic Stress*, *31*(5), 631–642. https://doi.org/10.1002/jts.22320

Srinivasan, N. (2020). Consciousness without content: A look at evidence and prospects. *Frontiers in Psychology, 11*, Article 1992. https://doi.org/10.3389/fpsyg.2020.01992

St. Arnaud, K. O., & Sharpe, D. (2023). Entheogens and spiritual seeking: The quest for self-transcendence, psychological well-being, and psychospiritual growth. *Journal of Psychedelic Studies, 7*(1), 69–79. https://doi.org/10.1556/2054.2023.00263

Stanley, S., Purser, R. E., & Singh, N. N. (2018). *Handbook of ethical foundations of mindfulness.* Springer. https://doi.org/10.1007/978-3-319-76538-9

Stauffer, C. S., Anderson, B. T., Ortigo, K. M., & Woolley, J. (2021). Psilocybin-assisted group therapy and attachment: Observed reduction in attachment anxiety and influences of attachment insecurity on the psilocybin experience. *ACS Pharmacology & Translational Science, 4*(2), 526–532. https://doi.org/10.1021/acsptsci.0c00169

Stavropoulos, A., Haire, M., Brockman, R., & Meade, T. (2020). A schema mode model of repetitive negative thinking. *Clinical Psychologist, 24*(2), 99–113. https://doi.org/10.1111/cp.12205

Stevens, F. L. (2014). Affect regulation styles in avoidant and anxious attachment. *Individual Differences Research, 12*(3), 123–130.

Stevens, F. L. (2019). Affect regulation and affect reconsolidation as organizing principles in psychotherapy. *Journal of Psychotherapy Integration, 29*(3), 277–290. https://doi.org/10.1037/int0000130

Stevens, F. L. (2021). *Affective neuroscience in psychotherapy: A clinician's guide for working with emotions.* Routledge. https://doi.org/10.4324/9781003150893

Straver, F. R. (2017). *A theoretical model of substance use based on schema therapy concepts* [Master's thesis, Utrecht University].

Strentz, T. (1980). The Stockholm syndrome: Law enforcement policy and ego defenses of the hostage. *Annals of the New York Academy of Sciences, 347*(1), 137–150. https://doi.org/10.1111/j.1749-6632.1980.tb21263.x

Struhl, K. J. (2020). What kind of an illusion is the illusion of self. *Comparative Philosophy, 11*(2), Article 8. https://doi.org/10.31979/2151-6014(2020).110208

Stuart-Parrigon, K., Kerns, K. A., Movahed Abtahi, M., & Koehn, A. (2015). Attachment and emotion in middle childhood and adolescence. *Psychological Topics, 24*(1), 27–50.

Sui, J., & Humphreys, G. W. (2015). The integrative self: How self-reference integrates perception and memory. *Trends in Cognitive Sciences, 19*(12), 719–728. https://doi.org/10.1016/j.tics.2015.08.015

Sui, J., & Rotshtein, P. (2019). Self-prioritization and the attentional systems. *Current Opinion in Psychology, 29*, 148–152. https://doi.org/10.1016/j.copsyc.2019.02.010

Sujiva, B. (2000). *Essentials of insight meditation practice: A pragmatic approach to vipassana.* Buddhist Wisdom Centre.

Sundag, J., Zens, C., Ascone, L., Thome, S., & Lincoln, T. M. (2018). Are schemas passed on? A study on the association between early maladaptive schemas in parents and their offspring and the putative translating mechanisms.

Behavioural and Cognitive Psychotherapy, 46(6), 738–753. https://doi.org/10.1017/S1352465818000073

Tacikowski, P., Berger, C. C., & Ehrsson, H. H. (2017). Dissociating the neural basis of conceptual self-awareness from perceptual awareness and unaware self-processing. *Cerebral Cortex*, 27(7), 3768–3781. https://doi.org/10.1093/cercor/bhx004

Tackman, A. M., Sbarra, D. A., Carey, A. L., Donnellan, M. B., Horn, A. B., Holtzman, N. S., Edwards, T. S., Pennebaker, J. W., & Mehl, M. R. (2019). Depression, negative emotionality, and self-referential language: A multi-lab, multi-measure, and multi-language-task research synthesis. *Journal of Personality and Social Psychology*, 116(5), 817–834. https://doi.org/10.1037/pspp0000187

Talbot, D., Smith, E., Tomkins, A., Brockman, R., & Simpson, S. (2015). Schema modes in eating disorders compared to a community sample. *Journal of Eating Disorders*, 3(1), Article 41. https://doi.org/10.1186/s40337-015-0082-y

Tangney, J. P. (2015). Psychology of self-conscious emotions. In J. D. Wright (Ed.), *International encyclopedia of the social and behavioral sciences*. Elsevier.

Tangney, J. P., & Dearing, R. (2002). *Shame and guilt*. Guilford.

Teicher, M. H., Gordon, J. B., & Nemeroff, C. B. (2022). Recognizing the importance of childhood maltreatment as a critical factor in psychiatric diagnoses, treatment, research, prevention, and education. *Molecular Psychiatry*, 27(3), 1331–1338. https://doi.org/10.1038/s41380-021-01367-9

Teicher, M. H., Samson, J. A., Polcari, A., & McGreenery, C. E. (2006). Sticks, stones, and hurtful words: Relative effects of various forms of childhood maltreatment. *American Journal of Psychiatry*, 163(6), 993–1000. https://doi.org/10.1176/ajp.2006.163.6.993

Tejaniya, A. (2014). *Awareness alone is not enough*. Auspicious Affinity.

Tenore, K., Mancini, F., & Basile, B. (2018). Schemas, modes and coping strategies in obsessive-compulsive like symptoms. *Clinical Neuropsychiatry*, 15(6), 384–392.

Thal, S., Engel, L. B., & Bright, S. J. (2022). Presence, trust, and empathy: Preferred characteristics of psychedelic carers. *Journal of Humanistic Psychology*, Article 00221678221081380. https://doi.org/10.1177/00221678221081380

Thomas, K., & Malcolm, B. (2021). Adverse effects. In C. S. Grob & J. Grigsby (Eds.), *Handbook of medical hallucinogens*. Guilford Press.

Thompson, E. (2008). Neurophenomenology and Francisco Varela. In A. Harrington & A. Zajonc (Eds.), *The Dalai Lama at MIT*. Harvard University Press.

Thompson, E. (2014). *Waking, dreaming, being: Self and consciousness in neuroscience, meditation, and philosophy*. Columbia University Press. https://doi.org/10.7312/thom13709

Thompson, R. A., Simpson, J. A., & Berlin, L. J. (Eds.). (2021). *Attachment: The fundamental questions*. Guilford Press.

Timmermann, C., Kettner, H., Letheby, C., Roseman, L., Rosas, F. E., & Carhart-Harris, R. L. (2021). Psychedelics alter metaphysical beliefs. *Scientific Reports*, 11(1), Article 22166. https://doi.org/10.1038/s41598-021-01209-2

REFERENCES

Timmermann, C., Watts, R., & Dupuis, D. (2022). Towards psychedelic apprenticeship: Developing a gentle touch for the mediation and validation of psychedelic-induced insights and revelations. *Transcultural Psychiatry*, 59(5), 691–704. https://doi.org/10.1177/13634615221082796

Timuľák, L. (2015). *Transforming emotional pain in psychotherapy: An emotion-focused approach*. Routledge.

Timuľák, L., & Keogh, D. (2021). *Transdiagnostic emotion-focused therapy: A clinical guide for transforming emotional pain*. American Psychological Association. https://doi.org/10.1037/0000253-000

Timuľák, L., & Pascual-Leone, A. (2015). New developments for case conceptualization in emotion-focused therapy. *Clinical Psychology & Psychotherapy*, 22(6), 619–636. https://doi.org/10.1002/cpp.1922

Tiwari, P., Berghella, A. P., Sayalı, C., Doss, M. K., Barrett, F. S., & Yaden, D. B. (2023). Learned helplessness as a potential transdiagnostic therapeutic mechanism of classic psychedelics. *Psychedelic Medicine*, 1(2), 74–86. https://doi.org/10.1089/psymed.2023.0010

Tracy, J. L., & Robins, R. W. (2006). Appraisal antecedents of shame and guilt: Support for a theoretical model. *Personality and Social Psychology Bulletin*, 32, 1339–1351. https://doi.org/10.1177/0146167206290212

Tronick, E. (2007). *The neurobehavioral and social-emotional development of infants and children*. W. W. Norton & Company.

Tronick, E., & Gold, C. (2020). *The power of discord: Why the ups and downs of relationships are the secret to building intimacy, resilience, and trust*. Little, Brown Spark.

Trungpa, C. (2002). *Cutting through spiritual materialism*. Shambhala.

Twenge, J. M., & Campbell, W. K. (2009). *The narcissism epidemic: Living in the age of entitlement*. Free Press.

Underhill, E. (2019). *Mysticism: A study in the nature and development of man's spiritual consciousness*. Wentworth Press.

Vago, D. R., & Silbersweig, D. A. (2012). Self-awareness, self-regulation, and self-transcendence (S-ART): A framework for understanding the neurobiological mechanisms of mindfulness. *Frontiers in Human Neuroscience*, 6, Article 296. https://doi.org/10.3389/fnhum.2012.00296

van der Kolk, B. A., Wang, J. B., Yehuda, R., Bedrosian, L., Coker, A. R., Harrison, C., Mithoefer, M., Yazar-Klosinki, B., Emerson, A., & Doblin, R. (2024). Effects of MDMA-assisted therapy for PTSD on self-experience. *PLoS One*, 19(1), Article e0295926. https://doi.org/10.1371/journal.pone.0295926

van der Wijngaart, R. (2021). *Imagery rescripting: Theory and practice*. Pavilion Publishing & Media.

van Elk, M., & Yaden, D. B. (2022). Pharmacological, neural, and psychological mechanisms underlying psychedelics: A critical review. *Neuroscience & Biobehavioral Reviews*, 140, Article 104793. https://doi.org/10.1016/j.neubiorev.2022.104793

van Gordon, W., Shonin, E., Diouri, S., Garcia-Campayo, J., Kotera, Y., & Griffiths, M. D. (2018). Ontological addiction theory: Attachment to me, mine, and I. *Journal of Behavioral Addictions*, 7(4), 892–896. https://doi.org/10.1556/2006.7.2018.45

van Gordon, W., Shonin, E., Dunn, T. J., Sapthiang, S., Kotera, Y., Garcia-Campayo, J., & Sheffield, D. (2019). Exploring emptiness and its effects on non-attachment, mystical experiences, and psycho-spiritual wellbeing: A quantitative and qualitative study of advanced meditators. *Explore*, 15(4), 261–272. https://doi.org/10.1016/j.explore.2018.12.003

van Vreeswijk, M., Broersen, J., & Schurink, G. (2014). *Mindfulness and schema therapy: A practical guide.* John Wiley & Sons.

VanderKooi, L. (1997). Buddhist teachers' experience with extreme mental states in western meditators. *Journal of Transpersonal Psychology*, 29(1), 31–46.

Varela, F. J. (1999). *Ethical know-how: Action, wisdom, and cognition.* Stanford University Press.

Vasilopoulou, E., Karatzias, T., Hyland, P., Wallace, H., & Guzman, A. (2020). The mediating role of early maladaptive schemas in the relationship between childhood traumatic events and complex posttraumatic stress disorder symptoms in older adults (> 64 years). *Journal of Loss and Trauma*, 25(2), 141–158. https://doi.org/10.1080/15325024.2019.1661598

Vaughan, F. (1986). *The inward arc: Healing and wholeness in psychotherapy and spirituality.* Shambhala.

Veilleux, J. C., Chamberlain, K. D., Baker, D. E., & Warner, E. A. (2021). Disentangling beliefs about emotions from emotion schemas. *Journal of Clinical Psychology*, 77(4), 1068–1089. https://doi.org/10.1002/jclp.23098

Velotti, P., D'Aguanno, M., De Campora, G., Di Francescantonio, S., Garofalo, C., Giromini, L., Petrocchi, C., Terrasi, M., & Zavattini, G. C. (2016). Gender moderates the relationship between attachment insecurities and emotion dysregulation. *South African Journal of Psychology*, 46(2), 191–202. https://doi.org/10.1177/0081246315604582

Villiger, D. (2022). How psychedelic-assisted treatment works in the Bayesian brain. *Frontiers in Psychiatry*, 13, Article 812180. https://doi.org/10.3389/fpsyt.2022.812180

von Franz, M. L. (2000). *The problem of the puer aeternus.* Inner City Books.

Vonk, R., & Visser, A. (2021). An exploration of spiritual superiority: The paradox of self-enhancement. *European Journal of Social Psychology*, 51(1), 152–165. https://doi.org/10.1002/ejsp.2721

Vörös, S. (2016). Sitting with the demons: Mindfulness, suffering, and existential transformation. *Asian Studies*, 4(2), 59–83. https://doi.org/10.4312/as.2016.4.2.59-83

Vybíral, Z., Castonguay, L., Danelová, E., Hodoval, R., Kulhavý, V., Plchová, R., & Přibylová, H. (2010). Kolik je na světě psychoterapií? *Psychoterapie*, 4(1), 39–55.

Walach, H. (2015). *Secular spirituality: The next step towards enlightenment.* Springer. https://doi.org/10.1007/978-3-319-09345-1

Walach, H. (2008). Narcissism: The shadow of transpersonal psychology. *Transpersonal Psychology Review*, 12(2), 47–59. https://doi.org/10.53841/bpstran.2008.12.2.47

Walpola, P., Walpola, I., & Toneatto, T. (2022). A contemporary model for right mindfulness based on Theravada Buddhist texts. *Mindfulness, 13*(11), 2714–2728. https://doi.org/10.1007/s12671-022-01988-3

Walsh, R., & Roche, L. (1979). Precipitation of acute psychotic episodes by intensive meditation in individuals with a history of schizophrenia. *The American Journal of Psychiatry, 136*(8), 1085–1086. https://doi.org/10.1176/ajp.136.8.1085

Walsh, R., & Vaughan, F. (1993). *Paths beyond ego: The transpersonal vision.* Tarcher/Penguin.

Wampold, B. E., & Imel, Z. E. (2015). *The great psychotherapy debate: The evidence for what makes psychotherapy work.* Routledge. https://doi.org/10.4324/9780203582015

Waszczuk, M. A., Zimmerman, M., Ruggero, C., Li, K., MacNamara, A., Weinberg, A., ... & Kotov, R. (2017). What do clinicians treat: Diagnoses or symptoms? The incremental validity of a symptom-based, dimensional characterization of emotional disorders in predicting medication prescription patterns. *Comprehensive Psychiatry, 79,* 80–88. https://doi.org/10.1016/j.comppsych.2017.04.004

Watson, G. (2018). *Beyond happiness: Deepening the dialogue between Buddhism, psychotherapy and the mind sciences.* Routledge. https://doi.org/10.4324/9780429472404

Watson, J. B. (1913). Psychology as the behaviorist views it. *Psychological Review, 20*(2), 158–177. https://doi.org/10.1037/h0074428

Watson, D., Levin-Aspenson, H. F., Waszczuk, M. A., Conway, C. C., Dalgleish, T., Dretsch, M. N., Eaton, N. R., Forbes, M. K., Forbush, K. T., Hobbs, K. A., Michelini, G., Nelson, B. D., Sellbom, M., Slade, T., South, S. C., Sunderland, M., Waldman, I., Witthöft, M., Wright, A. G. C., ... & Krueger, R. F. (2022). Validity and utility of Hierarchical Taxonomy of Psychopathology (HiTOP): III. Emotional dysfunction superspectrum. *World Psychiatry, 21*(1), 26–54. https://doi.org/10.1002/wps.20943

Watts, R., Day, C., Krzanowski, J., Nutt, D., & Carhart-Harris, R. (2017). Patients' accounts of increased "connectedness" and "acceptance" after psilocybin for treatment-resistant depression. *Journal of Humanistic Psychology, 57*(5), 520–564. https://doi.org/10.1177/0022167817709585

Watts, R., & Luoma, J. B. (2020). The use of the psychological flexibility model to support psychedelic assisted therapy. *Journal of Contextual Behavioral Science, 15,* 92–102. https://doi.org/10.1016/j.jcbs.2019.12.004

Wayment, H. A., Bauer, J. J., & Sylaska, K. (2015). The Quiet Ego Scale: Measuring the compassionate self-identity. *Journal of Happiness Studies: An Interdisciplinary Forum on Subjective Well-Being, 16*(4), 999–1033. https://doi.org/10.1007/s10902-014-9546-z

Weber, J. (2017). Mindfulness is not enough: Why equanimity holds the key to compassion. *Mindfulness & Compassion, 2*(2), 149–158. https://doi.org/10.1016/j.mincom.2017.09.004

Weder, B. J. (2022). Mindfulness in the focus of the neurosciences: The contribution of neuroimaging to the understanding of mindfulness. *Frontiers in Behavioral Neuroscience, 16,* Article 928522. https://doi.org/10.3389/fnbeh.2022.928522

REFERENCES

Wegela, K. K. (2014). *Contemplative psychotherapy essentials: Enriching your practice with Buddhist psychology*. W. W. Norton & Company.

Weinhold, B. K., & Weinhold, J. B. (2013). *How to break free of the drama triangle & victim consciousness*. CICRCL Press.

Wei, M., Russell, D. W., Mallinckrodt, B., & Vogel, D. L. (2007). The Experiences in Close Relationship Scale (ECR)-short form: Reliability, validity, and factor structure. *Journal of Personality Assessment, 88*(2), 187–204. https://doi.org/10.1080/00223890701268041

Weiser Cornell, A. (1996). *The power of focusing: A practical guide to emotional self-healing*. New Harbinger Publications.

Weissman, D. G., Bitran, D., Miller, A. B., Schaefer, J. D., Sheridan, M. A., & McLaughlin, K. A. (2019). Difficulties with emotion regulation as a transdiagnostic mechanism linking child maltreatment with the emergence of psychopathology. *Development and Psychopathology, 31*(3), 899–915. https://doi.org/10.1017/S0954579419000348

Wei, M., Vogel, D. L., Ku, T. Y., & Zakalik, R. A. (2005). Adult attachment, affect regulation, negative mood, and interpersonal problems: The mediating roles of emotional reactivity and emotional cutoff. *Journal of Counseling Psychology, 52*(1), 14–24. https://doi.org/10.1037/0022-0167.52.1.14

Welwood, J. (1996). Reflection and presence: The dialectic of self-knowledge. *Journal of Transpersonal Psychology, 28*, 107–128. https://www.atpweb.org/jtparchive/trps-28-96-02-107.pdf

Welwood, J. (2002). *Toward a psychology of awakening: Buddhism, psychotherapy, and the path of personal and spiritual transformation*. Shambhala.

Wheeler, M. S., Arnkoff, D. B., & Glass, C. R. (2017). The neuroscience of mindfulness: How mindfulness alters the brain and facilitates emotion regulation. *Mindfulness, 8*(6), 1471–1487. https://doi.org/10.1007/s12671-017-0742-x

Whitehead, R., Bates, G., Elphinstone, B., Yang, Y., & Murray, G. (2018). Letting go of self: The creation of the nonattachment to self scale. *Frontiers in Psychology, 9*, Article 2544. https://doi.org/10.3389/fpsyg.2018.02544

Wielgosz, J., Goldberg, S. B., Kral, T. R., Dunne, J. D., & Davidson, R. J. (2019). Mindfulness meditation and psychopathology. *Annual Review of Clinical Psychology,15*,285–316.https://doi.org/10.1146/annurev-clinpsy-021815-093423

Wilber, K. (2006). *Integral spirituality: A startling new role for religion in the modern and postmodern world*. Shambhala.

Wilber, K. (2016). *Integral meditation*. Shambhala.

Williams, P. (2022a). A holistic needs-based model of diagnosis. In E. Maisel & Ch. Ruby (Eds.), *Humane alternatives to the psychiatric model*. Ethics International Press.

Williams, P. (2022b). A holistic needs-based model of support. In E. Maisel & Ch. Ruby (Eds.), *Humane alternatives to the psychiatric model*. Ethics International Press.

Williams, J. M. G., & Kabat-Zinn, J. (2013). *Mindfulness: Diverse perspectives on its meaning, origins and applications*. Routledge. https://doi.org/10.4324/9781315874586

Winkelman, M. J., & Sessa, B. (Eds.). (2019). *Advances in psychedelic medicine: State-of-the-art therapeutic applications*. ABC-CLIO.

Winnicott, D. W. (2017). *Playing and reality*. Routledge.

Winnicott, D. W. (2018a). Ego distortion in terms of true and false self. In V. Richards & G. Wilce (Eds.), *The person who is me: Contemporary perspectives on the true and false self*. Routledge. https://doi.org/10.4324/9780429482700

Winnicott, D. W. (2018b). *The maturational processes and the facilitating environment: Studies in the theory of emotional development*. Routledge. https://doi.org/10.4324/9780429482410

Winnicott, D. W. (2018c). *Through paediatrics to psychoanalysis: Collected papers*. Routledge. https://doi.org/10.4324/9780429484001

Winterheld, H. A. (2015). Calibrating use of emotion regulation strategies to the relationship context: An attachment perspective. *Journal of Personality*, 84(3), 369–380. https://doi.org/10.1111/jopy.12165

Winter, U., LeVan, P., Borghardt, T. L., Akin, B., Wittmann, M., Leyens, Y., & Schmidt, S. (2020). Content-free awareness: EEG-fcMRI correlates of consciousness as such in an expert meditator. *Frontiers in Psychology*, 10, Article 3064. https://doi.org/10.3389/fpsyg.2019.03064

Witkiewitz, K., & Villarroel, N. A. (2009). Dynamic association between negative affect and alcohol lapses following alcohol treatment. *Journal of Consulting and Clinical Psychology*, 77(4), 633–644. https://doi.org/10.1037/a0015647

Wittmann, M. (2018). *Altered states of consciousness: Experiences out of time and self*. MIT Press.

Wolff, M., Evens, R., Mertens, L. J., Koslowski, M., Betzler, F., Gründer, G., & Jungaberle, H. (2020). Learning to let go: A cognitive-behavioral model of how psychedelic therapy promotes acceptance. *Frontiers in Psychiatry*, 11, Article 5. https://doi.org/10.3389/fpsyt.2020.00005

Wolfson, E. (2023). Psychedelic-supportive psychotherapy: A psychotherapeutic model for, before and beyond the medicine experience. *Journal of Psychedelic Studies*, 6(3), 191–202. https://doi.org/10.1556/2054.2022.00192

Woodman, M. (1988). *Addiction to perfection: The still unravished bride: A psychological study*. Inner City Books.

World Health Organization (2018). *International classification of diseases 11th revision*. World Health Organization.

Wright, A. G., & Edershile, E. A. (2018). Issues resolved and unresolved in pathological narcissism. *Current Opinion in Psychology*, 21, 74–79. https://doi.org/10.1016/j.copsyc.2017.10.001

Xiao, Q., Yue, C., He, W., & Yu, J. Y. (2017). The mindful self: A mindfulness-enlightened self-view. *Frontiers in Psychology*, 8, Article 1752. https://doi.org/10.3389/fpsyg.2017.01752

Yaden, D. B., & Newberg, A. (2022). *The varieties of spiritual experience: 21st century research and perspectives*. Oxford University Press. https://doi.org/10.1093/oso/9780190665678.001.0001

Yakeley, J. (2018). Current understanding of narcissism and narcissistic personality disorder. *BJPsych Advances*, 24(5), 305–315. https://doi.org/10.1192/bja.2018.20

REFERENCES

Yankouskaya, A., & Sui, J. (2022). Self-prioritization is supported by interactions between large-scale brain networks. *European Journal of Neuroscience*, 55(5), 1244–1261. https://doi.org/10.1111/ejn.15612

Yehuda, R., & Lehrner, A. (2018). Intergenerational transmission of trauma effects: Putative role of epigenetic mechanisms. *World Psychiatry*, 17(3), 243–257. https://doi.org/10.1002/wps.20568

Young, J. E., Klosko, J. S., & Weishaar, M. E. (2003). *Schema therapy: A practitioner's guide*. Guilford Press.

Yurchenko, S. B. (2022). From the origins to the stream of consciousness and its neural correlates. *Frontiers in Integrative Neuroscience*, 16, Article 928978. https://doi.org/10.3389/fnint.2022.928978

Zaman, S., Arouj, K., Irfan, S., & Yousaf, I. (2021). Maladaptive schema modes as the predictor of post-traumatic stress disorder among trauma survivors. *JPMA. The Journal of the Pakistan Medical Association*, 71(7), 1789–1792. https://doi.org/10.47391/jpma.01-013

Zanesco, A. P., King, B. G., Conklin, Q. A., & Saron, C. D. (2023). The occurrence of psychologically profound, meaningful, and mystical experiences during a month-long meditation retreat. *Mindfulness*, 14(3), 606–621. https://doi.org/10.1007/s12671-023-02076-w

Zarate-Guerrero, S., Duran, J. M., & Naismith, I. (2022). How a transdiagnostic approach can improve the treatment of emotional disorders: Insights from clinical psychology and neuroimaging. *Clinical Psychology & Psychotherapy*, 29, 895–905. https://doi.org/10.1002/cpp.2704

Zeifman, R. J., Spriggs, M. J., Kettner, H., Lyons, T., Rosas, F., Mediano, P. A., Erritzoe, D., & Carhart-Harris, R. (2023a). From Relaxed Beliefs Under Psychedelics (REBUS) to Revised Beliefs After Psychedelics (REBAS): Preliminary development of the Relaxed Beliefs Questionnaire (REB-Q). *Scientific Reports*. https://doi.org/10.31234/osf.io/w8j6t

Zeifman, R. J., Wagner, A. C., Monson, C. M., & Carhart-Harris, R. L. (2023b). How does psilocybin therapy work? An exploration of experiential avoidance as a putative mechanism of change. *Journal of Affective Disorders*, 334, 100–112. https://doi.org/10.1016/j.jad.2023.04.105

Zessin, U., Dickhäuser, O., & Garbade, S. (2015). The relationship between self-compassion and well-being: A meta-analysis. *Applied Psychology: Health and Well-Being*, 7(3), 340–364. https://doi.org/10.1111/aphw.12051

Zeynel, Z., & Uzer, T. (2020). Adverse childhood experiences lead to transgenerational transmission of early maladaptive schemas. *Child Abuse & Neglect*, 99, Article 104235. https://doi.org/10.1016/j.chiabu.2019.104235

Zhou, H. X., Chen, X., Shen, Y. Q., Li, L., Chen, N. X., Zhu, Z. C., Castellanos, F. X., & Yan, C. G. (2020). Rumination and the default mode network: Meta-analysis of brain imaging studies and implications for depression. *Neuroimage*, 206, Article 116287. https://doi.org/10.1016/j.neuroimage.2019.116287

Zimmermann, P. (1999). Structure and functions of internal working models of attachment and their role for emotion regulation. *Attachment and Human Development*, 1(3), 57–71. https://doi.org/10.1080/14616739900134161

Žvelc, G. (2010). Relational schemas theory and transactional analysis. *Transactional Analysis Journal*, *40*(1), 8–22. https://doi.org/10.1177/036215371004000103

Žvelc, G., & Žvelc, M. (2021). *Integrative psychotherapy: A mindfulness- and compassion-oriented approach*. Routledge. https://doi.org/10.4324/9780429290480

Zweig, C. (2023). *Meeting the shadow on the spiritual path: The dance of darkness and light in our search for awakening*. Simon and Schuster.

Index

Note: Page numbers in **bold** refer to tables, and those in *italics* refer to figures.

Abandoned Self 64, **68**, 103, 142, *150*, 163; and core beliefs 65, 94n1; and emotions 51, 65, 91; and unmet needs 2, 108, 162; *see also* Wounded Self

abandonment (feeling) 27, 135; in case fragments 14, *41*, 66, 127, 142; as a core pain 17n6, 28, 48, 117; in exercise 86; *see also* core pain; fear of abandonment; loneliness

Abhidhamma 54n1, 129n4, 154–155, 162; and conceit 82, 174; and dependent origination 95n4, 159n4; and hatred 124; and intention 116; and meditation 162, 164; and mental defilements 16n5, 52, 123n7, 182n3; and neuroscience 159n3n4; and *nibbāna* 159n7; and transpersonal development 184–185; *see also* Buddha's teachings

absolute reality 6, 7n2, 101, 176, 178

acceptance 89, 102, 161, 167, 169n2, 176; of anger 102, 104, 126; of core pain 128n3, 157, 165, 176, 178; in exercises 22, 45, 50, 69–70, 122; of experience 80, 100–101; of fear 57; of feelings 48, 115, 141, 165, 172; by God 143; of limits 80, 99, 167, 175, 179; of oneself 43, 174–175, 179; of phenomena 49, 102, 142, 154–155, 179; of sadness 119; unconditional 81, 133, 135, 143

Acceptance and Commitment Therapy 5, 152n5, 170n4, 185n2

adult responsibility *see* responsibility

adverse childhood experiences 18–20, 22n2; *see also* corrective experience; developmental trauma; early experiences

afterglow period 147n7

altered states of consciousness 97, 139–140, 161, 165–166; and Abhidhamma 184; and compassionate attitude 179; in exercise 168; and meditation 153; and perinatal experiences 21; phenomenological map of 164; and psychedelic therapists 164; and psychedelics 146n5; and transpersonal development 153, 165; *see also* non-dual awareness; psychedelic experience

ambivalent attachment **62**

Anālayo, B. 102, 149, 154

anattā see Not-Self

anger *see* protective anger; reactive anger

anxious-preoccupied attachment **62**

INDEX

Assagioli, R. 24, 139–140, 150, 160n11, 164
attachment 131–134, 137n1, 144
attachment anxiety 130, 133–135, 144, 176; and defense mechanisms 135; and fear of abandonment 131; and the *phenomenological model of maladaptive schemas* 138n4; in romantic relationships 132
attachment avoidance 130, 132–133, 176; and close relationships 130; and defense mechanisms 135; and emotion regulation 134; and fear of closeness 132, 134–135; illusion of independence 135, 141; and the Mindful Zombie 130, 172; and the *phenomenological model of maladaptive schemas* 138n4; and psychedelic experience 144; in romantic relationships 132; and shame 132
attachment security priming 50
attachment style 31, 54, 134; in the Abandoned Self **68**; in the Inferior Self **76**; in the Inflated Self **85**; in the Lost Self **62**
attachment theory 2, 7n1, 18, 20, 130–131
Authentic Self 93, 97–98, *150*; and core beliefs 108; development of the 2–3, 100, 135, 180; differentiation of the 184–185; in exercises 45, 85, 145–146, 181; flexibility of the 151–152; manifestation of the 179, 181; narrative of the 140, 152n2, 167; quiz 145–146; and relationships 133, 145; and transpersonal experiences 175–176; utilization of the 178; and vulnerability 130; *see also* Narrative Self; Wounded Self
authoritarian parenting 79, 82; *see also* parenting styles
authoritative parenting 79; *see also* parenting styles
autobiographical self *see* Narrative Self
awakening 6; full 180–181; levels of 155–156, 160n8, 170n3, 174; *see also* seven factors of awakening

bare attention 149, 151, 172
Barendregt, H. 129n4, 141, 149, 154–155, 159n5, 162
basic developmental needs *see* developmental needs
Baumrind, D. 79
being mode 3, 100, 178–179, 181; *see also* doing mode; ego state; state of mind
Berne, E. 24, 99–100, 107–108, 129n4
Bernstein, A. 149–150
Bible 127, 180
Billy Elliot 72
Bodhi, B. 24–25, 54n1, 93, 101, 129n4, 146n3, 159n6, 164, 174, 179, 181
Bowlby, J. 18, 24, 130
Brach, T. 73
Brewer, J. 43, 95n4
Brown, B. 105, 123n4n9, 136, 141, 175
Brown, D. P. 66, 118, 153, 160n8
Brown, K. W. 30, 45, 151
Buddha 179–181; in comparison with Freud 8n3; on five aggregates of clinging 93; on mental formations 24–25; on mindfulness 101
Buddha's teachings 1, 162, 171–172; and the attainment of *nibbāna* 155; on the Noble Eightfold Path 101; on the seven factors of awakening 106n3; on the three refuges 159n6; *see also* Abhidhamma
Burbea, R. 25, 95n4, 164

Campbell, J. 178, 180
Carhart-Harris, R. L. 143, 167, 169n2
Castonguay, L. G. 4n3, 89, 143, 184
CCC model *see* Compassion-Comprehension-Commitment model
ceremonies 142–143, 173–175
clinging 36, **52**, 102, 141, 156, 181; in exercise 85; and meditation and psychedelic experiences 179; and the pleasure principle 105; to the Wounded Narrative Self 126
close relationships 115, 130, 136; and the afterglow period 147n7; and attachment anxiety 130, 132; and attachment avoidance 130;

237

in Buddha's teachings 159n6; in case fragments 173; and corrective emotional experiences 136; maintaining 2, 11, 38; and maladaptive schemas 91, 136, 138n2, 173; and the Mindful Zombie 172–173; and personal development 140–141, 158, 173; and the relational Self 133, and transpersonal development 158, 175; and transpersonal experiences 157; *see also* closeness

closeness 20, 31, 66, 108, 130–131; and the Abandoned Self 2, 64–65, 108, 162; and attachment anxiety 135; and attachment avoidance 132, 134; avoidance of 172; in case fragments 109; emotional 136; and mindfulness 5, 136; need for 14, 53, 64, 102; in personality disorder 40; physical 64; in therapist-client dialogue 68; and transpersonal experiences 166; *see also* courage to be close; fear of closeness

cognitive map 164, 168

cognitive reappraisal 3, 28, 49, 112, 115–116; as only a complementary strategy 91–93, 157, 166; as an emotion regulation strategy 134; and meditation or psychedelic experiences 161, 166, 169n2; and mindfulness 26, 93; in therapist-client dialogue 27

cognitive science 159n3n4

cognitive-behavioral therapy 25–26, 28, 90, 92; representative of 94n1; third wave of 5

common factors 10–11, 15, 47

compassion 18, 97, 124–125, 127, 166; and altered states of consciousness 161; and assertion 102; in case fragments 61, 118, 121, 142, 163; with the child 137n1; and close relationships 173; and core beliefs about emotions 116; and defense mechanisms 48, 89; and emptiness 152; in exercises 16, 22, 69, 181; and the "master of two worlds" 181; mechanisms of 47; meditation 159n6; and meditation or psychedelic experiences 179–180; of meditation teacher 162–164; and non-dual awareness 158; as a prerequisite for cognitive reappraisal 93; and psychedelic experience 144; as a relational experience 50n2, 55n3, 162–164; of the therapist 162, 166; in therapist-client dialogue 76; and the *Transdiagnostic Theory of the Wounded Self* 184; and transformation of maladaptive schemas 48; and transpersonal experiences 167, 175; and trauma 100; and understanding of needs 48, 136; and the Wounded Self 181; *see also* compassionate attitude; compassionate wrath; Compassion-Comprehension-Commitment model; fierce compassion; self-compassion

compassionate attitude 47, 178–179; in case fragments 43, 127; toward core pain 28, 48, 92, 114n3, 117, 128n3; toward emotions 136; in exercises 16, 22, 45, 77, 112, 122; toward feelings 85, 172; toward loneliness 66; toward maladaptive schemas 49; and *memory reconsolidation* 89; of the therapist 6, 165–166

compassionate wrath 124–127, 128n3; *see also* protective anger

Compassion-Comprehension-Commitment model 165–166, 170n5

conceptual self *see* Narrative Self

constant mindfulness 151, 153–154; *see also* mindfulness; momentary mindfulness

constructive dependency 136

content-free awareness *see* non-dual awareness

conventional reality 7n2, 159n4, 176, 178

core belief 26, 28, 88, 90–91; in alcohol dependence 43–44; in anorexia nervosa 42–43; and attachment 131; and the Authentic Self 108; on a billboard (exercise) 93–94; and the Buddha 93; in case fragments 104; and cognitive neuroscience 29n1; cognitive reappraisal of 3, 92, 112, 135, 157, 166;

INDEX

and cognitive-behavioral therapy 94n1; and dependent origination 95n4; in depressive disorder 36–37; development of 18–20, 26, 73, 82; and developmental trauma 61, 91, 108; and ego states 99, 110; as an element of maladaptive schema 2, 14, 33; about emotions 116; example of 58, 65, 73, 82; in exercises 45, 77, 93–94; and the Inferior Self 73, 94n1; and the inner critic 94n2; and life scripts 107; and the Lost Self 94n1; and maladaptive schemas 25, 117; and mindful diagnosis 51; and mindfulness 15, 92, 100, 105, 112, 178; and the Narrative Self 151 in obsessive-compulsive disorder 35, 36; in personality disorder 40, 41; in post-traumatic stress disorder 38, 39; in psychotherapy 9, 11, 28, 49, 89, 92; rigidity of 167; as "secret program" 17n7; and self-conscious emotions 115; and semantic memory 90; in social anxiety disorder 32–33, 34; in therapist-client dialogue 84; and transpersonal experiences 143, 156, 161, 168, 169n2; uncovering 33, 37, 39, 41, 44, 174; understanding the origin of 15, 49, 53; and the Wounded Self 117

core pain 48, 66, 88–89, 100; acceptance of 128n3, 157, 165, 176, 178; in alcohol dependence 43, 44; and anger 124; in anorexia nervosa 43; in case fragments 83, 103, 121, 174; compassion for 126, 166; compassionate attitude toward 28, 48, 92, 114n3, 117, 128n3; and corrective relational experiences 28, 50n2; courage to consciously confront 136, 173; and defense mechanisms 19, 53, 91, 135, 138n4, 174; and dependent origination 95n4; in depressive disorder 37; as an element of maladaptive schema 2, 25, 88, 112; emergence of 14, 25, 112; and emotional breakthrough 166; in exercises 45, 69, 137, 169; in the Lost Self 61; and *memory reconsolidation* 89–90; and mindful diagnosis 15, 52; and mindfulness 15, 49, 66, 73, 88, 93; and the Narrative Self 117; in obsessive-compulsive disorder 35, 36; origin of 18, 23n5; in personality disorder 40, 41; in post-traumatic stress disorder 39; and psychedelic experience 161–162; and responsibility 113; and scripts 107; and self-compassion 135; in social anxiety disorder 33, 34; in therapist-client dialogue 13, 27, 74; three variations of 17n6, 51, 88, 90, 94n1, 117; transforming 68, 89, 125; and transpersonal experiences 168; uncovering 9, 135, 173; understanding the origin of 66; *see also* abandonment (feeling); existential dread; inferiority (feeling); loneliness; shame

corrective experience 3, 6, 89–90, 92, 116; and the afterglow period 147n7; in case fragments 14, 66, 118, 121, 142; and close relationships 136; cognitive interventions 95n5; and core pain 28; and defense mechanisms 48; and developmental needs 53, 90; and insecure attachment 135; and maladaptive schemas 157; and meditation experiences 175; and *memory reconsolidation* 61, 73, 92, 94n3, 166, 182n1; and psychedelic experience 157, 162; and psychotherapeutic change 184; within the therapeutic relationship 114n3; in therapist-client dialogue 70n1; and transpersonal experience 165, 175; and the Wounded Self 3, 157, 162, 165; *see also* adverse childhood experiences; developmental trauma; early experiences

courage to be close 99, 130, 136–137

courage to separate 99, 130; *see also* fierce compassion

Cozolino, L. 20

crisis of duality 175

239

Dalai Lama 124, 127
Dambrun, M. 156, 179
dark night of the soul 154, 171
decentering 149–150
default mode network 16n1, 46n2, 131, 152n4
defense mechanisms 65, 88–89, 94n2, 114n2, 180; and Abhidhamma 182n3; and adverse childhood experiences 19; in alcohol dependence 44; in anorexia nervosa 43; and attachment anxiety 135; and attachment avoidance 135; in case fragments 14, 103; commitment to overcoming 144; and compassion 48, 89; conceit, as a 174; and core pain 19, 53, 92, 135, 138n4, 174; in depressive disorder 37; dissociation, as a 23n4; as an element of maladaptive schema 2, 112; in exercises 45, 69, 76; and existential dread 138n4; and loneliness 138n4; and meditation and psychedelic experiences 161; and mindful diagnosis 15, 49, 51–52, 135; and mindful therapist 53; and mindfulness 102; and Mindfulness-Informed Integrative Psychotherapy16n5, 49, 52, 89; in narcissism 83; in obsessive-compulsive disorder 36; omnipotent guilt, as a 117, 123n7; origin of 25, 48–49; in personality disorder 41; and the *phenomenological model of maladaptive schemas* 25; in post-traumatic stress disorder 39; rejecting attitude toward 49; and scripts 107; and shame 138n4; in social anxiety disorder 34; and the "Taming the Demons Within" technique 49, 89; and trauma 99, 130; uncovering 9, 11; *see also* defilements
defilements 16n5, 48, 52, 156, 182n3; *see also* defense mechanisms
Deikman, A. 100, 150–151, 178
dependent origination 24–25, 95n4, 159n4
developmental needs 21, 51, 53, 54, 65, 80; and attachment 131–132;

in exercise 21; and the Pesso Boyden System Psychomotor Therapy 55n3; and the *Transdiagnostic Theory of the Wounded Self* 183
developmental trauma 2, 19, 21, 48, 136, 172; and core beliefs 61, 91, 108; *see also* adverse childhood experiences; corrective experience; early experiences
Dharmapala, A. 184
Dialectical Behavior Therapy 5, 185n2
Diagnostic and Statistical Manual of Mental Disorders *see* DSM-5
Discourse on Dependent Origination 24
disidentification 88, 149–150, 158
dismissing-avoidant attachment 85
disorganized attachment **68, 76**
dissociation 20, 23n4, 134, 172, 179
doing mode 3, 100, 178–179, 181; *see also* being mode; ego state; state of mind
drama triangle 107, 109–111, 114n3; and automatic thoughts 103; in exercise 113; and externalization 83, 110; lens of the 109, 126–127, 176; liberation from the 111–113; and shifting responsibility 117, 120
DSM-5 1, 9, 51; depersonalization-derealization disorder in the 63n4; and the HiTOP model 16n3; and mindful diagnosis 14; narcissistic personality disorder in the 82; personality disorders in the 46n3, 86n2

early experiences 20–21, 23n5, 136; and attachment 130; and core beliefs 26, 91, 116; and self-compassion 49, 128n2; and parent-child interactions 18, 91, 131; and unmet needs 21, 56, 64; *see also* adverse childhood experiences; corrective experience; developmental trauma
Ecker, B. 47–48, 66, 89–90, 94n3, 147n7, 184
ego inflation 86n4, 173
ego state 24, 25, 26, **52–53**, 129n4; Adult 99, 105, 109, 117, 133; in alcohol dependence 44; in anorexia

nervosa *43*; archaic 2, 88, 105, 107, 110, 133; in case fragments 61, 103–104; Child 99, 103, 105, 107, 111, 117; and core beliefs 99, 110; and dependent origination 95n4; in depressive disorder *37*; as an element of maladaptive schema 51–53, 88, 112; and games 107; in the Inflated Self 82; labeling 49, 54n2; and mental disorders 51; mindful Adult 100, 111, 129n4, 168, 178; mindful awareness of 88; in obsessive-compulsive disorder 35–36; Parent 99, 105, 107–109, 111; in personality disorder *41*; in post-traumatic stress disorder *39*; in schema therapy 51; in social anxiety disorder 33–34; *see also* being mode; doing mode; state of mind
Emotion-Focused Therapy 7, 53, 55n3, 124, 185n2; and core pain 17n6, 25
emotion regulation 2, 15, 48, 112, 116, 134; and Adult ego state 99; and adverse childhood experiences 20; in case fragments 12; and closeness 131; in exercise 158; and personal development 140, 176; in personality disorder 40; and self-compassion 124
emotional breakthrough 162, 166
emotional resonance 165–166
emotional schema therapy 116
empty chair dialogue 66, 73–75, 78n1, 166
Engler, J. 6–7, 140–141, 153, 160n8, 164, 176, 185
Enlightened Nerd 3, 158, 171–172, 175; *see also* spiritual bypassing
enlightenment *see* awakening
Epstein, M. 100, 108, 129n4, 146n4, 155, 162, 179, 181
Erikson, E. 18, 175
existential dread 26, 48, *54*, 61; in case fragments 35, *36*, 61, 109, 112, 120; and core beliefs 26; as a core pain 17n6, 28, 51, 88, 117, 165; and defense mechanisms 138n4; and developmental trauma 61; in exercise 121; in the Lost Self 56–57, 117, 162; in meditation 154–155, 159n6; and mindfulness 61, 118, 155; and the need for security 53; and transpersonal experiences 168; *see also* core pain
existential fear *see* existential dread
existential horror *see* existential dread
existential nausea 154

factors of awakening *see* seven factors of awakening
fear of abandonment 131, 134–135, 138n4, 144; in exercise 137; and mindfulness 112
fear of closeness 138n4, 144; and attachment avoidance 132, 134–135; in case fragments 163; and mindfulness 172; in narcissism 86n6; *see also* closeness; courage to be close
fear of intimacy *see* fear of closeness
fearful-avoidant attachment 20, **68**, **76**
fierce compassion 124, 127
focusing (technique) 12, 41, 166
Frankl, V. E. 175–176
Freud, S. 8n3, 18, 24, 99, 102, 114n1
Fromm, E. 121
Frýba, M. 7, 95n4, 101–102, 116, 164

Gallagher, S. 2, 26, 30, 150
Gendlin, E. T. 12, 41, 117, 141, 166
Germer, Ch. K. 5–6, 184
global distress 48, 61
Goldstein, J. 155, 172
Grabovac, A. 154, 162, 164, 168
grandiose self *see* Inflated Self
Greenberg, L. S. 7, 47, 50n3, 53, 167, 183; and anger 124, 126; and attitude toward a feeling 115; and case formulation 1, 12, 51; and core pain 25; and corrective emotional experiences 114n3, 136; and "maladaptive emotion schemes" 24; and *memory reconsolidation* 90
Grof, S. 21, 24, 146n5, 162

Harlow, H. F. 64
Harris, T. A. 54, 108
Hayes, S. C. 105, 157, 178

healthy selfishness 3, 121; *see also* selflessness; self-referrential processing
Hierarchical Taxonomy of Psychopathology *see* HiTOP
HiTOP 11, 16n3
Holotropic Breathwork 21, 161
hungry ghosts 108
hyperarousal 100, 111, 117, 131
hypoarousal 100, 111, 117, 132

ICD-11 1, 9, 51; in case fragment 14; complex post-traumatic stress disorder in 22n3; depersonalization-derealization disorder in 63; and HiTOP model 16n3; personality disorders in 39, 46n3; social anxiety disorder in 32
ideal parent 92, 123n8; in case fragment 66–67, 118–120; in exercise 62–63; in therapist-client dialogue 67–68, 119–120; *see also* Ideal Parents Technique
Ideal Parents Technique 49, 50n3, 66, 73, 118, 166
implicit semantic memory 26, 48, 90
inadequacy (feeling) 112, 165; in exercise 16; *see also* inferiority (feeling); shame; worthlessness (feeling)
inadequate responsibility 61–62, 113, 117, 125; in therapist-client dialogue 60; *see also* omnipotent guilt; responsibility
Inferior Self 71, **76**, 83, *150*; and attachment 172; and core beliefs 73, 94n1; and emotions 51, 71, 82, 91; in exercise 76–77; and meditation practice 174; and unmet needs 2, 108, 162; *see also* Wounded Self
inferiority (feeling) 30, 76–77, 82; as a core pain 17n6, 88; in case fragments 33, 43–44, 74, 103; in exercise 76; in the Inflated Self 173; in meditation 141; in therapist-client dialogue 85; *see also* inadequacy (feeling); shame; worthlessness (feeling)
Inflated Self 79, 82–83, **85**, *150*, 175; and attachment 138n4, 144, 172; in the drama triangle 111; and emotions 51, 79, 91, 126, 132, 173; and mental disorders 87n9; and unmet needs 2, 108, 135–136, 162; *see also* Wounded Self
insecure attachment 133–134; *see also* attachment anxiety; attachment avoidance
intensive meditation 140, 151, 153, 155, 159n1; and *constant* mindfulness 151, 154; and the dark night of the soul 154–155, 157; and maladaptive schemas 156–157; and meditation teacher 162–164; and Not-Self 30, 156; and observer perspective 178; and psychedelic experiences 140, 161, 169n1, 175, 178; and transpersonal experiences 161, 175; *see also* long-term meditators; mindfulness and insight meditation; retreat
International Classification of Diseases *see* ICD-11

James, W. 150, 184
Jesus 127
John of the Cross 154, 171, 177n1
Johnson, S. 136
Jung, C. G. 86n4, 98, 135, 138n3, 173

Kabat Zinn, J. 101–102, 106n2
Karpman, S. 109
kilesa see defilements
Kohut, H. 65, 80, 98
Kornfield, J. 142, 144, 156, 158, 173, 180

Laing, R. D. 31
Lambert, M. J. 6, 143
Lane, R. D. 47–48, 66
Leahy, R. L. 24, 116, 122n3, 126
learned helplessness 18, 99, 122, 161
Letheby, C. 157, 161, 164, 180, 185
Levine, P. A. 38, 100
life positions 54, **62**, **68**, **76**, **85**, 108
life scripts *see* scripts
Linehan, M. 5
loneliness 26, *54*, 132; in the Abandoned Self 64, 162; in case fragments 20, 37,

39, 103, 142, 174; and core beliefs 14; as a core pain 17n6, 51, 88, 90, 165; and defense mechanisms 138n4; and developmental trauma 26, 72; in exercise 69; in meditation 141; and mindfulness 14; and the need for closeness 14, 53, 64; and self-compassion 66; in therapist-client dialogue 13; *see also* abandonment (feeling); core pain

long-term meditators 139, 157, 160n9, 164, 184; *see also* intensive meditation; retreat

Lost Self 54, 56, 58, **62**, 136, *150*; and attachment 138n4; 144; core beliefs 94n1; and dependency on others 132, 135; in the drama triangle 110; and emotions 51, 90, 109, 117, 126, and mental disorders 61, 63n4; and the Stockholm syndrome 63n3; and taking responsibility 57; and unmet needs 2, 108, 162; *see also* Wounded Self

Mahāsi, S. 102, 154, 170n3, 171
Maitri Breathwork 21, 161
maladaptive schemas 3, 24, 28, 144, 151; and the Abandoned Self 64–65; activation of 11, 26, 90–92; and advanced meditators 156; and adverse childhood experiences 19; in alcohol dependence 43, *44*; in anorexia nervosa *43*; and archaic ego states 133; and awakening 156; awareness of 100; in case fragments 14, 103–104, 142, 163; and close relationships 91, 136, 138n2, 173; and core beliefs 25, 117; and core pain 88, 138n4, 178; and corrective experiences 94n3, 142, 147n7, 182n1; deactivation of 112; in depressive disorder 36, 37; elements of 15, 20, 25, 54, 73, 88; and emotional vulnerability 90; in Enlightened Nerd 175; in exercises 45, 69, 169, 174, 181; formation of 19–20, 23n5, 48; and games 107, 110; healing of 141–142; and "hungry ghosts" 108; and implicit semantic memory 48, 90; and the Inflated Self 79; and intensive meditation 156–157; and the Lost Self 56; and *memory reconsolidation* 90; and mental disorders 1, 7n1; and mindful therapist 53; and mindfulness 6–7, 49, 105, 112, 126; and the Narrative Self 93; and neuroimaging methods 131; and *nibbāna* 155; and non-dual awareness 157; and observing perspective 157; in obsessive-compulsive disorder 34–35, 36; and parenting styles 86n1; in personality disorder 40, 41; phenomenology of 20–21; in post-traumatic stress disorder 38, 39; and psychedelic experiences 143, 157, 164; and psychotherapy 145, 157, 159n2; reconsolidation of 61, 66, 90, 182n1; and schema therapy 52; and self-perception 99; and shifting responsibility 117; in social anxiety disorder 32–33, 34; and splitting 109; and therapeutic relationship 143; in therapist-client dialogue 27; and the *Transdiagnostic Theory of the Wounded Self* 183; transformation of 1, 6, 45, 48, 73, 89; transgenerational transmission of 21; and transpersonal development 142, 164; and transpersonal experience 168; and trauma 21; typology of 51, 54; understanding the origin of 92, 136; and the Wounded Self 2, 136, 168; *see also phenomenological model of maladaptive schemas*

Maslow, A. H. 98, 121, 141
Masters, R. A. 124, 126–127, 135–136, 141, 158, 172–173, 175, 180
Maté, G. 100, 108
McLean, K. 31, 97, 99
meditation retreat *see* retreat
meditation *see* mindfulness and insight meditation
memory reconsolidation 89–90, 92, 95n5, 120, 123n8; and core pain 66, 89; and corrective emotional experiences 3, 61, 73–74, 166, 182n1; and psychedelics

169n2; and transformation of maladaptive schemas 6, 47–48, 53, 90, 157; *see also reconsolidation window*
mental defilements *see* defilements
mental formation 24–25, 54n1, 155
mental scripts *see* scripts
meta-awareness 149–150, 152n1
micchādiṭṭhi see wrong understanding
micchā-sati see wrong mindfulness
Mikulincer, M. 7n1, 18, 130, 132–133
mindful Adult 101, 105, 135, 178; in case fragments 108; as an ego state 100, 111, 129n4, 168, 178; in exercise 113
mindful awareness 48–49, 61, 85, 102; in case fragments 14, 61; of core beliefs 91–93; of core pain 15, 128; of ego state 88
mindful disintegration 159n5
mindful diagnosis 9, 11, 16n3; in case fragments 14; of maladaptive schemas 2; perspective of 34, 43, 51, 135
mindful discernment 101, 106n2, 117, 129n4, 146n3, 155; in exercise 85; of defense mechanisms 135; in depressive disorder 36; of mental defilements 52; in obsessive-compulsive disorder 35
mindful perspective 5, 9, 47, 135, 157, 184; and diagnosis of mental disorders 14–15
mindful processing 166
mindful therapist 6, 165, 167; in exercise 15; and uncovering the client's inner processes 4n3, 9, 11, 15, 47, 53
Mindful Zombie 3, 141, 171–173; *see also* spiritual bypassing
mindfulness 5, 88, 97, 102, 164, 170n3; and acceptance 102, 115, 128n3; and anger 124–126; and the Authentic Self 99; and authenticity 98, 105; versus bare attention 149, 172; in Buddha's teachings ; in case fragments 12, 103, 112, 142; and closeness 5, 136; and cognitive reappraisal 26, 93; as a common factor 47; and core beliefs 15, 92, 100, 105, 112, 178; and core pain 15, 49, 66, 73, 88, 93;

and decentering 149; and defense mechanisms 48, 52, 89, 102, 135; definition of 1; development of 101, 149, 160n9, 172, 176, 180; and depression 88; and developmental trauma 61, 100; and disidentification 88, 149–150; and drama triangle 111; and early childhood experiences 18; enthusiasts 101, 140, 174; and ethical-psychological connections 102, 180; in the etiology of mental disorders 2; and evaluation 101–102, 106n2; and existential dread 61, 118, 155; and fear of closeness 172; and fear of abandonment 112; of feelings 48, 115, 124, 126, 141, 179; and games 111; and insight 26, 87n10, 93, 153, 162; lack of 2, 15, 150, 157, 172; and loneliness 14; and maladaptive schemas 6–7, 49, 105, 112, 126; as a means of self-discovery 1; mechanisms of 47, 115, 184; and mental defilements 25, 52; and mental disorders 1, 9, 17n8, 184; and the Narrative Self 99, 105, 125, 157; and the Noble Eightfold Path 101; and non-judgment 101–102, 106n2; and phenomenological reduction 50n1; and psychedelic experiences 160n9; and psychotherapeutic change 2, 14–15, 47, 126, 184; in psychotherapy 2, 6, 162, 184; research 139, 164, 184; and self-transcendence 5, 175, 180; and structure of experiencing 47; versus thinking 47–48, 50, 93, 105, 182n2; and the Transcendent Self 151–152, 178; and transformation of maladaptive schemas 44, 48–49; understanding 3, 4n3; *see also* constant mindfulness; mindfulness and insight meditation; momentary mindfulness; right mindfulness; wrong mindfulness
mindfulness and insight meditation 97, 153–155, 169n1; aim of 6, 141, 151; and bodily feelings 141; and cognitive understanding

101; and the Transcendent Self 178; *see also* intensive meditation; *vipassanā-bhāvanā*
Mindfulness and Compassion-Oriented Integrative Psychotherapy 7
Mindfulness-Based Cognitive Therapy 5
Mindfulness-Based Stress Reduction 5
Mindfulness-Informed Integrative Psychotherapy 3, 4n3, 5, 7, 28, 53; aim of 47; and defense mechanisms 16n5, 52, 89; and maladaptive schemas 49; techniques of 73, 89
Minimal Self 26, *150*, 151–152; *see also* Narrative Self; Transcendent Self
mismatch 90; *see also* memory reconsolidation
mode *see* being mode; doing mode; ego state
momentary mindfulness 151, 159n2; *see also* constant mindfulness; mindfulness
monkeys *see* rhesus monkeys
Murphy, R. 143–144
mystic death 162
mysticism 151, 171
mystics 171, 180

Nagarjuna 7n2, 152
Ñāṇamoli, B. 174, 180–181
Ñāṇārāma, M. S. 154, 171
Narada, M. 54n1, 129n4, 164
narcissism 82; epidemic 86n3; and highly sensitive people 87n8; and narcissistic personality disorder 86n2; and parenting styles 80, 82; spiritual 175, 177n1; *see also* Spiritual Narcissist
Narrative Self 1–2, 30, *150*, and the brain 20, 26, 46n1; as a construct 45, 152n5; and core belief 33, 35, 37, 44, 104; and core pain 117; development of the 26; differentiation of the 30–31, 133, 150–152; and the drama triangle 110; in exercises 105, 176; function of the 97, 151; and identification with phenomena 149; in insecure attachment 133; and mental disorders 28, 31–32, 34, 40, 42; and mindfulness 99, 105, 125, 157;

social dimensions of the 133, 152n2; transformation of the 93, 100, 109; and transpersonal experiences 144, 156–157, 160n9; *see also* Authentic Self; Minimal Self; Transcendent Self; Wounded Self
Neff, K. D. 124
neuroscience 2, 48, 122n1, 159n3, 184; and altered states of consciousness 139; and attachment theory 131; and early childhood experiences 20, 22n1; and free will 159n4; and high-level priors 29n1; and long-term meditation 160n10; and the Narrative Self 46n1; and self-prioritization effect 26
nibbāna 155, 159n7, 171
Noble Eightfold Path 101, 171
non-dual awareness 7, 151, 153, 155, 162; and "ego dissolution" 156; and maladaptive schemas 157; and Not-Self 152n3, 156; and personal development 171; and self-compassion 158; *see also* altered states of consciousness
Norcross, J. C. 6, 143, 183, 185n1n2
Not-Self 30
Nyanaponika, T. 141, 149, 159n6, 182n3
Nyanatiloka, T. 106n3, 129n4

Observing Self *see* Transcendent Self
omnipotent guilt 11, 57–58, 61, 117, 120; in case fragments 35, 109, 117, 120; and the Child ego state 117; and endless remorse 123n7; in exercises 62–63, 121; ridding oneself of 113; and shifting responsibility 117; *see also* inadequate responsibility; responsibility
omnipotent responsibility *see* omnipotent guilt
ontological addiction theory 2, 45
ontological shock 167
optimal frustration 56, 65

paradigm shift 184
parenting styles 79–80, 86n1n3; *see also* authoritarian parenting; authoritative parenting; permissive parenting

pattern theory of self 2
permissive parenting 79, 82; *see also* parenting styles
personal boundaries 3, 82, 115, 121, 176; in the Lost Self 57, 61, 117
personal development 2, *140*, 145, 171, 176, 185; and the Authentic Self 151; challenges of 175; and close relationships 140–141, 158, 173; phases of 171, 175, 180; theory of 164; and transpersonal experiences 171; *see also* transpersonal development
Pesso, A. 53, 63n1
Pesso Boyden System Psychomotor psychotherapy 7, 55n3
phenomenological model of maladaptive schemas 2, 25, 138n4, 184
pleasure principle 102, 105, 156
prediction error 90; *see also* memory reconsolidation
Prochaska, J. O. 183, 185n1
protective anger 3, 124–127, 128n3; in case fragment 61, 120; and empty chair dialogue 74; in exercise 127–128; *see also* reactive anger
psychedelic experience 180; and absolute reality 176; and acceptance 142, 179; and attachment 144; classic book on the 141; and cognitive reappraisal 161, 166, 169n2; and compassion 179–180; and core beliefs 143; and core pain 161–162; and corrective experiences 142–143, 157, 162; and defense mechanisms 161; destabilizing 139; and emotional breakthrough 162; in exercise 168; and impermanence 179; and intensive meditation 140, 161, 169n1, 175, 178; and life values 180, 182n4; and maladaptive schemas 143, 157, 164; and *memory reconsolidation* 169n2; and mindfulness 160n9; models for integrating 165; and the Narrative Self 156–157; and observer perspective 157, 161, 178; and ontological shock 167; preparation for the 143; and psychotherapy 143–144, 164, 185; and self-compassion 144;

and social connectivity 161; in a therapeutic context 139; and the *Tibetan Book of the Dead* 141; and transpersonal development 140, 144, 185; and two worlds 178; and the Wounded Self 144, 151, 156, 174–175, 182n1; *see also* altered states of consciousness; non-dual awareness
psychedelic-assisted psychotherapy 143–144, 162, 164, 169n1
psychedelics 2, 139–141, 146n1; and altered states of consciousness 161; and attachment 144; and corrective experiences 3; effects of 180, 185; legal use of 146n2; and mental disorders 139, 164; and the Narrative Self 160n9; and out-of-body experiences 179; and the *reconsolidation window* 147n7; and relational experiences 143, 145; research on 161, 180, 185; and selflessness 3; therapeutic use of 164–165, 185; and transpersonal experiences 141; *see also* psychedelic experience; psychedelic-assisted psychotherapy
psychonauts 142, 144, 157, 171, 180, 182n4; definition of 146n5
psychosis 16n3, 31–32
psychotherapeutic change 45, 47–48, 139, 143, 184; in case fragment 61, 118; mechanisms of 15, 90, 151, 167, 169n2, 183; trajectory of 89; and the *Transdiagnostic Theory of the Wounded Self* 2
purification 101, 106n1, 171

RDoC 11
reactive anger 83, 124–127; in case fragment 12, 14, 41, 66, 129n5; and drama triangle 111; in exercise 15–16; in therapist-client dialogue 12–13; *see also* protective anger
reappraisal *see* cognitive reappraisal
reconsolidation *see memory reconsolidation*
reconsolidation window 94n3, 147n7
Research Domain Criteria *see* RDoC

responsibility 81, 112, 115–116, 136; avoiding 172; boundaries of 112–113, 115, 120; in case fragments 109, 118; in the drama triangle 110–111; in the Lost Self 91; moral 159n4; parental 122n2; shifting 117, 120, 132; taking full 117, 176; in therapist-client dialogue 60; therapist's 166; *see also* inadequate responsibility; omnipotent guilt

retreat 153–155, 159n1, 162, 164; in case fragment 142, 163; and transpersonal experiences 175; *see also* intensive meditation; long-term meditators

rhesus monkeys 64

right mindfulness 3, 101, 149, 173; *see also* mindfulness; wrong mindfulness

right understanding 101–102, 105, 162

Rogers, C. R. 16n4, 30, 98, 150

Röhr, H. P. 17n7, 83, 107, 132

rumination 36, 46n2, 88, 92, 134, 163

ruthless compassion *see* fierce compassion

sammā-sati see right mindfulness
saṅkhāra see mental formation
satta sambojjhaṅgā see seven factors of awakening

schema therapy 25, 54n2; in alcohol dependence 44; in anorexia nervosa 42; in depressive disorder 37; modes, 51, 52–53; in obsessive-compulsive disorder 35; in personality disorder 41; in post-traumatic stress disorder 39; in social anxiety disorder 33

scripts 7n1, 99, 107, 131, 163

secular ethics 164

secular spirituality 164

self-compassion 99, 116, 124, 126, 128n1, 151; and anger 66, 74, 102, 120, 124, 128; and authenticity 98; and boundaries of responsibility 120; in case fragments 14, 61, 66, 103, 108, 112; as a common factor 47; and core beliefs about emotions 116; and core pain 48, 50n2, 73, 92–93, 135; cultivating 7, 49, 55n3, 131; and defense mechanisms 89; and early childhood experiences 128n2; in exercises 21, 45, 122, 128, 137, 146; lack of 15; and loneliness 66; and maladaptive schemas 1–2, 44, 49, 182n1; and the "master of two worlds" 179, 181; and *memory reconsolidation* 92; and mental disorders 2; and the mindful Adult 100; and needs 136; and non-dual awareness 158; processing 166; and protective anger 61; and psychedelic experience 144, 160n9; and psychotherapy 2; and relational experiences 2, 48, 166

self-conscious emotions *see* core belief; self-conscious feelings

self-conscious feelings 28, 43, 51, 88, 115, 122n4

selflessness 3, 175, 180, 185; versus dissociation 172; and happiness 156; versus self-denial 179; *see also* healthy selfishness; self-referential processing

self-prioritization 26, 156

self-referential processing 26, 44–45, 178, 184; and core beliefs 28; and mental disorders 32; and *nibbāna* 155; *see also* healthy selfishness; selflessness

seven factors of awakening 106n3, 155

shame 22n3, 30, 32, 40, 54; in attachment avoidance 132; in the brain 123n6; in case fragments 34, 43–44; and core beliefs 26, 115, 135; as a core pain 17n6, 28, 48, 51, 88, 117; and defense mechanisms 138n4; and developmental trauma 26; differentiation of the 78n2, 123n6; in the drama triangle 111; in exercise 76–77; in the Inferior Self 71, 73, 76, 162; in the Inflated Self 79–80, 82–83; and the need for recognition 53, as a self-conscious emotion 115, 117; in therapist-client dialogue 75; *see also* core pain; inadequacy (feeling); inferiority (feeling); worthlessness (feeling)

Shaver, P. R. 2, 18, 130–132, 134

Shonin, E. 2, 32, 45, 184
Siegel, D. J. 20, 26, 48, 86n5, 131, 137n1, 140, 152n1, 166, 175
Socrates 98
Sogyal, R. 175
Sohmer, O. R. 98, 133
spiritual bypassing 164, 171–172, 176; *see also* Enlightened Nerd; Mindful Zombie; Spiritual Narcissist
spiritual gluttony 177n1
spiritual materialism 173
Spiritual Narcissist 3, 171–173, 177n1; *see also* narcissism; spiritual bypassing
splitting 109, 111
state of mind 27, 39, 88, 142, 150, 163; in Abhidhamma 129n4; in exercise 85; *see also* being mode; doing mode; ego state
Stauffer, Ch. 144
Stevens, F. L. 48, 89, 134, 136, 184
still-face experiments 56
Sujiva, B. 141–142

Taming the Demons Within 49, 89
Tangney, J. P. 78n2, 117
therapeutic change *see* psychotherapeutic change
Thompson, E. 179, 184
Tibetan book of living and dying 175
Tibetan Book of the Dead 141, 146n4
Timuľák, L. 1, 7, 17n6, 25, 48, 51, 53, 66, 74, 90, 124
trance of unworthiness 73
transactional analysis 54, 99, 109, 185n2
Transcendent Self 30, 98, 100, 145, 149, *150*; and Abhidhamma 164; development of the 2, 151, 180; differentiation of the 152n5, 184–185; in exercise 181; and mindfulness 151–152, 178; and *nibbāna* 159n7; and observer perspective 152, 154–155, 157, 161, 179; utilization of the 181; *see also* Minimal Self; Narrative Self
Transdiagnostic Theory of the Wounded Self 1–2, 165, 183–184

transpersonal development 2–3, *140*, 141, 145, 152; and Abhidhamma 185; and altered states of consciousness 153, 165; challenges of 173; and close relationships 158, 175; and maladaptive schemas 142; and observer perspective 150; and personal development 2, 140–141, 164, 181, 185; phases of 171, 175, 180; and psychedelic experiences 144; and psychotherapy 164; theory of 164, 171; *see also* personal development
transpersonal psychology 139, 171, 175, 184
trauma *see* developmental trauma
Tronick, E. 56, 63n3, 65
Trump, D. 97, 173
Trungpa, Ch. 173, 175

Underhill, E. 151, 162, 171, 174, 180
unpleasure principle 102, 105, 156

values 79, 97–98; in exercises 77, 181–182; and meaning 105; and the Narrative Self 99, 133; reevaluation of 161, 180, 182n4
van Gordon, W. 2, 30, 45, 156, 158
Varela, F. J. 180
vipassanā-bhāvanā see intensive meditation; mindfulness and insight meditation
vulnerability 32, 73, 98, 135; acknowledging 127, 136, 161, 175; beliefs about 26, 58, 91; and defense mechanisms 125, 132; existential 56; to harm **62**; heightened emotional 15, 90; revealing 130, 132, 136; *see also* vulnerable narcissism
vulnerable narcissism 82, 87n8

Wampold, B. E. 4n3, 143
Welwood, J. 73, 136, 153, 155, 164, 171, 173
Whitehead, R. 105, 156, 179
Wilber, K. 139–140, 164, 175
Winnicott, D. W. 18, 57, 98, 138n3

worthlessness (belief) 36, 73, 92, 94n1, 151; *see also* worthlessness (feeling)

worthlessness (feeling) 11, 27, 79, 85; *see also* inadequacy (feeling); inferiority (feeling); shame; worthlessness (belief)

Wounded Self 51, *54*, *150*; and the brain 91, 131; and core beliefs 117; and corrective relational experiences 3, 157, 162, 165–166; and ego states 133; in exercises 85, 121, 137, 146, 169; healing of the 32, 88, 93, 135, 165, 180; and maladaptive schemas 2, 136, 168; narrative of the 91, 100; and meditation or psychedelic experiences 144, 151, 156, 174–175, 182n1; as an opportunity for growth 181; rigidity of the 152, 167, 178; types of the 49, 53–54, 90, 108; *see also* Abandoned Self; Authentic Self; Inferior Self; Inflated Self; Lost Self; *Transdiagnostic Theory of the Wounded Self*

wrong mindfulness 101; *see also* mindfulness; right mindfulness

wrong understanding 172, 174

Young, J. 24, 51, 53–54

Young's schemas **62**, *68*, **76**, **85**

Žvelc, G. and M. 5, 7, 24, 90, 99–100, 105, 107, 129n4, 150, 166, 179